ARCHITECTURE AND THE SCIENCES

EXCHANGING METAPHORS

Antoine Picon and Alessandra Ponte, editors

Foreword by Ralph Lerner

PRINCETON ARCHITECTURAL PRESS

PRINCETON PAPERS ON ARCHITECTURE

CONTENTS

FOREWORD

Architecture and science have long benefited from their love-hate relationship. The essays collected here will do little to help reach a more balanced relationship, which may be to the lasting benefit of each discipline. As the eleven scholars make clear, each field feels free to borrow metaphorically from the other, and the results reinforce their (often) unacknowledged dependence. From the perspective of a school of architecture within a basic research university, it appears that architectural method and the current vogue for the term *research* in design remain light-years away from the parallel universe of scientific method and the use of the term *research* in the sciences.

Architecture and the Sciences: Exchanging Metaphors is a high-water mark for the School of Architecture at Princeton University, which sponsored the symposium in November 2000 from which this book emerged. Its essays underscore and broaden the architect's view relative to what is at stake in contemporary design thinking. Written from the perspective of architecture, they are directed at people interested in the theories of design that inform and motivate the work of architects. As one reads the essays, particularly those that rely upon work in other disciplines such as history, philosophy, and literature, one comes away with the sense that it is the thorough examination of the architectural method of inquiry that is the volume's ultimate subject. A subset of this examination is the particular, long-held fascination that architects have with transposing various aspects of science and technology into their work. As the editors' introduction makes clear, this is most timely because science has been a particularly important source of ideas for architects over the last decade and as such deserves careful examination.

The Princeton symposium was the second gathering of this sort that the school has recently held. In 1996 it cosponsored with the chemistry department a symposium entitled "The Architectonics of

Nature" under the direction of professor of chemistry Clarence Schutt. The meeting brought together a broad array of scientists, artists, and art historians to exchange viewpoints around the topic of what each discipline has learned and may learn from the other. Speakers included Barbara Maria Stafford, Arthur Danto, Gerald Edelman, Chuck Hoberman, Don Ingiber, and Roger Penrose. Our goal then, as with this project, was to establish a critical inquiry into the motivations and methods utilized by artists and architects, as well as scientists, in drawing meaning from developments in science.

In terms of the education of an architect, the more recent symposium (and by extension, this book) extends and enriches the school's educational strategy—to provide its graduates with the critical abilities and learning skills that will enhance their capacity to master new realms of knowledge throughout their careers. Given the profound impact of the scientific and technological breakthroughs of the last quarter century and the expanding roles being assigned to architects, this emphasis is absolutely essential. The school's programs are designed to produce educated individuals capable of understanding, analyzing, and applying what they have learned to the complex issues in architecture and its related disciplines. *Architecture and the Sciences* is an important addition to the school's curriculum because it broadens our research into the specific ways architecture responds to other spheres of knowledge without presuming that architecture is determined by these spheres.

I want to personally thank professors Picon and Ponte for their efforts in bringing together the symposium and sticking with the project to produce this book. They are scholars and teachers of exceptional merit, spirit, and insight into our discipline. Their contributions in this regard are both obvious and, as the reader may discover, quite subtle. Additionally, I want to thank Kevin Lippert of Princeton Architectural

Press, who has played a pivotal role in the last decade in bringing the school's activities to the attention of a wider audience through his publication of the Princeton Papers on Architecture and other works.

Ralph Lerner, FAIA
Dean and George Dutton '27 Professor of Architecture

INTRODUCTION

Since the time of Vitruvius and Leonardo, the sciences have served as a source of images and metaphors for architecture and have had a direct influence on the shaping of built space. In recent years, architects have been looking again at science as a source of inspiration in the production of their designs and constructions. This volume attempts to evaluate the interconnections between the sciences and architecture from both historical and contemporary perspectives.

Each essay in this collection attempts to show how scientific paradigms migrated to architecture and to illuminate what caused the migration to take place. Architecture has provided images for scientific and technological discourse also. Accordingly, this volume investigates the status of the exchange between the two domains.

The first part of this book explores various places of experiment, whether they are cosmographic representations, zoological laboratories, or testing sites in the atomic age. The second part examines the role of specific concepts, such as types, norms, and figures of being, of living, and of entropy. Focusing on bio-informatics, artificial intelligence, and the virtual realm, the third part investigates the all-encompassing computer-designed environments of new mechanic assemblages, new thinking machines, and possibly a new thinking architecture itself.

As often in history, the question of why conditions the question of how. The many reasons capable of justifying connections between the history of architecture and the history of science and technology require interrogation. How is it possible to deal with the relation between these two domains, which are so different in terms of chronology, means, and techniques of analysis? Many pitfalls lie on the path of historians and theorists attempting to discover homologies or homotopies between them. Our aim is not an exhaustive coverage of research in the field;

rather, it is a specific examination of problems and issues of method that seem to us to be the most urgent task. Hoping to provide a fertile field of encounters, we deliberately invited historians both of architecture and of science to rise to the challenge of specifying how one discipline can furnish a model or paradigm for the other.

We conceived this project against a distinct background of work—some recent, some not so recent. It is impossible not to cite the overwhelming analysis of Michel Serres, who has traced themes across domains such as literature, philosophy, science, and art, combining, for instance, Joseph M. William Turner's vaporous paintings, Jules Michelet's energetic history, and Emile Zola's steamy subjects with Sadi Carnot's thermodynamics.[1] It is worth mentioning the work of French pioneers before the time of Serres, such as Gaston Bachelard, Georges Canguilhem, and their illustrious followers, which include Jacques Guillerme, the physicist and historian of techniques and technology who was also an art and architectural historian.[2] Guillerme's seminal intuitions connected the crystallography of Jean-Baptiste Romé de Lisle and Renée-Just Haüy with the systematic exposition of architecture as found in Jean-Nicolas-Louis Durand's course given to the engineers at the École Polytechnique in Paris at the beginning of the nineteenth century.[3] It should be noted, parenthetically, that crystallography would become a geometrical science that would lead to the conceptualization of the elements of symmetry in crystals and their limited number of combinations, a theoretical acquisition that would later help physicist Pierre Curie write his general theory of the symmetry of physical phenomena themselves.

That the method of producing the history of the sciences is shifting toward the various fields of cultural studies is illustrated by recent projects such as Martin Kemp's opus *The Science of Art*, Peter Galison and Emily Thompson's *The Architecture of Science*, and

ANTOINE PICON AND ALESSANDRA PONTE

Barbara Maria Stafford's sublime *Body Criticism* and *Artful Science*, which demonstrated wonderful connections among optical cabinets, baroque machines, enlightened experiments, and museum displays.[4] Also noteworthy is Jonathan Crary's *Suspensions of Perception*, which opened a meandering path through nineteenth-century optical science and visual analysis.[5] This kind of history creates the conditions for new kinds of enterprises, such as the *Dictionnaire culturel des sciences*, in which the sciences are viewed not from the interior, as is usual, but from the exterior—that is, from sites and places interfacing with other fields of knowledge and culture.[6] For some historians, only in that condition—in that new juxtaposition and vicinity—do the sciences acquire their full meaning. It is not by chance that the work of Eugène Emmanuel Viollet-le-Duc has provided the occasion for many studies, for the inspiration of his architecture was actually to be found in nineteenth-century biology: hence Caroline van Eck's *Organicism in Nineteenth-Century Architecture: An Enquiry into Its Theoretical and Philosophical Background*, Laurent Baridon's *L'Imaginaire scientifique de Viollet-le-Duc*, and Martin Bressani's dissertation, *Science, histoire et archéologie: Sources et généalogie de la pensée organiciste de Viollet-le-Duc*.[7]

Today, the sciences, instead of announcing speed, progress, and well-being, open the way to the possibility of mass destruction, the devastation of the environment, the depletion of resources, and the transformation of human genetics. Even while science threatens the amenity of our life, it still provides art and architecture with a fertile source of analogies and metaphors. In literary theory and cultural studies, and in various departments of comparative literature and architecture, it is common to refer to chaos theory, the genome project, string theory, fuzzy logic, and the recent developments in molecular biology. These references are usually superficial, but nonetheless they do bear witness to the displacement that has occurred within the last few years, a kind of fascination with technology and industry. Although the architects of the so-called modern movement had dreamt mainly of transposing analogically the methods of industry to life in the city, recently artists and architects have been drawn toward science, as opposed to technology proper, for their inspiration.

For this new type of connection between architecture and science, the computer, of course, is central. The numerical simulation that it orchestrates represents something truly experimental, transcending the usual distinctions between doing and understanding. It also transcends traditional boundaries between art and science. Its use authorizes multiple *détournements*, or "misappropriations"; software applications created for precise scientific use can be hijacked to generate simulations of different forms and environments. These "virtual realities" find their interpretation and application in very different domains, opening up new fields of knowledge and action. It follows that the interpretation of numerical models requires a sensibility capable of pioneering further unprecedented connections between different practices in science and art. Our interest in the interrelations between these practices derives from such a novel sensibility and is intended to foster it.

One of the dangers that threatens historians as soon as they proceed to map the plausible connections between the history of architecture and the history of the sciences lurks in the false belief that there exists something like "the spirit of the time," a *Zeitgeist*, the hypothetical existence of which would allow them to find similarities in cultural fields that are far from adjacent. They encounter analogies that are seductive but implausible. At the beginning of his *Patterns of Intention*, art historian Michael Baxandall fiercely criticizes this kind of analogy, denouncing, for instance, the parallels sometimes advanced between

ANTOINE PICON AND ALESSANDRA PONTE

cubist art and Einstein's theory of relativity.[8] By what means could Picasso have acquired any knowledge of the postulates of relativity, Baxandall asks, when the painter and the physicist belonged to very different worlds that hardly communicated? Far from condemning the historian's aspirations for mapping connections between the arts and sciences, Baxandall asks only that one put in evidence the effective possibility of mediation between these different orders of reality. For instance, he reveals very convincing relations between the French painter Jean-Baptiste-Siméon Chardin and the science of optics in the seventeenth and eighteenth centuries. His solid demonstration is based on the patient and well-argued reconstruction of the multiple threads tying together pictorial production and the physiology of vision, as illustrated in published works that acted as intermediaries between the worlds of art, philosophy, and science—works that Chardin without a doubt knew.

The identification of points of contact and mediation constitutes the indispensable beginning of any attempt to establish a connection between two distinct cultural environments. Such a starting point is to be observed in the contemporary translation of the "critical method," as demonstrated by Antoine Prost in his *Douze leçons sur l'histoire*.[9] In addition to individuals and their productions, points of contact may be offered by institutions, academies, and salons, and also by the art market, where buyers and dealers measure up their different systems of values. The market plays an important role in another book by Baxandall, *Painting and Experience in Fifteenth-Century Italy*, where he focuses on the links between the mercantile culture of Renaissance Florence, which was obsessed with the notion of measure, and paintings based on the use of perspective.[10] In the field of architecture, networks of clientele and modalities of reception constitute the background for similar issues of mediation.

Superficial or even false analogies are often based on an excessively wide-ranging vision of the culture of a period. One might forget that the various aspects of a culture depend upon very different systems of temporality. The rhythms of the history of art and architecture are not similar to those of mathematics and physics; the interruptions and disjunctions in their development do not usually occur at the same moment. Often chronological coincidences are only random effects, chance events generating an illusion of cross-fertilization. By failing to test these correspondences, one risks oversimplification or complete misunderstanding.

The true interest of this kind of crossing-over between architecture and the sciences, and between architecture and technology, does not lie in an ideological emphasis on "tectonics" or in the mere reiteration of the love affair between architects and industry, but rather, it resides in a definite and demonstrable connection, susceptible to theoretical analysis. One of these themes is the articulation of representations and practices; another is the embodiment of immaterial elements of culture, such as theories, in material constructs. In the case of the sciences, this embodiment is never simple or artless. It is true that, with the emphasis on the interconnections between architecture and science, one is actually confronted with many unworthy contaminations, often a freakish impregnation of architectural design with vulgarizations of scientific knowledge. Nevertheless, these *détournements*, these unorthodox misappropriations, can perhaps become the most interesting examples of cross-pollination, capable of producing the effects at which architecture excels—namely, the transposition and materialization of the most original ideas of an epoch.

Antoine Picon and Alessandra Ponte
Cambridge, Massachusetts, and Princeton, New Jersey, April 17, 2002

NOTES

1. Michel Serres, *Hermes: Literature, Science, Philosophy*, ed. Josué V. Harari and David F. Bell (Baltimore: Johns Hopkins University Press, 1982); idem, *Eclaircissements*, trans. *Conversations on Science, Culture, and Time*, trans. Roxanne Lapidus (Ann Arbor: University of Michigan Press, 1995).

2. Gaston Bachelard, *Subversive Humanist: Texts and Readings*, ed. Mary McAllester Jones (Madison: University of Wisconsin Press, 1991); François Delaporte, ed., *A Vital Rationalist: Selected Writings from Georges Canguilhem*, trans. Arthur Goldhammer (New York: Zone Books, 1994); Jacques Guillerme, ed., *Les Collections: Fables et programmes* (Seyssel: Champ Vallon, 1993).

3. Jean-Nicolas-Louis Durand, *Précis des leçons d'architecture données à l'Ecole polytechnique*, English trans. *Précis of the Lectures on Architecture; with Graphic Portion of the Lectures on Architecture*, with an introduction by Antoine Picon, trans. David Britt (Los Angeles: Getty Research Institute, 2000).

4. Martin Kemp, *The Science of Art: Optical Themes in Western Art from Brunelleschi to Seurat* (New Haven: Yale University Press, 1990); Peter Galison and Emily Thompson, eds., *The Architecture of Science* (Cambridge, Mass.: MIT Press, 1999); see also, Caroline A. Jones and Peter Galison, eds., *Picturing Science, Producing Art* (New York: Routledge, 1998); Barbara Maria Stafford, *Body Criticism: Imaging the Unseen in Enlightenment Art and Medicine* (Cambridge, Mass.: MIT Press, 1991); idem, *Artful Science: Enlightenment, Entertainment, and the Eclipse of Visual Education* (Cambridge, Mass.: MIT Press, 1994).

5. Jonathan Crary, *Suspensions of Perception: Attention, Spectacle, and Modern Culture* (Cambridge, Mass.: MIT Press, 1999). See also, idem, *Techniques of the Observer: On Vision and Modernity in the Nineteenth Century* (Cambridge, Mass.: MIT Press, 1990); and Carl Havelange, *De l'oeil et du monde: Une histoire du regard au seuil de la modernité* (Paris: Fayard, 1998).

6. Nicolas Wittkowski, ed., *Dictionnaire culturel des sciences* (Paris: Editions du Regard, 2001).

7. Caroline van Eck, *Organicism in Nineteenth-Century Architecture: An Enquiry into Its Theoretical and Philosophical Background* (Amsterdam: Architectura & Natura Press, 1994); Laurent Baridon, *L'Imaginaire scientifique de Viollet-le-Duc* (Paris: Harmattan, 1996); Martin Bressani, *Science, histoire et archéologie: Sources et généalogie de la pensée organiciste de Viollet-le-Duc* (doctoral dissertation, Université de Paris IV, 1997). For eighteenth-century connections among architecture, landscape design, and botanical sciences, see Alessandra Ponte, *Le paysage des origins: Le voyage en Sicile (1777) de Richard Payne Knight* (Paris: Les Éditions de l'Imprimeur, 2000).

8. Michael Baxandall, *Patterns of Intention: On the Historical Explanation of Pictures* (New Haven: Yale University Press, 1985).

9. Antoine Prost, *Douze leçons sur l'histoire* (Paris: Le Seuil, 1996).

10. Michael Baxandall, *Painting and Experience in Fifteenth-Century Italy: A Primer in the Social History of Pictorial Style*, 2nd ed. (Oxford and New York: Oxford University Press, 1988).

II. CONCEPTUAL FRAMEWORKS

III. TOOLS AND METAPHORS

I. PLACES AND SITES

PTOLEMY AND VITRUVIUS: SPATIAL REPRESENTATION IN THE SIXTEENTH-CENTURY TEXTS AND COMMENTARIES

Denis Cosgrove

Between 1550 and 1620, Europeans experienced dramatic and unsettling changes in their capacities to conceptualize and represent space. This was true not only for the new material spaces described by heliocentricity and oceanic and continental geography, and for the action spaces of geopolitics, but equally for the theoretical and representational spaces of mathematical understanding and technical representation. Applied geometry in ballistics and triangulation in survey, use of the grid and graticule in mapping and of perspective theory and practice in drawing and painting, together with the mechanization of vision by the camera obscura and lens, fundamentally transformed European "spatialities."[1] Movable type and the emerging print culture of the later fifteenth century were crucial, not only to the communication and thus the social impact of these changes, but to their actual achievement.[2] The debate between ancient classical and ecclesiastical authority on one hand and contemporary experience on the other was negotiated through printed texts; "new worlds" were communicated and represented in print and engraving, and the consistency of calculations and scientific illustrations was secured for a geographically scattered scholarly and scientific community. Newly revived scientific practices such as geography and architecture, which had a shared interest in conceptualizing and representing material space and in understanding the ways humans transform the physical world, were profoundly impacted by these processes.

This paper traces aspects of the overlapping intellectual history of geography and architecture as spatial disciplines in the Renaissance by examining the fate of two texts then considered foundational to their respective practices.[3] Geography was transformed in theory and practice by the reappearance in the West of Claudius Ptolemy's second-century AD work *The Geography*, while Vitruvius Pollio's *Ten Books of Architecture*, dating from a century earlier, had a similar impact on architecture. Each offered a technical manual for its respective spatial practice: classifying, recording, and mapping places on the one hand; engineering, planning, and building places on the other. Each located its specific knowledge and practices within a broader conception of spatial order that reached from the cosmos itself to individual locations. And each emphasizes the graphic representation of that spatial order, emblematized in their common iconographic use of the *sphaera mundi* and the compass (figs. 1, 2). Apparent in both the texts themselves and the summaries and commentaries that derived from them are the epistemological and practical tensions that accompanied the West's spatial revolution, notably between humanist rhetoric and mechanical *techne*. Such tensions could not remain disconnected from sixteenth-century Europe's bitter divisions of faith and religious practice.

VITRUVIUS AND PTOLEMY: ARCHITECTURE AND GEOGRAPHY

Architecture had no place in the medieval classification of the liberal arts; indeed, the disciplinary concept scarcely existed, while the work of the mason was regarded as strictly mechanical—scarcely the subject of written treatises. Scholastic education placed geography, alongside astronomy, within the ambit of cosmography as descriptive parts of Aristotelian natural philosophy, although there was a long medieval tradition of written descriptions of the Earth's surface.[4] It was through humanist and courtly interest that the two classical treatises by Vitruvius and Ptolemy became the focus of scholarly attention, translation, and commentary from the early decades of the fifteenth century. Because each work places its technical discussion of terrestrial space within the broader cosmological framework, both were readily swept into the circuits of early Renaissance speculation, description, and illustration of a geocentric Aristotelian cosmos, divinely patterned from the outer reaches of the firmament to the core of terrestrial space.[5]

Vitruvius's concern for architecture as *scientia*, or formalized, theoretically founded knowledge, is apparent from Book I. He requires the architect to pay close attention to matters of astronomy, astrology, and geography in site selection, in building choice and plan, and in construction. His reference to the human body as microcosmic measure of the world machine had a significant impact on Renaissance readers, while his strictures on the breadth of an architect's educational foundation were elaborated by Leon Battista Alberti and in every subsequent architectural treatise.

Interest in Vitruvius was stimulated by discovery of a manuscript copy at Montecassino in 1414. This was the basis of Alberti's closely modeled

(fig. 1)

The cosmographer, from a fifteenth-century cosmographic text

PTOLEMY AND VITRUVIUS

work *De re aedificatoria*, written about 1450 and printed in 1486, and for Fra Giocondo's illustrated edition of 1511. Translations of Vitruvius's text, as well as commentaries and architectural treatises closely modeled on it, appeared regularly during the sixteenth century, culminating in Vincenzo Scamozzi's *Idea dell'architettura universale* (1615).[6] Here the focus is on illustrated and published works rather than manuscript sources, for it was the medium of print that brought the text out of the orbit of courtly humanism and into a wider sphere of discourse and practice.

Among the most influential printed "Vitruvian" texts were the pseudo-Vitruvian *Hypnerotomachia Poliphili* (1499);[7] Caesare Caesariano's Italian translation of Vitruvius (1521), the first to contain a modern commentary and significant illustration;[8] and Sebastiano Serlio's pivotal *De architettura* (1537/1575), which set full-page images opposite the text, echoing the form of contemporary "scientific" treatises.[9] Daniele Barbaro's *Vitruvius* (1567, in Latin; 1586, in Italian) contained lengthy commentaries drawn from his extended scientific contacts with mathematicians, engineers, surveyors, naturalists, and astronomers and illustrations drafted by Andrea Palladio.[10] *I quattro libri dell'architettura* (1570), by Palladio himself, was the first architecture book to give greater emphasis to its author's own experience and designs than to those recorded by Vitruvius, although it also drew heavily on Palladio's detailed field measurement of Roman structures.[11] Pietro Rusconi's *De architettura* is known only through its striking illustrations of architectural practice; it was published in 1590 from a lost text by a student of the mathematician Nicolò Tartaglia.[12] Vincenzo Scamozzi's *Idea* (1615), often regarded as the last of the genre, is a massive two-volume work that unashamedly proclaims architecture a "universal" science (fig. 3).[13]

The above-mentioned works have been studied with varying intensity, and the cosmological aspects of their attention to geometry, proportion, and music, as well as their reworking of medieval ideas of the human microcosm, have been given close attention. The parallels between these and the corpus of specifically cosmographic writing, however, have received less study. Beyond a shared use of cosmological and cosmographic illustrations, to which I shall return, there are marked historical similarities in the publishing history of Vitruvian works and Renaissance cosmographic texts (fig. 4). The texts held a common appeal to scholars from the time of Alberti himself, who not only practiced architecture and modeled his treatise *De re aedificatoria*

(fig. 2)

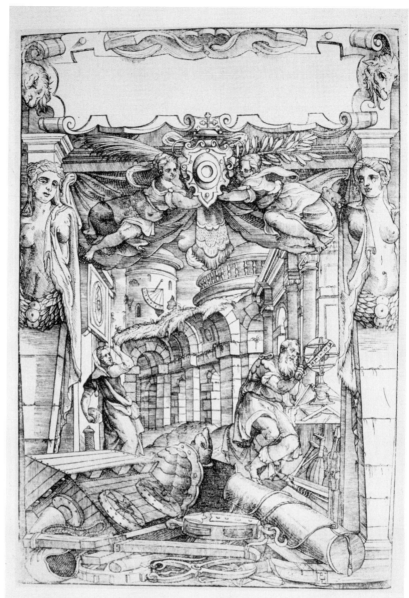

8. L'architetto, uomo di scienza, studia la *machina* del mondo: D. Barbaro, *I dieci libri* (1556), *verso* di frontespizio.

The architect as universal figure, from Daniele Barbaro, translation of Vitruvius (1556)

closely upon Vitruvius but whose fascination with mathematical games seems to have encouraged his application of Ptolemy's coordinate method to his "map" of Rome.[14]

Like Renaissance architecture, Renaissance geography also recovered a text at the turn of the fifteenth century that transformed its theory and practice. Claudius Ptolemy's *Geography* summarized and applied to the mapping of the world much of the same cosmographic knowledge on which Vitruvius had drawn for his own science. Ptolemy's second-century work was part of the Alexandrian's broader cosmological and cosmographic project, which included writings on both astronomy (*Almagest*) and astrology (*Tetrabiblos*).[15] In Renaissance printings, personifications of both architecture and cosmography hold a compass, quadrant, or rule, signifying their status as a priori discourses of reason, measure, and order, while gesturing also to the role of *techne* and instrumental skill in their practice.

The transformative texts of architecture and cosmography in early modern Europe thus both originated as products of an imperial scientific culture, in Rome and Alexandria. Both were treated as "rediscovered" ancient knowledge by fifteenth-century humanists and were therefore invested with the authority of classical science as scholars set about the philological tasks of restoring textual corruptions and translating and commenting on their

(fig. 3)

Title page from Vincenzo Scamozzi, *Idea dell'architettura universale* (1615)

(fig. 4)

COSMOGRAPHY	ARCHITECTURE
1480	
Ptolemy, *Geography* (Bologna: 1477;	Alberti, *De re aedificatoria* (1486)
Rome: 1478; Berlinghieri, Ulm: 1482)	First printing of Vitruvius (1486)
1500	
Geography, Waldseemüller (1513)	*Hypnerotomachia Poliphili* (1499)
Waldseemüller, *Cosmographia Introductio* (1502)	Fra Giocondo, *Vitruvius* (1511)
1520	
Geography, Frisius (1522); Pirckheimer (1525)	Caesariano, *Vitruvius* (1521)
Apian/Frisius, *Cosmographicus* (1524/33)	
1540	
Geography, Münster (1540)	Serlio, *Architettura* (1537/75)
Münster, *Cosmographei* (1544)	
Copernicus, *De revolutionibus* (1543)	
Vesalius, *De humani corporis fabrica* (1543)	
Tartaglia, Italian trans. of Euclid's *Elements* (1543)	
1560	
Geography, Ruscelli (1561); Mercator (1570)	
Ortelius, *Theatrum* (1570)	Palladio, *I quattro libri* (1570)
Thevet, *Cosmographie universelle* (1575)	
Mercator, *Atlas, sive Cosmographicae* (1569/94)	
1580	
	Rusconi, *De architettura* (1590)
1600	
Fludd, *Utriusque cosmi* (1617)	Scamozzi, *Architettura universale* (1615)

Comparative publication dates of cosmographic and architectural texts, 1480-1620

contents. Both were technical treatises, dealing with matters of spatial cognition and representation, and in the opinion of fifteenth-century scholarship both had originally been illustrated. In this sense, Vitruvius and Ptolemy shared characteristics that did not extend to the majority of ancient texts revived and restored at this time, which included much of Aristotle's writing, most of Plato, and a large body of poetry, drama, history, and political thought. These latter works had not originally been illustrated, so that graphic additions were extensions to the classical text. However, neither the nine to eleven original illustrations for Vitruvius nor Ptolemy's twenty-six maps had survived; they therefore had to be reconstructed from the texts.[16]

This chapter traces the publishing history of the two works themselves and of their associated sixteenth-century literatures and, focusing on selected influential works, examines their shared conceptions of space and cosmic order before returning to the question of illustration. The idea of a spatial structure governed by geometry but concealed below the level of appearance seemed to offer to both cosmographers and architects a conceptual grid for experience, observation, and technique. But contradictions between conception and experience affected the ways that such order could be made visible in printed images. As the two texts moved out of the exclusive control of humanists and into a wider world of practice, so they followed

(fig. 5)

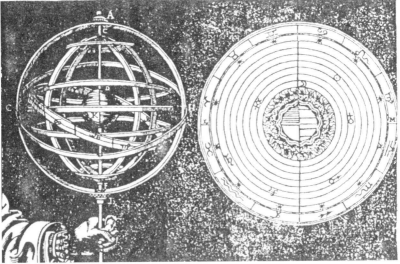

Armillary and celestial spheres, from Caesare Caesariano, *Vitruvius* (1521)

somewhat parallel paths, from authoritative source of ancient—and thus privileged—scientific knowledge, through attempts to harmonize the ideal measures they proposed with empirically observed, often instrumentally recorded form, to more critical treatment of their claims. In each case this resulted in their displacement by the early seventeenth century from canonical text to historical document, becoming more of antiquarian than of practical value. There remained however, even among the most influential practitioners, a strong commitment to an overarching "universal" science, through which geography could describe the terrestrial part of the world machine and whence architecture could take its guiding principles. This evolution in the reception and use of Ptolemy and Vitruvius saw rhetoric, observation and measure, and understanding of causes variously deployed as guarantors of scientific truth.

THE PRINTED COSMOGRAPHY 1480–1620

In his "Preface to Euclid" of 1570, the English polymath John Dee defined cosmography as "the whole and perfect description of the heavenly, and also elementall parte of the world, and their homological application, and mutuall collation necessarie."[17] Geography, which described the surface form and pattern of the elemental sphere, had thus to conform in some way to the celestial order. Descriptions of the heavens relied for the most part theoretically on Aristotle's *Physics* and *De Caelo*, and empirically on Ptolemy's *Almagest*, both known and studied in the West since about 1300. In the late medieval schools these were familiar largely through summaries such as Albertus Magnus's *De Caelo et Mundo* and Sacrobosco's *Tractatus de Sphera*, the latter remaining a basic educational text for science well into the seventeenth century. The cosmographic argument was expressed in two familiar images: the armillary sphere and the concentric diagram of four elemental and seven crystalline spheres reaching to the zone of fixed stars, the prime mover and the empyrean (fig. 5). Much of the work of astronomers was devoted to explaining the apparent divergences between the perfect motion described by Aristotle's theory and observed movements in the heavens, work that became significantly easier when astronomical observations and predictions could be collated and distributed between distant places as published calendrical tables. Among the earliest and most significant figures in this work was the Nuremberg scientist and publisher Regiomontanus, whose printed

Ephemerides contributed to the theoretical revolution in cosmology begun by Copernicus in 1543.

Regiomontanus died before his own edition of Ptolemy's *Geography* could be completed and published. *The Geography* was central to the cosmological project because it offered the means by which "homologicall application, and mutuall collation" between celestial and elemental parts of the world system could be practically demonstrated in the patterns of location on the Earth's surface. The work had been available in Latin from 1410, but its circulation remained largely restricted to lavish codices studied by court humanists and some monastic scholars. Printed editions became available in Italy and southern Germany from 1477, a few years before Vitruvius's *Ten Books* and Alberti's *On Building* were published. But these, too, were exclusive products, their costs elevated by the expense of reproducing large numbers of maps, and it was the appearance of the single-sheet world map based on Ptolemy's method and accompanied by a descriptive text that spread the new way of mapping space widely across Europe. The influence of *The Geography* was thus considerable. It revived cosmography as a practical endeavor through Ptolemy's use of a graticule of numbered meridians and parallels as the coordinating device for recording the precise location of places on the Earth's surface. This allowed a scaled spatial image of terrestrial space to be mapped onto the sphere or, by means of projection, to be transferred onto a planisphere. The parallels and meridians of the graticule are determined from geocentric observation of the celestial bodies, whose movements are graphically illustrated by the sphere of axes and circles of the *sphaera mundi*. Modeling their work on a hybrid of Sacrobosco and Ptolemy, with borrowings from encyclopaedic history, late fifteenth- and sixteenth-century cosmographers undertook the task of mapping the world and harmonizing an increasingly adventitious pattern of terrestrial distributions with observed celestial order.

The printed cosmographic treatise and map evolved rapidly from the early 1500s as the presses—now capable of setting color and incorporating woodcut or copperplate images—disseminated the reports of ocean navigation and revised the world map received from Ptolemy. The printed text, summarizing mathematical cosmography and describing the parts of the world, accompanied a globe or world map, reconstructed on Ptolemy's principles, the former an explanatory handbook for the latter. Thus Martin

Waldseemüller's *Cosmographia introductio* (1502) outlined the construction and contents of his revolutionary globe and world map while printing Amerigo Vespucci's narrative of his Columbian voyage. Peter Apian's pocket-size *Cosmographicus Liber* of 1524 (1533 with Gemma Frisius's chapter on triangulation as a method of mapping terrestrial space) also accompanied a globe and world map (fig. 6). In both texts a mathematical section defined simplified principles of Euclidean spherical geometry, illustrated by diagrams, while a second section gave a geographical description of the continents and countries on the terrestrial globe.[18] Apian's text was widely translated across Europe, reprinted and consulted throughout the century, and principally valued for its practical mathematical and technical clarity. But by the 1540s the volume of descriptive cosmography resulting from geographical discovery was clearly outstripping the mathematical side and seriously undermining the authority of Ptolemy's original geography. In Sebastian Münster's hugely influential *Cosmographei* (1544), printed in Basel, and in less widely translated works—for example, those by the French cosmographers Guillaume Postel and André Thevet, the Englishman William Cuningham, and the Italian Giacomo Gastaldo—mathematical cosmography tended to be "quickly formulated in some ritual definitions at the beginning of the work" and illustrated by an often highly elaborate *typus* of the world machine.[19] These cosmographers, and their counterparts in Spain and Portugal, were different in background and training from earlier humanist scholars who had studied Ptolemy's text, such as Francesco Berlinghieri, whose 1482 poetic translation of Ptolemy emerged from the intellectual context of Ficino's Florentine academy. Although sixteenth-century cosmographers sought and often obtained royal patronage of their work, they had been trained as doctors,

(fig. 6)

Title page from Peter Apian, *Cosmographei* (1540)

engineers, and instrument makers; they advised on navigation, trained pilots, and actively embraced the mechanical arts.[20] They were "moderns" who placed a greater emphasis on experience and instrumental measure than on philology and style of argument.

Descriptive cosmography expanded continuously as the volume of information returned from navigation exploded, threatening the simple regulatory order of mathematical cosmography, which was simultaneously under challenge after 1453 from Copernicus's new picture of the celestial spheres. Reconciling the a priori order of Aristotelian science with the disparate elements of observation and practice produced a midcentury crisis for cosmography.[21] The extended delay in publishing Gerardus Mercator's multivolume *Atlas, sive Cosmographicae Meditationes de fabrica mundi et fabricati figura*, conceived in 1569 but finally published posthumously and unfinished in 1594, and the reception of Thevet's *Cosmographie universelle* of 1575 are indicative of this crisis. In his cosmographic project, Mercator simply set himself too universal a task to complete if he were to retain its scientific and intellectual integrity. Thevet, less scrupulous, ended with an uncoordinated miscellany of facts and fables. As Anthony Grafton comments of Münster, from midcentury the cosmographer was unable either to "create a sound new vessel nor dam the stream of information that threatened to overwhelm him. Instead, he varnished the surface of the old one, plugged its leaks, and ignored the water that still poured in."[22]

The crisis was at once theoretical as much as practical, but it was cut across by a third dimension that for many appears to have lent a special urgency to retaining the cosmographic image of universal harmony.[23] To maintain Dee's "whole and perfect description" of a single "world machine," cosmographers necessarily negotiated a growing divergence between the information available to them and that offered by the ancients, and especially by Ptolemy, whose *Geography* gave their work its technical foundation and historical legitimation. Waldseemüller, Apian, Münster, and Mercator all edited Ptolemy's *Geography* (fig. 7), indicating its continued influence. But their editions incorporated new maps. Ptolemy's original image of the ecumene, stretching from the Atlantic coast to Indochina and from the Arctic Circle to the southern coasts of an enclosed Indian Ocean, was now accompanied by modern maps of four or five continents: the original three, America, and an unknown southern continent beyond the Cape of Good Hope and the Straits

(fig. 7)

Title page from Gerardus Mercator, *Geographiae* (1569)

of Magellan. An ever increasing number of new *tabulae*, or maps, of regions unrecorded by Ptolemy further illustrated the tension between "ancient" and "modern" knowledge. Finally, in 1570, Abraham Ortelius's *Theatrum Orbis Terrarum*, the first collection to bind in a single volume standardized contemporary maps of every known continent and region, accompanied by written description on the recto page, opens with only a modern world map. Ptolemy's *tabulae* are relocated to an entirely separate volume, the *Parergon*, where they appear alongside maps of antiquarian, exegetical, and humanist rather than "scientific" interest, such as those of Ulysses or St. Paul's voyages. Toward the end of the century, the impact of Copernicus's *De Revolutionibus Orbium Celestium* (1543) began to be felt in cosmography, so that from the 1590s cosmographers incorporated within the margins and interstices of their planispheres and double-hemisphere world maps images of the competing world systems (Ptolemaic, Tychonian, Copernican). These appeared alongside conventional summaries of mathematical cosmography and inset maps of the ancient ecumene, effectively ignoring the theoretical contradictions posed by cosmography's dependence on geocentricity.

The most practical challenges to sixteenth-century cosmography, however, were to incorporate "discoveries"—experience—into Ptolemy's spatial template, and to provide its representation with a legitimacy equivalent to that derived from the latter's classical authority. While Ptolemy's empirical measures and mappings simply could not be reconciled with terrestrial and celestial observations recorded by contemporary navigators and, with the aid of the telescope, by astronomers, his graticule remained the key ordering device for geographical location, and his applied spherical geometry was the basis for developments in projection by cosmographers such as Frisius and Mercator. The apparent objectivity and precision of numbered meridians and parallels offered a legitimating device for experience by fixing locations within measurable space. In his *Cosmographie universelle*, Thevet consistently refers to his personal maritime experience (although it was limited) to the eyewitness truth of his illustrations, and to the numerical coordinates of latitude and longitude of every phenomenon, however arbitrary these actually were.[24] Mathematical coordinates lent authority to even the most bizarre claims, and, given the inability to fix the longitude at sea and the problems of conveying new knowledge back to the cosmographer's study, recorded coordinates were indeed often quite arbitrary. Yet, in seeking to legitimate and harmonize new and disparate elements, cosmography contributed to changing notions of scientific truth.

In so doing, the cosmographic project ultimately self-destructed as an empirical endeavor. The separation of geography and astronomy into distinct sciences, resisted by Mercator if anticipated in Ortelius's project, was one outcome of the growing theoretical recognition that no necessary or harmonious connection between the patterns of celestial and elemental space existed. But geographical diversity left open the question of cause and, in an age that had rejected Aquinas's separation of faith and reason, this was deeply disturbing. More disturbing still for educated and cosmopolitan cosmographers in the closing decades of the sixteenth century was the savagery of religious intolerance that surrounded them in every part of Europe. In such circumstances the practice of pietism and an urgent belief in ideals of universal love and harmony among peoples were widespread and understandable responses, widely adopted by many of the most intellectually progressive minds in Europe, and especially in the Low Countries, the Venetian Republic, and England.[25] These included the principal European centers of map making and printing, and, although by definition such spiritual allegiances had to be clandestine, we know that Ortelius and Mercator embraced neo-Stoicism's position of the rational, disengaged, yet mindful contemplation of the world machine, and that they expressed these beliefs emblematically in their cartographic work. Ortelius's use of "theater" as the title for his atlas arises directly out of the cosmological trope of the *teatrum mundi*, while the quotations from Seneca and Cicero with which he surrounds his 1587 world map make his philosophical allegiance immediately apparent.[26]

Cosmography's universalist embrace of a single, rationally ordered celestial and terrestrial space chimed perfectly with the metaphysical turn apparent in so much of philosophy, literature, and art at the turn of the seventeenth century. It is most dramatically apparent in Robert Fludd's *Utriusque Cosmi Maioris scilicet et Minoris Metaphysica* (1617), a heroic restatement of the cosmographic project as a universal spatial science working through graphic images in the face of increasing empirical refutation coming from the mechanization of vision by means of telescope and microscope. Kepler, who sought empirical warranty for the new mathematical cosmology, challenged Fludd's cosmography on epistemological grounds in a famous polemic.[27] Galileo's sunspot images of 1610–13 offered such empirical evidence, dramatically demonstrating how the image was shedding its metaphorical role for a mimetic role in science, and rendering Fludd's highly illustrated cosmography an elaborate conceit.

THE VITRUVIAN CORPUS 1480–1620

For Vitruvius's *Ten Books of Architecture* and its associated Renaissance literature, a similar pattern of publication and commentary can be traced. Initial reverence for ancient authority, philological inquiry, and critical study of its author's theoretical claims yielded to attempts to harmonize the ideal measure of the original with the empirical measure of observed forms, and to incorporate contemporary experience into the received conceptual framework. Like *The Geography*, by the end of the sixteenth century the *Ten Books* was being displaced as a canonical work to the position of historical document, of antiquarian more than practical value. This trajectory, too, saw rhetoric, observation and experience, and the knowledge of causes variously deployed as measures of scientific truth. And, as in the Ptolemaic corpus, graphic images played a significant role within the shifting authority and meanings of the text.

Before tracing this evolution in the "scientific" status of Vitruvius's text, it is important to record that there is sufficient cross-referencing between it and Ptolemeic science to indicate that the mutual awareness between the projects of cosmographers and architects already evident in Alberti's work continued through the Renaissance. The island of Cythera in the *Hypnerotomachia Poliphili*, for example, draws upon classical references such as Circe's islands and the Vitruvian story of Aristippus, to be sure, but its description and mapping draw upon the same cosmographic models as Buondelmonti's island book, and its narrative structure may be based on parallels between the hydrological cycle and the circulation of blood in the human body.[28] The *Hypnerotomachia's* publication date of 1499 coincides with a period of contemporary excitement over islands in the Ocean Sea, whose description by the cosmographers drew heavily on conceptions of the *locus amoenus*. Caesariano accompanies his map of Italy with a passage on cosmography and chorography that anticipates Apian's extension of Ptolemy's conventional scalar distinction of geography and chorography to include cosmography (fig. 8). The map itself probably owes its westerly distortion of Calabria to Ptolemy's own inaccuracies in mapping the peninsula.[29]

DENIS COSGROVE

Daniele Barbaro and Andrea Palladio debated and corresponded about cosmographic questions with Jacomo Gastaldi and Gianbattista Ramusio.[30] Antonio Santucci taught cosmography at the Venetian Accademia del Disegno, while Rusconi was the pupil of Nicolò Tartaglia, translator of Euclid, and author of the "New Science."[31]

Cosmography and architecture faced similar dilemmas in coordinating theory and practice, authority and experience. Like *The Geography*'s humanist editors and commentators, Leon Battista Alberti and Fra Giocondo were principally concerned with demonstrating the contemporary value of the restored classical text within a discourse of "renewal." Alberti demands of the architect no more than pragmatic acquaintance with cosmographic skills:

> The arts which are useful, and indeed absolutely necessary to the Architect, are painting and mathematics. I do not require him to be deeply learned in the rest....Nor need he be a perfect astronomer, to know that Libraries ought to be situated to the North.[32]

Like his contemporary Waldseemüller, who incorporated the new fourth continent into his descriptive cosmography simply by appending Vespucci's

(fig. 8)

(fig. 9)

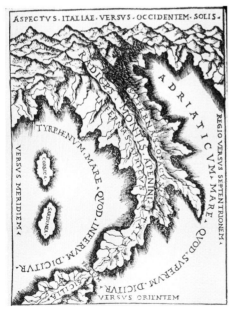

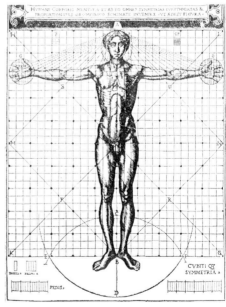

Chorographic map of Italy, from Caesare Caesariano, *Vitruvius* (1521)

Measured Vitruvian figure from Caesare Caesariano, *Vitruvius* (1521)

report of Columbus's voyage, Fra Giocondo did not stray far from the classical model. But by the 1520s, Caesare Caesariano, like Apian and Frisius, was more willing to cast the received text in the light of contemporary thought and practice and to offer critical commentary. Incorporating woodcut illustrations further opened the significance of their texts to readers, as is detailed below. As in the case of *The Geography*, the lack of original models for these graphics opened a space for the technical skills of artists and practitioners to gloss the text, which humanists were unable to provide. Caesariano's two renderings of the human body set within circle and square drew upon the geometrical methods used by the architects and surveyors of his day, and his commentary indicates the use of the measured grid for both drawing figures and measuring a land surface (fig. 9). But his written instructions for reproducing the diagram are unclear, suggesting that Caesariano's approach remains idealist and rhetorical more than empirical and technical.

It is Serlio's seven books, contemporary in their appearance with Münster's work and with cosmography's crisis years of the early 1540s, that shifted the architectural treatise toward an explicit attention to empirical measure. The change is apparent in Serlio's overall organization, which abandons Vitruvius's structure for one founded on initial propositions and on Serlio's own technical experience, made most explicit in his seventh, posthumously published, book. It is found also in the prominence, location, and precision of his measured illustrations, which can be compassed, like a scale map (fig. 10). Serlio's first book outlines the same principles of Euclidean geometry with which the mathematical cosmography opened. Applied to material space, these gave meaning to the *sphaera mundi* through whose logic architecture could shape its interventions to the spatial structure of nature. From geometry derives Serlio's concept of architectural *linee occulte*, "a continuous invisible network within which the planes and facades of buildings, and the spaces around them, were defined."[33] These hidden lines, like the parallels and meridians within which cosmographers sought to capture and represent an ordered, global geography, give precise form and order to a building's visual appearance. Serlio insists on these principles being learned through the technical skills of drafting and drawing, as the cosmographer might learn from the instructions of Apian, Frisius, or Oronce Fine to use compass and ruler in order to construct the graticule, project the sphere onto the plane, and thus map geographical space. In Serlio, as in the midcentury cosmographers, humanist scholarship is being displaced by practitioners' *techne*.

(fig. 10)

Liqual gracilità per eſſer due inſieme, & di poco rilieuo, non è uitioſa. Le miſure del tutto ſi
no nell'ordine Ionico, al quarto mio libro. Sopra la cornice ſi metterà la Tribuna, oueramente cu-
ra laquale ſarà una lanterna per dar luce al corpo del Tempio. La miſura ſua ſi trouerà con li
coli nella pianta ſegnati. L'altezza delle colonne tonde del portico, ſi farà di piedi xiij. ſopra
ſarà l'architraue d'un piede, ſopra delquale poſerà l'arco, & ſopra quello ſarà una cornice di tât'al-
unto è groſſa la colonna partita, come il capitello Dorico : ma le colonne ſaranno Doriche. La
ſotto ſegnata A, rappreſenta una di quelle capelle che eſcono fuori del muro tre piedi, & queſta
ta la parte di fuori, laquale uà coperta di mezo tondo come ſi uede.

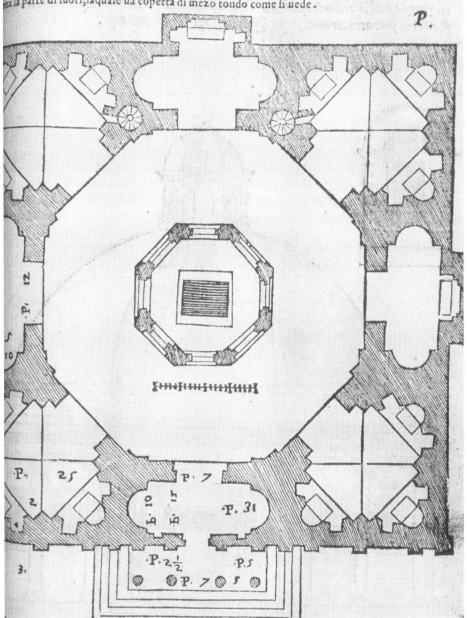

For Serlio, too, as for Münster and Thevet, the formal rule and order of geometry explicitly connected the material world with "mankind," *homo fabens*. In Book I, Serlio states:

> Bodies which are more perfect have more power than bodies which are less than perfect. It is the same with mankind. The closer man gets to the mind of God, which is perfection itself, the more goodness he has in himself. The further man moves away from God, taking pleasure in earthly things, the more he loses that initial goodness which was granted to him in the beginning.[34]

His obsession with architectural order and license, and with the moral implications of the bizarre and the monstrous—illustrated, for example, in "rustic" timber structures inhabited by "those who live dissolute and devil-may-care lives"—goes beyond Vitruvius, whose borrowings from Hesiod and Lucretius on the use of fire and the origins of shelter in the Golden Age had been illustrated by Caesariano.[35] It should be read in the light of the increasingly urgent questions surrounding irregularities of celestial and ter-restrial space and the possible connections between newly discovered and ancient peoples that cosmographers were forced to confront in dealing with discovery. Serlio's writing coincided with the polemic between Las Casas and Sepulveda over the human status of Native Americans and with Pope Paul III's encyclical *Sublimis Deus* of 1537, which declared New World peoples to have souls.[36] Münster's 1544 cosmography also figures these men and women as both perfect beings inhabiting the Golden Age and monstrous races on the edges of the space of redemption.

In Serlio, too, a growing tension can be seen between the received authority of Vitruvian theory and practical experience in the contemporary world, echoing that faced by the cosmographers. While Vitruvius remains "a guide and infallible rule," for Serlio the visual appearance of a building—revealed in illustration through the application of specific technical skills, as we have seen—should determine the final judgment (*giudicio*) of its deco-rum.[37] *Giudicio* is a rhetoric term, but, as John Onians explains, Serlio's "metaphors of stylistic description were rooted in direct sensory response rather than being transferred at secondhand from the world of literature," unlike Colonna's and Caesariano's.[38] Thus, Serlio was the first to incorporate and illustrate modern buildings into the architectural text alongside those of the ancient world, paralleling the increasing domination of technically sophisticated modern maps within the Ptolemaic corpus. The questions confronting Serlio in the 1540s mirror those facing the cosmographers in the same decade: how to resolve growing contradictions between the absoluteness of the ratios and measure implied by their respective classical authorities and the empirical measures of human and geographical forms that their technical skill permitted them to illustrate and examine; how to reconcile a conception of the whole with its myriad individual parts; and how to render form visually satisfying in practice, in buildings, and in maps, respectively.

With Palladio's *I quattro libri*, published in the same year as Ortelius's atlas, the elevation of modern experience over ancient authority is explicit. Palladio is the first to illustrate ancient buildings *all'antica*, distanced by a "Gothic" interlude from the present even as they offer to the present a language of form that his own structures demonstrate. In the same way, Ortelius physically removes Ptolemy's maps from his atlas, even as he adopts *The Geography*'s structure of planisphere and regional maps to present a picture of the theater of the world. Palladio and Ortelius share a desire to elevate the significance of the graphic image—architectural drawing and map—over the written text. Palladio's words are distinctly subordinate to his illustrations, just as Ortelius confines his written descriptions to the recto side of the maps. Each reinforces his technical claims through attention to consistent "scale," assuming a trained eye capable of using scale and measure in order to make judgments directly from the image itself without necessary recourse to the text. This necessitates a shift from schematic to precise, mimetic illustration, while the authority of the image is established more by the technical abilities of author and reader to measure and calculate than through a priori theoretical statements, which both works avoid. As Alina Payne points out, by the 1570s,

> [T]he skills of the cartographer, land surveyor, and *idrostatico* were increasingly swelling those of the traditional fifteenth-century *mecanico*.... Barbaro's scientific interests..., Rusconi's discipleship with Tartaglia, Galileo's early successes in Padua and Venice, to say nothing of the growing publications industry focused on scientific subjects, are only some of the best-known examples of this trend.[39]

There are dangers, however, in pressing a progressive model of "scientific advance" onto this narrative, for the boundaries of science and art, letters and *techne* were fluid. And architects, no more than cosmographers, could remain immune from the social and doctrinal struggles being waged around them. Scamozzi's *Idea dell'architettura universale* makes an appeal to universalism, to the figure of the world machine and the trope of *theatrum mundi*, that places it in the same intellectual context as Fludd's work. Like Fludd, Scamozzi emphasizes the scientific nature of his work, taking science to mean rational knowledge of the world rather than the method of empirical observation and experiment that Galileo was demonstrating and Francis Bacon was theorizing in these same years. Like Fludd, too, Scamozzi privileges the imaginative over the physical eye as an instrument of vision that can penetrate appearances. It is the *oculus imaginationis* that allows us to discern the causes of things and it does so by close attention to images.

Scamozzi's text is structured through a series of dialectics: of form and matter, universal and particular, architecture and building, theory and practice, the ideal and the corporeal. In Payne's opinion, he reduces the architectural orders and the material remains of antiquity to a minor place in his text, because, tellingly, "modern discourse requires no *visual* validation from the past."[40] A universal "science" is not founded on strict empiricism but, like contemporary cosmographers, Scamozzi offers a more emblematic reading of images. He illustrates the wind rose, a convention of the empirical *carta marina* rather than of the planisphere, suggesting that practical rather than theoretical knowledge is critical for the architect. But his image of the cosmos and his title are telling: this is architecture as a "universal" science. "More than any other of his predecessors, Scamozzi hints at a whole universe collapsed into a study whence the artist-scientist peeks into the larger world"; science may operate by means of "keyholes" offered by telescopes, specimens, field notes, maps, texts, and carved fragments.[41] Scamozzi is concerned to raise the status of the mechanical practices and techniques that Serlio, Palladio, and Rusconi had brought into the architectural treatise to the level of natural philosophy. Like his contemporary Fludd, Scamozzi moves toward the metaphysical, regarding form as neither purely imitative nor purely inventive but the expression of a universal mathematical certainty. His image of the human microcosm is surrounded by geometrical figures but is not itself scaled or gridded, leaving the reader to undertake the work

DENIS COSGROVE

of measure. While Alberti required of the architect a general familiarity with the practices listed by Vitruvius, Scamozzi seeks an architectural metascience, "sublime in speculation, unchallenged in demonstration, ennobled by its subject . . . excellent in its method," an architecture that should embellish the whole of the world.[42] The scope and embrace of his language is reminiscent of the prefatory poems and eulogies that Ortelius had printed in the opening pages of the *Theatrum*. For Scamozzi and Fludd, architecture and cosmography are parallel material expressions of a totalizing cosmological science. In their writings and images, architecture and cosmography seem drawn toward the perfection of metaphysical space as consolation for a material world broken by strife.

The shared role of graphic illustration in cosmography and architecture that both Ptolemy and Vitruvius were understood to have used to illustrate their texts was an invitation to their modern followers to incorporate graphics into their own editions. These quickly moved beyond drafting into maps of the coordinates of Ptolemy's *tabulae* or depictions of those structures described by Vitruvius that still existed, such as the Pantheon in Rome or the Temple of the Winds in Athens. Indeed, the number, inventiveness, and sophistication of graphic illustrations provide a measure of their authors' distance from humanist scholarship and their technical rather than philological approach to the texts. Apian's cosmography, for example, is remarkable for its inclusion of *vovelles*, including his *speculo cosmographico*; printed instruments that invited the reader to make complex calendrical and astronomical calculations based on the mathematical and geometrical principles enunciated in the text. Caesariano's contemporary edition of *Vitruvius* is richly illustrated with woodcuts of Caesariano's own design, including a sophisticated allegory of his own life, in which Vitruvius's commentator applies to himself the earlier architect's remarks about early instruction in art. Loosely modeled on the story of the ancient artist Apelles's struggle against those who sought to calumniate him, Caesariano presents himself, holding both paintbrush and compass, as having moved from the elemental realms of poverty to the ethereal spaces of fame and honor. The allegory draws upon cosmographic images of the spheres for its basic spatial structure, emphasizing *techne* as a key foundation for Caesariano's claims to honor.

Cosmography's homologies between the spheres and architecture's principles of order and decorum both depended upon Euclidean geometry and invited graphic demonstration. The *typus* or armillary diagram illustrating the formal relationships of poles, axis, great circles, and ecliptic was effectively a visual exercise in spherical geometry, and it appears regularly in publications of both Ptolemy and Vitruvius. Corollary cosmographic images, illustrating the pattern of days, nights and seasons, eclipses, climates and zones of habitability, and the distribution of lands and seas on the surface of the Earth appear in architectural as well as cosmographic texts, following Vitruvius's grounding of architectural principles in a profound understanding of location, climate, and environment. Thus Caesariano copies his armillary and world-system diagrams directly from printed editions of Sacrobosco, whose ideas he references in his commentary on the perfection of the world machine (see fig. 5).[43] Other illustrations are original and make connections between cosmographic and artistic practice. For example, the verso figure on page xi connects the use of the cross-staff in determining the declination of celestial bodies to the visual cone described by Alberti as the basis for constructing linear projection (fig. 11). Caesariano illustrates, too, the use of the gnomon to determine latitude by measuring the sun's meridian shadow at diverse locations. The technical accuracy of these images is variable, although Caesariano had drawn on the help of friends including doctors "of medicine, philosophy, and astrology."[44] The consequence was often an amalgam of Vitruvian and early Renaissance science, sometimes quite inaccurate in its rendering of the former, as seen, for example, in Caesariano's diagram illustrating connections between the latitudinal climates and the pitch of the human voice, where the variations are stretched over a single hemisphere rather than from pole to pole. The many cosmographic images in Vitruvian texts range in scale from such universal diagrams to chorographic maps. Caesariano's map of Italy lacks scale, graticule lines, or other mathematical notation, unlike other illustrations in his text (see fig. 8). It seems to follow literally Ptolemy's distinction of chorography and geography wherein the former sought to give the visual impression of a place rather than its proportioned relations of geographical space, thus was dependent more upon skills of drawing and painting than those of measure and calculation.

Caesariano's illustrations may in turn have influenced those of cosmographers. His woodcuts showing the origins of fire and the construction of the first shelter using the trunks and branches of trees (the beginnings of architecture) draw upon Golden Age iconography, recalling Piero di Cosimo's illustrations of Lucretius's narrative of civilization (familiar to Vitruvius himself). Such images, echoed in Serlio's treatment of rustic architecture and the satyric scene, were taken up by cosmographers illustrating New World peoples. Thevet's *Cosmographie universelle* of 1575 and, to an even greater extent, Theodore de Bry's images of Virginia, Hispaniola, and Peru, later used by cosmographers such as Giuseppe Rosaccio to fill the blank continental spaces of American maps, may betray a Vitruvian inspiration.[45] Such ethnographic and narrative illustrations came to dominate in later sixteenth-century written cosmographies as the space devoted mathematical principles declined.

The changing role and significance of such images over the course of the sixteenth century were partly an expression of a growing emphasis on autopsy and empirical evidence rather than on received authority and a priori reasoning. The lack of formal symmetry in the elemental sphere (as in the geographical pattern of lands and waters), although long pursued—for

(fig. 11)

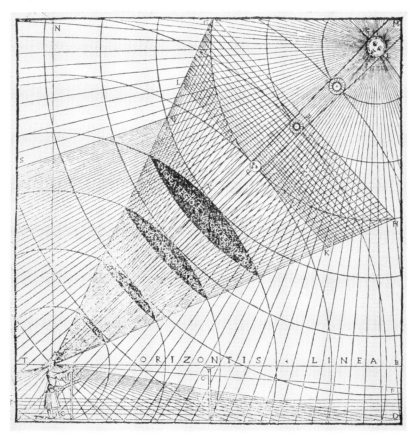

Illustration showing the use of the cross-staff, from Caesario Caesariano, *Vitruvius* (1521)

example, in the cartographic survival of a great southern continent—could be explained away by Aristotle's principle of corruptibility in the sublunar realm. But theoretical questions became subordinated as descriptive cosmography strengthened, so that by midcentury, simply and even ritually defined in the opening pages, mathematical cosmography hardly balanced "the thousands of profuse pages that contain the many-hued descriptions of countries, regions, towns and islands."[46] These descriptions called for illustration: Münster's text offers a plethora of urban and architectural graphics, as does the urban companion to Ortelius's atlas, Braun and Hogenberg's *Civitates orbis terrarum* from 1580. It is for research to determine the extent that these draw upon either specific models or principles of urban and architectural illustration to be found in the Vitruvian corpus.

CONCLUSION

Within our general understanding of the role of classical texts in sixteenth-century scientific and epistemological debates, there remain questions of the specific relations between individual works and the discourses surrounding them. Here, some such questions concerning the relations between Ptolemy's *Geography* and Vitruvius's *Architecture* and between the fields of cosmography and architecture have been opened. The histories of both works have been individually well studied and their connections occasionally noted, but the latter have not been systematically explored. The parallels in reception, commentary, and illustration of the two texts indicate a fertile zone for further research, which might throw light on broader questions of scholarship, science, metaphor, and image between 1450 and 1650. Such research might concentrate around shared characteristics of the texts. One is their common role as technical and scientific works whose publication took place within the context of continuing practice, generating new experience and knowledge unknown to their authors. Another, related to the reciprocal connections of text and practice, is how far the absence of whatever graphic materials had originally accompanied the classical texts opened a space not only for imaginative reconstruction of images but for images to take on an active role in producing meaning from the texts. Such meaning reflected the works' passage from humanist scholarship to more technical expertise.

Graphic illustration increased in significance as editors and commentators emphasized the technical and practical significance of Ptolemy and

DENIS COSGROVE

Vitruvius, while simultaneously revealing their own competence. Illustration thus came to offer an alternative way of "reading" the texts themselves. Cosmography and architecture were opened visually to readers not necessarily able themselves to use the instruments necessary to their practice. Ortelius's *Theatrum*, for example, proclaims its consistently scaled and colored maps as agents for vicarious travel across the globe through their faithful rendering of the terrestrial space, so the eye travels across the mountains, hills, and plains of the map as the body might do over actual space; it abandons, however, even a cursory summary of the mathematical cosmography. Empirical example and simple numerical measure tended to gain in authority over principles of geometry and proportion in both of cosmography's successor sciences, geography and astronomy, rather less so in architectural treatises. Palladio's illustrations are drawn predominantly from his own projects tagged to specific construction sites in the Veneto, and like Ortelius in the same year he keeps theoretical claims to a minimum. Nonetheless, the numerical measurements he prints on his plans and sections, while apparently related to actual structures, have often been altered in order to maintain Vitruvian principles of eurhythmy—an indirect statement similar to Ortelius's emblematic hints rather than direct proclamations of continuing belief in cosmography's universalism. This desire to maintain the consolations of universalism and harmony implicit in the cosmographic model seems to have increased in the later years of the century, possibly in response to the growing violence of doctrinal division. Thus, both Scamozzi and Fludd use images in their published works as a way of sustaining a metaphysical unity inscribed in the cosmos and to be realized in architecture, a unity finding diminishing empirical support from geography and astronomy.

Hasty conclusions about the status of images in these texts, however, are best avoided—for example, contrasting Fludd's and Scamozzi's metaphysical images on the one hand with Joan Blaeu's scientific planispheres or Galileo's mechanically made astronomical images on the other. Mario Biagioli has recently suggested that simple distinction between schematic or diagrammatic pictures (such as the armillary, the celestial diagram, or the climatic zones) favored by cosmographers and architects, and realistic or mimetic illustration (such as the Ptolemaic planisphere, or the telescopic image of lunar mountains) is difficult to maintain. Indeed, Galileo's observations themselves became known through their redrawing for publication even though their authority was founded on the claim of mechanical origin. Lacking, as was inevitable before these images themselves established it, a notion of the "real" against which to evaluate the truth claims of any image, "eye witness" authority actually derived less from mimesis than from the strength of the existing authority it challenged. In 1600, Aristotelian orthodoxy remained so absolutely defined that any experience that deviated from it had to gain a large measure of conviction from the technical expertise of its production.[47] Thus, the graphic image itself played something of the role of metaphor in Aristotle's sense of giving form and name to nameless things, but it was obliged to work with the language of the known. In mapping celestial certainty onto elemental flux, the cosmographer's world machine offered a powerful metaphor in a time of social collapse and seems to have offered architecture, too, the promise of a more harmonious and stable space.

NOTES

1. By "spatialities" I mean the ways in which people experience, think about, and imagine material spaces. The literature on the subject is, predictably, enormous. Among the most useful general statements are Edward Grant, *Planets, Stars and Orbs: The Medieval Cosmos, 1200–1687* (Cambridge: Cambridge University Press, 1994) on cosmology; Maria Boas Hall, ed., *Nature and Nature's Laws: Documents of the Scientific Revolution* (New York: Walker and Company, 1970) for key scientific texts; Lisa Jardine, *Worldly Goods: A New History of the Renaissance* (London: Macmillan, 1996) on the commercial and intellectual implications of oceanic trade and discovery; David Woodward, ed., *The History of Cartography*, vol. 3, *Cartography in the European Renaissance* (Chicago: University of Chicago Press, forthcoming), and David Buisseret, *Monarchs, Ministers and Maps: The Emergence of Cartography as a Tool of Government in Early Modern Europe* (Chicago: University of Chicago Press, 1992) on mapping and cartography; Martin Kemp, *The Science of Art: Optical Themes in Western Art from Brunelleschi to Seurat* (New Haven and London: Yale University Press, 1990), Svetlana Alpers, *The Art of Describing: Dutch Art in the Seventeenth Century* (London: John Murray, 1983), and Walter S. Gibson, *Mirror of the Earth: The World Landscape in Sixteenth Century Flemish Painting* (Princeton, N.J.: Princeton University Press, 1989) on art. The classic architectural work is Rudolf Wittkower's *Architectural Principles in the Age of Humanism* (London: Alex Tiranti, 1962).

2. Elizabeth L. Eisenstein, *The Printing Press as an Agent of Change: Communications and Cultural Transformations in Early-Modern Europe* (Cambridge: Cambridge University Press, 1979); Anthony Grafton et al., *New Worlds, Ancient Texts: The Power of Tradition and the Shock of Discovery* (Cambridge, Mass.: Belknap Press, 1992).

3. Tony Campbell, *The Earliest Printed Maps, 1472–1500* (London: British Library, 1987); Vaughan Hart and Peter Hicks, *Paper Palaces: The Rise of the Architectural Treatise* (New Haven and London: Yale University Press, 1998).

4. Natalia Lazovsky, *"The Earth Is Our Book": Geographical Knowledge in the Latin West, ca. 400–1000* (Ann Arbor: University of Michigan Press, 2000).

DENIS COSGROVE

5. The cosmological aspects of the Vitruvian corpus were first systematically explored by Rudolf Wittkower in *Architectural Principles*. More recent work is summarized in John Onians, *Bearers of Meaning: The Classical Orders in Antiquity, the Middle Ages and the Renaissance* (Cambridge: Cambridge University Press, 1988), and Lionel March, *Architectonics of Humanism* (Chichester, England: Academy Editions, 1992). On the cosmological connections of Ptolemy's *Geography*, see Denis Cosgrove, *Apollo's Eye: A Cartographic Genealogy of the Globe in the Western Imagination* (Baltimore: Johns Hopkins University Press, 2001).

6. Since Onians's *Bearers of Meaning* (1988), the Vitruvian treatises have received renewed scholarly attention from Anglophone scholars, in part through their translation into English. A 1996 translation of perhaps the most influential of them—Sebastiano Serlio's *Tutte l'opere d'architettura*, an incomplete collection of seven books published between 1537 and 1575—stimulated Hart and Hicks's edited volume. This was supplemented in 1999 by Alina A. Payne's *The Architectural Treatise in the Italian Renaissance* (Cambridge: Cambridge University Press).

7. For a useful summary of literature and current debates on this perplexing text, see the collection of papers edited by John Dixon Hunt in *Word & Image* 14, nos. 1/2 (1998).

8. Caesare Caesariano, *De architectura* (Como, 1521), with an introduction and index by Carol Herselle Krinsky (Munich: Wilhelm Fink, 1969).

9. Sebastiano Serlio, *On Architecture*, Vol. I, Books I–V, in Sebastiano Serlio, *Tutte l'opere d'Architettura et Prospetiva*, trans. Vaughan Hart and Peter Hicks (New Haven and London: Yale University Press, 1996).

10. *I dieci libri dell'architectura di M. Vitruvio Pollio*, with commentary by Sig. Daniele Barbaro (Venice, 1586).

11. Andrea Palladio, *I quattro libri dell'architettura* (Venice, 1570).

12. Pietro Rusconi, *De architettura* (Venice, 1590). Tartaglia was the translator of Euclid's *Elements* into Italian and a popularizer of an empirical, mathematically based "new science" of ballistics.

13. Vincenzo Scamozzi, *Idea dell'architettura universale* (Venice, 1615).

14. Recent work by Mario Carpo casts an interesting new perspective on Alberti's relationship with Ptolemy's text, suggesting that Alberti's famously "lost" map of Rome (*Descriptio Urbis Romae*) never actually existed because its inventor, like Ptolemy, was demonstrating that cartographic knowledge could most accurately be conveyed by *tabulae*, lists of coordinates. Any person with sufficient technical skill could reproduce the map personally from the numbers provided, thus avoiding the inevitable inaccuracies of copying a linear drawing.

15. Ptolemy's *Almagest*, literally "The Great Work," named thus by Arab scientists because it summarized ancient theoretical and empirical knowledge of the heavens and their movements, was known in the Latin West from the late thirteenth century. *The Geography*, which came to Florence from Byzantium about 1400 and was translated into Latin by 1410, summarized ancient geographical knowledge and offered a systematic procedure for mapping the sphere onto a planisphere; its *tabulae* gave coordinates for 1,500 places across the ecumene, or habitable earth. On the reception and publication of *The Geography*, see Marica Milanesi, "Geografia e cosmografia in Italia tra XV e XVII secolo," in *Atti del Convegno La Cultura Astronomica e Geografica in Italia dal XV al XVII Secolo*, Memorie della Società Astronomica Italiana 65, 2 (1994): 443–68.

16. There was some disagreement about the numbers of maps that could be reconstructed from *The Geography*'s twenty-six *tabulae*. Vitruvius's illustrations were thought to number thirty.

17. John Dee, "The Mathematical Preface to the *Elements of Geometrie . . .*" (1570) (New York: Science History Publications, 1975).

18. In Waldseemüller these consist of 1. Elements of geometry; 2. Meaning of sphere, axis, poles, etc; 3. Circles of the heavens; 4. Theory of the sphere according to the system of degrees; 5. Five celestial zones in heavens and Earth; 6. Parallels; 7. Climates; 8. Winds; 9. Divisions of the Earth and distances between places.

19. Frank Lestringant, "The Crisis of Cosmography at the End of the Renaissance," in *Humanism in Crisis: The Decline of the French Renaissance*, ed. Philippe Desan (Ann Arbor: University of Michigan Press, 1991), 156.

20. Ursula Lamb, *Cosmographers and Pilots of the Spanish Maritime Empire* (Aldershot and Brookfield, Vt.: Variorum, 1995); E. G. R. Taylor, *The Mathematical Practitioners of Tudor and Stuart England* (Cambridge: Cambridge University Press, 1954).

21. Lestringant, "The Crisis of Cosmography." This crisis was itself exacerbated by religious strife, as the careers of both Mercator and Ortelius bear witness. As I suggest below, this had implications for the metaphysical appeal of cosmography in the later sixteenth century.

22. Grafton, *New Worlds, Ancient Texts*, 111.

23. Lestringant, "The Crisis of Cosmography," 153–80.

24. Frank Lestringant, *Mapping the Renaissance World: The Geographical Imagination in the Age of Discovery* (Cambridge: Polity Press, 1994).

25. Frances Yates, *The Rosicrucian Enlightenment* (London: Routledge and Kegan Paul, 1972); Giorgio Mangani, *Il "Mondo" di Abramo Ortelio: Misticismo, geografia e collezionismo nel rinascimento dei Paesi Bassi* (Ferrara: Franco Cosimo Panini, 1998).

26. On the metaphor of theater in late sixteenth-century cosmography and on literary culture more generally, see Ann Blair, *The Theatre of Nature: Jean Bodin and Renaissance Science* (Princeton, N.J.: Princeton University Press, 1997).

27. Robert S. Westman, "Nature, Art, and Psyche: Jung, Pauli, and the Kepler-Fludd Polemic" in *Occult and Scientific Mentalities in the Renaissance*, ed. Brian Vickers (Cambridge: Cambridge University Press, 1984): 177–230.

28. Roswitha Stewering, "The Relationship between World, Landscape and Polia in the *Hypnerotomachia Poliphili*," *Word & Image* 14, nos. 1/2 (1998): 2–10.

29. Caesariano, *Vitruvius*, xlvi r, where he directly acknowledges the work of Ptolemy and other cosmographers.

30. Cosgrove, *Apollo's Eye*, 143–47.

31. Payne, *Architectural Treatise*, 207–10.

32. Leon Battista Alberti, *Ten Books of Architecture*, trans. Leoni (London: Alex Tiranti, 1955).

33. Serlio, *On Architecture*, 458.

34. Ibid., 19.

35. Ibid., 90; Onians, *Bearers of Meaning*, 282–86.

36. Cary J. Nederman, *Worlds of Difference: European Discourses of Toleration c1100–c1550* (State College, Penn.: Pennsylvania State University Press, 2000), 99–115.

37. Serlio, *On Architecture*, 136.

38. Onians, *Bearers of Meaning*, 270.

39. Payne, *Architectural Treatise*, 207.

40. Ibid., 215.

41. Ibid., 211.

42. Vincenzo Scamozzi, *Idea*, 5 ("[E]lla è sublime nella speculatione, indubitata nelle dimostrave, nobilissima per il sogetto...ecellentissima per il methodo...perche lei sola abellisse il Mondo tutto").

43. Caesariano, *De Architectura*, xlix r.

44. Ibid., Introduction, 24.

45. These images from the 1590s predate by nearly a century those of Caramuel de Lobkowitz, which Joseph Rykwert connects to Caesariano's work (*On Adam's House in Paradise* [Cambridge, Mass.: MIT Press, 1997], 137–40).

46. Lestringant, *Mapping the Renaissance World*, xxx.

47. Mario Biagioli, "Picturing and Convincing: The Discovery and Illustration of Sunspots," paper delivered at the University of California at Los Angles, October 2000.

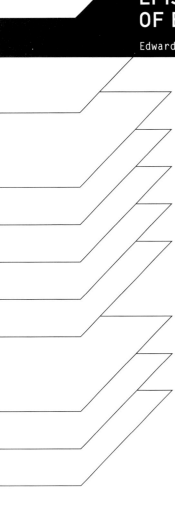

THE PLACE OF DISTRIBUTION:
EPISODES IN THE ARCHITECTURE
OF EXPERIMENT

Edward Eigen

Un point grave et capital, c'est le choix de l'habitation.

—Jules Michelet, *La Mer*

In his compendious *Eléments et théorie de l'architecture* of 1905, the academician Julien Guadet declared the subject of the laboratory "absolutely modern."[1] During France's Third Republic, the laboratory became the focus of a state-sponsored cult of science, the site of a strategic alliance of research and pedagogy. Reflecting the concomitant specialization within the scientific disciplines, Guadet delineated the actual distribution of institutional spaces proper to emerging fields of study, each of the so-called ensembles designated metonymically by the name of the "chair" inscribed at its entrance. Each ensemble was composed of representational spaces such as lecture halls, libraries, and collections rooms; in addition, place was to be made for preparation and storage rooms, drawing and photographic studios (the latter requiring its own laboratory), and finally crematoria for the cadavers of animals sacrificed in the dissection amphitheater. In an echo of J.-N.-L. Durand's protoscientific analysis of composition, Guadet reduced the program of the ensemble to the elements of air, space, and light.[2] Synthesized in adequate—and "absolutely different"—measure, these elements of architecture were to catalyze the advance of science itself. Yet the classificatory rigor of Guadet's (re)distribution of the spaces of the laboratory was belied by the contingency of laboratory life. Having no fixed formal structure apart from evolving methods of experience and practice, this very contingency is what validated the laboratory's claim to being absolutely modern. In order to grasp the events for which the laboratory is the scene—the laboratory's fate of place[3]—the dynamics of distribution (the task of managing resources and keeping things in their proper place, as it were) must be identified. To render account of this manner of planning, the laboratory's evolutionary (and premodern) sources must also be seen in their proper cultural and cognitive context.

Originally understood as the place where the fire was kept, the laboratory was part and parcel of the practical tasks of managing the household economy. As the site and engine of material change—and arguably as the origin of experiment—the foyer (literally the fire) required ongoing maintenance and material investment. As Claire Salomon-Bayet explains in her history of experiment, in the predominantly rural world of the Ancien Régime, the foyer was the place of lodging for those who tended the familial hearth.[4] It designated at once a physical habitation and the familiar structure of its inhabitants, bound as they were by social and economic functions. That this domestic economy entailed issues of distribution went beyond the task (as defined in terms of *convenance* by Jacques-François Blondel) of "maintaining" the *enfilade*, or sequence of rooms in a house. As Salomon-Bayet observes, the laboratory's affiliation with household life stems from the need to identify and place in close proximity the experimenter and the means of experiment.[5] If this need can be met with rudimentary architectural elements or means of spatial division, it nonetheless calls into being the habits of the prudent housekeeper-experimenter who ensures that these quantities are sensibly employed. Indeed, the model of (domestic) economy preceded the laboratory's plan in strictly architectural terms, just as the task of watching the fire anticipated any experimentation. Written after the fact, as it were, Guadet's own classification of plan types ran the risk of mistaking the effect for the cause; the domestic space circumscribed a differentiated terrain from which experimentation evolved. Distribution implied a network of exchanges that made place for laboratory life.[6] Plan followed suit, by design or otherwise.

The above notion of economy is apparent in the crucial distinction Guadet drew between laboratories designed for the experimental and for the mathematical sciences. The mathematical sciences, he allowed, were "abstract" and could be conducted in virtually any setting. In the experimental sciences, however, it is possible to speak of the priority of place. Natural history in particular required a "very different combination [of spaces], in virtue of the special nature of its experimental subjects."[7] Simply put, its subjects were living beings. The museum—the wonted theater of nature's spectacle—would be displaced as the site for naturalists' research. In the evolution of natural history from a descriptive to a historic and finally experimental science, with its concern with organic development, the question of how things lived could no longer be abstracted from the milieu in which they lived. Understanding the distribution of living kinds—the study of which was a key predecessor to evolutionary theory—meant taking account of large-scale factors of geography and climate as well as the intra- and extraorganic conditions of physiological labor and reproduction.

Given the necessity of properly combining the architectural elements of the laboratory with regard to these emerging priorities of research, what rationality was to dictate the location of the laboratory itself? One prescient response was offered by the physiologist Claude Bernard (1813–1878)—who suggested that the branches of natural history should be established in naturally favorable sites where they could be most productively cultivated, rather than concentrating them in urban and university centers. The opportunities for research that these extramural sites offered would attract scientific talent to them.[8] In this way the household of science would be arranged according to nature's own economy. Notably, Bernard's recommendation was made in a private communication to the Emperor Napoleon III following a meeting at the Tuileries Palace in March 1868 at which he and other scientific luminaries, including Louis Pasteur and Henri Milne-Edwards, voiced their collective despair over the appalling state of research facilities in Paris.

Curiously, Guadet's principal example of the modern laboratory offered in his *Eléments* was the marine research station at Saint-Vaast (fig. 1). What lends interest to Saint-Vaast, situated on an island in the Bay of the Seine, is that it was an outpost, if not an outgrowth, of the storied Muséum d'histoire naturelle in Paris. Bernard's recommendation came at a time when the edifice of French science was in disarray, its restoration involving a strategy of administrative bookkeeping that would capitalize on already existing sites for research wherever they could be identified. Creating localized exceptions to the long-standing juxtaposition of Paris and the provinces (or, more generically, the center and periphery), nearly uninhabited but potentially

(fig. 1)

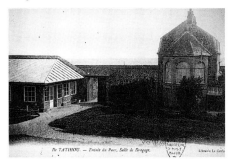

View of the Muséum d'histoire naturelle's laboratory in a converted lazaret on the Ile Tatihou

productive regions such as Saint-Vaast were poised to become epicenters of science and to define new directions of research. To wit, Guadet's discussion of Saint-Vaast was based entirely on the description provided by its architect. The failure of the Paris-based academician to inspect the place in person was no doubt attributable to its location, which was remote if not geographically distant. Saint-Vaast thus assumed a central role in Guadet's taxonomy of the laboratory, without the startling anomaly of its situation changing in any way the architectural syntax on which his systemization was based. Arguably only a visit to the frontier of France (and of science) would have affected such a necessary change.

That Guadet commented on Saint-Vaast at all warrants some attention. One observer who actually toured the marine laboratories that eventually dotted the French coast commented that even the most famous of them, at Roscoff in Brittany, lacked the "harmonious appearance and architectural beauty characteristic of buildings designed by state architects" (fig. 2).[9] In terms of official aesthetics, clearly defined character was the desired product of any well-conceived composition. Yet rather than being seen as lacking architectural interest, these laboratories were the source of renewal of the scientific edifice. Considered "annexes" and even "colonies" of urban institutions including the Muséum, the Sorbonne, and the Collège de France, their anomalous plan was the product of a flexible approach to facilitating new forms of research. Deriving from embryological discourse, the term *anomalous* refers here to structures that responded to the particularities or irregularities of terrain. By contrast, *design* implies a normal approach to planning, normal in the sense suggested by Georges Canguilhem as involving the use of a T square.[10] These laboratories' lack of harmony can be regarded as a form of naturalism unconstrained by artistic laws. The same reasons that make it unproductive to seek their place within the architectural canon suggest the usefulness of understanding how the laboratories represented a particular mediation of new programs and new sites, albeit at a lower level than that of architectural theory.

(fig. 2)

Construction of *Roland II* at the Arago Laboratory, Banyuls-sur-Mer

This is not to say that Saint-Vaast was without a plan. The layout of its scientific campus was overseen by an assistant to Jules André, the Paris Muséum's state-appointed architect. But, as was the case at Roscoff, its architect was not responsible for the design of a new building but rather for remaking an existing structure into a facility for advanced research. Indeed, much of Saint-Vaast's furnishings consisted of architectural salvage from the Muséum's cabinet of natural history, which at the time was being replaced by André's Grand Gallery. While the conversion of Saint-Vaast certainly did not tax its architect's expertise, the mutually inflected status of the Muséum and its research station points to a changed emphasis in their respective architectural meanings. The isolation of Saint-Vaast was perfectly suited to its original function, that of a military quarantine station.[11] The Muséum was a prized landmark of Paris's institutional landscape; the streets surrounding it bear the names of its great naturalists. Thus, Guadet, who was André's student, paid his master the compliment of calling the Grand Gallery a veritable "Louvre of science."[12] The ease with which this apotheosis of museum-based science was fit into an urban monumental tradition only highlights the distance between it and the scene of experimental research at Saint-Vaast. To be sure, this distance once might have been bridged by the conception of the Muséum as the "metropolis of the natural sciences," supplied by a vast hinterland of specimens and talent. But the Muséum had instead become nature's "necropolis."[13] A great collector of dust, the museum was no place to study living nature.

This sentiment, expressed by Muséum scientist and Saint-Vaast founder Edmond Perrier, reflected a practical understanding that it was not stately walls that gave rise to "modern" science. In terms of architecture, the innovation represented by Saint-Vaast and Roscoff was precisely that it was established beyond the Muséum's walls.[14] The laboratory's migration *extra muros* represents a critical moment in a spatial narrative that began with the movement that shaped Perrier's own efforts to reconfigure the Muséum's institutional identity. This narrative was set in motion by the naturalists Milne-Edwards and Victor Audouin's *Recherches pour servir pour l'histoire naturelles des côtes de France* (1828–32), in which they claimed that the sciences of life could no longer be pursued "amid collections and the silence of the cabinet."[15] The Paris Muséum was indeed a vast and invaluable store of specimens that were the source of countless contributions to science. If, however, the use of arsenical soaps and other preservation measures made possible the emergence of fields such as ornithology,[16] the fluids used for preserving marine specimens distorted their true form and color. The evidence such specimens offered of shapeless forms and indifferent hues was but a symptom of the more troubling aspect of working amid collections: absent was the vital functioning of life itself. The Muséum's glass-fronted vitrines and endless ranks of specimen jars provided the instruments of research for naturalists and the object of curiosity for visitors including the architect Gottfried Semper, who found in them confirmation of primordial architectural types. But although the penetration of the scientific glance or the drama of dissection might in a visual and narrative sense recall these specimens to life, they were in no sense actually living.

In Foucault's dramatic telling it was the great anatomist Georges Cuvier (1769–1832) who was to "topple the glass jars of the Museum, smash them open and dissect all the forms of animal visibility that the classical age had preserved in them." His act of vandalism, if not iconoclasm, had evidently not gone far enough (fig. 3).[17] For the naturalists inspired by Milne-Edwards and Audouin's work, the innate transparency of the organisms to be found along the shore offered new opportunities to observe the emergence of organic being. It was not the smashing of the glass jars but the rolling of the surf and the "pulsation of life" that shattered the silence of the cabinet. These sights and sounds provided the new rhythms of research staged by the tides. Thus it was during their 1828 expedition to the Chausey Islands that Milne-Edwards and Audouin wrote to their Muséum colleagues explaining their need to "transport their seat of observation" to the places where their subjects lived (fig. 4).[18] Their mobile seat of observation mediated the physical and phenomenal features that separated the institutional aims of the Muséum and the untested practices set to work along shore.

The silence of the cabinet was as much the product of shuttering out distractions as closing in the objects upon which the naturalist's gaze was fixed; the cabinet, of course, was also the site of interior journeys. In making their seat of observation a portable property, one lacking the properly architectural principles of inclusion and exclusion, Milne-Edwards and Audouin were forced to mediate open space. But when the cabinet is seen as a trope in the careers (those exemplary spatial narratives) that were focused on the Muséum, it becomes clear that Milne-Edwards and Audouin's expedition to the coast was not a rite of initiation but one of return.

(fig. 3)

Intérieur du Cabinet d'anatomie comparée.

Georges Cuvier's Cabinet d'anatomie comparée, Muséum d'histoire naturelle, Paris, illustrated in Jules Janin and Pierre Boitard. *Le Jardin des plantes* (1842)

THE PLACE OF DISTRIBUTION

In the person of Cuvier can be found a particular form of disaffection that betrayed the costs that the cabinet, as instrument of research and privacy, presented. With his "conquest of the city," as Cuvier's biographer Dorinda Outram has described it, Cuvier became a permanent denizen of the Muséum. He began to regard open space as an epistemological threat.[19] The uncertainty of fieldwork, the myriad particulars and variables confronted by the naturalist, threatened his ambition to elevate natural history to the status of the "exact sciences." Once ensconced within the Muséum's institutional confines, however, Cuvier became "distanced" from the places where it was possible to make the kind of observations that originally won his place at the Muséum.[20] Aside from Cuvier's own scientific precocity, these observations were attributed to the "conditions in which they were made,"[21] namely, a prolonged stay along the coast of Normandy where he had access to living specimens. In returning to these same sites, Milne-Edwards and Audouin remade the camera obscura of the cabinet into a fugitive eye, tracing the salient features of the field as they progressed through it.

Upon returning from the Chausey Islands to continue his work at the Muséum, Milne-Edwards commented that many of the specimens in the cabinet of invertebrates were marked with the same label regardless of the "real locality" of their origin.[22] The problem was not one of labeling per se but rather the inevitable result of the traffic in specimens themselves. Much if not most of the Muséum's infinitely diverse collection was provided by so-called *naturalistes voyageurs* who were sent on an errand to collect nature's bounty on behalf of the Muséum's professors.[23] Occupied as they were with the institutional mission of the Muséum, the latter were largely sheltered from the rigors of fieldwork and, as a consequence, forgetful of their deputies' labors while benefiting from them. For the specimen labels to serve as signs of reference to the external world, the nature of the errand itself would have to be transformed from a form of service carried out on behalf of someone

(fig. 4)

ILES CHAUSEY. — Le Village BLAINVILLAIS. La ferme

Village of Blainvilais fishermen on the Grand Ile of the Chausey Islands

EDWARD EIGEN

else to the business with which a well-trained observer occupied himself; the field itself would have to be made into a viable place of sustained occupation. The other option—one that was widely pursued—was to instruct field-workers in the art of observation. The evidence of Milne-Edwards and Audouin's success during their first expedition to the coast—their experiments on living specimens contributing to an important revision to the similitude of form and function that was so grandly demonstrated in Cuvier's Cabinet d'anatomie comparée (gallery of comparative anatomy)—suggests that their purpose was not strictly to report material back to the Muséum. Rather, the work carried out in the field was in a crucial sense proper to an understanding of life in the field; it also meant carrying the means of experimentation to the field. In order to understand how an act formerly regarded as an errand took on meaning in its own right, it is necessary to pose the following question: What facilities, if not buildings, made naturalists feel as if at home while abroad in the field of research? In other words, what significance can be found in the fact that the naturalists regarded the success of their scientific adventures to the coast as inextricable from the seemingly quotidian concerns of housekeeping, if not homemaking?

While Guadet defined the composition of the laboratory in terms of its architectural elements, the problem for the naturalists was how they were to mediate their own circumstances in the field. This problem turned on the issue of whether the field was an eligible place for a laboratory, even or especially one of a temporary nature. The nonreducibility of Saint-Vaast to its architectural elements, or rather the recognition of a new manner of their composition, is expressed in Guadet's identification of its so-called double program: research and habitation. The type of the marine laboratory was essentially hybrid, literally occupying an in-between place where land and water met and exchanged states according to the time of day. Guadet attributed the double program to the simple need for the naturalists to find lodging in a remote place that was cut off from the mainland each day by the tides. But it is in the nature of the place that the complicated origins of the marine laboratory are to be found. It was not the case that design had failed to articulate adequately these programmatic functions; rather, they arose together and were provided for with the same selected elements of the laboratory and the household that the naturalists transported to the field. Especially when provided in the most rudimentary setting, they were never in fact separate.

In historic terms, the founding of Saint-Vaast in 1888 and its redefinition of the Muséum stands at the end of the narrative that began with Milne-Edwards and Audouin's first expedition of 1828. Spanning these two historical markers are a variety of attempts, notably at Roscoff, to translate the naturalists' mobile seat of observation into a structural form, permanent or not. Their research practices also shaped a more complex understanding of distribution than architectural discourse was as yet equipped to confront.

What distinguishes the marine laboratory's double program from the scholarly fastness of the monastery or even from the Muséum's tradition of resident naturalists are the particular traits of distribution (conceptual, spatial, and natural) of its field of operation. Experimental zoology as defined in practice by Milne-Edwards and Audouin forced to the fore both meanings of the term *occupation*, that of intellectual orientation and that of habitation. Theirs was a science based on principles of domestic economy, mirroring, in part, what they perceived to be nature's own economy. The initial impression of the laboratory-household as a curious and necessary instance of architectural bricolage is only enhanced by the extant cracks in the French scientific edifice. The infamous penury of the scientific budget meant that even Louis Pasteur was forced, in his words, to negotiate with the minister for "light, air, and space," the very elements Guadet so liberally distributed in his theoretical text.[24] Bernard, another critic of what was a veritable spatial crisis within the most esteemed Parisian research institutions, famously claimed that laboratories were the tombs of France's greatest scientists.[25] Amid such humid, dark, and poorly ventilated laboratories, Pasteur noted balefully, the scientist could not even be sure whether his experimental subjects expired due to the very conditions in which they were kept.

Despite the perspicacity of his proposal to establish research centers in the places where nature provided the objects of study, Bernard's own experimental method is, for the most part, antithetical to that of zoology. The physiologist drew a distinction between the (passive) Observer, who considers phenomena in the "conditions where nature offers them to him," and the (active) Experimenter, to whom facts appear in "conditions of which he himself is the master."[26] Although it employed precise anatomical methods, zoology was not to be regarded as an active science until it, too, possessed the means to master the conditions, if not the final outcome, of experimentation on living beings. Mastery in this context meant wedding field-based research to laboratory science in the absence of any laboratories in the field to accommodate it. This paradox was not lost on the first generation of naturalists to visit the coast, whose activity was largely consumed in judging its very eligibility for research. As later retold in terms that stressed the naturalists' Crusoe-like resourcefulness, there they were pushed back to first principles. Milne-Edwards and Audouin and their wives, who accompanied them on their first expedition to the Chausey Islands, improvised a ménage at turns brilliant and drastic in a sadly dilapidated farmhouse.[27] Though Audouin was pleased to report that at least one room had a window to illuminate their microscopes, it was rather the house's location, its walls practically "lapped by the incoming tide," that proved invaluable.

The equability of the Chausey Islands as a site of research was in some sense overdetermined by the first series of observations Milne-Edwards and Audouin performed. As if recapitulating the ritual-cum-experimental method of establishing the viability of a site where a camp was to be established by inspecting the livers of the animals that lived there,[28] Milne-Edwards and Audouin inspected the viscera of animals they kept alive until the time of experiment in an "open air" observatory. The latter consisted of a basin dug into the ground beside their farmhouse and a channel that fed it directly with seawater. In terms of managing the resources of the nascent laboratory-household, with its stock of specimens, the naturalists could pace themselves and avoid the fate of the *naturalistes voyageurs* who, having run out of time to work in the field, were forced to base their observations on specimens conserved in liquid.[29] If it was not fire that animated their experiments, it was rather the initiation of this hydrological economy that made the preparation of their site complete. Having husbanded this stock of specimens— local inhabitants noted that the naturalists "consumed" a great number but ate none—they proceeded with their experiments on the physiology of circulation.[30] Circulation, a term central to the emergence of modern social and economic thought, was theirs to manage in their improvised observatory and formed the object of their experimental scrutiny.

Milne-Edwards and Audouin's experiments proceeded by their injecting a dye into the circulatory system of crustaceans, their very act of living rendering them graphically visible to the naturalists. By tracing the circulation of vital fluids through their bodies, the naturalists recorded the "formless" (*informe*) lacunae between organs. The indirect evidence of these spaces and the functions they performed belied the similitude of form and function on which the topography of living form had been based.[31] Evidently the anatomicophysiological traits of organic texture and structure that were made legible by Cuvier's famed Cabinet d'anatomie comparée were an incomplete rendering of what took place in the act of life itself. In comparing the linear, ramifying circulation of vital matter through well-defined "paths of communication" to the pooling of mixed liquids in formless, intraorganic cavities, they found evidence for reestablishing the analogies between living beings and the organization upon which life was based. Instead of descriptively mapping and classifying the components of the "the living machine,"[32] Milne-Edwards sought the laws governing the progressive division of physiological labor along the scale of organized being. That this notion would be interpreted by Darwin in geographic terms as a factor of evolution lent force to Milne-Edwards's contention that these experiments gave a new understanding to how vital functions were "localized" in the animal economy.[33] Its conceptually proleptic value notwithstanding, the significance of the division of labor for the emergence of the laboratory gives shape to a logic of distributing resources that needed to be in place for experiments of the same sort to be possible.

Milne-Edwards and Audouin's experimental resources on the Chausey Islands were severely restricted. Their furnishings were limited to the carefully selected elements of home and laboratory, the objects of personal and scientific necessity that could be transported with them into the field. Their sole table served for meals and dissections. Further suggesting the state of domestic affairs prior to the division of labor, if not space, the wives' hands, Audouin reported, were occupied at one moment with cooking meals, the next with a broom, and then with pens to describe the specimens the men had collected along the shore. In this setting the expectation of privacy afforded by the cabinet was not remotely relevant. The juxtaposition of the husbands' mobility outside the house and the wives' labors inside correspond to traditional gendered division of space. With the absence of women on subsequent missions, a less localized but more pervasive concern with domesticity nonetheless manifested itself in the naturalists' writings. The program of researching the domestic coast of France was framed by the naturalists explicitly in terms of contrast to the heroic circumnavigations that were the contemporary measure of masculinity. Though highly productive, ocean-bound research had none of the predictability or continuity that the makings of the household-laboratory promised. Rather than providing a true sense of adventure, the self-understood hardships of the first naturalists to visit the coast—the oft-repeated tales of making laundry basins into aquariums, of living in bivouacs—speaks of a frustrated desire to domesticate the site of research, inside and out.

It was this tradition of "making do," in Perrier's words, that preceded the "period of foundation" of marine research stations. While Milne-Edwards and Audouin's first visit to the coast was highly productive in its own right, their success did not predict the emergence of permanent stations, as opposed to mutable research outposts. Indeed, Milne-Edwards's first proposal for a research station involved a navy ship moored semipermanently above an active coral reef, which would serve as a diving platform. If by "foundation" Perrier meant edification in the true sense of preparing ground for a permanent structure, it was clearly the case that the structuring principles of the household, or *oikos*, preceded the building of any households of science.[34]

The term *economy* nominates root operations through which the elements of space, time, and circumstance are mutually arranged. From *oikos*, meaning "household" (and the family it houses) and *nomos*, or the "law" (of distribution), *oikonomia* (and its Latin cognate *distributio*) appears in Vitruvius's *Ten Book of Architecture* with regard to the advantageous use of materials and site.[35] Fittingly, along with the elements of design, the Vitruvian architect was educated in physiology, or the workings of the physical universe. From the circumscribed limits of the household, the practical intelligence of economy extended to an understanding of the *oikoumene*, or the inhabited part of the Earth, with all its inequalities and cultural differences. These various meanings of economy were accentuated rather than forgotten in the early modern period, when the meaning of physiology referred more specifically to the workings of living nature, but the search continued for nature's own plan. Milne-Edwards's notion of the physiological division of labor helped pave the conceptual ground connecting Linnaeus's classical notion of nature's own providentially self-regulating economy and Ernst Haeckel's definition—in evolutionary terms—of ecology as "nature's own housekeeping."[36] Milne-Edwards wrote that the principles followed by nature were the same as those articulated by modern economists. Employing what he identified as "the language of technology," he explained that low-order organisms were like "poorly directed workshops" in which each worker is responsible for every operation.[37] The division of labor in more fully formed beings resulted from the balanced agency of the law of variety and the law of economy. Looking beyond metaphoric migrations between disciplines, however, which are nonetheless significant of their own accord, the observations Milne-Edwards and Audouin conducted along the shore lent meaning and significance to all that was later implied by the double program of the laboratory-household. Stated as a question, What ideas concerning economy—a term that in architectural literature was long analogous to, if not identical with, distribution—made the naturalists' narrative of space cohere?

The naturalists had displaced themselves from the Muséum to the end of the world (the administrative department of Finistère [including Brittany], i.e., finis terre). Indeed, during part of their expedition they were guided by the hydrographer Charles-Francois Beautemps-Beaupré (1766–1854), who at the time was mapping the region's dusting of reefs and tidal islands for his maritime atlas of France.[38] But being on site to witness the emanation of life itself did not necessarily mean that conditions were always (or ever) favorable for their observations. Reducing their still structurally undefined seat of observation to a level even more fundamental than Guadet's architectural elements, Milne-Edwards and Audouin wrote of the need to master time, place, and circumstance.[39] The level of the tides and the season of the year were among the particularities of place that set the rhythm of a day's work, though a passing cloud could temporarily draw things to a close. It is possible to place their desire for mastery alongside the practice of maritime insurers, who constantly gathered information in order to "domesticate risk," applying to it the same principles necessary to the preservation of a family's fortune.[40] What these practices shared was the recognition that formless circumstances "distribute" themselves around even the best-laid plans.[41] Milne-Edwards and Audouin, too, hedged their bets. They wrote of repeated visits to specific points along the coast that were especially productive, measuring in terms of a simple ration of time spent and specimens collected. As with fishermen since antiquity, they employed the concept of metis, a "principle of economy" by which the maximum effect was derived from the minimum force.[42] It implied knowing the proper place and the proper moment to seize (or, in the naturalist's case, make intelligible) one's prey. They openly expressed the fact that their strategy represented a balance of risk and reward; it was often "only by chance" that their observations progressed.

Milne-Edwards and Audouin's *Recherches* documents the effort to translate the particularities of the field and the contingencies that attended their research into patterns of distribution. Perhaps no section of their richly composite text does so better than Audouin's "distribution" of shipwrecks along the coast of France (fig. 5).[43] Based primarily on salvage claims, Audouin sought to establish a correlation between "accidents" of terrain and the rate of shipwreck, going further to link their frequency to the season of the year.[44] Related practices of record keeping had a place in the naturalists' own work. The detailed daily inventories of the specimens they collected and the locations they collected them from served as the basis for the four "regions" of habitation between the limits of the high and low water marks that Milne-Edwards and Audouin established for the first time in the section of the *Recherches* headed "Distribution."[45] Although their limited time alongshore did not allow them to establish "precise rules" for the physiological correlation between organism and the nature of the terrain (the basis for modern ecology), their observations were an important contribution to the burgeoning field of animal geography, which sought to establish global patterns. Thus, Milne-Edwards analyzed the "localism" and "cosmopolitanism" of species with regard to how topography, climate, and finally the shape of time affected their distribution.[46]

The same factors applied to human populations. On a terrestrial scale, the notion of the *oikoumene* addressed the unequal distribution of peoples and the boundaries (physical, cultural, and racial) that divided densely inhabited from desolate regions.[47] In the same year that he made his first

(fig. 5)

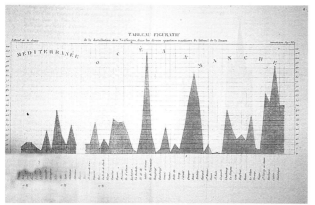

Jean-Victor Audouin, "Figurative tableau of the distribution of shipwrecks in the diverse maritime quarters of the French coast," illustrated in Jean-Victor Audouin and Henri Milne-Edwards, *Recherches pour servir à l'histoire naturelle du littoral de la France* (1832)

expedition to the coast, Milne-Edwards worked with the social hygienist Louis René Villermé on a statistical account of the effect of the relative density of housing distribution on the "physiological economy" of a population.[48] In a later report on the progress of science in the provinces, Milne-Edwards touched on the cultural aspects of the distribution of specialized communities within the general population. There was no reason to doubt the advantages of concentrating the best and the brightest in well-endowed urban institutions, he wrote, but the benefits were often counterbalanced by the myriad "inconveniences inherent to agitated [city] life," in particular the immoderate desire for celebrity that caused professors to publish too much and too often.[49]

The same interest in the location, density, and kinds of populations figures prominently in the broad range of statistical information that the naturalists caused to be published in the *Recherches*. Following type, Milne-Edwards's analysis of the fisheries proposed a "natural" classification of fishing communities according to the "sedentary" or "migrant" habits of the catch.[50] Perrier explained that the very "circumstances" of Milne-Edwards and Audouin's expedition, notably the support they received from "friends of science" stationed in each locality they visited (naval officers, fisheries inspectors, engineers from the Corps des ponts et chaussées, members of Linnaean societies), made it advantageous for them to address a range of "economic questions."[51] From descriptive accounts of agricultural production to literacy levels and even the dispersion patterns of fumes from the soda-ash burners, statistics was a tool for taking stock of the current if not initial and final state of things at widely varying dimensional and temporal scales. The prevalence of statistics in the *Recherches* was not an isolated phenomenon but rather reflected a general epistemological shift in the life sciences from mechanistic analogies to analogies stemming from political economy.[52] This shift manifested itself in Milne-Edwards's theory of the physiological division of labor no less than Perrier's studies of animal "colonies."[53] But just as important to an understanding of their place in the naturalists' work is the argument that territory was for the statistician what the spaces of the herbarium, cabinet, and botanical garden were for the naturalist.[54]

The implications of this argument are twofold. First, the field became a legitimate object of research, sharing the same epistemological status as the immured cabinets and manicured grounds of the Muséum. Second, it became incumbent upon the naturalists to provide a precise description of how the field would be made into a site for research. Milne-Edwards and Audouin's desire to master this field reflects what Leroi-Gourhan, in defining domestication, described as "taking charge" of time and space. Domestication as such did not necessarily involve the construction of physical enclosures but rather the control of the social and physical rhythms of the domestic site.[55] Notably, in his account of the site of Milne-Edwards and Audouin's original laboratory-household, Armand de Quatrefages gave particular attention to the circumstances and seasons that determined the movements of "nomadic" fishermen, seaweed harvesters, and quarrymen who came to exploit the Chausey Islands' resources. While retracing his teacher Milne-Edwards's itinerary as a pedagogic exercise in its own rite, Quatrefages noted that beginning with the autumnal equinox, these nomadic populations departed one after another until the islands were largely bereft of life during the winter months.[56] Each "tribe" had its settlement of rudimentary shelters; the naturalists, nomads too, were no different. And if Quatrefages lamented that the "magic velocity of the rail" had not yet (as many argued it would) collapsed the distance between Paris and the coast, of greater concern to naturalists were the precise steps to make themselves at home in the field.

The question of movement, be it historic, migratory, or transitory, seems immanent in Perrier's periodization of fieldwork into the "nomadic life" and the subsequent "foundation of permanent" (architectural) structures of research. Historically the interval spans Milne-Edwards and Audouin's expedition of 1828 and the establishment of a laboratory-household at Roscoff in 1872 by Milne-Edwards's student, Henri de Lacaze-Duthiers. It also corresponds to a change in the status of the field as a result of Milne-Edwards and Audouin's efforts to domesticate it. Yet one final layer of significance may be added to the concept of distribution by examining what was at issue in the evolution from the laborious and time-consuming nomadic life to the creation of institutions of research. This layer is to be found in works such as L'Habitation humaine (1892), by the architect Charles Garnier and the anthropologist Auguste Ammann, in which they provide a history of the racial stock of France consisting of the "Celts," identified etymologically (and falsely) as tent dwellers, and the "Galls," who cultivated the land and lived in fixed habitations (fig. 6).[57] Perrier was likely aware of the significance his periodization had in the anthropological discourse of his day.[58] The problem nonetheless remains the same: What rules governed the evolution of the household itself?

Along with Garnier, architects such as Eugène Emmanuel Viollet-le-Duc (1814–1879) drew on racialistic anthropological discourse, offering that the national home was nothing more than the wagon of the nomad that had come finally to rest, its wheels being replaced by a solid foundation.[59] Quatrefages's own claim that his training as a field naturalist prepared him for his appointment to the newly created chair in the Natural History of Man (later to be renamed Anthropology) at the Muséum in 1854 suggests that his change of specialty represents less of a disciplinary transgression than it might appear. And whether the question was posed with regard to the races of man and the peopling of the globe or to the far more specific problem of how to establish the laboratory-household, the amalgamation of architecture, anthropology, and by extension zoology provided a simple but crucial insight into the nature of housekeeping. Once nomadic tribes were "liberated" from the absorbing necessity of interpreting an anomalous territory, the management of the household cultivated the foresight of the prudent manager who made provision for times of want.[60] The evolution of the permanent habitation was not primarily a structural innovation, but an evolutionary advance in the science of distribution.

The foundation of a permanent laboratory-household at Roscoff put an end to nomadic life. During his first visit to the coast as Lacaze-Duthiers's

(fig. 6)

Mobile habitation of Aryan migrants, illustrated in Charles Garnier and Auguste Ammann, *L'Habitation humaine* (1892)

student, Perrier was on hand to transcribe the lease that transformed a "simple country house" into an "official laboratory of the Sorbonne." At first, only modest improvements were made, including plumbing to supply basins in which embryos taken directly from the sea would be kept until they were put under the microscope. Yet it was not Lacaze-Duthiers's original intention to settle down; he instead indicated that the "laboratory would have been able to be transported from locality to locality and thus would have been established the zoological inventory of our coasts."[61] The laboratory itself was conceived as a "central station" that would supply the provisions for "scientific caravans" that would go out to explore the coast in an ever wider radius.[62] The meaning of "station" here is close to that of an *étape*, in the allied sense of the distance covered in a day's march and the corresponding daily ration.[63] In a seeming effort to convince himself of the domestic virtues to be gained in giving up the nomadic life, during the first year of Roscoff's existence Lacaze-Duthiers commissioned a report on the famed "flying research station" constructed by the Dutch Zoological Society (fig. 7). Made of standardized lightweight panels that could easily be assembled and disassembled, the station could be transported from place to place along the coast as changing research interests dictated; at the end of the summer it was packed in a train car and stored in the attic of the Leyden Natural History Museum until the next season. In his report on the flying station, Léon Fredericq joined the scientific press in praising its structural ingenuity, but he concluded that the hospitality made possible with the permanent establishment of Roscoff greatly offset the loss in freedom of movement. The difficult work of domestication would give way finally to the joys of hospitality.[64]

The moral economy that governed Roscoff was reflected in Lacaze-Duthiers's expectation that the naturalists who visited the laboratory-household would repay their debt of hospitality by placing their scientific work in the pages of its scientific organ, the *Archives de Recherches expérimentale et générale*. With its table of scientific contents serving as a de facto register of Roscoff's occupation, the *Archives* recorded both elements of the double program. Lacaze-Duthiers's investment in Roscoff amortized itself in its pages. He wrote that

(fig. 7)

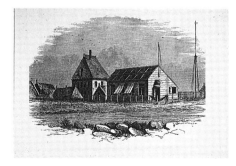

The "flying research station" of the Dutch Zoological Society, illustrated in *La Nature*, 20 January 1877

while a "grand and handsome facade" might lend an air of distinction to a research institution, the number and quality of publications it produced was the true measure of its success.[65] Milne-Edwards's earlier comments about the fever to publish that raged in academic centers notwithstanding, the statement reflects a notion of cultural capital. It also reveals a characteristic ledger-book mentality applied to the management of the laboratory-household (fig. 8). Lacaze-Duthiers's temperamental sensitivity to the costs of conducting research is evident in the notebooks in which he kept minute accounts of train fares, meals, and hotel rooms while scouting a site for his station.[66] His scientific training instilled in him the notion of a static balance in nature's economy, expressed in Jean-Baptise Dumas's dictum "Nothing is created, nothing is lost." The experiments Lacaze-Duthiers devised early in his career to study these exchanges of organic matter took on another shape in the laboratory-household in which the principal function was mediating nature (fig. 9).

In terms of the instruments of mediation, the exceedingly house-proud Lacaze-Duthiers took particular pleasure in the U-shaped desk and accompanying swivel chair of his own design (fig. 10). The arrangement allowed the naturalist to turn effortlessly from the specimens kept on the left to the microscope in the center, facing the window, to the drawing table on the right. Thus was completed the circuit whereby specimens taken directly from the sea were made ready to appear in the pages of the *Archives*. One visitor to Roscoff commented that having become accustomed to this setup, he was never at ease with any other arrangement.[67] Indeed, the swivel chair has a place in the archaeology of comfort. According to architectural historian Sigfried Giedion, the nineteenth century saw the emergence of furniture for highly specialized tasks, "the best posture for any given moment is the constant aim, differentiated mobility, the means."[68]

For Lacaze-Duthiers, whose own practical training as a naturalist consisted of arduous expeditions in which he made do as circumstances dictated, the relative comfort of Roscoff posed a moral threat. The ardor for work would atrophy if the opportunity to work were not hard won, the argument went. Loneliness, (mild) suffering, and self-reliance were the elements of masculinity requisite for work in the field. The risk was that guests would become dependent on the undifferentiated and thus unlocatable labor that the wives of Milne-Edwards and Audouin originally provided; their place in the domestic economy was eventually formalized by the "service," to whom visitors were obligated in the form of a gratuity. It is clear, however, that to Lacaze-Duthiers, a lifelong bachelor, the laboratory-household represented a desire for home, for the sweetness of the foyer, which was never clearly expressed but never left in doubt.

The very words *douceur du foyer*, as Hans Robert Jauss discusses, associated in an untranslatable fashion a social ideal and the poetry of everyday life: the joy to be found in repose amid family at the end of the day.[69] It was in this private realm that the normative values of bourgeois life were reproduced. The foyer referred not only to the notion of warmth and security, but also to the economic role of the family as a unit of organized consumption as well as of hierarchical integration.[70] The moral economy enforced in Lacaze-Duthiers's laboratory-household instilled in visitors the proper regard for the hospitality extended to them. All the material wants would be met,

(fig. 8)

Campagne de 1886.

Nos	Noms	Date de l'arrivée	Date du départ	Cotisation	Logement	Place de travail	Sujet de travail
1	Delage	16 avril	31 août	40	Chambre du directeur	Cabinet du directeur	Recherches sur les Poissons
2	Joubin	16 juin	20 Septembre	30	Chambre du préparateur	Cabinet du préparat.	Recherches sur les Némertes
3	Cuénot	18 mai	7 août	10	École no 1	Stalle 7	Recherches sur les Astéries
4	Guitel	28 mai	18 août	30	Laboratoire no 2	Stalle 5	Recherches sur le Lepadogaster
5	Costes	20 juin	1 Septembre	30	École no 4	Stalle 1	Recherches sur les Crustacés
6	Hérouard	20 juin	2 Septembre	30	École no 3	Stalle 3	Recherches sur les Holothuries
7	Lacroix	25 juin	26 juillet	20	École no 2	Stalle 4	Licence
8	Curtel	27 juin	26 juillet	20	Laboratoire no 5	Stalle 8	Licence
9	Meurisse	27 juin	28 juillet	10	École no 5	Stalle 7	Licence
10	Laguesse	29 juin	3 août	15	Laboratoire no 7	Stalle 9	Licence
11	Martin	29 juin	3 août	15	Laboratoire no 6	Stalle 6	Licence
12	Nusbaum	30 juin	7 août	5	Laboratoire no 4	Stalle 8	Recherches sur l'Embryol. des Mysis
13	Coupin	4 juillet	11 août	10	Laboratoire no 3	Stalle 2	Licence
14	Hervé	6 juillet	6 juillet	0	—	—	Recherches sur les Isopodes
15	Citerne	10 juillet	10 août	10	Laboratoire no 8	Stalle 1	Licence
16	Boutan	13 juillet	5 août	20	Chambre du Maître de Conférences	Cabinet de M. [illegible]	Recherches sur les Mollusques
17	Joux	13 juillet	11 août	10	En ville	Stalle 5	Licence
18	Gorecki	14 juillet	18 juillet	5	En ville	Stalle 3	Licence
19	Lapicque	22 juillet	19 août	10	En ville	Stalle 4	Licence
20	Le Marc'hadour	23 juillet	14 août	10	En ville	Stalle 8	Licence
21	Lahille	24 juillet	9 septembre	10	En ville	Stalle 2	Recherches sur les Synascidies
22	De Seigneux	24 juillet	19 août	15	En ville	Stalle 7	Licence
23	Marvenoux	30 juillet	22 août	20	En ville	Stalle 10	Licence
24	Cathelineau	31 juillet	2 septembre	5	En ville	Stalle 10	Licence
25	Lerfve	31 juillet	19 Septembre	15	École no 5	Stalle 6	Pratique des injections
26	Chevrel	31 juillet	20 Septembre	30	Laboratoire no 7	Stalle 4	Recherches sur les [illegible]
27	Pruvôt	1 août	18 Septembre	30	Chambre du Maître de Conférences	Chambre de M. [illegible]	Recherches sur les Annélides
28	Dereims	4 août	24 août	10	Laboratoire no 5	Stalle 9	Licence
29	Lefèvre	4 août	24 août	10	Laboratoire no 6	Stalle 6	Licence

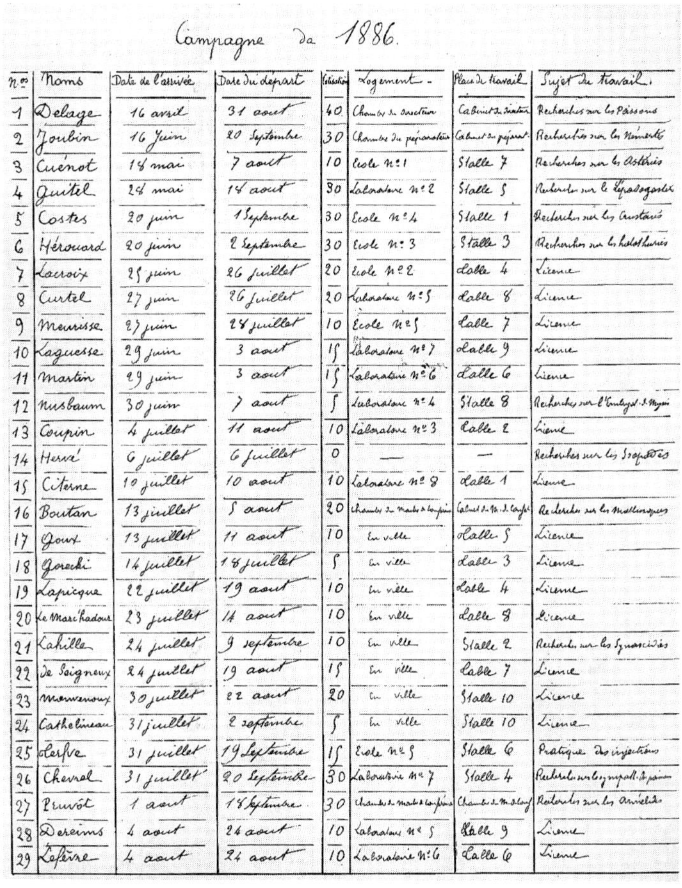

Entry log from the laboratory at Roscoff, 1886

but only in "proportion" to what was dictated by prudent research methods. If the management failed to put constraints in place, then eventually "liberality takes the form of license." The laboratory-household was a nursery for *homo economicus*. In satisfying both modes of occupation implied by the double program, however, it rationalized the foyer while producing associations of home, the life of the family. The evolution of the laboratory-household from the nomadic life to the permanent habitation followed exactly the trajectory Garnier had traced in his history of human habitation, culminating in the well-kept world of the bourgeoisie. The naturalists were finally at home in the field.

Like characters of a bildungsroman, the movement of these naturalists from the known to the unknown, their discoveries at the margins of the social discourse, and their ultimate reincorporation into new institutions provide a rich spatial narrative. As a representative departure from the institutions of the city, Lacaze-Duthiers wrote that in "plunging himself into the sea," Milne-Edwards "went far from his family, far from his [academic] chairs."[71] He was referring to his teachers' donning a diving helmet to collect embryos in the very medium in which life began. But the description equally suggests exactly what Guadet meant when he contrasted the abstract sciences to the natural history that demanded a highly particular arrangement of space. To wit, Lacaze-Duthiers's veritable protestation of faith in the founding of Roscoff: "I am here to create a laboratory of zoology, of that zoology which I call experimental in opposition to that which seems to me based too much on collections."[72] If such eligible sites were to replace the silence of the cabinet as the site to study life, it meant immersion in the dense particularities of place and the definition of practices for managing them properly. The plan for structure in such a setting was to become the embodied force of circumstance. The expedition to the coast, plunging into the sea, was not the formula for the composition of architectural elements; it demanded the birth of a hopeful monster, the hybrid laboratory-household.

(fig. 9)   (fig. 10)

Arago Laboratory, Banyuls-sur-Mer, circa 1881

Three-sided research table with swivel chair, Arago Laboratory

As the plan for work at Saint-Vaast took shape, the Muséum inaugurated its new Grand Gallery during the Paris Universal Exposition of 1889. The progressive critic César Daly described the monumental classical facade that clad its vast iron and glass atrium as "conservative," in the most positive sense of the term.[73] The classical elements had been recomposed for the purposes of a modern institution of science. But the laboratory was not a site of conservation, or primarily even of representation, but of mediation. The contents of an opaque sea passed through it and were made visible and knowable. If the laboratory offered any "conservative" element, it was in the form of hospitality; as the Renaissance humanist Justus Lipsius observed, a defining purpose of the original museum—or temple of the muses—was to provide food and lodging to all students, freeing them from cares. Tellingly, the 1889 exposition was also the site of Garnier's *L'Habitation humaine*, an exhibition of over forty historically and geographically diverse houses that recapitulated the evolution of the habitation from natural shelters to the bourgeois townhouse. In terms that echo Milne-Edwards's critique of cabinet-based study, Garnier wrote of the need to go beyond the "mute evidence" of the past that was meticulously arranged along the walls of museums. Garnier wrote that reanimating these domestic scenes gave the visitor access to the inhabitant's "foyer" and the opportunity to share in the most intimate secrets of domestic life.[74] One of those secrets is the practice of prudent management or, more grandly, the laws of distribution that served as the ideogenesis of modern scientific and architectural rationality.

NOTES

1. Henri Bergson, "La Philosophie" [1913], in *Claude Bernard, extraits de son oeuvre*, ed. E. Dhurot (Paris: Presses universitaire de France, 1939), 19. Lending credence to this claim, Bergson wrote that the nineteenth century gave birth to the "laboratory sciences," which were confirmed in the tenets of Claude Bernard's experimental method.

2. On the role of analysis in architectural reasoning, see Antoine Picon, introduction to *Précis of the Lectures on Architecture* by Jean-Nicolas-Louis Durand, trans. David Britt (Santa Monica, Calif.: Getty Institute, 2000), 36–44.

3. For a discussion of how notions of place imply a structure of events, see Edward Casey, *The Fate of Place* (Berkeley: University of California Press, 1997).

4. Claire Salomon-Bayet, *L'Institution de la science et l'expérience du vivant* (Paris: Flammarion, 1978), 378–79.

5. Ibid., 378–79.

6. Yvette Conry, *L'Introduction du Darwinisme en France au XIXe siècle* (Paris: Vrin, 1974), 335.

7. Julien-Azaïs Guadet, *Eléments et théorie de l'architecture* (Paris: Librairie de la construction moderne, 1901), 283.

8. Claude Bernard, "À S. E. Monsieur le ministre de l'instruction publique," in Ashley Miles, "Reports by Louis Pasteur and Claude Bernard on the Organization of Scientific Teaching and Research," Notes and Records of the Royal Society of London 37 (1982–83): 106.

9. A. Ménégaux, "Le Laboratoire de Roscoff," Bulletin de l'Institut général psychologique, 1905: 77.

10. Georges Canguilhem, The Normal and the Pathological, trans. Carolyn Fawcett (New York: Zone Books, 1989), 125.

11. The architect Théodore Dauphin was responsible for the redesign of the lazaret that had been built by Napoleon III for the troops returning from his adventure in Mexico between 1861 and 1867. Archive Nationale, Paris, AJ^{15} 850 (Muséum. Ile Tatihou). Bibliothèque centrale du Muséum Nationale d'histoire naturelle, Paris, Registre des procès-verbaux des séances de l'assemblée des professeurs administrateurs du Muséum d'histoire naturelle 60, no. 16 (10 January 1882–27 December 1889).

12. Julien Guadet, "Jules André architecte, notice sur sa vie et ses oeuvres," Journal de l'architecture, June 1890: 13.

13. Edmond Perrier, "Le Laboratoire maritime du Muséum d'histoire naturelle," in La Nature 794 (18 August 1888): 186. See also Camille Limoges, "The Development of the Muséum d'histoire naturelle of Paris, c. 1800–1914," in The Organization of Science and Technology in France, 1808–1914, ed. Robert Fox and George Weisz (Cambridge: Cambridge University Press, 1980), 211–40.

14. Paul Lemoine, "Le Muséum d'histoire naturelle," in Archives du Muséum national d'histoire naturelle, volume du tricentenaire (Paris, 1935), 18.

15. Henri Milne-Edwards and Victor Audouin, Recherches pour servir a l'histoire naturelle de la France, ou, Recueil de mémoires sur l'anatomie, la physiologie, la classification et les mœurs des animaux de nos côtes (Paris: Crochard, 1832), I: ii.

16. See Paul Lawrence Farber, "The Emergence of Taxidermy and the History of Ornithology," Isis 68 (1977): 550–66.

17. Michel Foucault, The Order of Things: An Archaeology of the Human Sciences (New York: Vintage Books, 1970), 139.

18. Michel de Certeau, The Practice of Everyday Life, trans. Steven Rendall (Berkeley: University of California Press, 1984), 122. Following Michel de Certeau's discussion of the founding of places, it may be observed that this specific formulation, "transporting themselves to the places themselves" (se transportaient sur les lieux), recalls the ancient legal tradition of visiting the scene of a case over property at issue. For the naturalists, the boundary in dispute was the space opened by their own expedition.

19. Dorinda Outram, "New Spaces in Natural History," in Cultures of Natural History, ed. N. Jardine, J. A. Secord, and E. C. Spary (Cambridge: Cambridge University Press, 1996), 260.

20. Henri Daudin, Cuvier et Lamarck, les classes zoologiques et l'idée de série animale, 1790–1830 (1927; reprinted, Paris: Editions des archives contemporaines, 1983), 98. Cuvier depended on correspondents such as Milne-Edwards and Audouin to provide him with the material on which his Histoire naturelle des poissons was based. On the composition of this monumental work, see my "Overcoming First Impressions: Georges Cuvier's Types," Journal of the History of Biology 30 (1997): 179–209.

21. Henri de Lacaze-Duthiers, "Discours de M. Lacaze-Duthiers," in Discours prononcés aux obsèques de M. H. Milne-Edwards (Paris: Gauthier-Villars, [1886?]), 17.

22. Henri Milne-Edwards, "Recherches anatomiques, physiologiques et zoologiques sur les eschares," in Annales des sciences naturelles, 23 February 1835: 41.

23. Jules Janin and Pierre Boitard, *Le Jardin des plantes, description et mœurs des mannifères de la ménagerie et du Muséum d'histoire naturelle* (Paris: J. J. Dubochet, 1842), 22–23.

24. Louis Pasteur, "Quelques réflexions sur la science en France," *Oeuvres de Pasteur* 7 (1939): 204, n. 1; originally published as "Le Budget de la science," *Revue des cours scientifiques*, 1 February 1868.

25. Ibid., 200.

26. Claude Bernard, *Rapport sur les progrès de la physiologie générale en France* (Paris: Imprimerie générale, 1867), 132.

27. Audouin's letters from this period are excerpted in Jean Théodoridès, "Les débuts de la biologie marine en France: Jean-Victor Audouin et Henri Milne-Edwards, 1826–1829," in *Communications du premier congrès international d'histoire de l'océanographie, Monaco 1966* (1968), 453–65.

28. The practice of inspecting livers was still a matter of discussion in Pierre Patte's *Mémoires sur les objets les plus importants de l'architecture* (1769), in which the author makes reference to its source in Book I, Chapter IV of Vitruvius, *On Architecture*.

29. Milne-Edwards and Audouin, *Recherches*, I: 70.

30. Based on the report of Cuvier, their research won them the Prix Moynton. See Georges Cuvier and Georges Duméril, "Rapport sur deux mémoires de MM. Audouin et Milne-Edwards, contenant des recherches anatomiques et physiologiques sur la circulation dans les crustacés, fait à l'Académie des sciences 19 mars 1827," *Annales des sciences naturelles* 10 (1827): 394–99.

31. "Dans nos écoles, on admettait sans discussion que tout phénomène physiologique dépend de l'action d'un organe particulier et ne peut se produire que là où l'instrument existe et fonctionne; que, par conséquent, là où la fonction est remplie, l'agent spécial ne saurait être absent, et que la similitude dans les actes vitaux suppose la similitude dans la structure de la machine vivant." Milne-Edwards, *Rapport sur les progrès des sciences zoologiques en France* (Paris: Imprimerie impérial, 1868), 186.

32. Ibid.

33. Henri Milne-Edwards, *Histoire naturelle des crustacés* (Paris: Librairie encyclopédique de Roret, 1834), I: 58.

34. On economy in architecture, see Mark Wigley, "Untitled: The Housing of Gender," in *Sexuality and Space*, ed. Beatriz Colomina (New York: Princeton Architectural Press, 1992), 334.

35. See E. Laroche, *Histoire de la racine Nem—en Grec ancien* (Paris: Librairie C. Klincksieck, 1949), 141–42.

36. On the metaphoric migration of economy, see Robert Stauffer, "Haeckel, Darwin, and Ecology," *Quarterly Review of Biology* 32 (1957): 138–44; Donald Worster, *Nature's Economy: A History of Ecological Ideas* (Cambridge: Cambridge University Press, 1977).

37. Milne-Edwards, *Histoire naturelle des crustacés*, I: 56. See Camille Limoges, "Milne-Edwards, Darwin, Durkheim and the Division of Labour: A Case Study in Reciprocal Conceptual Exchanges between the Social and the Natural Sciences," in *The Natural Sciences and the Social Sciences*, ed. I. B. Cohen (Dordrecht: Kluwer Academic Publishers, 1994), 338 n. 18.

38. Milne-Edwards and Audouin, *Recherches*, I: 86.

39. "Plus maître de son temps, on peut alors choisir les localités convenables, y demeurer davantage, et ne négliger aucune des circonstances propres à faciliter les travaux, aucune des précautions qui en garantissent l'exactitude." Henri Milne-Edwards and Jean-Victor Audouin, "Résumé des recherches sur les animaux sans vertèbres, faites aux Iles Chausey," *Annales des sciences naturelles* XV (1828): 7.

40. Lorraine Daston, "The Domestication of Risk," in *The Probabilistic Revolution*, ed. Lorenz Krüger, Gerd Gigerenzer, and Mary Morgan (Cambridge, Mass.: MIT Press, 1990), I: 254.

41. Henri de Lacaze-Duthiers, "Leçon d'ouverture du cours à la Sorbonne 1873–1847," *Archives de zoologie expérimentale et générale* 3 (1874): 23. Lacaze-Duthiers recounts the fate of the great hydrographer Ernest Mouchez, who, having been commissioned to observe the Venus transit of 1874, made the voyage to the South Seas and set up a station well in advance of the astronomical event. But in spite of his ability to calculate the precise location and time of his observation, there was no way of predicting that at the very moment of the transit dense fogs and clouds would obscure the horizon, preventing Mouchez from seeing anything. While sensitive to the epistemological implications of Mouchez's dilemma, Lacaze-Duthiers's own interpretation participates in a metaphorical tradition that views voyaging as a cultural criticism of the steady occupation and predictable rewards of domestic life.

42. Marcel Détienne and Jean-Pierre Vernant, *Les Ruses de l'intelligence. La Mètis des Grecs* (Paris: Flammarion, 1974), 23–25.

43. Daston, "Domestication of Risk," 248.

44. Ibid., 379.

45. Milne-Edwards and Audouin, *Recherches*, I: 139. In *The Philosophical Naturalists, Themes in Early Nineteenth-Century British Biology* (Madison: University of Wisconsin Press, 1983), 133–34, Philip Rehbock separates the small-scale, local distribution of species, including vertical zonation, with large-scale, regional patterns. The first relied more on the immediate physical and biological circumstance (such as the tide), the latter with historical events and the play of isolation, by means of migration or other geographical means. The two processes, however, shared the terminology of "stations" (physical settings) and "habitations" (geographic locations) that originated with Linnaeus's *Economy of Nature* (1753).

46. Milne-Edwards, "De la distribution géographique des crustacés," *Histoire naturelle des crustacés*, III: 556–57.

47. Clarance Glacken, *Traces on the Rhodian Shore* (Berkeley: University of California Press, 1967), 17.

48. René Villermé and Henri Milne-Edwards, "De l'influence de la température sur la mortalité des jeunes enfants," in *Société philomatique de Paris, extraits des procès-verbaux des séances* (1829; reprinted, 1838), 119–22.

49. Henri Milne-Edwards, "Discours sur les progrès des sciences dans les départements pendant la dernière période décennale," *Revue des sociétés savantes* 1 (1862): 54.

50. Milne-Edwards and Audouin, *Recherches*, I: 262.

51. Edmond Perrier, "Henri et Alphonse Milne-Edwards," *Nouvelles archives du Muséum d'histoire naturelle*, no. 4, 2 (1900): xl.

52. See Georges Canguilhem, *Études d'histoire et de philosophie des sciences* (Paris: Librairie J. Vrin, 1968), 330–31.

53. On the development of Milne-Edwards's ideas of organic "aggregation" and "association" into a full-fledged metaphorics of animal societies, see Edmond Perrier, *Les Colonies animales et la formation des organismes* (Paris: Masson, 1881).

54. Marie-Noëlle Bourguet, *Déchiffrer la France, la statistique départementale à l'époque Napoléonienne* (Paris: Éditions des archives contemporaines, 1989), 83.

55. André Leroi-Gourhan, *Le Geste et la parole* (Paris: A. Michel, 1964), II: 139–40.

56. Armand de Quatrefages, *Souvenirs d'un naturaliste* (Paris: Charpentier, 1854), I: 39.

57. Charles Garnier and Auguste Ammann, L'Habitation humaine (Paris: Hachette, 1891), 404.

58. Perrier's final work, La Terre avant l'histoire (1920), was part of the series L'Évolution de l'humanité, which also included Lucien Febvre's La Terre et l'évolution humaine (1922).

59. Arthur de Gobineau, Essai sur l'inégalité des races humaines (1853), quoted in Laurent Baridon, L'Imaginaire scientifique de Viollet-le-Duc (Paris: L'Harmattan, 1996), 113.

60. Garnier and Ammann, L'Habitation humaine, 65.

61. Henri de Lacaze-Duthiers, Enquètes et documents relatifs à l'enseignement supérieur, Ministère de l'instruction publique et des beaux-arts, laboratoire maritimes XIII (Paris: Imprimerie Nationale, 1884), 3.

62. Georges Pruvot, "Henri de Lacaze-Duthiers," Archives de zoologie expérimentale et générale 10 (1902): 40.

63. At the beginning of his career, Lacaze-Duthiers taught the course in zootechnology (the "economy of livestock") at the newly established Institut agronomique de Versailles. His chief research concern was calculating the daily ration of cavalry horses and those that worked the Paris omnibus lines, a staple that varied according to climate, locality, and the conditions of service; see Edmond Lavalard, Le Cheval dans ses rapports avec l'économie rurale et les industries de transport (Paris: Firmin Didot, 1888).

64. Léon Fredericq's report consisted of a partial translation and commentary upon Paulus Petrus Hoek, "Bericht ueber die zoologische station der niederlaendischen zoologischen gesellschaft," Niederlandisches Archiv fur Zoologie 3 (1876–77): 309–15.

65. Henri Lacaze-Duthiers, "Les Améliorations matérielles des laboratoires maritimes de Roscoff et de Banyuls en 1894," Archives de zoologie expérimentale et générale 3 (1895): 11.

66. Georges Petit, "Henri de Lacaze-Duthiers (1821–1901) et ses 'Carnets Intimes,'" in Communications du premier congrès international d'histoire de l'océanographie, Monaco 1966 (1968), 453–65.

67. George Dimmock, "The Arago Laboratory at Banyuls," Science 28 (26 October 1883): 558.

68. Sigfried Giedion, Mechanization Takes Command (New York: Oxford University Press, 1948), 406.

69. Hans Robert Jauss, Aesthetic Experience and Literary Hermeneutics, trans. Michael Shaw (Minneapolis: University of Minnesota Press, 1982), 266.

70. See Monique Eleb-Vidal and Anne Debarre-Blanchard, "Architecture domestique et mentalités, les traités et les pratiques, XVIème–XIXème siècle," in Extenso 2 (1984): 151–52.

71. Pruvot, "Lacaze-Duthiers," 18.

72. Henri Lacaze-Duthiers to Alexandre Agassiz, Roscoff, 12 August 1872, Museum of Comparative Zoology, Harvard University, Special Collections, Ag544.10.1.

73. Note by César Daly in F. Monmory, "Le Nouveau Muséum d'histoire naturelle au Jardin des plantes de Paris," Revue générale de l'architecture et des travaux publics 4, no. 10 (1883): 19 n. 2.

74. Garnier and Ammann, L'Habitation humaine, 3.

DESERT TESTING

Alessandra Ponte

For this is the age of experimentation, and we have not yet learned to read its protocols.

—Avital Ronell, "The Test Drive"

For Nietzsche, it is the experimental character of modern science that has caused the collapse of ecclesiastical cathedrals, which, in turn, has been conducive to the ruin of moral systems founded on the faith in absolute, divine truths. In one of the first aphorisms of *The Gay Science*, Nietzsche points to a new, immense, and paradoxical field of study, opened up by the triumph of scientific atheism over the Christian faith, which will be the analysis of moral matters. According to Nietzsche, it would require whole generations of scholars to accumulate, sort, and compare data, and investigate the customs and passions of every age and people. To achieve this, it would be necessary to write histories of love and envy, avarice and cruelty. Comparative histories of laws and punishments, the moral influence of food, and a philosophy of "moral climates" should also be written. Experiments on collective life would have to be attempted, and a dialectic of matrimony and friendship developed. Having accomplished this colossal task, the integral essence of moral judgment could be established. At this point, Nietzsche explains:

> [T]he most insidious question of all would emerge in the foreground: whether science can furnish goals of action after it has proved that it can take such goals away and annihilate them; and then experimentation would be in order that would allow every kind of heroism to find satisfaction—

centuries of experimentation that may eclipse all the great projects and sacrifices of history to date. So far, science has not yet built its cyclopic buildings; but the time for that, too, will come.[1]

Nietzsche's second edition of *Gay Science*, published in 1887, is one of his most thorough attempts to reform the language of past metaphysics. As a philosopher, the reformer opposes science, and, also as a philosopher, he opposes art. At the same time, however, he objects to the past philosophy and to the language associated with this past. Philosophy, as a discipline, must disappear, but philosophers, or thinkers, must remain. They must learn to talk in an unprecedented way, with novel words, by borrowing new forms of communications from what precisely survives of the past philosophy: from science and from art.[2]

In a recent essay titled "The Test Drive," Avital Ronell has located in Nietzsche's *Gay Science* the starting point for an interpretation of the scientificity that dominates our technologically oriented world. This Nietzschean notion of scientificity would be capable of embracing "the qualities both of destructive and artistic modes of production."[3] What Nietzsche started to conceptualize is that both science and art go repeatedly through a series of experiments, or tests.[4] The primacy of the test is coextensive with the recognition of the modern experimental disposition. This particular disposition can be detected in the fields of political theory, cybernetics, and artificial intelligence. Moreover, the trend also has effects on language, truth, probability, and process. For Ronell, this is why "experimentation is a locus of tremendous ethical anxiety...that travels way beyond good and evil."[5]

The American desert provides an ideal locus in which to test the meaning of experimentation across the sciences and the arts. Attempts to conceptualize the topos, the logic, the aesthetics, of spaces in our society may also be interrogated so as to read again how inscriptions (texts), circumstance, and happenstance connect with one another in a testing situation.[6]

(fig. 1)

"One Hundred Tons of TNT,
Trinity Crater," three stills
from *Trinity and Beyond: The
Atomic Bomb Movie*, directed by
Peter Kuran, Visual Concept
Entertainment, 1995

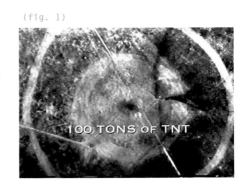

The desert could also be used as a test site for the last few decades of critical theory, though here critical theory is as likely to come back with a blunted edge or a shattered perspective.

—Rebecca Solnit, "Scapeland"

In his *Nuclear Landscapes* of 1991, Peter Goin presented a number of impressive photographs, portraying sites used by the United States to build and test atomic weapons: the Nevada Test Site, the Hanford Nuclear Reservation, and the Bikini and Enewetak atolls. In Goin's career, the exploration of nuclear landscapes came after the completion of previous projects investigating the blending of human artifacts in the landscape.[7] During 1977 and 1978, the first series involved extensive traveling throughout Central America and revealed his overwhelming encounter with the ruins of pre-Columbian architecture, especially the more mysterious sites not identified in archaeological maps. This was followed by a survey of contemporary ruins in the American South and then, by photographs of the abandoned Erie Canal network in New York State and of the overgrown Mesabi Iron Range in Minnesota. In 1984, Goin began a vast survey of the Mexican-American border, involving more then three years of field- and darkroom work.[8] The project, in the words of the author, "sought to reflect not just the geography of the border but also to imply the social, economic, and political complexity created through the artificial division of a shared landscape."[9] It was also the catalyst that helped define the nuclear landscape project.

In 1984, Goin moved to Nevada and became fascinated with the awe-inspiring landscape of the radioactive test site. He was one of the first outsiders authorized to photograph what he designates as a landscape of fear. This site of invisible and uncontainable danger echoed for Goin the enigma and magnificence of the pre-Columbian ruins. He writes about the perilous site:

Subsistence craters, created by underground detonations, are everywhere. Is that slight depression a subsistence crater, or is it simply an earthen depression that I am interpreting as dangerous? Are the Mayan mounds an archaeological site, or are they earthen mounds created by the forces of erosion?[10]

Goin could have asked himself even more questions: Those ruins, do they not appear as landscapes of fear? Or does their antiquity, the mystery still surrounding this civilization and its apocalyptic disappearance, inspire a different aesthetic judgment? And, if this is the case, how do Mayan remains relate to the nuclear "ruins"? The photographer appears to teeter on the brink of admitting to the "beauty" he sees in both kinds of ruins, but for ethical reasons he also draws back from the perception of the nuclear landscape as beautiful.

Also in 1991, Patrick Nagatani published *Nuclear Enchantment*, a series of photographs begun in 1983. These carefully constructed *tableaux vivant* were produced initially in Los Angeles, in collaboration with the painter Andrée Tracey, and later in New Mexico with the help of students working as actors or set painters.[11] Even before he moved to New Mexico, the location of the first atomic test, Nagatani's work was already revolving around atomic themes; not too surprisingly, since he was born on 19 August 1945—thirteen days after the first fission bomb was dropped on Hiroshima—of Japanese-American parents who had been interned in a camp during the war. To the Los Angeles period belongs "Alamagordo Blues, 1986," a tableau influenced by the more playful, ironic approach of Tracey. It is a wry reference to a famous 1946 photograph of a group of scientists sitting out in beach chairs in the desert, protected only by sunglasses, watching an atomic bomb test. In the Nagatani/Tracey version, blue-skinned Japanese experts, shooting Polaroids, are placed against a fantastic desert background painted in red. Japanese tourists, taking photos of each other next to the obelisk commemorating the first atomic test at the Trinity site, eating sushi while contemplating rockets at the National Atomic Museum in Albuquerque, or holding miniature souvenir versions of the Nike-Hercules Missile Monument at St. Augustine Pass, appear also in a number of tableaux, created later in New Mexico and presented in *Nuclear Enchantment*.

Nagatani is one of a few artists who address the question of atomic tourism, a widespread phenomenon, the success of which is attested to by the Bureau of Atomic Tourism, a Web site "dedicated to the promotion of tourist locations around the world that have either been the site of atomic explosions, display exhibits on the development of atomic devices, or contain vehicles that were designed to deliver atomic weapons."[12] Making fun of the conventional image of Japanese tourists, and reversing the blame on the victim, is hardly the only object of Nagatani's careful "atomic" cartography of New Mexico. Other actors animate Nagatani's landscapes: Boy Scouts, schoolchildren, and Native Americans. Hopi and Navajo are portrayed, for instance, playing a leisurely game of Scrabble while the story of a nuclear waste site is being broadcast on the evening news. Or they are seen performing one of their ritual dances next to a missile range or dwelling in a village close to a contaminated site. Their kachinas hover above missiles and radioactive rivers. In Nagatani's New Mexico, traces of the nuclear age coexist with the multiple layers of the state's history, and those signs become especially poignant when they encounter the still preserved Native American culture. The mysterious ruins left by the ancient inhabitants of their desert territory produce a haunting impression, captured by Nagatani in "F-117A Stealth Fighter, Pueblo Bonito, Chaco Culture National Historical Park, New Mexico, 1990." Nagatani's photographs depict the double "enchantment" of New Mexico, the state that at the same time embodies both the "threat" and "glory" of the atomic age and caters to the needs of generations of fugitives escaping from modernity and technology in their quest for the "primitive." It is the encounter with the unspoiled culture and beliefs of the "other" that unshackles the new self in a purified nature.

Photographs by Goin and Nagatani were included in *Nuclear Matters*, an exhibition held at San Francisco's Camera-works in 1991, curated by Timothy Druckrey and Marnie Gillett, who, accordingly, sought to explore "the issues surrounding the nuclearization of culture," a phenomenon that did not come to an end with the thawing of the Cold War and was still "laden with an insidious sense of universal destruction."[13] The exhibition catalog included photographic works of the Atomic Photographers Guild, together with works of Berlyn Brixner, who was assigned the job of filming the first atomic explosion at the (code name) Trinity site fifty miles from Almagordo, New Mexico. Also exhibited were the five photographs that Yoshito Matsuhige, a newspaper and army reporter, took in the city of Hiroshima on 6 August 1945. These were the only photographs taken in the city the day the bomb exploded.

For the curators of the exhibition, one of the main issues is how to address these troubling images: are they mere documents, or are they art that can be exposed in galleries or in museums? For Druckrey, however, Matsuhige's images suggest that the "dimensions [of the event] were unimaginable."[14] He recalled Theodor Adorno's famous remark that poetry after Auschwitz was impossible. For the curators, the challenge of photographs representing massive destruction leads to the notion of the unrepresentable. Photography, inheritor of both science and the tradition of art, either romantic or realist, is called upon to represent the total annihilation of reality. This is certainly a paradox—the nihilism inherent in technological societies—that cannot be fathomed within the confines of common sense or pragmatic judgment. Thus, it remains for us to ponder the controversial status of these photographs.

The events of 1945—Trinity, Hiroshima, and Nagasaki—have been characterized through aesthetic appraisals. One observer characterized what he saw at Trinity site on Monday, 16 July 1945, at 5:30 A.M. this way:

> And just at that instant there rose from the bowels of the earth a light not of this world, the lights of many suns in one. It was a sunrise such as the world had never seen, a great green super-sun...Up it went, a great ball of fire about a mile in diameter, changing colors as it kept shooting upward, from deep purple to orange, expanding, growing bigger, rising as it expanded, an elemental force freed from its bounds after being chained for billions of years. For a fleeting instant the color was unearthly green, such as the one seen only in the corona of the sun during a total eclipse. It was as though the earth had opened and the skies had split. One felt as though one were present at the moment of creation when God said: "Let there be light."[15]

In its references to the sun, the rainbow of interstellar colors, the eclipse, the opening earth, and the splitting skies, and, finally, the biblical "Fiat lux!"

(fig. 2)

ALESSANDRA PONTE

combining natural and supernatural entities, the description borrows from the vocabulary of art, from baroque epiphanies to sublime and romantic commentaries. The sublime, as it were, is a rhetorical trope that was interpreted by the pseudo-Longinus. It referred to what was called the elevated style of speech. During the eighteenth century, first Edmund Burke and then Immanuel Kant transmuted this style of speech into an aesthetic notion. While classical beauty is characterized by what is measurable through harmony and proportion, the sublime refers to the unmeasurable, to the limitless. Doubtless, observers of Trinity did not know much about aesthetics; nonetheless their vocabulary conveys that kind of meaning. For both Burke and Kant, "beauty" was supposed to induce pleasure in the beholder, whereas the "sublime" indicated the particular representation of that which elicits pain and fear.

In 1990, Richard Misrach, together with his wife, Myriam Misrach, published *Bravo 20: The Bombing of the American West*. This collection of spectacular photographs depicts the landscape "sculpted" by decades of test bombings by the U.S. Navy, which have devastated vast desert areas of Nevada.[16] The introduction describes progressive appropriation of Nevada as a proving ground by the Navy, Army, and Air Force and the extreme harm exacted on the environment and its inhabitants by this usurpation, which actually began in 1942. It recounts also the struggle of citizens against the military to force withdrawal of the Navy from Bravo 20. At the end of the book, Misrach presents his project for a sixty-four-square-mile site that would have been America's first environmental memorial.[17]

In 1996, photographs from *Bravo 20* were included in *Crimes and Splendors: The Desert Cantos of Richard Misrach*, an exhibition presenting this artist's epic series undertaken from 1979 on. It presented stunning images of death, where the themes of tourism, ecological disaster, and technological feat blend in the American desert.[18] In *Crimes and Splendors*, a book based on the exhibition, four new cantos were devoted to military abuses of desert areas in the United States. Canto VI, "The Pit," disclosed awesome images of a pit for dead animals in Nevada, where locals deposit livestock that have died,

"Cameramen shooting an atomic explosion," two stills from *Trinity and Beyond*

often for "unknown" reasons. Canto IX, "The Secret (Project W-47)," revealed desolate views of the abandoned Wendover Air Base in Utah, theater of still classified stages in the development of atomic bombs. Canto X, "The Test Site," depicts the Nuclear Test Site in Nevada: Snow Canyon in Utah, an area exposed to fallout from early atomic testing, and Rocky Flat Mesa in Colorado, a site heavily contaminated by a nuclear weapons plant. Canto XI, "The Playboys," framed the bullet-ridden pages of two issues of *Playboy* magazine used for target practice and found near the Nuclear Test Site, a stern commentary on the contradictions of American culture.

As a prologue to the nineteen cantos, Misrach inserted views of desert sites in Egypt and Israel, matching them with disturbingly similar views taken in Nevada and California. Most of the photographs—for example, the first pair, "Swimmers, Pyramid Lake Indian Reservation, Nevada, 1987" and "White Man Contemplating Pyramids, Egypt, 1989"— seem to echo a tradition typical of American landscape photography, that of comparing geological formations in the New World with celebrated monuments in the Old. Such comparison could imply the possibility of construing American desert features through biblical associations. Nevertheless, other photographs—especially the last two, "Pyramid and Sphinx, Las Vegas, Nevada, 1994" and "Tennis Courts and Pyramids, Giza, Egypt, 1989"—suggest perhaps a different, more complex interpretation. The suburban features that characterize the banality of both views evoke a shared cultural background, but, in this case, it is the American landscape that provides the clues for interpreting contemporary views of the biblical desert. In other words, Misrach's carefully organized sequence of photographs seems to describe a pervasive phenomenon: the "Americanization" of the landscape—in this case, the desert—through the global extension of the marketplace, which threatens to erase millennia of cultural and religious associations.

Where does Misrach find his stance in relation to the sites he photographed for two decades? In his rather extensive introduction to *Bravo 20*, Misrach follows the conventional opinion, denouncing ecological and human catastrophes. It appears that his convictions would then align themselves with the political positions of other "postapocalyptic" photographers. But, as the film critic and novelist David Thomson has observed in his volume *In Nevada: The Land, the People, God, and Chance*,

"His pictures, I think, are more profound than the book's text."[19] This opinion seems to be shared by Rebecca Solnit in her essay prefacing *Crimes and Splendors*. Addressing the issue of beauty in Misrach's oeuvre, Solnit writes:

> In the present, it often seems that the Left would like to deny beauty as a motivating force altogether, to deny the power of form and embrace content alone—as though the two were separable. Beauty is profoundly undemocratic. In bodies it is especially the property of the young, some more than others—and as a quality of women it is enormously problematic, grounds for objectification, discrimination, and obsession, commonly called a myth and a trap; while exceptional beautiful property itself—such as land and great works of art—is likely to be a privilege of the wealthy. Perhaps the Left equates beauty with evil. The Right follows Aquinas and endeavors to deny and suppress those beauties that tempt, the nonalignment of the ethical and the aesthetic.[20]

Solnit hypothesizes that it may be the language that contemporary critics use in their discussion of beauty that makes beauty contrary or, at least, problematic. She writes of the degeneration of the aesthetic language in the last century, recalling how the eighteenth century, the period that pervasively interrogated the aesthetic of the landscape in all its forms (in painting, poetry, garden design, and scenic tourism), critics had introduced three distinct aesthetic categories to discuss what now is simply labeled beauty: the Beautiful, the Picturesque, and the Sublime. The Beautiful, explains Solnit, is best represented by peaceful and radiant, idealized and pastoral landscapes of antiquity, as in the paintings of Claude Lorrain. Such icons gave inspiration for many landscape gardens of the British aristocracy, with their green lawns and placid rivers and lakes. The Sublime is the aesthetic of the terrifying, experienced from a distance. Solnit quotes Edmund Burke: "The passion caused by the great and sublime in nature, is astonishment; and astonishment is the state of the soul, in which all its motions are suspended, with some degree of horror."[21] The Picturesque, according to Solnit, is "the territory of the rough, the irregular, the idiosyncratic—[as illustrated by] Thomas Gainsborough ruined cottages."[22]

A DIALECTICAL AESTHETIC

The picturesque, far from being an inner movement of the mind, is based on real land; it precedes the mind in its material external existence.
—Robert Smithson. "Frederick Law Olmsted and the Dialectical Landscape"

Picturesque (*pittoresco* in Italian) was literally anything that was judged proper enough to be transposed into a picture or a painting (*pittura*). To Solnit's observations, perhaps, one should add the fact that the Picturesque emerged primarily as an aesthetic of decay. For an educated elite, it justified the visual enjoyment of objects previously excluded by the classical theory of representation; if the bright, the new, the whole, the symmetrical, the strong, and the smooth pertained to the Beautiful, the decayed, the worn, the aged, the dirty, the ragged, and the unevenly lit characterized the Picturesque. It may be said that the eighteenth-century notion of the Picturesque prefigured the Kantian perspective of "disinterested pleasure," detaching the visual appearance of things from their existence in a social, political context. This peculiar aspect of Picturesque provoked, even amid its theorists, ethical angst. Uvedale Price, for example, warned the enthusiastic owners of rural estates against the preservation of picturesque broken-down cottages in the villages, reminding them that morality should take precedence over aesthetic pleasure. William Gilpin admitted that industrious factory workers presented a more morally pleasing picture than idle, ragged peasants, adding nevertheless that the first were unsuitable for painting while the latter were eminently appropriate.

The most radical criticism of the Picturesque as a form of "immoral" aesthetic, came, however, from John Ruskin, writing during the Victorian period, almost eighty years after the introduction of the notion. In *Modern Painters*, Ruskin censured the Picturesque as "heartless":

> In a certain sense, the lower picturesque ideal is eminently a *heartless* one: the lover of it seems to go forth into the world in a temper as merciless as its rocks...The shattered window, opening into black and ghastly rents of wall, the foul rag or straw wisp stopping them, the dangerous roof, decrepit floor and stair, ragged misery or wasting age of the inhabitants—all these

conduce each in due measure, to the fullness of his satisfaction. What is it to him that the old man has passed his seventy years in helpless darkness and untaught waste of soul? The old man has at last accomplished his destiny, and filled the corner of a sketch, where something of an unshapely nature was wanting.[23]

Ruskin thus inaugurated a trend of critical thinking, which expanded from painting to photography and still survives today. But it must be recalled that the detached visual pleasure of the Picturesque did open the way to the abstraction of the modernist vision and offered a framework within which artists could begin thinking about the representation of the trivial, the shattered, the overlooked. Questioning Ruskin's Victorian position, it may be possible to reject the idea of the Picturesque as an "immoral" aesthetic and rethink it as an aesthetic, "beyond good and evil," that offers freedom to artists who operate in uncharted territories.

From this point of view, the resuscitation of the Picturesque by Robert Smithson in the 1960s offered a novel perspective and an aesthetic that eluded the trap of moral judgment, both by undoing the Scholastic association of pulchrum and honestum and by overcoming the neoclassical linkage between ethics and aesthetics. In his famous essay about Frederick Law Olmsted's work in New York City's Central Park, Smithson wrote:

> Inherent in the theories of Price and Gilpin, and in Olmsted's response to them, are the beginnings of a dialectic of the landscape. Burke's notion of "beautiful" and "sublime" function as a thesis of smoothness, gentle curves, and delicacy of nature, and an antithesis of terror, solitude, and vastness of nature, both of which are rooted in the real world, rather than in the Hegelian Ideal. Price and Gilpin provide a synthesis, with their formulation of the "picturesque," which is on close examination related to chance and change in the material order of nature. The contradictions of the "picturesque" depart from the static formalistic view of nature. The picturesque, far from being an inner movement of the mind, is based on real land; it precedes the mind in its material external existence. We cannot take a one-sided view of the landscape within this dialectic... As a result we are not hurled into the spiritualism of

Thoreau[v]ian transcendentalism, or its present day offspring of "modernist formalism" rooted in Kant, Hegel, and Fichte. Price, Gilpin, and Olmsted are forerunners of a dialectical materialism applied to the physical landscape. Dialectics of this type are a way of seeing things in a manifold of relations, not as isolated objects. Nature for the dialectician is indifferent to any formal ideal.[24]

The picturesque is a synthesis of the beautiful and the sublime: it is a superior notion, inasmuch as it introduces chance and change in art, and it is based on concrete land, the actual physical landscape. Neither a projection of the mind nor an ideal object of modernist formalism, it enables the artwork to establish a dialectical relation with materials, with matter, with the real land.

Perhaps, to understand fully Smithson's fascination with Olmsted's parks, one needs to forget the recurrent narratives, recounting the construction of vast pastoral ranges and large swaths of grass in the heart of the metropolis that provide physical recreation and moral improvement to its inhabitants. While he remains remote from the landscape architect's social mission, Smithson also stays far from any kind of transcendental, romantic, or even ecological vision of the landscape. He envisions Central Park in terms of an engineering masterpiece, like the work of a herculean artist, able to compose with the land itself. He compares Central Park's feat to having "an orchid garden in a still mill, or a factory where palm trees would be lit by the fire of blast furnaces."[25] He is enchanted by the vision of an army of laborers, moving 10 million horse-cart loads of earth, transforming a wasteland into a man-made landscape through a process of permanent change. This is why he celebrates—something unusual for him—the creation of a green space. As a rule, Smithson is suspicious of gardens; he dislikes their being green and dank; he associates them with the kind of late modernist art he despises, such as, for instance, a perfect metallic form set up amid a befittingly trimmed, grassy swath. He dismisses especially sculpture gardens of any kind as sites of display unduly wet and quaint or excessively snug and neat. Certainly he would have disliked the most famous, even legendary, one—the Abby Aldrich Rockefeller Sculpture Garden, designed by Philip Johnson in the Museum of Modern Art, which opened in 1953.[26] Avoiding the dampness of the "sculpture garden," which for Smithson is nothing more then a "limbo of modern isms," the artist should move to the desert:

> Depreciation of aridity means that one would prefer to see art in a dewy green setting—say, the hills of Vermont, rather than the Painted Desert. Aristotle believed that heat combined with dryness resulted in fire: where else could this feeling take place than in a *desert* or in Malevich's head? "No more 'likenesses of reality,' no idealistic images, nothing but a desert!" says Malevich in *The Non-Objective World*. Walter De Maria and Michael Heizer have actually worked in the Southwestern deserts. Says Heizer, in some scattered notes, "Earth liners installed in Sierras, and down on desert floor in Carson-Reno area." The desert is less "nature" than a concept, a place that swallows up boundaries. When the artist goes to the desert he enriches his absence and burns off the water (paint) on his brain. The slush of the city evaporates from the artist's mind as he installs his art. Heizer's "dry lakes" become mental maps that contain the vacancy of Thanatos. A consciousness of the desert operates between craving and satiety.[27]

Smithson transports the artist toward the American desert as a site of experimentation that frees him from the confines of the studio, "the snares of craft and the bondage of creativity."[28]

In urging the artist to leave the studio, Smithson is reacting against the "idealistic" relation with technology implied by objets d'art created by artists such as David Smith and Anthony Caro, who during the 1950s and 1960s in New York had fervidly embraced the industrial, modernist legacy and had boldly proclaimed to be working as "steel welder" and as "laboratory technician."[29] According to Smithson, this led to a fetishization of steel and aluminum as a medium. "Painted or unpainted," Smithson wrote, "molded steel and cast aluminum are machine manufactured, and as a result they bear the stamp of technological ideology."[30] Such late modernist artists considered steel a technologically purified material, with industrial, specific properties, such as hardness and resistance to corrosion. In the United States, the moment of birth of this formalist trend may be situated with the *Machine Art* exhibition of 1934, curated by Philip Johnson for the Museum of Modern Art, which displayed sculpturally abstract, flawlessly manufactured objects, including a motorboat propeller and a circular saw.[31] Yet for Smithson, the most important property of steel was precisely that it could rust. This happens when the fetishistic "steel sculpture" begins to oxidate, which is for Smithson "an interesting non-technological condition."[32] Accordingly, the artist now must immerse the ideally formed, timeless "art object" into the flow of time, where it will face the hardships of duration. Then he will explore residues left behind by the industrial processes of matter's purification as well as the degradation of its purified form when subjected to time and weather. Things then reveal their cracked surfaces, expose their "corroded moments"—patina, disuse, waste, inactivity, entropy, ruin. For Smithson, "burnt-out ore or slag-like rust is as basic and primary as the material smelted from it."[33]

To abandon the studio and the city for the desert is not equivalent to a romantic return to nature. Nature had no feeling. It was neither good nor bad; it was just as it was. It could be cruel, even sadistic. "Sadism," Smithson writes, "is the end product of nature, when it is based on the biomorphic order of rational creation."[34] The American deserts of the 1960s and 1970s were the sites of relentless tests of nuclear devices, disintegrating matter at an enormous scale. Here, science and technology were stamping the most staggering marks on the land, and also stacking tremendous heaps of residues. Given the premises outlined by Smithson, they became the privileged sites for the experimentations of De Maria, Heizer, and Smithson himself. During a famous interview with Julia Brown, Heizer told how he began traveling, assembling notes, drawings, and paintings in Nevada and in the Mojave Desert after 1967: "[A]t the time I wasn't even attempting to make sculpture. I was attempting to make a remark about art and society. My purpose was merely to observe and respond, so I just did that. I didn't question what I was doing, I was experimenting, I'd been experimenting for years."[35]

TEST SITE

The H-bomb, that's the ultimate sculpture.
—Michael Heizer. "Works of Earth"

In 1957, while planning the "pacific" use of atomic explosions in massive engineering projects, the Atomic Energy Commission (AEC) launched

Project Plowshare. One of the main sponsors of the program, which lasted sixteen years, was the Hungarian émigré Edward Teller, a star of nuclear physics and the "father of the H-bomb." Teller was well known to the American public, as he had been on the winning side of two major issues after World War II, the first concerning the rapid development of the hydrogen bomb and the second relating to the creation of the Livermore Radiation Laboratory in 1952, a national center for research on atomic weapons, set up to compete with Los Alamos. Teller, although enthusiastically embracing his role as national scientist, argued in 1957 against the banning of nuclear tests. He also tried to convince President Eisenhower of the feasibility of developing a "clean bomb" in a short period of time, with little or no radioactivity, if testing were permitted to proceed.[36] One year later, Teller coauthored an article for Life magazine, "The Compelling Need for Nuclear Tests," arguing against the suppression of nuclear tests.[37] His case against disarmament was informed by three things: his deep mistrust of the Soviet Union's resolution to disarm or to respect treaties; his conviction that the public had a false perception of the risks posed by fallout, which he set out to minimize; and, finally, the urgent need for "defensive" nuclear weapons, to be used tactically against enemy forces, avoiding the destruction of cities and the annihilation of civilian populations.

In concluding the Life article, Teller praised "the spirit of adventure" and the "fearless exploration of the unknown" in science and technology of past centuries:

> When we talk about nuclear tests, we have in mind not only military preparedness but also the execution of experiments which will give us more insight into the forces of nature. Such insight has led and will lead to new possibilities of controlling nature. There are many specific political and military reasons why such experiments should not be abandoned. There also exists this very general reason—the tradition of exploring the unknown. It is possible to follow this tradition without running any serious risk that radioactivity, carelessly dispersed, will interfere with human life.[38]

(fig. 3)

"Dr. Edward Teller, nuclear physicist, father of the hydrogen bomb," a still from *Trinity and Beyond*

In 1968, a book entitled *The Constructive Uses of Nuclear Explosives* was published by Teller, together with Wilson K. Talley, professor of applied science at the University of California, Davis; Gary H. Higgins, Plowshare division leader at the Livermore lab; and Gerald W. Johnson, director of the Navy labs in Washington, D.C. In the preface to the volume, the authors recounted how, during the crisis aroused by the Egyptian blockade of the Suez Canal in 1956, a group of scientists of the Lawrence Radiation Lab, at Livermore, began to explore the possibility of excavating a new canal through friendly territory, utilizing nuclear explosives. Of course, the project was never implemented, but this was the initial impulse that gave life to the Plowshare program. The idea of digging a canal with nuclear bombs was proposed again the following year, this time for use as an alternative to the Panama Canal. This kind of endeavor was still under consideration more than ten years later, when *The Constructive Uses of Nuclear Explosives* was published. Along with canals, the Plowshare scientists proposed to dig artificial harbors.

Between 1956 and 1961, the so-called Project Chariot was planned to offer a blueprint for future constructions. Atomic tests in the Pacific were considered unsatisfactory because the craters had been "punched," rather than excavated, in the atolls. A site in a remote area of the Alaskan coast was chosen. A complete ecological survey of the area was made, but the project was first delayed and then abandoned. In 1969, a collaborative survey of the feasibility of a nuclear harbor on the west coast of Australia, at Cape Keraudren, was jointly announced by United States and Australian authorities. Thanks to the efforts of Australian scientists who feared the destructive effects of the operation on the environment, the survey was canceled a month after it was announced. According to the sponsors, this new, cheap, and relatively safe "earth-moving" technology was to be employed also to "improve" California's system of dams and canals, and to facilitate the opening of more efficient railroad and highway passages through the Bristol Mountains.[39]

In the preface to *The Constructive Uses of Nuclear Explosives*, the scientists account for the failure to bring to completion their schemes with two types

(fig. 4)

Opening image from *Plowshare*, United States Atomic Commission, 1968, unclassified per U.S. Department of Energy, Nevada Operations Office

of justification: the first emotional and the second political. The emotional reasons are explained thusly:

> A nuclear device is an energy source orders of magnitude above the conventional, and its effects are not in the range to which constructive use of high explosives have accustomed our thinking. In addition, the first use of nuclear explosives, in war, displayed their destructive potential, and this characteristic still captures the imagination.[40]

Then follows the political argument:

> In any major civil construction local politics must be considered. An economical nuclear-explosive project may be so large that it is brought to the attention of the entire world. . . . Furthermore, international agreements or treaties which are designed to limit the development of nuclear weapons may, unfortunately, apply to the peaceful uses of nuclear explosives as well.[41]

Even if Plowshare projects were not implemented because of such "emotional" and "political" reasons, the scientists did manage to set in place an impressive testing program that was carried out, mainly at the Nevada Test Site, but also in New Mexico. One of Nagatani's tableaux actually depicts a test site in Carson National Park, New Mexico, where a small plaque was put up to commemorate Project Gasbuggy, a twenty-nine-kiloton explosion in December 1967. Another nuclear device was detonated during Operation Gnome in December 1961, thirty miles southeast of Carlsbad. The most spectacular and well-publicized test of Project Plowshare was the one that swiftly shoveled Crater Sedan in the Nuclear Test Site, which today represents a major attraction for the public tour. David Thomson writes in *In Nevada*:

> Here on July 6, 1962, only months before the Cuban missile crisis, they exploded a device yielding 104,000 tons, buried feet under the ground. The crater is like a geometric form, by which I mean to say that there is no apparent irregularity. All the sides descend and slope inward at the same angle. These walls seem raked. The lip of the crater is tidily round. But I have not conveyed the scale. It is 320 feet deep, and 1,282 feet across. As much

as 12 million tons of earth were vaporized or moved. It is, I think, next to Hoover Dam, the most beautiful man-made thing in the state of Nevada. Indeed, it is already on the National Register of Historic Places, which means, I suppose, that even if the Test Site came to be abandoned one day, no one could spoil this bleak wonder.[42]

For the scientists involved, Project Sedan was mainly an exercise in rhetoric: they meant to display dramatically the capability, and also the safety, of nuclear earth-moving technology.[43] The test was approved in the wake of the public controversy that culminated with the cancellation of Project Chariot in Alaska, where members of the local university, polar scientists, and Eskimos challenged the authority of the Plowshare experts, forcing them to withdraw to the seclusion of the Test Site in Nevada. How was the Nevada desert initially selected as a testing site? The words that open the chapter "Test" in Teller's *Our Nuclear Future* are inspiring:

> Testing of atomic explosives is usually carried out in beautiful surroundings. There is a good reason for this: the radioactive fallout. Because of the fallout, the test site must be isolated. The presence of human population does not improve nature (with exceptions which are quite rare and the more notable). Also, to keep the site clean, tests must be carried out in the absence of rain. Therefore, at the site one usually finds sunshine and solitude. For the participants the beauty of nature forms the backdrop to preparations of experiments which are difficult and exciting to everyone involved. At the end, the atomic explosion is always dwarfed by its setting. But the work that culminates in the detonation is rewarded by something quite different from a flash and a bang.[44]

Who knew that cloaked under the mysterious veil of the physicist and the hardened skin of the Cold War warrior, whose character inspired Stanley

(fig. 5)

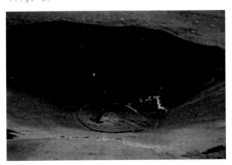

"Sedan Crater," a still from *Plowshare*

Kubrick's movie *Dr. Strangelove, or How I Learned to Stop Worrying and Love the Bomb* (1963), was literally hidden not only a poet but also an artist?

In 1972, Michael Heizer left New York and moved to Nevada. Generations of his family had lived in Nevada since the 1880s. One grandfather had been a mining engineer, the other a geologist. His father was an archaeologist, an expert on the Great Basin of California and on the Yucatán Peninsula, who worked also in various fields in Egypt, Bolivia, and Peru. When he died, he was writing a book on ancient systems of transporting heavy stones. It was Heizer who led Smithson and De Maria to the discovery of Nevada's vast, barren spaces, which were quite familiar to him.[45] As he has stated a number of times, he was the first to leave the constraints of the city in search of a place to create "American art." What brought him there was in no way the "beauty" of the desert landscape or its vistas. In a conversation with an art critic of *The New York Times* in 1999, he repeated almost literally what he had expressed previously:

> I have no interest in landscape in terms of art. I think American landscape art is one thing, but my work doesn't have anything to do with that, it has to do with materials. I went to those places for material. When I bought property in Nevada, I bought it because I had done studies and found sands and gravel that could make concrete, and clay soils that could be used for soil cements, and running water. These were all raw materials.[46]

There was another reason, however, to choose Nevada, as he had already explained during his interview with Julia Brown in 1984:

> **HEIZER:** It interested me to think about building *Complex One* on the edge of a nuclear test site in Nevada, and having the front wall be a blast shield. We had specifications for seismic conditions for the strength of the concrete that were the highest specifications that could be achieved. We measured all our water, we washed all our sand, we mixed carefully and had laboratory shear that surpassed what the engineer said we were required to have.
>
> **BROWN:** Your land in Nevada is next to a nuclear test site?
>
> **HEIZER:** Yes, it's a highly charged area, but I am reluctant to discuss it that much.

BROWN: But it's part of your planning?

HEIZER: Part of my art is based on an awareness that we live in a nuclear era. We're probably living at the end of civilization.[47]

The "American art" Heizer chose to produce had to do with advanced technology and vast dimensions. It was a sort of petrification, or a materialization of what he called the "American sensibility." At the time he was considering leaving New York, Heizer read something that had a profound impact on him. It was about changes in the way phone calls were handled. The rerouting of New York calls through Denver led the artist to new thoughts about distance and measure. He was also fascinated by the jumbo aircraft being built and, in general, by things "being done that felt uniquely American—a lot of them had to do with size."[48] He felt the clock was ticking, the end of the world was coming, and that "the idea of living in the postnuclear age informed everything."[49]

Heizer was inspired by American deserts, inasmuch as their vastness allowed for the possibility of the technological manipulation of what he called "materials." This manipulation would be done on a scale comparable to the geographical engineering envisioned by the Plowshare Program. Completed in the summer of 1968, one of Heizer's early works in Nevada, *Nine Nevada Depressions*, consisted of sites arranged in a linear sequence, spreading over 520 miles.[50] Heizer even took on the vocabulary of Project Plowshare, borrowing the term *earth-moving* from their scientists. In 1969, he first used heavy machinery, such as bulldozers, to realize *Five Conic Displacements*, an aligned series of excavations on the ground of Coyote Dry Lake in the Mojave Desert, California. This work evokes certain sketches and models that were published by the Plowshare program representing the alignment of nuclear craters necessary to carve canals and highways.

With *Double Negative* (1969–70), the most spectacular of his sculpted negative spaces, Heizer actually deployed an astonishing array of industrial machines, including cranes, loaders, transports, and Redi-mix cement trucks. "The result," writes the art critic Germano Celant, "is titanic, and consists of a double incision in the sides of the Mormon Mesa, created by moving 240,000 tons of rocks and sand to make two cuts, each fifty feet wide and defined by 90-degree walls and two descending ramps at 45 degrees. In all, the sculpture measures 1,500 feet in length."[51] There are photographs of the high stacks of dynamite containers used to blast through the mesa's rocks. There is also a dramatic sequence of film stills, recording the initial, gigantic explosion. Without doubt, the sudden expansion of pulverized rocks, followed by the slow dissipation of dust clouds over Mormon Mesa echoed the development of a mushroom cloud above a nuclear testing site. While discussing the giant earth-moving gear used in creating his art works, the artist corroborates the undeniable connection: "The rental system allows the artist practically any application he desires. It is now possible to rent a nuclear explosion."[52] The "negative" forms Heizer has blasted out in the desert underscore how nuclear devices can carve the surface of the Earth, inscribing immense trenches.

This is not to say that Heizer simply mimics icons taken from nuclear scientists. In his search for an American art, Heizer looked not only at the most staggering and terrifying technoindustrial feats of the twentieth century, he also contemplated archaeological remains of the pre-Columbian era. He superimposed, so to speak, one source of inspiration over the other in order to evoke their power. In the work that followed *Double Negative*, this is particularly evident, for instance, in *Complex 1*, the first element of a titanic enterprise entitled *City*, begun in 1972 and still in progress. *Complex*, a term similar to *ensemble, compound*, or *ancient site*, is borrowed from archaeology, a discipline familiar to Heizer through his father's career. The idea for *City* came to Heizer in 1970 during a visit to the Yucatán, while he was preparing a study on the serpent motif in the ball court of Chichén Itzá. The Yucatán was not the only reference, as Heizer linked the project of *City* to other grandiose ensembles of pre-Columbian monuments—those of the Olmec, Maya, Inca, and Aztec.

Heizer has maintained that he is attempting to achieve what had been accomplished centuries ago but has since been forgotten. In the Nevada desert, next to the Test Site, three complexes are being built around a curved, sunken plaza, or pit. Each of the massive structures, based on a rectangular plan with sloped sides, looks like a mastaba. Commenting on *Complex 1*, the artist referred to the mastaba form that shaped the mound over the burial place of Zoser at Saqqâra. Both their primitive building techniques and monumental character intrigue the sculptor. The concrete banding and projection that define the "facade" of the mastaba are akin to the serpent motif at Chichén Itzá. Heizer points out that his use of cantilevered elements was an impossible engineering feat for the builders of Chichén.

The juxtaposition of ancient techniques of construction (for instance, the transportation of large stones) and advanced contemporary technologies is a recurring theme of the narrative that frames Heizer's work. Addressing his ever expanding use of machinery, he even becomes epic:

> Complex 1 required cranes, loaders, pumps, Cats, graders, mixer and water trucks, batch plants, forms, re-bar, scaffolds, surveying, drilling, welding and compacting equipment; everything, almost the whole encyclopedia of construction was used in that one sculpture.[53]

All of this equipment was used to build works able to instill the state of wonder and awe that ancient megalithic architecture had inspired. Heizer drew a distinction between two main types of societies: "megalithic" societies, which built large structures out of massive materials, and "piecemeal" societies, which likewise built large structures but out of small elements. For Heizer, contemporary society is a piecemeal society, which builds enormous structures out of "millions of fragments."[54] While megalithic architecture tends to be made out of smaller dimensions, it has a superior grandness that mightily impacts the observer, and this is the effect that Heizer attempts to replicate. He wants to establish a "dormant dialogue"[55] with the powerful monoliths of antiquity, discarding, in the process, the original intents behind the forms: "Who, in our time, wants processionals for spirits, sacrificial platforms, or ceremonial buildings? These functions are no longer meaningful but are interesting for contemporary society if phrased in terms it can identify with."[56] The question seems to be how to "rephrase" an ancient text in contemporary terms and offer secularized relics without the revival of forgotten or bygone values.

Gilles Tiberghien, a historian and art critic, has suggested that the Hegelian definition of "inorganic sculpture" (*unorganische Skulptur*) could apply to the works of sculptors such as Robert Morris, Smithson, or Heizer. For Hegel, any sort of building, from a house to a temple, was characterized by

(fig. 6)

"Front page of the *Los Angeles Times*," a still from *Plowshare*

its destination, its instrumental use (habitation, place of worship, locus of display), whereas sculptures (representations of men and gods) present themselves as ends in themselves. This meant that a sculpture did not need to be useful to exist. For Hegel, however, if one went back in time toward the dawn of civilization, when architecture and sculpture were not yet differentiated arts, the obelisk, the pyramid, and the colossal statues of ancient Egypt would offer examples of an architecture that existed for itself, without bearing on any external, hetero-directed need or functional use. Additionally, unlike sculpture (of kings or divinities), these primitive works of art were even dispensed from the necessity of revealing their interior meanings by their own exterior shapes.

Independent of circumstance and context, these archetypal works would operate like symbols, standing as something "autonomous," their meaning not to be found beyond themselves, in an exterior realm such as utility or instrumentality. Accordingly, for Tiberghien, such independent objects were neither sculpture nor architecture, but at the same time encompassed both spheres, an aspect that is echoed in minimalist art and works of land art.[57] By inscribing these works within the question of the "origin" of art and architecture, Tiberghien's interpretation is quite persuasive, accounting, as it does, for the fascination of American artists with ancient ruins. One might ask, then, what links such "original" forms to a technologically dominated "now," where, according to Heizer, nobody is looking for spiritual ceremonials, sacrificial rites, or consecrated expanses. Do these original forms still maintain their power and meaning when nobody kneels any longer in front of them? Perhaps the question should be whether, despite his pronouncements, the artist's work is really announcing the disappearance of the power of the original forms. Or, instead, is he actually envisioning, if not their restoration, at least their memory?

Or, in other terms, do those forms still retain an "aura," recalling Walter Benjamin's notion of this "strange wave of space and time"? Actually, in his famous essay on the work of art in the age of mechanical reproduction, Benjamin addresses the "decline of the aura" and not its death or disappearance. Art historian Georges Didi-Huberman has pointed out the apparently ambiguous position toward the aura held by Benjamin: was he really announcing the destruction of it, or, instead, thinking of its restoration? Benjamin does not eliminate the aura from the work of art, because aura always retains an "originary" capacity. In the Benjaminian sense, the origin is what emerges from the process of becoming and disappearing. The aura (of religious cult images, of icons) survives as something that is declining, eluding its dogmatic imposition.[58] Both the aura and its decline are present in an artist's work, possibly. This happens because the aura, being original, refers to questions of forgetfulness, memory, and reminiscence.[59] For Benjamin, as for Heizer, interpreting an image means accepting to rememorize an original significance that survives, while rejecting a nostalgic rebirth or revival.

TEST/TEXT

The living organism, in a situation determined by the play of energy on the surface of the globe, ordinarily receives more energy than is necessary for maintaining life; the excess energy (wealth) can be used for the growth of a system (e.g., an organism); if the system can no longer grow, or if the excess cannot be completely absorbed in its growth, it must necessarily be lost without profit; it must be spent, willingly or not, gloriously or catastrophically.

—Georges Bataille, *The Accursed Share*

In 1962, the U.S. Department of Defense, together with the Atomic Energy Commission, published a revised edition of a report entitled *The Effects of Nuclear Weapons*. Most of the illustrations are collected in the section dedicated to the scientific analysis of structural damage caused by air blasts to industrial, residential, commercial, and administrative structures and also to infrastructures, including roads, bridges, railroads, automobiles, trucks, train cars, suspension towers, transformers, and utility poles. With cold precision, some of the images document the devastation at Hiroshima and Nagasaki. Chilling captions inform the reader about the nature of the ruins represented: "Industrial-type steel-frame building (0.35 mile from ground zero at Hiroshima). Wooden beams should be noted"; "Destroyed industrial area showing smokestacks still standing (0.51 mile from ground zero at Nagasaki)"; "Three-story, reinforced–concrete frame building; walls were 13-inch-thick brick panel with large window openings (0.13 mile from ground zero at Hiroshima)"; "One-story, reinforced-concrete building with steel roof trusses (0.26 mile from ground zero at Nagasaki). Note the resistance offered by end interior walls when acting as shear walls."[60]

The majority of the photographs contained in *The Effects of Nuclear Weapons*, however, illustrate the results of tests conducted at the Nevada Test Site. There, scientists, in collaboration with the Army, laid out parking lots, built antenna towers, installed heavy machinery, and constructed steel-frame buildings and concrete houses in order to subject them, in controlled conditions, to the effects of nuclear explosions. Possibly the most compelling part in this series of photographs is devoted to residential buildings, portraying the structures before and after a detonation. A comprehensive selection of typical American suburban houses was reconstructed and then blasted. The process was documented with black-and-white images that uncannily evoke some of the artworks produced in the 1960s and early 1970s in America. The text that introduces the photographs reads as follows:

> A considerable amount of information on the blast response of residential structures of several different kinds was obtained in the studies made at the Nevada Test Site in 1953 and, especially, in 1955. The Nuclear device employed in the test of March 17, 1953, was detonated at the top of a 300-foot tower and the yield was about 16 kilotons. In the test of May 5, 1955, the explosion took place on a 500-foot tower and the yield was close to 29 kilotons. In each case, air pressure measurements made possible a correlation, where it was justified, between the blast damage and the peak over-pressure. The main objective of the tests on residential structures were as follows: (1) to determine the elements most susceptible to blast damage and consequently to devise methods for strengthening structures of various types; (2) to provide information concerning the amount of damage to residences that may be expected as a result of a nuclear explosion and to what extent these structure could be subsequently rendered habitable without major repairs; and (3) to determine how persons remaining in their houses during a nuclear attack may be protected from the effects of blast and radiations.[61]

Those stark images have been an ingredient for many desert movies, from Michelangelo Antonioni's *Zabriskie Point* (1970)—the dazzling final scene of which, featuring an explosion of a house and its contents in slow motion, represents perhaps a symbolic ending of consumer civilization—to Dominic Sena's *Kalifornia* (1993), which ends with a scene set on testing grounds where dummies represent radiated inhabitants.[62]

In 1967, Edward Ruscha published his small volume *Thirty-Four Parking Lots in Los Angeles*, which depicts empty parking lots in a series of black-and-white photographs taken from a helicopter on a Sunday. There are thirty-four images of oblique white lines drawn on dark asphalt, together with thirty-four captions recording only the address of the lots. Ruscha used the same technique of black-and-white photography with abridged captions in *Twenty-Six Gasoline Stations* (1962), *Some Los Angeles Apartments* (1965), and *Real Estate Opportunities* (1970), the latter, according to French art critic Yve-Alain Bois constituting "one of his most devastating books."[63] Bois's remark appears under the entry "Zone" in the exhibition catalog *Formless. A User's Guide*, recalling the concept of "thermodynamics in reverse." This idea was taken from Georges Bataille, who, in his theory of expenditure, implemented principles taken from thermodynamics. First developed by Sadi Carnot in 1824, this was a theory of the heat engine.[64] Carnot's cycle explains why motors create movement by consuming energy or power. This cycle produces circulation by means of reservoirs and differences of temperature, which generate residue at the end of the cycle. During the nineteenth century, as soon as one could theorize about heat machines or combustion engines, the notion of time changed. From this moment on, time has been endowed with a direction and is irreversible. Every thermodynamic system drifts from order to disorder, from a powerful difference to a state of dissolution from which no energy, no force, can arise.[65] This process of dissolution was called the law of entropy. Maximal energy is always upstream in an irreversible process. This law was applied to the cosmos in general by Hermann von Helmholtz, among others.

Because of the sun's surplus of energy, Bataille thought that we are condemned to a perpetually growing production and to a permanent surplus, a kind of "reverse entropy." This unbalanced growth creates a cosmic

(fig. 7)

"Test House," three stills from *Trinity and Beyond*

ALESSANDRA PONTE

disequilibrium, which is to be self-regulated by devices that would kick in as soon as unspent energy had accumulated. War would be a typical example of amassed energy that would be expended in an unproductive way. Two corollaries to this thesis of overproduction and expenditure existed: on the one hand, Bataille's radical optimism that envisioned humanity's future as a voluntary renunciation of utilitarian things and excessive riches, and as the multiplication of unproductive expenditure; on the other hand, Bataille's radical pessimism about the effects of overproduction—for instance, the entropic growth of nonassimilable residue, or waste. For Bataille, the emblem of waste's output was dust and the daily war that house help waged against it with brooms and vacuum cleaners. This battle, according to the philosopher, would end only with dust's victory, overpowering "abandoned buildings and deserted dockyards" with garbage and trash.[66] Bataille's prediction anticipates the failure of the domestic fight against dust and foresees its extension to all the city, creating formless "zones" more and more abandoned and overcome by residues.

These areas in cities force a need for a continuous process of recycling to stop the entropic proliferation, the extending of the wasteland. The "zone" consists of abandoned lots awaiting buyers. The numerous "For Sale" billboards in Los Angeles, photographed by Ruscha in *Real Estate Opportunities* (1970), are emblems of the "zone." In another instance, the "zone" is made up of the interstitial spaces, vacant and useless, that New York City sold for a very low price and that Gordon Matta-Clark bought and then photographed for his book *Reality Properties: Fake Estates* (1973). For Matta-Clark, these small properties, in the borough of Queens, had no value because they were too small to hold anything. False merchandise, fake "real estate," they reveal the repressed manifestation of entropy in the urban context.

Truly, Ruscha's and Matta-Clark's works belong to the same context. Both artists confront the false, the void, the empty, and perceive the formlessness that is triggered by entropy. This is well exemplified by some of Ruscha's other books, such as *Nine Swimming Pools and a Broken Glass* (1968), *A Few Palm Trees* (1971), and *Every Building on Sunset Strip* (1966). In the work of both

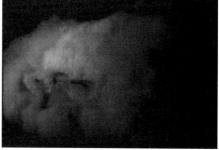

artists, it is worth observing also how the repetition of the photographs' format underlines the uniformity of the topic and the anonymity of the sites. And, in Bois's words, Ruscha's work specifically displays the will to simply elicit "a recognition of the same as nothing."[67] To Ruscha's intent, clear and nonjudgmental, the critic opposes the polemical denunciation of Dan Graham's *Homes for America* (1966) and Robert Venturi's "perverse admiration" for Levittown and Las Vegas. One could add other works accomplished during the same period, for example, Smithson's *Partially Buried Woodshed* (1970) or the destroyed objects of Gordon Matta-Clark, including *Splitting* (1974).[68] These works bear connections with the entropic testing in Nevada and also with the monotonous American urban and suburban landscape, with the wastelands and rust belts.

Bataille developed his post-Nietzschean thesis on the world's dynamics between two capital texts: "La Notion de dépense" (the notion of expenditure) (1933) and *The Accursed Share* (1949), concluding his political opus under the light, so to speak, of atomic explosions and as the Cold War began.[69] This new type of war would have taken place not on the battlefields of old but mainly on the testing sites of the two opposing powers. Bataille's central concern resides in the economic implications of such a war, the vast amount of wealth spent and the huge quantity of energy literally blown up during an arms race. Bataille tried to think about the nuclear threat, the fearsome raising of the stakes involved in the possible mortal conflict between the United States and the Soviet Union, placing himself on "alert consciousness," as opposed to actively fearing a foreseeable Armageddon. In *The Accursed Share*, he hypothesizes a nonmilitary competition between different methods of production and observes the awakening of the mind instigated by the situation's extreme danger. Remarking that a mental state of vigilance can result in some positive, clever cogitation, he writes:

> But while [the awakening] is the result of menace, and though it was once linked to the feeling of a useless effort, of the game already lost, the alert consciousness cannot in any way surrender to anguish; it is dominated rather by the assurance of the moment (the laughable idea that darkness alone will be the answer to the will to see). But, up to the last, it will not be able to give up the tranquil pursuit of good fortune. It will give up only in the happy event of death.

In this situation of absolute schism, what prevents one from believing war to be inevitable is the idea that under the present conditions "the economy," to alter Clausewitz's phrase, may "continue it by other means."[70]

Accordingly, Bataille suggests different outcomes for spending the excess of wealth produced by the American economy, which he considers to be "the greatest explosive mass the world has ever known."[71]

Bataille's new kind of "alertness" in the face of death and his refusal to surrender to the forces of "anguish" correspond to what Ronell alludes to in her essay, offering a possible idea of place defined by the test:

> The relation of testing to the question of site is essential. The test site, as protoreal, marks out a primary atopos, producing a "place" where the real awaits confirmation. The test site is not a home (unless you're a homunculus). Linked to a kind of ghostless futurity the site offers no present shelter. This explains perhaps why Nietzsche names the *gaya scienza* in the same breath that convokes "we who are homeless": "We children of the future, how could we be at home in this today—in this fragile, broken time of transition?"[72]

For Nietzsche, testing and experimentation are related to acts of negation and affirmation, and since they are conducted in the name of life, and also by life itself, they imply a strong, joyous personality. Ronell proceeds:

> But Nietzsche, being Nietzsche, knows how to affirm the unhinging of home as the preparation for another future, one not rooted in the ideologies of the homefront. The logic of the test site that we have not yet understood concerns precisely the relation of the site to life; we still know only how to leave the test site uninhabitable, mapping ever more deserts as eco-wasteland, unexploded arsenal, littered terrain, the "third world." The question that Nietzsche presses us on is therefore never merely one of affirming homelessness after metaphysics, but of rendering spaces habitable, multiplying trajectories for life and the living, refiguring the site of experimentation in such way as to ensure that it is not already the ensepulchered reserve of the living dead. In other words: why have we not yet thought the test site on the side of life?[73]

Nietzsche opposed the view that experiment implies objectivity and desubjectivization. The Nietzschean science has little to do with objective observation but belongs to the superior order of curiosity and experimental imagination. As a risk taker, the experimental spirit is not at home anywhere; he is a wanderer, a hermit. Furthermore, he disrupts the accepted knowledge, disentangles the mind from rules, and dissolves the "petrification of opinion."[74] Construing habitable desert spaces, multiplying trajectories for the living, refiguring the site of experimentation within an entropic economy: this has been the scope of artists such as Ruscha, Smithson, and Matta-Clark.

Is there an experiment that could lead to results that would place us on the other side of doomsday? One of Ruscha's books contains a visual narrative, contrary to most of the others. *Royal Road Test* (1967) illustrates a 1966 experiment carried out on a highway across the Nevada desert, 122 miles southwest of Las Vegas. The test consisted of throwing a typewriter out of the window of a Buick moving at 90 miles an hour. The photographs collect documents as if they were exhibits in a trial: objects, such as the site, the automobile, the car window, and the typewriter; participants, including a driver, a thrower, and a photographer; records of the distance the wreckage traveled and the point of impact; close-ups of the debris. The last photograph in the series portrays the carcass of the typewriter in the shadows projected by the performers, one of them pointing at it, the other looking closely, and the third taking the picture. The narrative of the book, as in the case of Heizer's work, cannot be reduced to a parody, or an ironic mimicry of the scientific tests in the desert. An elucidation is suggested by the choice of a typewriter, a machine with which to write that is destroyed by the speed of another machine, the automobile.

Ruscha's undoing of the typewriter seems to be connected to the production of Liquid Words, a series of paintings he produced between 1966 and 1969. These word-pictures were done by painting on horizontal canvases, expanding upon the technique already attempted by Jackson Pollock. Ruscha's letter-paintings have been viewed as belonging to the struggle of art, from Cézanne to Pollock, to overcome the phenomenological perpendicularity of (vertical) painting and (horizontal) writing. Additionally, the use of quirky materials in the writing of Liquid Words (beans, pieces of food, maple syrup, caviar, and substances like axle grease) has lead some critics to

ALESSANDRA PONTE

connect his research with Bataille's interest in raw and crude materials. The liquefaction to which the words are subjected has evoked the notion of entropy, since, in our contemporary society, languages are exposed to an irreversible process of devitalization, disarticulation, and erosion. Therefore, "liquid words" are depleted words, with little meaning left, forming an exhausted language. The coincidence of time between Ruscha's work and the publication of Jacques Derrida's *Of Grammatology* (1967) has also been noted, interpreting Ruscha's opus as an attempt to explore the unbridgeable, repressed gap between the sound of words and the silence of writing.[75] One may ask, however, what the wrecked typewriter is proclaiming: the end of Western logocentric thinking? A meltdown of language? The impossibility of communication in an entropic, postnuclear age? Probably none of the above. Ruscha's "liquidation" of a mechanical writing device is not the result of a will to destroy, which, in Bataille's words, would be a "surrender to anguish." The test does provide a text, a narrative, subject to never ending analysis, and it resists simple interpretation. The results of the test do not offer any "truth," nor do they moralize, condescend, or preach; they are forever provisional. However, on the aforementioned "side of life," they do open up the possibility of more tests, of an endless testing of sites that become the canvases upon which one can set out to write, to paint, or to build; or to incise, to wreck, and to ruin.

NOTES

1. Friedrich Nietzsche, *Die fröhliche Wissenschaft*, 2nd ed., 1887; idem, *The Gay Science*, trans. Walter Kaufmann (New York: Vintage Books, 1974), 82.

2. Giorgio Colli, introduction to the Italian translation, F. Nietzsche, *La gaia scienza* (Milan: Adelphi Edizioni, 1979), 6–7.

3. Avital Ronell, "The Test Drive," in *Deconstruction Is/in America: A New Sense of the Political*, ed. Anselm Haverkamp (New York and London: New York University Press, 1995), 201.

4. In this text I am using the terms *test* and *experiment* interchangeably, even if the first pertains more precisely to the technological domain and the second, to the scientific one. Historians of science tend to agree that "all the issues that recent sociology of science has raised about *experiment* in science can be raised about *testing* in technology." Donald Mackenzie "From Kwajalein to Armageddon? Testing and the Social Construction of Missile Accuracy," in *The Uses of Experiment: Studies in the Natural Sciences*, ed. David Gooding, Trevor Pinch, and Simon Schaffer (1989; reprinted, Cambridge: Cambridge University Press, 1993), 409–35.

5. Ronell, 201–02.

6. The experiment has been the subject of quite a number of studies published by historians of science in the last years. Their analyses tend to confirm the interpretations of the philosophers

about the issues raised by the test and the experiment. They describe the experiment as a way of "constructing knowledge" and point out the ever provisional nature of the results of the test. Here are some of the arguments, synthetically expressed: "No single experiment, by itself, can resolve a scientific controversy, because it is always possible, in principle, to challenge elements of experimental procedure. When an experiment produces a controversial result, it is generally possible for other scientists to find fault with the experiment or the methodology, and thus dismiss the result as spurious. When an attempt is made to replicate an accepted experimental finding, negative results can be explained away on similar ground." Benjamin Sims, "Concrete Practices: Testing in an Earthquake-Engineering Laboratory," *Social Studies of Science* 29, no. 4 (August 1999): 486. On the experiment, and on the seminal work of Bruno Latour in particular, see Bruno Latour and Steve Woolgar, *Laboratory Life: The Construction of Scientific Fact* (Princeton: Princeton University Press, 1986). On the "geography of science," see also David N. Livingstone, "The Spaces of Knowledge: Contribution toward a Historical Geography of Science," *Society and Space* 13 (February 1995): 5–34.

7. Peter Goin, *Nuclear Landscapes* (Baltimore and London: Johns Hopkins University Press, 1991). Goin, together with photographers from five countries, is a member of the Atomic Photographers' Guild, founded in 1986 by the Canadian Robert Del Tredici. Goin offers his own interpretation:

> The photographs in *Nuclear Landscapes* were not taken to convey the sense of beauty found in these areas. In fact, celebrating the beauty of these landscapes contradicts the subject and intent of the project. In contemporary landscape photography, there is a critical dialogue that centers on how photographers will address the role of beauty. How does a photographer convey content and still make the photograph appealing to the eye? Should a photograph appease and soothe the viewer, or challenge the viewer to think about the subject? Formal beauty can be a contradictory element in a photograph that comments critically on land use and land management. Many popular contemporary photographs do not attempt to reconcile aesthetic and content. This issue is central to the originality of this project.

Goin's arguments regarding the problem of the "beauty" of nuclear landscape photography are not far from the one elaborated in Deborah Bright, "Of Mother Nature and Marlboro Men: An Inquiry into the Cultural Meanings of Landscape Photography," in *The Contest of Meaning: Critical Histories of Photography*, ed. Richard Bolton (New York: Lustrum Press, 1989): 125–43.

8. Peter Goin, *Tracing the Line: A Photographic Survey of the Mexican-American Border* (limited ed. art book, 1987).

9. Peter Goin, prologue in *Nuclear Landscapes*, xvii–xxii.

10. Ibid.

11. Photographs by Patrick Nagatani, with an essay by Eugenia Parry Janis, *Nuclear Enchantment* (Albuquerque: University of New Mexico Press, 1991).

12. See www.atomictourism.com, "Graded 'A' by *Entertainment Weekly*," "Selected as 1 of 20 Web Gems by the *Wall Street Journal*," and "Rated Four Stars by the *Seattle Times*."

13. Preface in *Nuclear Matters*, ed. and curated by Timothy Druckrey and Marnie Gillett (San Francisco: Camerawork, 1991), 3.

14. Ibid., 6.

15. William L. Lawrence, *Dawn Over Zero: The Story of the Atomic Bomb* (New York: Alfred A. Knopf, 1946), 10–11.

16. Richard Misrach, with Myriam Weisang Misrach, *Bravo 20: The Bombing of the American West*

(Baltimore: Johns Hopkins University Press, 1990).

17. On this project, see Andrew Ross, "How to Occupy Your Own Country," *Documents*, fall/winter 1992: 12–19; in the same issue, see Miwon Kwon, "The Pleasure of Nature in Ruins": 20–26.

18. *Crimes and Splendors: The Desert Cantos of Richard Misrach*, exhib. cat., ed. Anne Wilkes Tucker (Boston and New York: Bulfinch Press/Little, Brown and Co. in association with the Museum of Fine Arts, Houston, 1996).

19. David Thomson, *In Nevada: The Land, the People, God, and Chance* (New York: Alfred A. Knopf, 1999), 154.

20. Solnit, "Scapeland," in *Crimes and Splendors*, 47.

21. Ibid., 48.

22. Ibid.

23. Quoted in Wolfgang Kemp, "Images of Decay: Photography in the Picturesque Tradition," *October* 54 (fall 1990): 106–07. The commentary on Price and Gilpin is also taken from this essay.

24. Robert Smithson, "Frederick Law Olmsted and the Dialectical Landscape," *Artforum*, February 1973, reprinted in *The Writings of Robert Smithson*, ed. Nancy Holt (New York: New York University Press, 1979), 119.

25. Ibid., 118.

26. Franz Schulze, *Philip Johnson: Life and Work* (New York: Alfred A. Knopf, 1994), 208–9.

27. Robert Smithson, "A Sedimentation of the Mind: Earth Project," *Writings of Robert Smithson*, 85. See footnote * for the quotation about sculpture gardens.

28. Ibid., 87.

29. The transformation of the artist's studio into a laboratory in postwar America is examined in depth in Peter Galison and Caroline A. Jones, "Factory, Laboratory, Studio: Dispersing Sites of Production," in *The Architecture of Science*, eds. Peter Galison and Emily Thompson (Cambridge, Mass.: MIT Press, 1999), 497–540.

30. Smithson, "Sedimentation of the Mind," 86.

31. Schulze, *Philip Johnson*, 98–99.

32. Smithson, "Sedimentation of the Mind," 86.

33. Ibid., 87.

34. Ibid.

35. Julia Brown and Michael Heizer, "Interview," in *Michael Heizer: Sculpture in Reverse*, ed. Julia Brown (Los Angeles: Museum of Contemporary Art, 1984), 8–43, 11.

36. This information is taken from Scott Kirsch, "Experiment in Progress: Edward Teller's Controversial Geographies," *Ecumene* 5, no. 3 (July 1998): 267–85. The essay is part of the themed section of the journal dedicated to "Nuclear Engineering and Geography," with three more essays on the Plowshare Program. On Plowshare, see also Dan O'Neill, *The Firecracker Boys* (New York: St. Martin's Press, 1994).

37. This article would subsequently be included in Teller's book, *Our Nuclear Future [...] Facts, Dangers and Opportunities* (New York: Criterion Books, 1958), 80.

38. Edward Teller and Albert L. Latter, "The Compelling Need for Nuclear Tests," *Life*, 10 February 1958: 72.

39. The last scheme, under the name of Project Carryall, was developed in collaboration with the California State Division of Highways and the Santa Fe Railway. Other proposals of the Plowshare scientists that were never implemented include Project Oil Sand, designed to recover oil sand from the Athabasca area in Alberta, and Project Ketch, a commercial scheme to create an underground gas-storage chamber in Appalachian Pennsylvania.

40. Edward Teller, Wilson K. Talley, Garry Higgins, and Gerald W. Johnson, *The Constructive Uses of Nuclear Explosives* (New York: McGraw-Hill Book Company, 1968), v.

41. Ibid.

42. Thomson, *In Nevada*, 244–45.

43. The test produced five times more radioactivity than predicted but was nevertheless considered a success by the Atomic Energy Commission.

44. Teller, *Our Nuclear Future*, 80.

45. Heizer insists on having been the first to discover the desert of Nevada as a new space of artistic experimentation. See, for example, his assertion during a conversation reported in Michael Kimmelman, "A Sculptor's Colossus of the Desert," *The New York Times*, 12 December 1999. Heizer's role and influence on the works of De Maria and Smithson are also mentioned by Germano Celant in *Michael Heizer*, exhib. cat., ed. Germano Celant (Milan: Fondazione Prada, 1997), xix. Celant does mention one antecedent—that of Jean Tinguely, who in 1962 realized the work *Étude pour une fin du monde n. 2* in a dry salt lake near Las Vegas.

46. Brown and Heizer, "Interview," 11. In *The New York Times* conversation (Kimmelman, "A Sculptor's Colossus"), Heizer recounts that in 1970 he hired a pilot from Las Vegas to help him find a property: "It had sand and gravel, running water from a creek, isolation, the right climate—and it was cheap."

47. Brown and Heizer, "Interview," 16.

48. Ibid., 10.

49. Ibid., 11.

50. Heizer's work was commissioned by Robert C. Scull, a New York taxi magnate.

51. Celant, *Michael Heizer*, xxvii–xxviii.

52. Michael Heizer, in "The Art of Michael Heizer," *Artforum* 5 (December 1969): 35.

53. Brown and Heizer, "Interview," 33.

54. Ibid.

55. Ibid.

56. Ibid.

57. Gilles A. Tiberghien, "Sculptures inorganiques," in *Land Art* (Paris: Éditions Carré, 1993), 61–83.

58. Georges Didi-Hubermann, "The Supposition of the Aura: The Now, the Then, and Modernity," in *Negotiating Rapture: The Power of Art to Transform Lives*, exhib. cat. (Chicago: Museum of Contemporary Art, 1996), 48–63; see esp. 49–53.

59. Georges Teyssot, "History as a Destructive Remembrance," *Lotus International* 81 (1994): 117–22.

60. Samuel Gladstone, ed., *The Effects of Nuclear Weapons*, report prepared by the U.S. Department of Defense, rev. ed. (Washington: U.S. Atomic Energy Commission, 1962), 218, fig. 5.55a; 221, fig. 5.60a; 238, fig. 5.86b.; 240, fig. 5.88c.

61. Ibid., 200.

62. Edward Dimenberg, "Beyond Cinema: Space, Time, and Entropy in *Zabriskie Point*," in *Paragrana, Internationale Zeitschrift für Historische Anthropologie* 7 (1998): 241–49.

63. Yve-Alain Bois, "Zone," in *L'informe: Mode d'emploi*, exhib. cat., eds. Yve-Alain Bois and Rosalind E. Krauss (Paris: Centre Georges Pompidou, 1996), 212–18; Yve-Alain Bois and Rosalind E. Krauss, *Formless. A User's Guide* (New York: Zone Books, 1997), 226.

64. Michel Serres, *Hermes: Literature, Science, Philosophy*, ed. Josué V. Harari and David Bell (Baltimore: Johns Hopkins University Press, 1982), 34–35, 54–62.

65. Ibid., 71–75.

66. Bois and Krauss, *Formless*, 226.

67. Ibid., 231.

68. See Pamela M. Lee, *Object to Be Destroyed: The Work of Gordon Matta-Clark* (Cambridge, Mass.: MIT Press, 2000).

69. On nuclear criticism and issues related to the Cold War, see also *Nuclear Criticism*, thematic issue of *Diacritics*, summer 1984, and in particular Jacques Derrida, "No Apocalypse, Not Now (Full Speed Ahead, Seven Missiles, Seven Missives)": 20–31. See also Richard Dellamora, ed., *Postmodern Apocalypse: Theory and Cultural Practice at the End* (Philadelphia: University of Pennsylvania Press, 1995).

70. Georges Bataille, *The Accursed Share: An Essay on General Economy*, trans. Robert Hurtley, 2 vols. (New York: Zone Books, 1988), 1: 171.

71. Ibid.

72. Ronell, "The Test Drive," 209, quoting Nietzsche, *The Gay Science*, 338.

73. Ronell, "The Test Drive," 209–10.

74. Ronell, "The Test Drive," 213, quoting Nietzsche, *The Gay Science*, 238.

75. Here again, see the crucial analysis of Yve-Alain Bois in "Liquid Words," in *Formless*, 124–29, and in *Edward Ruscha Romance with Liquid Paintings, 1966–1969* (New York: Rizzoli, 1993).

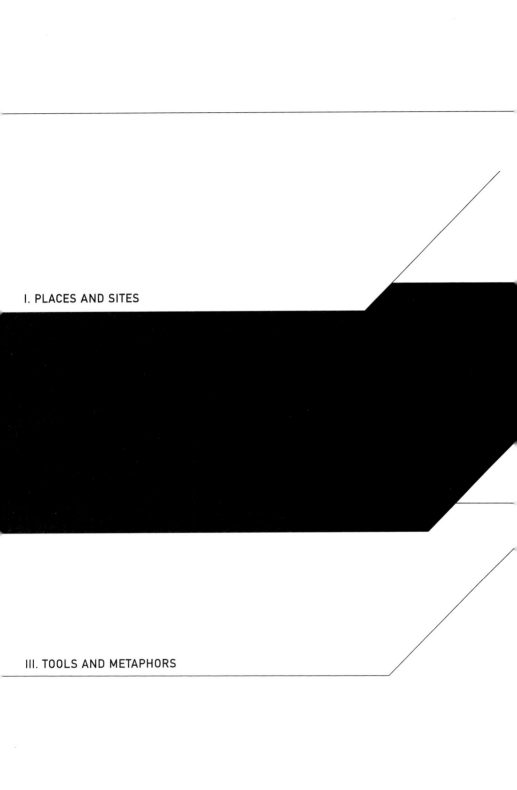

I. PLACES AND SITES

III. TOOLS AND METAPHORS

II. CONCEPTUAL FRAMEWORKS

VIOLLET-LE-DUC'S OPTIC

Martin Bressani

When discussing relationships between fields, it is wise to distinguish analogies proper from analogies metaphorical. The existence of concrete analogies may prevent rather than encourage the construction of metaphoric bridges. The central problem with architecture's relationship with modern science is not the distance that separates the two disciplines but, on the contrary, a closeness that prevents free metaphoric exchanges. A productive metaphor needs an inherent distance between the terms that it links together—the clash in meaning being the source of the resonance.

The nineteenth century is an era that illustrates well such a paradox. It is usually believed that the inertia of conventions alone prevented architects of the age of historicism to draw from modern materials and techniques. Yet modern feats of engineering were known and popular among the general public; witness the extraordinary attraction of the Crystal Palace. Its author, Sir Joseph Paxton (1803–1865), however, was no architect, and we can guess that the profession reacted to the great exhibition hall as a form of surrender to engineering and modern efficiency. It was too much an invasion of their own province to lead to any generous reevaluation of their methods. The reaction of Eugéne-Emanuel Viollet-le-Duc (1814–1879), the self-proclaimed rebel in French architecture of the nineteenth century, to the experiments of Boileau in iron construction is very telling in this regard: he treats Louis-Auguste Boileau (1812–1896) as an outsider, a bricoleur who tinkers with new materials without any serious investment in the "discipline" of architecture. Iron and modern engineering are too crude (and too close) to be truly engaging. Measured steps must be taken.

When architects do draw inspiration from scientific fields, it is from the least likely ones such as physiology, anatomy, and geology. The case of Viollet-le-Duc is again extremely revealing; the greatest apostle of rationalism in the nineteenth century, untiring advocate of structural determinism, a man heavily involved with practice, he remained totally aloof from developments in the modern science of structures. His enormous library, which numbered many thousands of books on a multitude of subjects, held not a single volume on the modern science of engineering.[1] And nowhere in his description of medieval construction does any trace of the scientific method as we generally know it appear.

Yet Viollet-le-Duc definitely envisaged his work as "science," his great medieval archaeological treatise, the *Dictionnaire raisonné de l'architecture française*, being intended as a foundation for a scientific approach to architecture. What was Viollet-le-Duc's own route to the scientific, then? In the preface to the *Dictionnaire raisonné* he explains that he will explore medieval architecture like an anatomist examining the human body, providing a structural physiology of the cathedral. Why anatomy rather than engineering? Only in retracing in detail the development of his mode of apprehension of the architectural object can we grasp the convoluted metaphoric operations.

For all his rationalism, Viollet-le-Duc considered monuments the objects of an extremely strong emotional relationship. As a young boy, he had been panic-stricken inside Notre-Dame in Paris and seized by vertigo in the ruins at Pierrefonds—interestingly, the two greatest of his future restoration works. Viollet-le-Duc recollects in great detail his "vivid childhood emotion" at Notre-Dame in the first of his *Entretiens sur l'architecture*,[2] a passage that seeks to explain the power and essential unity of all arts. Secure in the arms of an old family servant inside the crowded church, the young Eugène gazes, fascinated at the dazzling light of the sun-drenched southern rose window when suddenly the church's organ started. Transfixed, he imagines that it is the great rose itself that sings, its various translucent panels producing each a different sound. Trapped within a hallucination that grows progressively more acute despite the servant's efforts to reassure him, he is absolutely terrified and has to be taken out of the church immediately.

Very far from a romantic reverie, the experience related by Viollet-le-Duc is a tactile encounter. Like Rainer Maria Rilke's poem to the "cathedral's great window-roses" that "gripped a heart and pulled it deep into God,"[3] an experience that the poet likens to being subjected, face to face, to the unsettling wildness of a great feline, Viollet-le-Duc's childhood episode at Notre-Dame is an opening into the depth of a force the strength of which makes the young boy lose himself in otherness. If it is not, strictly speaking, a religious experience, it is essentially sacred in nature and defines an apex of possibilities. It is perhaps from this emotional whirlpool that Viollet-le-Duc's life work in architecture began. Relentlessly, he would set himself the task of mastering such chaos, not only transforming into rationality the unbridled architecture of the Middle Ages but measuring the nonmeasurable Mont Blanc, unmasking the logic of deadly battles of war, giving shape to the unruly world of industry. Viollet-le-Duc, however, never loses touch with his early emotional encounter at Notre-Dame. In the early 1840s, already touring for the Monument historique, he writes to his father of his enchantment among old French monuments, where pillars, walls, and cornices whisper intimate confidences to him, as he seeks "their illnesses, their sufferings."[4] There he feels great solace, forging an intimate link with the stone monument and the vast historical field it embodies: "We at last understand each other better," writes Viollet-le-Duc, "because few understand us, few know what we tell each other.... There is an indefinable charm in this sympathy, charm the stronger that it is unrecognized, that it is secret, intimate, silent."[5]

This special bond forms the basis of Viollet-le-Duc's archaeological method; he came to feel the monument's body endowed with its own secret life. Following Viollet-le-Duc's patient dismantling of a medieval building, in which absolutely no references to the science of engineering can be found, architecture becomes a combination of organs working together in a complex solidarity and subject to a single type-force akin to the stuff of life. To become aware of that metabolism is to get hold of the impulse at the origin of the building's making, renewing contact with a construction instinct.

Opening the Dictionnaire raisonné de l'architecture française du XIe au XVIe siècles is thus a form of initiation. The reader penetrates, with childlike innocence, a world previously hidden. Relatively uninterested in the liturgical space used by the clergy and the congregation, Viollet-le-Duc sounded instead the monument's own body, which acquired a new depth. His countless small perspective drawings of parts of medieval construction reveal a mysterious, often inchoate, inner world that demands explanation. The profusion of drawings is overwhelming. The woodcuts—very delicate, without accented shadows—have the fragility and preciosity of a palimpsest, an intricate web holding within their relationships the secret of medieval builders. Though drawn mostly in perspective, they are almost never of picturesque views of the monuments. Instead, they present a minute, myopic scanning of the fabric; the eye is brought into various hidden corners, shown partial views in which layers are peeled away in order to study the inner workings (fig. 1).

To consider his drawings is to get hold of Viollet-le-Duc's mind at its least conscious level. Drawing, for him, was a compulsive act, unquestionably the first means through which the hypersensitive child was able to gain a foothold on life. Always armed with a pencil or a pen, Viollet-le-Duc could never stop drawing. Whether sitting in committees, touring building sites, climbing mountains, or at work in the darkness of his study, he drew relentlessly. His need to draw was as obsessive as his need to work, a compulsion that led his uncle, the art critic Étienne Delécluze (1781–1863), to call him a "machine à dessiner."[6] The pleasure he drew from it was not of an artistic nature per se but of a technical sort, the satisfaction of having solved a difficulty—a means to have power over things, to take possession.

Viollet-le-Duc's drawings are not passive reproductions of reality. The figures of the *Dictionnaire raisonné* are often unfaithful to the actual state of the building they represent.[7] They either restore the fragment to an assumed original state or strip it of its "unnecessary" clutter, both processes amounting to the same thing. Drawing, for Viollet-le-Duc, was an active operation rather than a passive reproduction. The emblematic example, despite its uniqueness, is the celebrated exploded perspective of the springing point of the arch of the nave in a typical thirteenth-century church, a drawing published in 1859 in volume four of the *Dictionnaire raisonné* (fig. 2). It takes up a full page in the article "Construction." Both the view and the building are totally imaginary, the fictive arch seemingly in the process of being slowly assembled before the reader's eyes. The drawing summarizes not only Viollet-le-Duc's whole conception of the Gothic structure in equilibrium but also his method of drawing. To draw is a mental act of decomposition and recomposition.

(fig. 1)

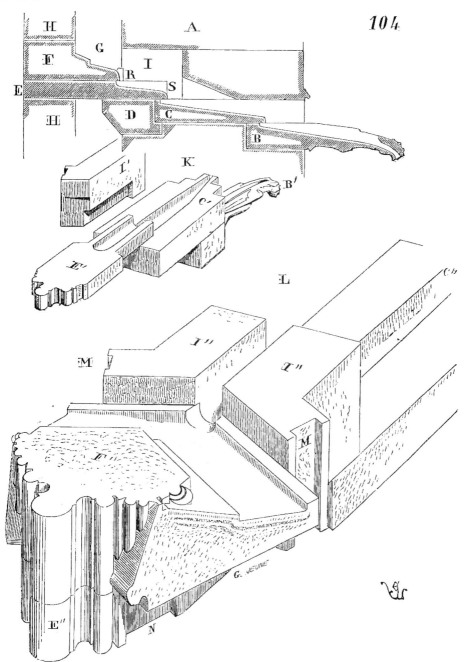

Detail of Gothic gutter, from "Construction." *Dictionnaire raisonné de l'architecture* 4: 187, fig. 104

The whole of the *Dictionnaire raisonné* follows this logic. Despite their remarkable clarity, the drawings contained therein, splintered into myriad disparate parts, have at first sight a rather disorienting effect. The text alone offers the thread that unifies the succession of illustrations. The reader's curiosity aroused by the pleasant intricacy of the drawings, he/she turns to the text and then is made to participate in a process of slow and progressive mental re-creation, from disjointed members toward a never reached totality.

Considering the history of the exploded perspective of the springing point of the arch, a drawing the form of which preoccupied Viollet-le-Duc for more than a decade before it reached its final resolution in 1859, is a good means to better understand the nature of Viollet-le-Duc's graphic imagination. In his earliest account of Gothic construction, written for the *Annales archéologiques* between 1844 and 1847, Viollet-le-Duc spent great energy on the problem of representing the springing points of the Gothic cathedral's great arches. Their first three-dimensional depiction in the *Annales* is a noteworthy drawing, being the earliest cutaway perspective ever published by Viollet-le-Duc. That form of *écorché* would have a great importance in the *Dictionnaire raisonné* for its capacity to clarify relationships among distinct but adjacent members. In the 1847 installment of that long article in the *Annales*, probing closer to the springing point of the arch, Viollet-le-Duc draws a series of detail elevations and three-dimensional cuts to expose the complex imbrication of stones (fig. 3). With the advantage of hindsight, it is easy to imagine how these dispersed drawings could become synthesized in the one exploded perspective of a decade later. Yet the vision that underlies these small drawings is essentially different from the later version. What is presented here is a kit of parts, stones the distinct shapes of which visibly fit into one another but lack the vital tension apparent in the great drawing of 1859.

In the first volume of the *Dictionnaire raisonné*, Viollet-le-Duc illustrates under the heading "Appareil" another stage in the evolution of the representation of the springing point of the rib-vault (fig. 4). This time the representation is an exploded perspective closely resembling the final disposition. The adjustments that will be made later, however, are crucial. By separating only one stone coursing, by spreading these stones far apart and omitting the course immediately below, and especially by neglecting to cast shadows and by erasing the geometrical matrix that gives such a strong visual structure to the final version, this early drawing of 1853 is devoid of the powerful

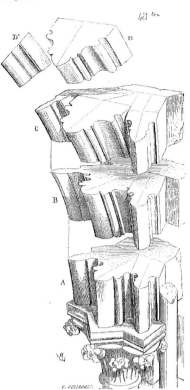

(fig. 2)

Exploded perspective of the springing point
of the arch of the nave of a typical thirteenth-century church, from "Construction,"
Dictionnaire raisonné de l'architecture 4:
93, fig. 48

(fig. 3)

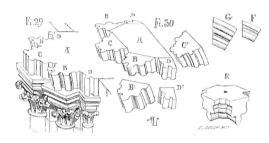

Detail of the springing point of the vault
of a typical eighteenth-century church, from
"De la construction des monuments religieux
en France," *Annales archéologiques* 6 (1847):
248-49, figs. 29 and 30

(fig. 4)

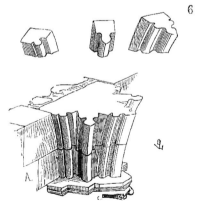

Springing point of the Gothic vault,
from "Appareil," *Dictionnaire raisonné
de l'architecture* 1: 30, fig. 6

corporeality that characterizes the one drawn in 1859. Its stones float as if deprived of weight.

From these few comparative remarks, it is easy to identify the final version's particular power. Not only does it immediately communicate a strong sense of unity, allowing the viewer to deduce at a glance the Gothic vault as a whole, but it does so with considerably greater dynamism, as if one stone metamorphoses into another. The drawing expresses all at once a strong feeling of the corporeality and weight of the stone and an inner vitality that runs through it.

Judging from such a progressive evolution, it is easy to forget that Viollet-le-Duc had a model for this type of representation in contemporary scientific illustration. An anatomical drawing contained in the first volume of Marc Jean Bourgery's *Traité complet de l'anatomie de l'homme* (1831) shows an extraordinary exploded perspective, a unique form of representation in the history of anatomical illustrations (fig. 5). That specific drawing, of a human skull, had been given the highest praise in the press by Viollet-le-Duc's uncle, a great admirer of the anatomical work of Bourgery (1797–1849), who was Delécluze's most intimate friend. Viollet-le-Duc was cognizant of the illustration, not only having read his uncle's raving description of it in the *Journal des débats* but also being himself closely acquainted with the eccentric Bourgery, who was very fond of him and shared his passion for the Gothic. Viollet-le-Duc had even acquired, at high cost, an entire set of the eight folios that make up this lavish anatomical publication.

Delécluze emphasized in 1834 that the most notable achievement of the *Traité complet de l'anatomie* was its illustrations, lithographs drawn by the painter Nicolas Henri Jacob (1782–1871), who, like Delécluze himself, had been a student of the great Jacques-Louis David (1748–1825). The *Traité complet* is generally recognized as a work that, more than any other treatise of the nineteenth century, studies drawing's capacity to represent exactly the human body in its intimate assembly as a whole.[8] According to Delécluze, the lithograph of the exploded skull is the one illustration most representative of the whole work, clearly demonstrating "each particular bone's diverse mode of articulation with its adjacent neighbors, and its relative position within the ensemble that makes up the skull."[9] It is indeed a remarkable visual demonstration of the great Baron Georges Cuvier's (1769–1832) comparative anatomy, at the time a leading scientific method that paid scrupulous attention to

MARTIN BRESSANI

(fig. 5)

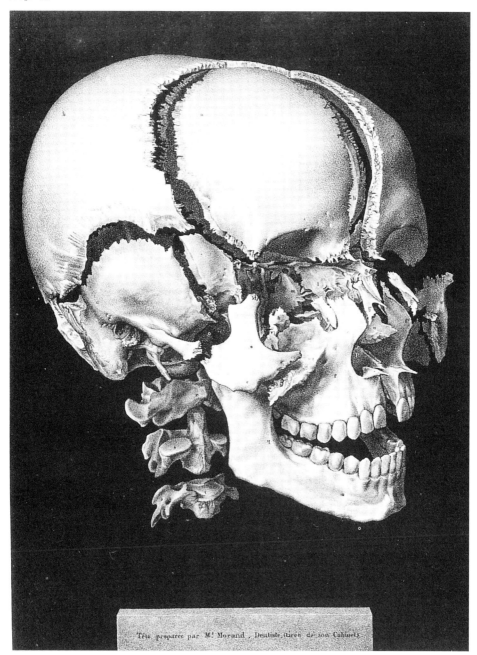

Tête préparée par M. Morand, Dentiste, tirée de son Cabinet

Exploded perspective of a human skull, drawn by N. H. Jacob, from Marc Jean
Bourgery, *Traité complet de l'anatomie de l'homme*, 8 vols. (Paris: Delaunay,
1832-1854), 1: pl. 30

each organ's role within the overall economy of living beings. But in his review of 1834, Delécluze insists not so much upon the drawing's illustration of scientific principles as upon its capacity to merge scientific merit with artistic purpose. Jacob's lithographs not only provide accurate scientific information regarding the human body, claims Delécluze, but they also propose an "artistic" view of it. By "artistic," the critic does not refer to some beautification of the body's inner parts, nor is he primarily thinking of the quality of Jacob's draftsmanship; he points, rather, to the lithographs' ability to make us "feel" the body's texture and volume. Scientists, claims Delécluze, are happy to keep to an abstract idea of the body, "forgetting, for instance, the sense of depth and the manifold directions that take the parts of a whole."[10] For their part, artists, left to themselves, are at risk of providing a representation devoid of the logic of the body's workings.

Working very closely, Bourgery and Jacob were able, according to Delécluze, to synthesize both artistic and scientific aspects together, combining a sense of abstraction with a truly realistic image. Instead of representing, as is usual, each layer of the body one by one, Bourgery devised special anatomical pieces in which the body has been cut transversally, "allowing Jacob to provide drawn sections which, though representing something real, nonetheless bring to mind an abstract conviction as would an orthogonal drawing."[11] By having cut into the depth of the body, by drawing out of it a newly discovered spatiality—similar to the spatialization Viollet-le-Duc would find within the cathedral's body—Jacob created images of a powerful palpability (fig. 6). In a subsequent article, published in the *Journal de Paris* in 1840, Delécluze summarizes succinctly his interpretation of Jacob's lithographs: "One who studies [the *Traité complet de l'anatomie*] is confronted and seized by two of his auxiliary organs, mind and sight, whose functions when operating simultaneously, render, as it were, truths palpable."[12]

Bourgery and Jacob's ideal of an exhaustive description is not only technically more advanced and daring than what came before but introduces a new way of deciphering corporeal space. Mind and sight must work conjointly. Their work reflects what the philospher Michel Foucault described in 1963 as the "clinical gaze," one endowed with a plurisensorial structure.[13] The "palpable truth" is the body revived in the mind of the clinician. The drawing of the exploded skull is therefore exemplary because it makes visible, with amazing vividness, the process of decomposition and restoration

(fig. 6)

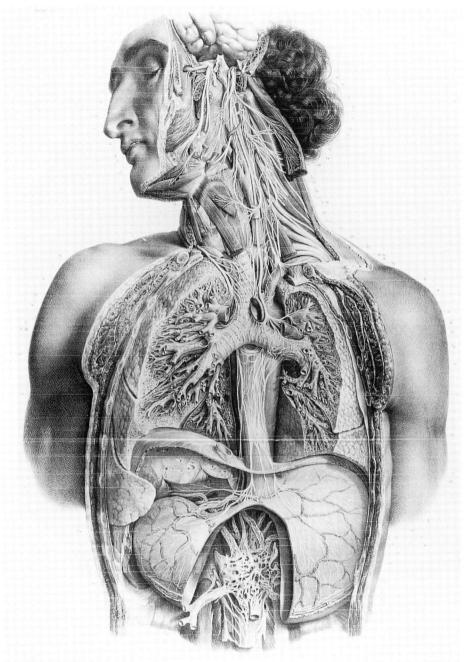

Nervous system of the human head and torso, drawn by N. H. Jacob, from Bourgery,
Traité complet 5: pl. 16

upon which the whole of the treatise is predicated. It is a portrait of the act of drawing itself.

Similar remarks could be made in regard to Viollet-le-Duc's exploded perspective of the Gothic vault. Viollet-le-Duc slowly evolved toward a representation that makes palpable each stone's specificity and position within a total ensemble. What especially distinguishes the last version, however, is its capacity to make us relive an action—stones falling into place. Like Jacob's lithographs as described by Delécluze, the drawing seamlessly merges the abstract with the corporeal; the viewer feels and is made to understand, participating sensorially and mentally in a temporal process.

Leaving aside Viollet-le-Duc's architectural training proper, it is revealing and quite fascinating to study the visual tradition in which the architect operated. The influence of Bourgery's anatomy is only a relatively late if crucial manifestation of a more general mode of apprehending the palpability of the world to which Viollet-le-Duc was introduced early in life. Several routes present themselves to the historian wishing to trace a genealogy of that influence, from Viollet-le-Duc's youthful interest in geology to the particular romanticism that pervaded the family house. These avenues of research, however, seem tangential when compared with his early training as a painter under the direction of Delécluze. It is difficult to overestimate the importance of the uncle for the young Viollet-le-Duc, a child whom Delécluze maintains was "born in my arms and never left me in childhood nor during his studies."[14] Recognizing very early young Eugène's talent, Delécluze conducted a kind of didactic experiment with his nephew. A key representative of a specific artistic current emerging from David's studio, Delécluze introduced Viollet-le-Duc to a visual tradition that, according to a recent study by a historian of science, had itself been a determinant influence in Bourgery and Jacob's anatomical work.[15] It is thus by moving farther away from architecture into the risky terrain of painting theory that this article attempts to develop an interpretation of Viollet-le-Duc's scientism as a form of optical trope.

Delécluze's ideas on art, antiromantic and tied to the classical school, were by no means characterized by a narrow academism. Profoundly influenced by his apprenticeship with David, he sought to regenerate art through a return to the great artistic principles of Greek antiquity, a return effected as a result of a systematic and rational investigation of the natural world and, above all, the human body. "Beauty is the goal, imitation is the means" is Delécluze's own succinct summary of the doctrine.[16]

There is in Delécluze a central idea taken up by Viollet-le-Duc, albeit in a classical guise: art's quasi-scientific link to reality. The term "quasi-scientific" is apt because Delécluze's approach was visual, based entirely upon drawing. "The study and the practice of art," he writes, "lead to the scrupulous observation of nature, to the search for its underlying laws, to the hidden cause of all phenomena, to the search for truth, in short, to science and philosophy."[17]

It is the *Précis d'un traité de peinture*, a small book published by Delécluze when Viollet-le-Duc was fourteen years old, that gives the first clues of the critic's rational art pedagogy. It rigorously sets the rule "of copying exactly *d'après nature*, all objects that one would wish to imitate."[18] Inspired by the teaching of David, who "admonished his students to look at nature with the innocence of a child,"[19] Delécluze advocates a methodical exploration of the truth of nature as a "compass" to orient the artist in his search for beauty. The art of perspective is the key agent of disclosure. It is an "elementary science" with which "the artist combines everything he sees and feels so as to make perception swifter, stronger and easier to other men."[20] There is a sort of magic to art, born of "love which vivifies everything"; it is only through such mysterious agency "that life emerges from chaos and death" and "the pupil feels he has finally become an artist."[21]

Asserting that the true artist's aim "is to penetrate nature's secret,"[22] Delécluze's short book on painting carries an investigative character. Investigation was a prominent idea of the school of David, embodied particularly in its interest in anatomy. The new corporeal aesthetic that developed in David's studio showed man's grandeur and perfectibility, his moral character linked to the organic life of the body.[23] Delécluze is rather discreet on the "anatomical theory" in his famous account of the school of David. It was probably too much a part of the artist's secret science, best kept to the privacy of the atelier. His diary is actually more forthcoming in revealing how his years in David's studio were spent studying anatomy every morning from five to eight o'clock.

An examination of the theoretical work of the painter Jacques Nicolas Paillot de Montabert (1771–1849) lends insight into the scientific method of drawing practiced in David's studio. Author of the monumental ten-volume *Traité complet de la peinture* (1828), Montabert actually ties together the two strands followed until now: serving as a guide for Jacob in his scientific illustrations for Bourgery's anatomy treatise,[24] Montabert—a student of David's—is also, according to Delécluze, the theoretician who codified into something reasonable and coherent the secret doctrine of David's studio.[25] He himself claims to have lifted the veil of lost ancient artistic knowledge, distinguishing among the Greeks "the public doctrine of painting from the secret one."[26] "Among moderns," Montabert claims, "the famous David is the only one to have recovered...the esoteric doctrine of drawing."[27] Delécluze pours the greatest praise in the *Journal des débats* for the work of Montabert, whom he calls a "philosophe-peintre."[28] Viollet-le-Duc himself will acquire the ten-volume work, small octavos that have some kinship to his *Dictionnaire raisonné.*

Montabert sought to avoid what he considered to be two pitfalls of contemporary artistic theory: misty metaphysics and the cult of genius. Art, claims Montabert, "must finally rely upon solid knowledge."[29] It must proceed from reason rather than sentiment.[30] In the opening pages of volume one, he makes a lengthy argument for the need to set rules to guide the artist. Montabert's rules are not the established recipes favored by the Académie des Beaux-Arts, an institution that he disparages throughout the *Traité complet*. He speaks instead of the necessity for students to unlearn,[31] wishing "to go back to the fundamental principles of art to construct a new theory."[32] Like Viollet-le-Duc, Montabert has the ambition to refound the discipline of art upon a scientific basis.

At the heart of Montabert's art theory is a method for learning how to see. Montabert points, of course, to Greek sculpture for guidance, antiquity being "the great preserver" or "the great regulator that teaches to see, to judge and to choose."[33] But beyond such devotion to antiquity, Montabert's realist stand forces him to define a new science of seeing structurally embedded within the painter's activity. Just as Viollet-le-Duc will identify construction as the core aspect of his new science of architecture, drawing—"the life of painting," following Montabert's expression[34]—makes up the core discipline of the *Traité complet*: it alone makes art a science.

The science of drawing is dealt with by Montabert along two distinct axes: anatomy, subject of volume five; and perspective and geometry, subjects of volume six. Surprisingly, art historians have paid absolutely no attention to these sections of the *Traité complet*. Yet a startlingly new kind of visuality emerges from these volumes. As hinted at only by Delécluze in his

Précis d'un traité de peinture, Montabert seeks to escape from the confines of normal subjectivity and reach a kind of heightened consciousness through the discipline of drawing. Art, he claims, must allow one to "sense more," to see objects "more forcefully."[35] It must develop a "power of optical existence."[36]

Anatomy is the foundation of Montabert's science of drawing, providing the necessary constructive knowledge of the human body. Most relevant to the present discussion, however, is not anatomy proper but the way Montabert conceives of drawing in anatomical terms: "To err in drawing is to err in anatomy…incorrectness in anatomy corresponding to graphic incorrectness."[37] Drawing is a reconstruction of the body.

Inspired by Renaissance art theory, Montabert aspires to a reenchantment of the art of perspective. He conceives of it as "the great fundamental science of art,"[38] the "universal reason of drawing,"[39] a *graphidos* that can overcome the necessary deception of the eye. The goal of "the vivifying perspective"[41] is not to "copy the world as we see it," since most often one sees wrongly, but "to give a just representation of the idea of what is."[42] The visual must give way to the intellect—Montabert even speaks of a battle between the sense of sight and the intelligence.[43] The spacing between our eyes, claims Montabert, allows a very special scanning of reality nonreproducible in two-dimensional representation. The artist must therefore "fortify his imitation through a vivifying, lively and expressive feeling for planes."[44] To know natural objects as a painter should, claims Montabert, is "to have [their] construction at one's disposal either as a collective or as pieces; it is to create and constitute that object, to modify it, to set it down, to site it anywhere at will, in short to possess it, to master it completely."[45]

A constructive action, Montabert's perspective science must proceed from geometrical and planar understanding. According to Montabert, only orthogonal or geometrical representations are truly "natural";[46] even the idea of man preserved in our mind is essentially orthogonal.[47] If the artist is to take full possession of the reality drawn, "he must therefore get to know the *naturel géométrique*."[48] Only then will the *unité d'apparence* and the *unité de construction* be complete, the drawing realizing the "strength of optical existence."[49]

Using this geometric knowledge of objects as a basis, Montabert makes axonometric drawings—what he calls stereographic drawings—a preparatory stage "absolutely necessary to the painter."[50] Because this type of representation originated "from the antique science of drawing,"[51] the artist can show "the dimension of surfaces, their character, their various assemblages, what, in short, constitutes the construction of solids."[52] It "provides a complete knowledge and analysis of objects" as they truly are rather than as they appear. Stereographic projections, writes Montabert, allow objects to be seen "inside, outside, above and below as if our eye were traveling around its sides, and as if the object were truly three-dimensional, with this difference . . . that . . . all sides are or have been turned toward our eye, which [has] remained motionless."[53] "It is the object itself," Montabert maintains, "that we possess."[54]

Despite such an enthusiasm for that type of projection, Montabert never forgets what constitutes the painter's proper goal: perspective drawing. Never envisaged as an end in itself, the axonometric is only a means for the painter to mentally "possess" his subject. The analysis it provides is a crucial but preliminary stage toward a new optically constructed space.

Significantly, at this stage the "science" of drawing gives way to a "*sentiment graphique des formes*," with which the artist "animates, as it were, his graphic language and vivifies his signs and expressions."[55] Montabert's description touches upon the erotic: "What has roused [the true] artist, what has sustained and excited him, what has fired him up, making his work penetrating and touching, is the graphic feeling for planes [*sentiment graphique des plans*], it is the tenacious will to render, to communicate, to forcefully express movements, bends, projections, half-projections, receding parts, etc. It is the violent and ambitious desire to make the image move [*faire remuer l'image*], by fortifying, as it were, nature's characters."[56]

Drawing is therefore a staged process that, beginning with a tension between the realms of the visual and the intellectual, must eventually resolve itself into a higher unity. "One first needs to feel," writes Montabert, "then to know, in order to subsequently feel better."[57] To draw is to dialectically overcome habitual perception. It is a winning over reality.

One searches in vain through the pages of Montabert's treatise for any examples of drawings endowed with the "sentiment graphique des formes." The engravings in the *Traité complet*'s volume of plates are diagrams that serve to illustrate various drawing procedures with no pretense of setting examples. Undoubtedly, Montabert assumed in his reader the direct study of the paintings of David and his school. It is probably toward the art of Manet and perhaps Cézanne that, within the history of painting, we could track the most daring and challenging interpretation of Montabert's internalization of the discipline of drawing leading to a heightened presence, a pictorial architecture endowed with a sense of the plane, of geometry, and of movement. In the present context, however, it is, of course, to the images contained in Viollet-le-Duc's *Dictionnaire raisonné* that we must turn, their quasi-magical optical presence providing a surprising manifestation of Montabert's theory translated within the field of archaeological illustrations.

True, Viollet-le-Duc never paid special attention to the drawing of the human body. Since early childhood, his focus had been almost exclusively on natural landscapes and architecture. But one can easily make the claim that a corporeal approach underlies his view of the world and of buildings. His love affair with mountains, for instance, reflects the Earth apprehended as a body. In his thousands of mountainscapes, starting from the earliest in 1831, we sense a will to apprehend the volumetric wholeness of the world, its archetypal cohesiveness, its cosmogonic formation through cataclysmic revolutions of a dynamic vitality. His masterful restoration of Mont Blanc is structural anatomy, the uncovering of the underlying archetype (fig. 7). Revealing what is beneath the skin, he represents a corporeal structure. The Earth drawn by Viollet-le-Duc is made of bulges and protrusions under great tension and strain. As with Montabert, all such vital forces can be understood through the "naturel géométrique."

It is within Viollet-le-Duc's archaeological drawings that the lessons of Montabert appear most fruitful. As Sauvageot[58]—an engraver and close collaborator with Viollet-le-Duc—has astutely observed, his sense of the

(fig. 7)

(fig. 8)

Detail of medieval shoulder armour, from "Spallièrre," *Dictionnaire raisonné du mobilier* 6: 291, fig. 14 © Estate of Robert Smithson/ VAGA, NY, NY

Primitive sight of the protogine massif, from Eugéne-Emmanuel Viollet-le-Duc, *Le Massif du Mont Blanc* (1876), 7, fig. 4

1. — Aspect primitif du massif.

plane,[59] his "more studied, more caressed"[60] *modelé*, and his uncanny sense of movement (fig. 8)—all qualities that he would consciously lay out as goals in his drawing pedagogy—are absolutely remarkable.

To illustrate the point, it is useful to compare Viollet-le-Duc's drawings with illustrations of a similar genre, in archaeological glossaries or dictionaries roughly contemporary with the *Dictionnaire raisonné*. The fourth edition of John Henry Parker's *A Glossary of Terms Used in Grecian, Roman, Italian and Gothic Architecture* (1845), a popular work that Viollet-le-Duc admired,[61] provides an obvious precedent to Viollet-le-Duc's own. It contains small woodcuts of great precision, mostly perspectives of portions of monuments interspersed within the text. Parker's figures provided a norm in nineteenth-century practical archaeological manuals and were copied both in England and France.

Parker's treatment of the base of the pillar, for instance, is textured and of a fine volume but is apprehended as a distant object statically depicted, one element in the construction of a conventional taxonomy of the style (fig. 9). We gain a quite different sense of presence from a woodcut under the article "Base" in volume two of the *Dictionnaire raisonné* (fig. 10). Here, Viollet-le-Duc allows a kind of optical possession of the base of the pillar. We are almost able to reach out to touch the object, the base tilting toward us, the circularity of the columns, the texture and weight of the stones delicately delineated by a very fine hatching, a graphic treatment Viollet-le-Duc always supervised closely, indicating to his engravers, in each case, the precise sense and density of the strokes he desired.[62]

The gain in palpability does not mean an increase in transparency. In this regard, Parker's conventional drawing, as a result of its schematic

(fig. 9)

Base of column from a medieval church (Saint-Peters, Northampton), from John Henry Parker, *A Glossary of Terms Used in Grecian, Roman, Italian and Gothic Architecture*, 2 vols. (Oxford: David Bogue, 1845), 2: pl. 23 (detail)

character, is definitely more successful: what we see is what we get. Not so with Viollet-le-Duc's drawing. It presents us with a strange, singular medieval fragment, the complexity of which takes time to comprehend. The slight effect of opacity is further reinforced by the addition of two small cut sections that almost align with the edge of the columnar drum whose base molding they constitute. Moving back and forth between the perspective view and the sections, our reading of that part of the church is enriched. But the movement also occasions a delay in dealing with the totality of the drawing. It exhorts the viewer's mental powers.

The comparison with Parker's *Glossary* demonstrates the accuracy of the words chosen by Prosper Mérimée to describe the novelty of the figures of the *Dictionnaire raisonné*. "Its plates," writes Mérimée, "render the description, as it were, palpable. . . . It is reality substituted for a convention." Viollet-le-Duc's myriad woodcuts of fragments, heterogeneously mixed with other modes of representation, offer an agile vision that seeks corporeal contact. Feeling the object, penetrating its various folds, we then turn to the text to relieve our increasing sense of the oddity of the form: "The image," writes Viollet-le-Duc, "must draw our curiosity in demanding an explanation."[63] The figures—fragments in the process of being restored—provide an incentive to know. Such is the "science effect" of Viollet-le-Duc's method: a gap between tactility and intelligibility, between mind and sight, allowed Viollet-le-Duc's nineteenth-century French readership to retake possession of the Middle Ages by directly grasping it quasi-physically, by forming it in their minds and thus marking it as theirs.

(fig. 10)

Base of nave columns at the cathedral in Laon, from "Base," *Dictionnaire raisonné de l'architecture* 2: 154, fig. 37

NOTES

1. See *Catalogue des livres composant la bibliotéque de feu M.E. Viollet-le-Duc* (Paris: Adolphe Lafaitte, 1880).

2. Eugène-Emmanuel Viollet-le-Duc, "Premier entretien" (1858), *Entretiens sur l'architecture* (Paris: Morel, 1863), 1: 22. This anecdotal passage was first printed in the pages of the *Magazin pittoresque* 27 (1859): 103–4.

3. Rainer Maria Rilke, "The Rose Window," *The Rose Window and Other Verse from New Poems* (Boston: Little, Brown, 1997). Thanks to Robert Jan van Pelt.

4. Quoted by Pierre-Marie Auzas, *Eugène Viollet-le-Duc, 1814–1879* (Paris: Caisse nationale des monuments historiques et des sites, 1979), 43.

5. Ibid.

6. Étienne Delécluze, *Lettres d'Italie*, 26 August 1836: 126.

7. Claude Sauvageot was the first to document these modifications in his very useful study of Viollet-le-Duc's drawings. See his "Viollet-le-Duc et son oeuvre dessiné," *Encyclopédie d'architecture* 9 (1880): 62–171. His observations were developed further in Françoise Boudon, "Le Réel et l'imaginaire chez Viollet-le-Duc: Les figures du *Dictionnaire raisonné de l'architecture*," *Revue de l'art* 1983: 95–114, and Laurent Baridon, *L'Imaginaire scientifique de Viollet-le-Duc* (Paris: L'Harmattan, 1996), 125–36.

8. See Tisseron and Antoine-Chrysostome Quatremère de Quincy, "Notice sur le docteur Bourgery," *Archives des hommes du jour* (Paris: Maulde et Renou, 1846), 1.

9. Étienne Delécluze, "Variétés. Traité complet de l'anatomie de l'homme...," *Journal des débats politiques et littéraires*, 15 November 1834. Translation by author.

10. Ibid.

11. Ibid.

12. Étienne Delécluze, "Des travaux anatomiques de M. le docteur Bourgery," *Revue de Paris* 17 (1840): 210.

13. Michel Foucault, *The Birth of the Clinic* (New York: Vintage Books, 1975), 124–46.

14. Étienne Delécluze to Mme L. Berthaux, Clermont-Ferrand, 29 July 1831, quoted by Robert Baschet, *E.-J. Delécluze, témoin de son temps, 1781–1863* (Paris: Boivin et compagnie, 1942), 210 n. 2.

15. Reinhard Hildebrandt, "Anatomie und Revolution des Menschenbildes," *Sudhoffs Archiv* 76 (1992): 1–27.

16. Étienne Delécluze, "Traité complet de les peintures ar Paillot na Montabert." *Le journal des débats*, 13 January 1830.

17. Étienne Delécluze, *Léonard de Vinci, 1452–1519* (Paris: Schneider et Langitand, 1841), 78, quoted by Baschet, *E.-J. Delécluze*, 254.

18. Étienne Delécluze, *Précis d'un traité de peinture* (Paris: Encyclopédie portative, 1828), 176–204, quoted by Baschet, *E.-J. Delécluze*, 249–50.

19. Étienne Delécluze, *Louis David: Son école et son temps* (Paris: Didier, 1855), 57, quoted by Baschet, *E.-J. Delécluze*, 24. This passage is also cited in Baridon, *L'Imaginaire scientifique*, 132.

20. Delécluze, *Précis*, 5.

21. Ibid., 149.

22. Ibid., 5.

23. I paraphrase Dorothy Johnson, *Jacques-Louis David: Art in Metamorphosis* (Princeton: Princeton University Press, 1993), 169.

24. Bourgery refers directly to Montabert's work in *Traité complet de l'anatomie de l'homme* (Paris:

MARTIN BRESSANI

Delaunay, 1839–1854). See also Hilderbrandt, "Anatomie und Revolution," 4–6.

25. Delécluze, *Louis David*, 97.

26. Jacques Nicolas Paillot de Montabert, *Traité complet de la peinture* (Paris: Bossange pére, 1828), 4: 35. Translation by author.

27. Ibid., 36.

28. Delécluze, "Beaux-Arts. Traité complet de la peinture," *Journal des débats*, 13 January 1830.

29. Montabert, *Traité complet*, 5: 20.

30. Ibid., 6: 160.

31. Ibid., 1: 75.

32. Ibid., 3: 83–84.

33. Ibid., 62.

34. Ibid., 5: 16.

35. Ibid., 25.

36. Montabert's term is *force d'existence optique*. Ibid., 6: 149.

37. Ibid., 5: 43.

38. Ibid., 6: 197.

39. Ibid., 126.

40. Ibid., 184.

41. Ibid., 149.

42. Ibid., 153.

43. Ibid., 159.

44. Ibid., 450.

45. Ibid., 134.

46. Ibid., 135.

47. Ibid., 137.

48. Ibid., 143.

49. Ibid., 149.

50. Ibid., 182.

51. Ibid., 197.

52. Ibid., 227.

53. Ibid., 242.

54. Ibid., 227.

55. Ibid., 446.

56. Ibid., 457.

57. Ibid., 445.

58. Sauvageot, "Viollet-le-Duc et son oeuvre dessiné," 86.

59. Ibid., 85.

60. Ibid., 133.

61. When traveling in England in 1850, Viollet-le-Duc met the archaeologist Parker at Oxford, perhaps not for the first time. Viollet-le-Duc had Parker's glossary in his library, but a late edition dating from 1866.

62. Sauvageot, "Viollet-le-Duc et son oeuvre dessiné," 136.

63. Viollet-le-Duc, in a letter to his editor, Hetzel, 20 July 1874; see *Lettres inédites de Viollet-le-Duc recueilliés et annotées par son fils*, ed. Eugène L. Viollet-le-Duc (Paris: Imprimeries réunies, 1902), 147.

NORM AND TYPE.
VARIATIONS ON A THEME

Georges Teyssot

It is characteristic of architecture to press towards standard types.
Typology, in its turn, spurns the abnormal and seeks the normal.

—Hermann Muthesius. "Die Werkbundarbeit der Zukunft"

During the 1960s in Europe and the United States, the formula
of "typology"—as opposed to neoclassical "type"—was applied to the plan
of buildings, while the term *morphology* was used in relation to the forms of
the city.[1] Both terms were borrowed from the biological sciences. This use
of the term *typology*, when applied to biology, was problematic, since it came
from a totally different background, unrelated to the architectural use of the
concept of type during the eighteenth and nineteenth centuries. Architects,
in fact, appeared to be unaware of this disciplinary difference, and the
result has been a terminological confusion between type and typology.
Perhaps for this reason, it is necessary to reexamine the real, and somewhat embarrassing, origin of the concept of typology in architecture during the nineteenth century. While the revival of the notion of type through
Antoine Chrysostome Quatremère de Quincy corresponded to a return of
architectural theory to Platonic ideals, the introduction of the term *typology*

put into circulation, unbeknownst to architects, ideas whose origin were actually to be found in nineteenth-century ethnography and criminology.

In the second half of the nineteenth century, beginning with Gottfried Semper, architects started to look for a "scientific" foundation for the origin of architecture. The classical notion of archetype (developed, for instance, by Quatremère de Quincy) referred to original ur-forms, such as the temple or the basilica, formed in Greek and Latin history. Semper extended those ur-forms to the different activities of "primitive" man, such as weaving, potting, and carpentry. Semper was one of the most prominent architectural scholars to investigate the regional production of domestic architecture in Europe. He connected medieval buildings of northern and southern Germanic countries to a number of primitive, and vanished, archetypes. In his work *Der Stil* (1860–63), he developed an interest in the *Fachwerk*—edifices that combine *Gezimmer* (structural carpentry) and *Gemäuer* (masonry, either stone or brick), which he illustrated with the example of a mill at Effretikon, near Zurich.[2] This inquiry into primitivistic architecture was pursued further in Viollet-le-Duc's *Histoire de l'habitation humaine* (1875), in which the author maintained that the first houses were those of the "Aryas" (by which he meant the Aryans), who built walls and roofs using logs and then stone (figs. 1, 2).[3] From the second half of the eighteenth century, travelers like the Frenchman Abraham-Hyacinthe Anquetil-Duperron (1731–1805) and the English poet and jurist William Jones were able to trace affinities between the language of Parsee and Sanskrit—the focus of their studies—and Greek and Latin. This would slowly lead to the creation of a new genealogy of the European nations, allowing, for instance, a historian like Henri Martin (1810–1883) to think of "the great Indo-European family...of which Arya, that holy land of the earliest ages, appeared to have been the cradle."[4] It was in France, through the work of the

(fig. 1)

The primitive house of the Arya, from Eugène-Emmanuel Viollet-le-Duc, *The Habitations of Man in All Ages* (1876)

paleontologist Baron Georges Cuvier (1769–1832) and later the historian Jules Michelet (1798–1874), that the difference between the Semitic world and the Indo-Germanic world was cast in terms of struggle. In Germany, one of the most influential promoters of the "Indo-German," or Aryan, myth was Jacob Grimm (1785–1863), who in his classic *History of the German Language* (1848) introduced a chapter entitled "Immigration" that gave an account of the successive invaders of Europe from the East.[5] This opposition, presented as a scientific thesis, was confirmed by the writings of other "Indomaniacs" like the writer Ernest Renan, the official ideologist of the Third Reich. It was this dangerous mixture of history, linguistics, and archaeology that would build, via Herbert Spencer's reading of Charles Darwin, the long-lasting myth of the Aryan.[6]

NEW ARCHETYPES

In his *Histoire d'un dessinateur* (1879), Viollet-le-Duc dedicated two chapters to what he called "lectures on comparative anatomy" similar to those of Cuvier.[7] In his *Dictionary of Architecture*, his organicist conception of architecture very much resembled Cuvier's anatomic notion of the correlation of the organs and the subordination of characters.[8] An organ existed only in relation to the whole, and each form could be explained only through its place, or placement, in the system. For Viollet-le-Duc, as for Goethe, there was an initial formal principle in the art, comparable to the one that the crystallographer René-Just Haüy had discovered in relation to minerals and to the cells of plants. It is not known if Viollet-le-Duc knew the work of Etienne Geoffroy Saint-Hilaire or his colleague Henri Dutrochet, who thought that vegetables and animals had the same cellular structure at their origin, within their different tissues.[9] They believed cells are agglomerated through pressure, which

(fig. 2)

The Aryan wagon, from Eugène-Emmanuel Viollet-Le-Duc, *Histoire de l'habitation humaine depuis les temps préhistoriques jusqu'à nos jours* (1875)

confers on them a polygonal form, a form similar to that which Viollet-le-Duc thought made up Gothic architecture. In the *Story of a Draftsman*, he published an image of compressed pipes of rubber that have acquired a hexagonal form in section (fig. 3).[10] This is exactly the cellular law of compression discovered by Dutrochet. While architecture would have to be organic, it still remained to be discovered how architecture's dwellings were to be constructed. In fact, Viollet-le-Duc's argument is based on both organic thoughts and ethnographic notations.

Viollet-le-Duc believed that the primitive type of architecture in the West was the *chalet*, the Alpine rural dwelling that Jean-Jacques Rousseau had described for the first time in his *Nouvelle Héloïse*.[11] An obvious source for the suburban and resort villa, the Swiss chalet in France or Germany was the equivalent of the cottage in England. In his article "House," published in his *Dictionary of Architecture*, Viollet-le-Duc stated that the dwelling in the West was the expression of the feeling that one's family was something distinguished; the Western house was a symbol of modern individualism, hence the definition of his term *individual edifice*.[12] He added, "Everyone desires their own house." Having established a specific equation between individuals and house, he drew a peculiar genealogy of the chalet; he considered it to be the structure nearest, at least in Europe, to the primitive abode.[13]

It is possible to postulate the influence on Viollet-le-Duc of the self-proclaimed "Count" Joseph-Arthur Gobineau's *Essay on the Inequality of Human Races* (1853–55), which offered a genealogy of Aryan migration and the theory of the superiority of the German Nordic races.[14] Viollet-le-Duc suggested that it was the chariots of these nomads (traveling abodes that would stop at a certain point and would immobilize themselves in a particular region or

(fig. 3)

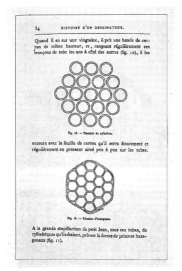

Section of compressed rubber pipes acquiring hexagonal forms, from Eugène-Emmanuel Viollet-le-Duc, *Histoire d'un dessinateur. Comment on apprend à dessiner* (1879)

site) that provided the archetype for the Swiss chalet, the Muscovite cabin, and the Norwegian peasant's hut.[15] He even extended this genealogy to include the rural houses of Normandy and the Vosges, which were still being built in wood during his lifetime. In addition to writing about these structures, he also built for himself his own version of this nomadic hut, a chalet in Lausanne he called "La Vedette" (1874–76).[16] The architectural myth of the chalet was also a political myth, probably one of the strongest during the nineteenth century, because it was able to collapse the multifarious sources of biology, ethnography, and history into a single image.[17]

On the occasion of the Paris Universal Exposition of 1889, and not long after the completion of Gustave Eiffel's new tower, Charles Garnier, the architect of the Paris Opéra, was named commissioner of an exhibition on the history of habitation. In a park along the Seine, a series of pavilions resembling small single-family houses in various styles (Assyrio-Babylonian, Etruscan, Merovingian, Aztec, Slavic, etc.) illustrated the form of dwellings from various civilizations past and present. Here, archaeology served as a pretext for pure invention, and even Garnier himself confessed that he followed an imaginative approach in the design of each building: "It is almost like closing one's eyes and, thereby, seeing as if in a dream how these past types have been formed."[18] In a book that appeared following the exposition, written in collaboration with Adolphe Ammann, a professor of history and geography at the Lycée Louis-le-Grand in Paris and entitled *Human Habitation*, Garnier reproduced the phantasmagoric and dreamlike melange that he had invented in the exhibition.[19] This mixture was clearly created both from a fictitious anthropology and the concept of architectural type derived from the intuitive methods of the Beaux-Arts artist. Garnier was not a scientist, and his dwelling types were almost entirely invented.

Meanwhile, in other parts of Europe and in the United States the idea of type was presented as a scientific truth, derived from scholarly research associated with site excavation. The German legacy of cultural history (*Kulturgeschichte*) would extend some of the assumptions exposed by Semper and Viollet-le-Duc, as evidenced by Franz Carl Müller-Lyer's *History of Social Development* of 1912: "The house of wood was typical of the early Aryan culture. According to Karl Weinhold, the famous German medievalist of the late nineteenth century, 'the Germans only built of wood, hence the connection of the word *bauen* = to build, and *baum* = tree.'"[20] In Germany, an original genealogy was "scientifically" traced, connecting culture with civilization; that is, the Aryan culture with the (German) wooden house. Thus, an archetype, wrapped in the authority of the academy, was born.

Later, in Paris, the Committee for Scientific and Historical Works, within the Ministère de l'instruction publique, decided at the end of the 1880s to conduct an inquiry into the condition of dwellings in France. A questionnaire was sent to local administrators in every French département asking for, in the words of Alfred de Foville (the editor of the ensuing book), a description of "typical houses" (maisons-types) in order to determine the habitual way of living in different parts of the country: "In nearly all the regions, there are, for the use of farmers (whether they are owners or not), hundreds, thousands of houses, more or less similar, and it is this typical house, this characteristic unity, which it is necessary to study, in order to define its elements" (fig. 4).[21] For de Foville, "each region showed a characteristic type, repeated a thousand times."

The important question, however, was whether the milieu influenced only the house, or whether the inhabitants themselves influenced their dwelling.

II. CONCEPTUAL FRAMEWORKS

> Man makes his house and in doing so, he must put into it something of himself. However, through the passage of time, the house makes man too, through the particular fold [pli] that it impresses on his daily life. Our house, for us, and above all for the laborers of the city and the fields, is therefore more than a mirror: it is also a mold, and our existence partly owes to it the form and the direction that it takes.[22]

De Foville's hypothesis is thus one of the reciprocal influences of milieu and inhabitant. In the conclusion to his discussion of the contemporary housing situation, he remarks that "each household wanted its own 'home,' its separate lodgings," bearing witness to a unanimous desire for independence. Only the autonomy of a self-supporting household will guarantee its moral, its hygiene, and its social use fullness. "The more the house is individual, the easier it is to modernize."[23] De Foville begins with a factual inquiry and survey, builds a theory, and then concludes with a normative dictate, following precisely the method of the engineer and sociologist Frédéric Le Play

146   GEORGES TEYSSOT

(fig. 4)

V. — LE VIGNERONNAGE ANCIEN

Après ces généralités, qui ont démontré à quelles causes profondes et permanentes était due l'amélioration des logements agricoles

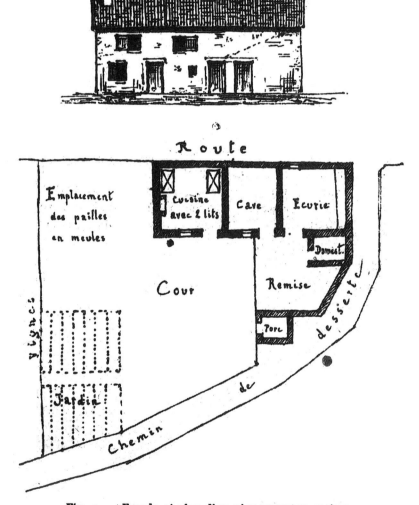

Fig. 1. — Façade et plan d'un vigneronnage ancien.

Facade and plan of a house in the Beaujolais region, from *Enquête sur les conditions de l'habitation en France. Les Maisons-types* (1894-99)

(1806–1882), who had written a history of family types and theory of "place-work-folk."[24] It need hardly be mentioned that the young Charles-Edouard Jeanneret (Le Corbusier) was an avid reader of de Foville's inquiry, which he studied before World War I at the Bibliothèque nationale in Paris.

IDEAL TYPE

At the very beginning of the nineteenth century, physiologist Xavier Bichat had expressed the hypothesis that all men were divided into three different classes, resulting in three different psychophysiological types. The three types were related to three different realms of human behavior: acting, thinking, and feeling. This fundamental division lead to a human typology that comprised the practical, the rational, and the emotive. Included in the first class of beings were administrators, workers, and engineers; in the second class were scientists; and in the third class were moralizers, artists, and poets.[25] This triadic division influenced the work of Henri Saint-Simon (1760–1825), who derived from Bichat's types his own classification: first, the "artiste" as creator; second, the "savant" as critic and scholar; and third, the "industriel" as executive. Later in his life, Saint-Simon would slightly modify his classification. New capacities replaced the old orders of the nobility and the clergy. The new aristocracy of talent was proclaimed, led by men of sensibility who showed Platonic capacity, including artists, poets, religious leaders, and ethical teachers. Those evidencing motor capacity formed the second, or industrial, class. Last came the scientists, who revealed Aristotelian capacity and belonged to the cerebral type.[26] To fight the malady of the modern age—an age of specialization dominated by the self-centered, egotistical, isolated individuals—one had to return to a principle of synthesis, transforming society into an organic whole. The means for this metamorphosis was a social physiology.[27]

Later in the century, both Le Play and Emile Durkheim shared the belief that the science of society, or "social science," should be a normative one. The difference is that Le Play, a conservative Catholic, wanted to defend private family life from the encroachments of public bureaucracies, while for Durkheim (1858–1917) and his followers, at home in the French academic system, families were expected to cooperate with the state in order to promote a kind of organic solidarity. The sociology of Vilfredo Pareto (1848–1923) in Italy, of Max Weber (1864–1920) in Germany, and Durkheim in France were all answers from the European universities to the challenge thrown out by Marxism.[28]

Le Play's followers were not Marxists either. One of them, Henri de Tourville (1842–1903), a founder of the periodical *La Science sociale*, accepted the principle of direct observation and the use of classificatory devices. Nevertheless, he criticized what he thought was the overly quantitative aspect of Le Play's monographic method, and he discarded Le Play's three types of family: the patriarchal, the stem, and the unstable.[29] He then created a broadened nomenclature, which became an instrument of social dissection: "a kind of sieve, which permits us to sift all elements of a social type, and to classify them, according to their qualities."[30] This new method, which put an emphasis on quality *versus* quantity, was used by another follower of Le Play, Edmond Demolins (1852–1907), who studied, for example, the migratory route of the nomads of the Asian steppes and the manner in which migration had determined the development of new types of families and societies (fig. 5). In his two-volume *Comment la route crée le type social* (1901–03), Demolins rejected Le Play's "three ages of work" (the age of pastures, of machines, and of coal) and proposed that the history of the people of the steppes was the key to understanding the origin of Western civilization.[31] The nomads, first settling in the western part of Scandinavia, evolved into "particularized families," which then migrated to England, America, Australia, and New Zealand. This was opposed to Mediterranean societies, which he claimed had retained the patriarchal family type for a longer period. "Particularized family," i.e., parents and their children, were autonomous, mobile, and capable of quick adaptation to the "modern" economy. Its opposed model was a patriarchal one: the large, extended family anchored in land and traditions. For Demolins, the

(fig. 5)

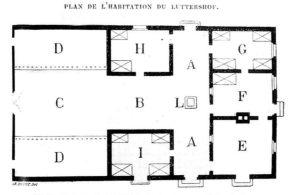

PLAN DE L'HABITATION DU LUTTERSHOF.

Franc and Saxon dwelling types, settlement of Luttershof, near Celle, from Edmond Demolins, *Comment la route crée le type social* (1901-03)

A, salle commune de travail *(flett)*; B, aixe; C, grange *(dehle)*; D, D, étables; E, salle commune de la famille *(dunzen)*; F, chambre des grands-parents *(kahmer)*; G, chambre des enfants et des servantes; H, chambre de l'héritier-associé *(anerber)*; I, chambre des célibataires et des domestiques; L, foyer.

connection between nomadism and individualism created the norm, or the "type," that modern society should follow. In this way, he provided the "scientific" basis for the sanitization and modernization of the family. Only a particularized family could be acted upon by reformers, doctors, hygienists, philanthropists, nurses, priests, and judges. Not by chance, Demolins would write a book that was immediately translated into English under the title *Anglo-Saxon Superiority: To What It Is Due* (1899).[32] The new, ideal "type" of family and household was to be North American: unconstrained by tradition, individualistic and nonconformist, self-governing and self-sufficient, and entrepreneurial. At the same time, Demolins defined the ideal type of family, Weber defined a theoretical notion of "ideal type" by trying to confer scientific objectivity to the selection, determination, and definition used in a social-scientific analysis of groups of people. Around 1900 he wrote:

> An ideal type is formed by the one-sided accentuation of one or more points of view, and by the synthesis of a great many diffuse, discrete, more or less present and occasionally absent concrete individual phenomena, which are arranged according to those one-sidedly emphasized viewpoints into a unified analytical construct.[33]

Just as "ideal-type" was defined by a slanted reading, the ideal family type was defined through a set of one-sided generalizations, in which the boundary between the typical and the normal was often lost.

Meanwhile, another kind of architectural "typology" originated in France. The Conseil municipal of Paris decided, in December of 1893, to create a "sanitary file" (*casier sanitaire*) of houses, similar to the criminal record of a person. The idea had already been announced by Sir John Simon (1816–1904), the medical officer of health in London, in 1849 and developed by John Snow (1813–1858), who drew maps of the city in 1855 showing the addresses of those who had died from cholera.[34] In Paris, the job was given to Paul Juillerat (1854–1935), chief of the Bureau of Sanitation, who organized the files by collating various kinds of data: administrative (house plans), technical (drainage plans), statistical (demographics), and scientific (quality of drinking water).[35] Juillerat united the traditional description of buildings with medical files, creating a laboratory dealing with unquestionable facts.[36] His method of collecting data in many

GEORGES TEYSSOT

ways resembled the one created for the study of criminal types compiled by Italian criminologist Cesare Lombroso in *Homo delinquens*, published in Milan in 1876. It was also analogous to the idea of creating a photographic archive for use by the police as irrefutable evidence in identifying suspects.[37] In all these examples, the issues at stake are related to the establishment of an archive, be it of diseased houses or of criminal men and women. Ideally, it was the making of such an archive through a rational, scientific procedure that permitted the elaboration of the typical and thus authorized the application of the normal.

The problem that photographic portraits of the same person could often appear totally different was explored by the creator of anthropometrics, Alphonse Bertillon (1853–1914), between 1883 and 1889. According to the chief of judicial identity of the Préfecture de police of Paris, the photographic portrait could be used for identification only if the principal traits of the person being photographed had been selected by the photographer in the process of archiving the image. Those singularities had to be described in words. One would "recite" the details of a face; hence the importance of what Bertillon called "speaking photographic portraits" or "speaking likeness" (*portraits parlés*), in which language did not define the ever changing particularities of real beings but only peculiar elements revealed by the photograph. The "speaking likeness" was a commentary not on a real face but on its photographic representation. To overcome the fact that photography could not reproduce the multiple phases of the aging of the face, Bertillon developed a "signaletic anthropometric," that is, the measurement on a living individual of the characteristic and invariant traits of the body, devoid of the envelope of the flesh and reduced to its structural nakedness. Man was now only a combination of lines and measurements that could be compiled in a catalog or displayed on a chart.[38]

Bertillon's archive attempted to associate images with words. Traditionally, the device that was used to couple images with words was called an allegory. However, allegory could easily lead to universal condensations of meaning (such as justice, strength, danger, etc.), which he considered too general or too abstract. What Bertillon attempted instead was a procedure connecting each individual to a general system, a system of representation capable of charting the diversity of the type.

MORPHOLOGICAL TYPES

Bertillon's method was derived in part from Franz Joseph Gall's physiology of the brain and craniology. Gall (1758–1828) affirmed that moral qualities and intellectual faculties of man are innate and that they depend on the cerebral morphology. By collecting craniums and casts that he compared and classified, the German physicist and biologist invented a kind of psychophysiology. He no longer attempted to define a common denominator for all humans, as had been undertaken during the eighteenth century. He wanted, instead, to connect the twenty-seven faculties that he had defined to a system belonging specifically to this or that individual.[39] Gall's organology was extended by his pupil Johann Gaspar Spurzheim (1776–1832), who emigrated to Great Britain from France and died of cholera in the United States in 1832. Spurzheim, the inventor of the term phrenology, became fashionable for detecting the character of individuals by reading the bumps on their cranium.[40] His ambition was to affirm the universal value of the physiological principle according to which form corresponds to function.[41] Following in Spurzheim's footsteps, in the 1830s Orson Squire Fowler (1809–1887) opened a "Phrenological Cabinet" in New York and gave character readings by mail.[42] By way of the theory that function created form Fowler invented his concept of a "home for all," convincing more than one thousand Americans to build a house on an octagonal plan, the figure nearest approaching the perfection of the circle.[43]

Another curious connection between architecture and science is the "Familistère," built by industrialist Jean-Baptiste André Godin (1817–1888) on the outskirts of Guise in northern France between 1858 and 1879 (fig. 6).[44] This philanthropist was a follower of Charles Fourier (1772–1837), who had dreamed and designed to erect a "phalanstery," a vast edifice housing the industrial "phalanx" that would have led to the foundation of a model community. Set in the pastoral countryside, its units would have contained 1,620

(fig. 6)

Summer sprinkling in the courtyard of the left wing, Familistère at Guise, France, built by André Godin, 1899

persons living fully in harmony by means of passional attraction. Godin, an industrialist who produced cast-iron coal stoves and furnaces, had joined the "École sociétaire" formed by Victor Considérant (1808–1893), a leader among Fourier's followers, a pupil of the École polytechnique and the author of many publications, including a volume "Social Considerations on Architectonics" (1834, 1848).[45] Godin rejected the notion of the phalanx, however, and attempted to adapt Fourier's plans by building a "family-stery," a kind of monastery for working families, organized around three rectangular courtyards, each with a glazed ceiling. Two-room apartments were organized around the courtyards, which provided ample light and ventilation. High standards of public health were insured by garbage chutes, drinking fountains, and sanitation blocks placed on each floor. Godin's plan also provided for amenities: a nursery and kindergartens following Friedrich Froebel's new methods; schools; a theater; a washhouse containing showers, a laundry room, and a swimming pool that used recycled hot water; a refectory; a bakery; various workshops; and a storage depot.[46] Like many during this period, Godin thought that human needs resided in a precise location in the body's organs. For instance, the sphenoidal part of the cranium housed the need for open space, light, and pure air (fig. 7). Because the Familistère responded to the requisites of human life, it improved its inhabitants. Godin maintained, "Intelligence is proportionate to the way in which light illuminates the house."[47] In a certain way, the Familistère was a phrenological construction.

The drive to compare craniums and brains was also pursued by the Turin-based scholar Cesare Lombroso (1835–1909), who actually analyzed the remains of Immanuel Kant, Alessandro Volta, Ugo Foscolo, and Carl Friedrich Gauss in his widely translated book *Man of Genius* (1891).[48] Using the principle of Gall's organology, Lombroso defined, by statistical methods, the frequency of the criminal type within the population of convicted perpetrators and honest people. The "delinquent type" was defined by "stigmata

(fig. 7)

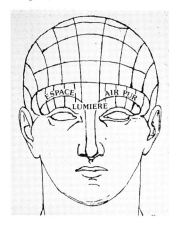

Localization of human needs in the cranium, from Jean-Baptiste André Godin, *Solutions sociales* (1871)

degenerationis," the stigma of the degenerate. Within his system of criminal anthropology, each stigma of the criminal contributed to the makeup of the criminal type. The criminal is such by nature, and, like a savage in a civilized country, he is an anachronism; by carefully isolating these types, society might free itself of them.[49]

The very notion of human type—the idea of a physiological mean in which the ideal would be deduced through the observation of the ordinary—was made possible by the Belgian sociologist Adolphe Quételet (1796–1874). In his *Treatise on Man* (1835), Quételet provided the statistical tools for the definition of a common type of human, proposing the concept of the "average man" as a "fictitious being."[50] Individual singularities were now to be observed only in light of the physiological mean or average. This was a reversal of the classical, neo-Platonic notion of type, which moved from singularity to the ideal. The new anthropology defined singularity only as a quantitative type, defined by statistics and means. This prosaic type, which erased the human being from any individuality, made concrete the exemplary figure of the "every man." Thus, Quételet showed that the extreme varieties of individuals conformed beyond their obvious appearances to a general and invariable law. Two consequences arose from this philosophy: the body was seen as an impersonal envelope, and every body was considered commensurate to a norm. This permitted the improvement of methods of identification, as it was then possible to measure identity by the degree of deviation from the statistical norm.[51]

Photography had been employed for judiciary purposes since 1860. As discussed previously, however, its use had been criticized, since two photographs of the same person could appear very different. This problem was solved by the aforementioned studies of Alphonse Bertillon, a great admirer of Quételet.[52] By selecting the principal traits of the face through words, Bertillon connected image with language. It was, literally, an "icono-logy." Under his system, only a divergence from the mean could produce notation, since the mean, or the norm, is unutterable and ineffable. Identity is defined by the measurement of invariant traits of the living body, for instance, the measurement of the cranium (fig. 8). The living being is reduced to segments, which are themselves brought down to the essence of geometrical lines. This combination of lines, weaving the organic with the geometric, does not imitate anymore but figures the invisible.

(fig. 8)

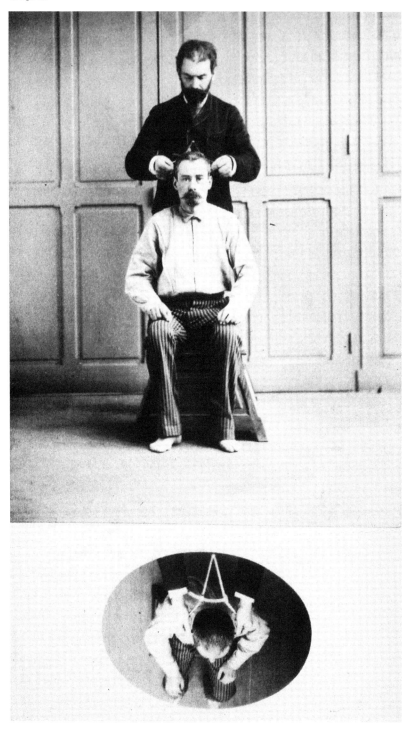

Alphonse Bertillon's measurement of the cranium, from *Alphonse Bertillon, Instructions for Taking Descriptions for the Identification of Criminals and Others by the Means of Anthropomorphic Indications* (1889)

This geometricization, which was also explored in the chronophotographs of Etienne-Jules Marey,[53] gave theorists and artists the opportunity to analyze the various morphological types of the human being. For instance, in France, Paul Richer (1849–1933), in his *Canons of Proportions of the Human Body* (1893) provided a renewed base to the study of human morphology, organized into types.[54] In Italy, the connoisseur Giovanni Morelli (1816–1891) devised a method of attribution of paintings based on "signature motifs" (*motivi sigla*), apparently insignificant details such as the representation of hair, nails, or ears that permit one to recognize the hand of an artist.[55] This geometricization would lead eventually to the rectangular division of the human body by Oskar Schlemmer (1888–1943), producing a "box man" (*Schachtelmensch*).[56]

It was Quételet's reduction of the body to a measurable type that permitted architects to think of the dwelling as a place that could be defined statistically, allowing the idea of normalization to be established. By reducing the analysis of the house to measurable data and to a diagrammatic scheme, Juillerat's sanitary cases created morphological domestic types that could then be used in a policy of intervention. In what was to become a new urban ecology, the French administration, between 1894 and 1904, was able to compile 80,000 files representing all the residential buildings within the walls of Paris.[57] These files were used to track the origin and path of disease, house by house. This sanitary file of houses was the moment of an encounter between medicine (the germ, the bacterium, the bacillus) and sociology (the insalubrious dwelling), creating a new definition of the type based not on a fictional narrative (the Aryans, for example) but on numbers. The aim of the files was to help eradicate "walls that kill." From now on, the authority of evidence established the "evidence" of authority, meaning that the authority had become conspicuous through the use of positive data and facts available as proof. This redefined authority was no longer moral but scientific; as in a criminal trial, it presented legal evidence, instituting a new semiotics of the house.

Following the creation of the sanitary files, a proposal was made to hang a plaque on each house indicating its sanitary condition. Interestingly, it was the owners, a group highly represented in parliament, that defeated this idea because they considered the hygienist state equivalent to the collectivist state.[58] As opposed to other northern European countries, which attacked the *disease* (of tuberculosis, for example), the government of France preferred to organize a hunt against the diseased—the infected persons. It demolished entire neighborhoods, disposing of their inhabitants in overcrowded hospitals or dispersing them to the farthest edges of the cities. This process of exclusion based on the notion of a diseased population could, of course, be easily extended to a "hygiene of race."[59]

ORGANIC HOUSEHOLD

To embed and wed the history of a nation with the history of a people (*Volk*) is an idea that can in part be credited to Wilhelm Heinrich Riehl (1823–1897) and his *The Natural History of the German People*, written largely between 1851 and 1855.[60] The literal title was "Natural History of the People as the Foundation of German Social Policy," showing that Riehl's sociology and anthropology of folklore (*Volkskunde*) had the precise conservative agenda of idealizing rural life while championing the virtues of neocorporatist social organization. In the first three volumes of his major opus, centered on "Civil Society," "Land and People," and "The Family," German society was presented as an organic totality, a natural work of art, the connection between the physical and the cultural topographies inscribed in the land forms. In the tradition of Johann Gottfried Herder (1744–1803) and Friedrich Schelling (1775–1803), Riehl exalted the Germanic folk ethos found in villages, guilds, and social estates as a bulwark against bureaucratic socialization and as an antidote to revolutionary egalitarianism. Stressing the traditional German opposition between culture and civilization, Riehl pontificated, "I raise my voice on behalf of the rights of forests over against fields, of mountains over against plains, of a natural popular culture over a homogeneous civilization."[61] His enemy was the fourth estate, what he called the "estate of the estateless," including factory workers, day laborers, bureaucrats, commercial travelers, commodity speculators, wholesale merchants, intellectuals, journalists, Jews, and gypsies. An academic authority in Germany, not a lonely lunatic, Riehl, a professor of social sciences at the University of Munich, presented the family as both model and metaphor for society at large. The very idea of family, he thought, had been disintegrated by modern life in Germany, by cosmopolitanism in France, by the nomadism of gypsies in the rest of Europe, and by the absence of roots in North America, where family life had almost completely disappeared "in the stampede to earn money."[62]

To resist the degeneration of the family—for Riehl, the origin of the decadence of modern societies—he would suggest the revival of a traditional setting, that of the "entire household" (*das ganze Haus*), which tended to disappear when the individual members of a family divided into separate groups. The site of the household, both architectural and within the landscape, contained the extended family, including not only relatives but servants and agricultural workers, and imposed "domestic discipline" on each of its members. "This expanded household," Riehl wrote, "extends the benefits of family life to entire groups who would otherwise be without family. . . . For the social stability of the nation as a whole, such a practice is a matter of the most profound significance."[63] Claiming that the renewal of society depended on a renewal of the home, he dismissed modern residential architecture, which he described as "miniature versions of box-like urban tenements, designed to be as cheap and profitable as possible." He lamented the disappearing large halls, the huge family hearths, and the ornamented galleries on each floor. Combining a medievalist resuscitation with an (*avant-la-lettre*) functionalist trend, Riehl claimed: "It is a fact of art history that the medieval house, castles, and churches were built from the inside out, that the exterior forms and proportions were freely arranged to suit the requirements of the interior, the practical uses of the building, whereas in our doctrinaire fashion we moderns routinely build from the outside in." He referred, as an example, to the models provided by the "authentic" German farmhouses and the so-called Swiss chalets, "which are constructed purely with a view to domestic utility, yet thanks to the instinctive aesthetic sensibilities of the common folk, are as lovely as folk song, as picturesque as peasant costume." Was Heinrich Tessenow (1876–1950), the German traditionalist architect, thinking of Riehl when he wrote in *House Buildings and Such Things* (1916), "Man must build a house from inside out"?[64]

Interestingly, in his praise for the Swiss chalet, Riehl foreshadowed the use of the same example by Semper and Viollet-le-Duc. All agreed

(fig. 9)

GEORGES TEYSSOT

(paradoxically, since Riehl despised the French attitude and manners) that the house of the future should be constructed "from the inside out." The family first had to be reconstituted, so that it could build a house in its own image. "Once we have reestablished a solid domestic tradition," wrote Riehl, "a new and organic residential architecture will also emerge, and architects will be at a loss to explain precisely how it came about—for the style will have come to them, not the other way around."[65] For him, the organic household had a name, grew like a plant, and was sung as a folkloric melody, while the modern house was changeable and temporary, mass-produced, and, even worse, rented. As such, it became a commodity, drawn into the maelstrom of larger urban capitalist society.

Riehl's work proved very influential in the further studies of the household and its settlement (Siedlung). Friedrich von Hellwald (1842–1892) wrote his Kulturgeschichte in 1876–77, a history of civilization from an evolutionary perspective that was considered authoritative in the Germanic countries.[66] This work was dedicated to German evolutionary biologist Ernst Haeckel (1834–1919), a specialist of marine fauna and author of the best-seller Artforms in Nature (1899).[67] Von Hellwald's Cultural History presented a curious, Wagnerian, Germanic warrior of the iron age, which he associated with Steinziet's funerary tumulus near Waldhusen.[68] Von Hellwald subsequently wrote a volume on the history of human settlements in 1888.[69]

Another example of Kulturgeschichte influenced by Riehl's work was The Prehistoric Man, edited by Wilhelm Baer (1874), which displayed an odd representation of the "the original German family" (Urgermanische Familie) (fig. 9).[70] In this volume, Ludwig Büchner wrote a chapter on "Races and History" expressing a belief in the congenital incapacity of "primitives" to raise their minds to the level of abstract ideas.[71] Riehl's presence may also be seen in the four-volume opus by August Meitzen, Settlement and the Essence of the Agrarian in West and East Germans, the Celts, the Romans, the Finns and the Slavs (1895), which was a cause of great concern for contemporary French scholars because it extended the Germano-Frank type of the house to half of France, denying the historical existence of the Gallo-Roman model.[72] In this way, scholars were already preparing for the next war.

HYGIENICS AND EUGENICS

Superficially, one could argue that proposals for housing reform in France at the end of the nineteenth century were less nostalgic, or reactionary, than those in Germany, but such an assertion would not be accurate. The major influence at the end of the century was the Arts and Crafts movement of William Morris (1834–1896), whose theories were disseminated in France by Dr. Henri Cazalis (1840–1909). Cazalis was a poet who belonged to the Parnassian group.[73] His talent was not limited to literature, however, but extended to philosophy, history, the fine arts, and music. He was also a physician involved in psychiatric therapy and eugenics, the medical improvement of the human race.

Writing under the name of Jean Lahor,[74] Cazalis published *W. Morris et le mouvement nouveau de l'art décoratif* in 1897, in which he described ugliness and beauty as something similar to "atmosphere," or the environment, possibly subject to contagion.[75] He referred to the book *Les Lois de l'imitation* by Gabriel de Tarde (1890), a sociological analysis of repetition, adaptation, and imitation by the lower classes of the traditions, habits, and fashions of the dominant classes, which provides a vivid history of the arts as well as of luxury, courtesy, and civility. Tarde argued that the eighteenth-century salon "would admit only equals, or equalized those it would admit," demonstrating that such instruments of civilization were also instruments of social leveling, producing democratic societies and a type of person governed by public opinion.[76] Picking up on Tarde's idea, Cazalis believed that bad taste could be communicated, like good taste, through the powerful social instrument of imitation. For art to remain elevated and pure, it was necessary that the mediocre or vile contagion "from below" be barred from spreading to the highest sphere.[77]

Both Jugendstil and art nouveau created parallels between aesthetics and hygienics. The curves of the "natural" body were brought into the building, while the building curved to receive the imprint of bodies. Cazalis praised for its restraint the French iron architecture of Paul Sédille (b. 1836) and Lucien Magne (1849–1916), the work of the architect Gustave Serrurier-Bovy (1858–1910) (founder of the school of Liège in Belgium and creator of the Pavillon bleu at the 1900 Parisian Exhibition), the art of Eliel Saarinen (1870–1950) from Finland (which he described as "very modern" but inspired by tradition), and the craftwork of Japan. In the English exhibit, he preferred the mirrored sideboards and the decor of the bathroom, and in the American display, the Tiffany lamps. The doctor was particularly anxious about hygiene: "For the first time since antiquity, this new art gives to hygiene the place which it rightly deserves in the design and organization of the building or the house."[78] He went on to mention an exhibition on the hygiene of hotels and inns, praising the simplicity and the cleanliness of the northern European countries and observing that aesthetics was obliged to occupy itself with these very humble virtues. Finally, quoting the experiments of the Lever Corporation at Port Sunlight, near Liverpool,[79] and the House of Cure built by the Krupp factory in Bensdorf, which were exhibited at the Parc de Vincennes in Paris, Cazalis uncovered his social and architectural program:

> We want art to be distributed to everybody, like air and light, and we want it to be everywhere, in the a house of the artisan, as in our own, from school to college, from those university barracks usually so ugly and always lugubrious, to hospitals, railway stations, and everywhere where human crowds, and especially popular ones, assemble.[80]

Nothing in this program appeared to be written by a racialist or by an extreme reactionary. This is because there was no contradiction between the racialist agenda and the socialistic program in Europe at that time. In both cases, the aim was unique: to target the human body through hygienics and eugenics.

THE ARYAN DWELLING

The reference to the "human crowds" in Cazalis's *L'art nouveau* was probably intended as an allusion to the right-wing theories of the physiologist Gustave Le Bon (1841–1931), who published a volume titled *Les Civilisations de l'Inde* in 1887 and whose book *Psychologie des foules* (1895) references Cazalis by name.[81] For Le Bon, the crowd was the receptacle of the unconscious and was opposed to the conscious elite. An inferior part of contemporary society, it had to be controlled by medical strategies. Le Bon warned that the crowd, with its "herd mentality," could bring about the psychological decline of races because its irrationality was the cause of mental contagion and left it open to manipulation by leaders. In this regard, it should be noted that *Psychologie des foules* went through eighteen editions by 1913 and was carefully read by, among others, Georges Sorel (1847–1922), the theoretician of the political use of violence, and Benito Mussolini (1883–1945). "A crowd is a serial flock that is incapable of ever doing without the master,"[82] wrote Le Bon. He remarked that men collected in a crowd are subject to "rapidly contagious" emotions, which explains not only the suddenness of panic but illnesses such as agoraphobia. An affirmation "sufficiently repeated," he thought, could lead, as in advertising and political campaigns, to the convincing of a truth by the "powerful mechanism of contagion"; the same mechanism was at work, so powerful that it could enforce "not only certain opinions, but certain modes of feeling as well."[83]

Le Bon was probably himself influenced by the psychophysiologist Jules Soury (1842–1915), an ultranationalist who used evolutionary biology to justify racial, as well as social, inequalities. These Frenchmen wanted to form an official society similar to Francis Galton's Eugenics Society, founded in London in 1867.[84] They believed in the new "science" of anthroposociology, which, through craniometry, would determine racial typologies. From 1875 to 1885, Rudolph Virchow (1821–1902), a prominent German liberal and physiologist, by arguing that Darwinism was more useful to socialists than to conservatives, launched a colossal inquiry, measuring the cephalic index of fifteen million schoolchildren, the aim of which was to establish a statistics of cranium morphology in all of Germany.[85] In a similar exercise in 1891, the social anthropologist Georges Vacher de Lapouge (1854–1936), aided by the poet Paul Valéry (1871–1945), measured six hundred craniums extracted from an old cemetery. Vacher de Lapouge, author of L'Aryen. Son rôle social (1899), believed that the "unfit" must be prevented from reproducing through a process of medical selection.[86] A follower of Galton and Haeckel, he would develop a racial classification between "brachycephalics" (round-headed men with brown hair and eyes) and "dolichocephalics" (men with long, narrow skulls, blond hair, and blue eyes, the heirs to the original "Aryans"). The dolichocephalics corresponded to the Homo Europaeus who emigrated to northern Germany, Great Britain, and the United States, while the brachycephalics engendered the Homo Alpinus who came from Asia Minor and the Balkans to Switzerland and France.[87]

(fig. 10)

Low-cost, hygienic furniture by León Benouville, published by Dr. Henry Cazalis [pseud. Jean Lahor]

A follower of Herbert Spencer (1820–1903), convinced of the biological determination of human destiny, Le Bon believed that the struggle for life would cause inferior people to die out and the best-adapted human races to survive. This racist theory was largely pessimistic, since the amelioration of the physical environment did not improve the human race.[88] Like Le Bon, Cazalis was also an advocate of social Darwinism: "Let's educate the majority, which is made up of the common people... to avoid destroying our own majority; because as a Darwinian, I repeat that innumerable masses, masters of today's life... are always a cause of mediocrity."[89] Cazalis advocated the institution of an authoritarian and elitist government that would erase the historical catastrophe which was the French Revolution (1789) and would rebuild a new democracy: "Hygiene, a branch of aesthetics—because health and cleanliness are necessarily the essential conditions of beauty—hygiene already attempts to give to people's habitations what has for too long been lacking, pure air, and the sun that kills pathogenic germs, and light, which is as much necessary for thought and the soul as it is for the body."[90] Cazalis signed his own name to his volume on eugenics, *Le Science et le mariage* (1900), dedicating it to nationalist author Maurice Barrès (1862–1923), who wrote the best-seller *Les Déracinés* (1897), a novel about the eradication of traditions and the unhappy life of uprooted people.[91] While William Morris thought that art should be made by the people, Cazalis thought that it had to be made for the people, as the title of his 1902 book, *Art for the People*, amply demonstrates.[92] His hygienic democracy was part of a general eugenics: the doctor wrote books on "scientific" marriage, prenuptial inspection, hereditary diseases, and the protection of health and race.[93] In this period, ethnic cleansing and aesthetic hygiene went side by side.

All of Cazalis's proposals converged in one of his last books, which described "low-cost dwellings and low-cost art" (1903) and was dedicated to Georges Picot, president of the housing society of France—the Société des habitations à bon marché (fig. 10).[94] He reminded the authorities that de Foville had already published a wondrous study of the types of houses and maintained, "We must prepare immediately for the workers of the most industrialized parts of the country types of individual houses, such as cottages, or chalets, which would be built in the regional style, blending harmoniously with the beauty and appeal of those rural parts."[95] This book was much more practical than his previous writings, publishing cooperative single dwellings in Puteaux (named "La Famille") and workers' houses near Beauvais (by Léon Benouville, who had also designed furniture for workers' homes in a very restrained art nouveau style), together with new barracks in Madagascar.[96] In the conclusion to the book, the doctor repeated his Darwinian credo that inequality between men is a universal, natural, and eternal law. Through the elimination of the weakest, the elite in France would win out: "Like true soldiers, they must think only of victory."[97] For humanity the battle was not only political but aesthetic. This aestheticiation of politics continued the fight of the Aryans, who inspired

> a religion, or a future philosophy that would help to make life more enticing and exciting for many spirits who are too doomed, too silent... while revealing all there is of mystery, all there is of prodigy, all there is that is human and divine, in the lesser animal and in the lesser plant, being able to recognize and to affirm according to the Aryan dogma the kinship that unites all beings.[98]

Another theoretician of *Kulturgeschichte*—Franz Carl Müller-Lyer, whose *History of Social Development* (1912) was read by many in Germany in the 1920s (including Walter Gropius)—put it this way:

> Just as in organic nature a progressive movement exists from the monad to the mammal, so is it in culture. And in both developments the movement goes from small to great, from simple to complex, from homogeneous to heterogeneous, and in these processes of increase, combination and differentiation... lies progress—and it lies in nothing else. That is the objective formula of the idea of culture progress. The happiness of the individual has no place therein. For Nature offers up the individual everywhere with cruel indifference on the altar of—the Type.[99]

What is given here as a kind of social program is the Darwinistic elimination of the individual on the "altar of the type."

Most likely, architects were not cognizant of all these connections when they began to use the term *typology* in the twentieth century. Although this does not diminish in any way the significance of their thinking, it is important to note that, as a consequence, architects did not discuss very clearly the profound difference between the classical type, as an ur-genesis that repeated the antique form, and the modern morphogenesis that established the abolition of mimesis, the institution of the norm, the repetition of the same, and the prescription of the new. The classical, and neoclassical, notions of type were based on the embodiment of ideals that referred through nature and time to principles and rules that conferred authority to the building, while typology led to disembodiment. The new abstract type was formed by means of calculation, determined by the laws of evolution, and grafted on to the skin by thousands of inscriptions. Although type no longer informed architecture (except as a revival), typology reorganized the environment in a thoroughly normative way.

In a period such as ours, when architects have often denounced any typological approach, while they have looked for a topological definition of the ground of architecture (which should also be analyzed one day for its methodological fictions), the analysis of how typology has structured social sciences and the arts in the last two centuries, and how normative and pre-scriptive it was and still is, may help us better understand the notion of the body as type, that is, the body as an entity to redesign, bringing it to the level of a prosthesis.

NOTES

1. See, for instance, Giulio Carlo Argan, "Sul concetto di tipologia architettonica," in *Progetto e Destino* (Milan: Il Saggiatore, 1965), 75–81; trans., "On the Typology of Architecture," in *Theorizing a New Agenda for Architecture*, ed. Kate Nesbitt (New York: Princeton Architectural Press, 1996), 240–46.

2. Gottfried Semper, *Der Stil in den technischen und tektonischen Künsten, oder praktische Aesthetik, ein Handbuch für Techniker, Künstler und Kunstfreunde*, vol. 1, *Die textile Kunst, für sich betrachtet und in Beziehung zur Baukunst* (Frankfurt am Main: Verlag für Kunst und Wissenschaft, 1860), vol. 2, *Keramik, Tektonik, Stereotomie, Metallotechnik, für sich betrachtet und in Beziehung zur Baukunst* (Munich: F. Bruckmann, 1863); trans., *Lo stile nelle arti tecniche e tettoniche o estetica pratica. Manuale per tecnici, artisti e amatori*, trans. Augusto R. Burelli (Rome: Editori Laterza, 1992), 2: 239–50.

3. Eugène-Emmanuel Viollet-le-Duc, *Histoire de l' habitation humaine depuis les temps préhistoriques jusqu'à nos jours* (Paris: Hetzel et Cie., 1875), 20; idem, *The Habitations of Man in All Ages*, trans. Benjamin Bucknall (Boston: James R. Osgood and Co., 1876), 8–23. Viollet-le-Duc owned a copy of Semper's *Der Stil*; see *Catalogue des livres composant le bibliothèque de feu M. E.Viollet-le-Duc* (Paris: A. Labitte, 1880).

4. Henri Martin, quoted in Léon Poliakov, *The Aryan Myth: A History of Racist and Nationalist Ideas in Europe*, trans. Edmund Howard (New York: Basic Books, 1974), 35, 189–90.

5. Jacob Grimm, cited in Poliakov, 298–99.

6. For an analysis of Darwin's seminal work, see the introduction, afterword, and commentaries by Paul Ekman in Charles Darwin, *The Expression of the Emotions in Man and Animals* (1872), 3rd ed. (Oxford and New York: Oxford University Press, 1998). See also Alessandra Ponte, "Fisiognomica," in *Dizionario critico illustrato delle voci piu utili all'architetto moderno,* ed. Luciano Semerani (Faenza: Edizioni C.E.L.I., 1993), 35–39.

7. Eugène-Emmanuel Viollet-le-Duc, *Histoire d'un dessinateur, comment on apprend à dessiner* (Paris: Bibliothèque d'éducation et de récréation, 1879).

8. Eugène-Emmanuel Viollet-le-Duc, *Dictionnaire raisonné de l'architecture française du XIe au XVIe siècles,* 10 vols. (Paris: B. Bance, then A. Morel, 1854–68).

9. Etienne Geoffroy Saint-Hilaire, "Sur des écrits de Goethe lui donnant des droits au titre de savant naturaliste," *Annales des sciences naturelles* February 1831: 192; Henri Dutrochet, *Mémoires pour servir à l'histoire anatomique et physiologique des végétaux et des animaux* (Paris: J. B. Baillière, 1837); François Duchesneau, *Genèse de la théorie cellulaire* (Montreal: Bellarmin, and Paris: Vrin, 1987), 21; Guido Cimino and François Duchesneau, eds., *Vitalisms: From Haller to the Cell Theory,* proceedings of the Zaragoza Symposium, XIXth International Congress History of Science, 22–29 August 1993 (Florence: L. S. Olschki, 1997); Laurent Baridon, *L'Imaginaire scientifique de Viollet-le-Duc* (Paris: Editions L'harmattan, 1996), 101–5.

10. Viollet-le-Duc, *Histoire d'un dessinateur,* 34.

11. Jean-Jacques Rousseau, *Julie, ou la nouvelle Héloïse: Lettres de deux amants habitants d'une petite ville au pied des Alpes,* part 4, "Lettre X à milord Edouard," text redacted by René Pomeau (Paris: Garnier, 1988), 127–30.

12. Viollet-le-Duc, *Dictionnaire raisonné,* 6: 214–300.

13. Ibid., 255–57.

14. Arthur, comte de Gobineau, *Essai sur l'inégalité des races humaines* (Paris: P. Belfond, 1967).

15. Viollet-le-Duc, *The Habitations of Man in All Ages,* 42–43. See also Stuart Piggott, *Wagon, Chariot and Carriage: Symbol and Status in the History of Transport* (London: Thames and Hudson, 1992).

16. See Jacques Gubler, "Une maison, histoire et contrepoint," in *Viollet-le-Duc et la montagne,* ed. Pierre A. Frey and Lise Grenier (Grenoble: Glénat, 1993), 34–42.

17. Baridon, *L'Imaginaire scientifique de Viollet-le-Duc,* 107–17.

18. See Alexandre Labat, "Charles Garnier et l'exposition de 1889: L'Histoire de l'habitation," in *1889: La Tour Eiffel et l'exposition universelle* (Paris: Editions de la réunion des musées nationaux, 1989), 130–47. See also Charles Garnier, *À travers les arts* (1869), reprinted as *Les Ambiguités de Charles Garnier* (Paris: Picard, 1985).

19. Charles Garnier and Adolphe Ammann, *L'Habitation humaine* (Paris: Hachette, 1892).

20. Franz Carl Müller-Lyer, *Die Entwicklungsstufen der Menschheit. Eine Gesellschaftslehre in Überblicken und Einzeldarstellungen,* 2 vols. (Munich: J. F. Lehmann, 1910–12); trans., *The History of Social Development,* trans. Elizabeth Coote Lake and E. J. Lake (New York: Alfred A. Knopf, 1921), 146. Perhaps this is one of the sources of Martin Heidegger's disputed equation between *Bauen* and *Wohnen,* even if he did not connect building to the tree. Martin Heidegger, *Being and Time,* trans. John Macquarrie and Edward Robinson (San Francisco: Harper, 1962), 80.

21. *Enquête sur les conditions de l'habitation en France: Les Maisons-types,* introduction by Alfred de Foville (Paris: E. Leroux, 1894–99), 2: 2.II.

22. Ibid., XIV–XV.

23. Ibid., XL.

24. Le Play is quoted by Charles Booth, and through Booth he had a great influence on the biologist and founder of English urban studies, Sir Patrick Geddes; Alessandra Ponte, "Building the Stair Spiral of Evolution: The Index Museum of Sir Patrick Geddes," *Assemblage* 10 (1990): 46–69; trans., *Les Collections: Fables et programmes*, ed. Jacques Guillerme (Paris: Champ Vallon, 1993), 297–307.

25. Frank E. Manuel, *The Prophets of Paris* (Cambridge, Mass.: Harvard University Press, 1962), 103–48, esp. 121. See also Xavier Bichat, *Recherches physiologiques sur la vie et la mort* (Paris: Brosson, Gabon et Cie., year VIII [1799/1800]); trans., *Physiological Researches upon Life and Death*, trans. Tobias Watkins (Philadelphia: Smith and Maxwell, 1809). On Xavier Bichat, see Nicolas Dobo and André Role, *Bichat: La Vie fulgurante d'un génie* (Paris: Perrin, 1989), and Philippe Huneman, *Bichat, la vie et la mort* (Paris: Presses universitaires de France, 1998).

26. Manuel, *Prophets of Paris*, 123–29, 142. On Claude Henri de Rouvroy, comte de Saint-Simon (1760–1825), see Frank Edward Manuel, *The New World of Henri Saint-Simon* (Cambridge, Mass.: Harvard University Press, 1956). See also the classic work Sébastien Charléty, *Histoire du saint-simonisme, 1825–1864* (Paris: P. Hartmann, 1931).

27. Manuel, *Prophets of Paris*, 115–18.

28. Zeev Sternhell, *La Droite révolutionnaire: Les Origines françaises du fascisme, 1885–1914* (Paris: Editions seuil, 1978), 21. On typology, see also Françoise Arnault, *Frédéric Le Play, de la métallurgie à la science sociale* (Nancy: Presses universitaires de Nancy, 1993), 87–99.

29. See Frédéric Le Play, "Family Types: Patriarchal, Stem, Unstable," *La Réforme sociale* (Tours: Mame, 1872), 352–58; trans., *On Family, Work, and Social Change*, ed. and trans. Catherine Bodard Silver (Chicago: University of Chicago Press, 1982), 259–62. See also "La Nomenclature sociale," after F[rédéric] Le Play, "La Science sociale est-elle une science?" by M. Henri de Tourville, "Les Lois du travail," by M. Prosper Prieur, extracted from *La Science sociale*, December 1886 (Paris: Firmin-Didot, 1887).

30. Introduction by C. Bodard Silver, in Le Play, *On Family, Work, and Social Change*, 118.

31. Edmond Demolins, *Les Grandes routes des peuples: Essai de géographie sociale, comment la route crée le type social*, 2 vol. (Paris: Firmin-Didot & Cie., 1901–03). See also idem, *Le Play et son œuvre de réforme sociale* (Paris: Bureaux de la "Réforme sociale," 1882).

32. Edmond Demolins, *À quoi tient la supériorité des Anglo-saxons* (Paris: Firmin-Didot et Cie, 1897); trans., *Anglo-Saxon Superiority: To What It Is Due*, trans. Louis B. Lavigne (New York: R. F. Fenno & Company, 1899).

33. Susan J. Hekman, *Weber, the Ideal Type, and Contemporary Social Theory* (Notre Dame, Ind.: University of Notre Dame Press, 1983), 31. Weber's emphasis added. See also Rolf E. Rogers, *Max Weber's Ideal Type Theory* (New York: Philosophical, 1969).

34. Lion Murard and Patrick Zylbermann, *L'Hygiène dans la République: La santé publique en France ou l'utopie contrariée, 1870–1918* (Paris: Fayard, 1996), 73–76.

35. See Paul Juillerat, *La Tuberculose et l'habitation*, report presented by Paul Juillerat and Louis Bonnier to the Congrès international de la tuberculose, Paris, 2–7 October 1905 (Paris: Masson, 1905); idem, *Le Choix d'un logement, son aménagement, son entretien*, conference held at the Grand-Palais, 23 October 1905, extract from *Progrès médical*, 6 January 1906 (Paris: Rousset, 1906); idem, *Une*

Institution nécessaire: Le Casier sanitaire des maisons (Paris: J. Rousset, 1906).

36. Paul Juillerat and Louis Bonnier, République française, Préfecture du département de la Seine. Direction des affaires municipales, Rapport à M. le préfet sur les enquêtes effectuées en 1906 [−1907] dans les maisons signalées comme foyers de tuberculose (Paris: Chaix, 1907−08); idem, L'Hygiène du logement (Paris: C. Delagrave, 1909); Paul Juillerat and A. Fillassier, Dix années de mortalité parisienne chez les enfants de 0 à 14 ans (97.885 décès) [...], extract from the Revue philanthropique, 15 juin 1914 (Paris: Masson, 1914); idem, République française. Préfecture du département de la Seine. Direction des affaires municipales. Rapport à M. le préfet sur les recherches effectuées au bureau du casier sanitaire pendant l'année 1908 [1909, 1910, 1915−1916−1917], relatives à la répartition de la tuberculose et du cancer dans les maisons de Paris (Paris: Imprimerie de Chaix, 1909−18).

37. Cesare Lombroso, L'Uomo delinquente studiato in rapporto alla Antropologia, alla Medicina Legale ed alle discipline carcerarie (Milano: Hoepli, 1875−76); trans., L'Homme criminel, trans. Regnier et Bournet (Paris: F. Alcan, 1882). trans., Cesare Lombroso, with Giuseppe Ferrero, La femme criminelle et la prostituée, trans. Louise Meille (Paris: F. Alcan, 1896); trans., Cesare Lombroso, The Female Offender (New York: D. Appleton, 1895). See also Gina Lombroso-Ferrero, Criminal Man According to the Classification of Cesare Lombroso (New York: Putnam, 1911); Nancy Anne Harrowitz, Antisemitism, Misogyny, and the Logic of Cultural Difference: Cesare Lombroso and Matilde Serao (Lincoln: University of Nebraska Press, 1994). On typology, see Renzo Villa, Il deviante e i suoi segni: Lombroso e la nascita dell'antropologia criminale (Milano: F. Angeli, 1985), 184−95.

38. Alphonse Bertillon, La Photographie judiciaire: Avec un appendice sur la classification et l'identification anthropométriques (Paris: Gauthier-Villars, 1890). See also Henry T. F. Rhodes, Alphonse Bertillon, Father of Scientific Detection (New York: Greenwood Press, 1968), esp. 102−09; idem, Alphonse Bertillon's Instructions for Taking Descriptions for the Identification of Criminals and Others by the Means of Anthropomorphic Indications, trans. Gallus Muller (1889; reprinted, New York: AMS Press, 1977); Christian Phéline, L'Image accusatrice: Les Cahiers de la photographie (Laplume: ACCP, 1985); Eugenia Parry, Crime Album Stories, Paris, 1886−1902 (Zurich and New York: Scalo, 2000).

39. F[ranz] J[oseph] Gall, Recherches sur le système nerveux en général et sur celui du cerveau en particulier: Mémoire présenté à l'Institut de France, le 14 mars 1808, suivi d'observations sur le rapport qui en a été fait à cette compagnie par ses commissaires (1809; reprinted, Amsterdam: E. J. Bonset, 1967). See also Georges Lanteri-Laura, Histoire de la Phrénologie: L'Homme et son cerveau selon F. J. Gall (Paris: Presses universitaires de France, 1970); David de Giustino, Conquest of Mind: Phrenology and Victorian Social Thought (London: Croom Helm and Totowa, and N.J.: Rowman and Littlefield, 1975); Sigrid Oehler-Klein, Die Schadellehre Franz Joseph Galls in Literatur und Kritik des 19. Jahrhunderts: Zur Rezeptionsgeschichte einer Medizinisch-biologisch Begrundeten Theorie der Physiognomik und Psychologie (Stuttgart and New York: Gustav Fischer Verlag, 1990).

40. J[ohann] G[aspar] Spurzheim, The Physiognomical System of Drs. Gall and Spurzheim, 2nd. ed. (London: Baldwin, Cradock, and Joy, 1815).

41. [Johann Gaspar] Spurzheim, Phrenology, in Connexion with the Study of Physiognomy (Boston: Marsh, Capen & Lyon, 1833). See Claudio Pogliano, "Entre forme et fonction: Une nouvelle science de l'homme," in L'Âme au corps: Arts et sciences, 1793−1993, ed. Jean Clair, exhib. cat., Galeries Nationales du Grand Palais, October 1993−January 1994 (Paris: Réunion des musées nationaux, Gallimard/Electa, 1993), 238−65.

42. O[rson] S[quire] Fowler and L[orenzo] N[iles] Fowler, Phrenology Proved, Illustrated, and Applied

(New York: self-published, 1837); O[rson] S[quire] Fowler, *Fowler's Practical Phrenology* (Philadelphia and New York: n.p., 1840); idem, *The Illustrated Self-Instructor in Phrenology and Physiology* (1849; reprinted, New York: Fowler and Wells, 1857). See John D. Davies, *Phrenology, Fad and Science, A Nineteenth-Century American Crusade* (New Haven: Yale University Press, 1955).

43. O[rson] S[quire] Fowler, *Home for All , or a New, Cheap, Convenient, and Superior Mode of Building* (New York: Fowler and Wells, 1848); idem, *A Home for All, or The Gravel Wall and Octagon Mode of Building* (New York: Fowler and Wells, 1854); reprinted as *The Octagon House: A Home for All* (New York: Dover Publications, 1973).

44. On J.-B. André Godin (1817–1888), see Annick Brauman and Michel Louis, eds., *Jean-Baptiste André Godin, Le Familistère de Guise ou les équivalents de la richesse*, 2nd ed. (Brussels: Archives d'architecture moderne, 1980); Guy Delabre and Jean-Marie Gautier, eds., *Jean-Baptiste André Godin et le familistère de Guise: Une utopie socialiste pratiquée en pays picard* (Vervins: Société archéologique de Vervins et de la Thiérache, 1983); idem, eds., *Godin et le Familistère de Guise à l'épreuve de l'histoire* (Reims: Presses universitaires de Reims, 1989).

45. Charles Fourier and Victor Considérant, *L'Avenir: Perspective d'un phalanstère ou palais sociétaire dédié à l'humanité* (Bordeaux: Imprimerie de H. Faye, n.d.); idem, *Considérations sociales sur l'architectonique* (Paris: Les Libraires du Palais Royal, 1834); idem, *Description du phalanstère et considérations sociales sur l'architectonique*, 2nd ed. (1940; reprinted, Paris: Guy Durier, 1979); idem, *Exposition abrégée du système phalanstérien de Fourier*, 3rd ed. (Paris: Librairie Sociétaire, 1845).

46. Jean-Baptiste André Godin, *La Richesse au service du peuple: Le Familistère de Guise* (1874; reprinted, Neuilly: Guy Durier, 1979).

47. Jean-Baptiste André Godin, *Solutions sociales* (Paris: A. Le Chevalier, 1871), 501; idem, *Solutions sociales*, ed. Jean-François Rey and Jean-Luc Pinol (Quimperlé: La Digitale, 1979); trans., *Social Solutions*, trans. Marie Howland (New York: J. W. Lovell Co., 1886). The *Familistère* was also the subject of an American novel written by Marie Howland, entitled *Papa's Own Girl: A Novel* (1874; reprinted, Philadelphia: Porcupine Press, 1975). The novel was translated into French by Marie-Adèle Moret, the wife of Godin, as *La Fille de son père, roman américain* (Paris: A. Ghio, 1880). Howland subsequently translated Godin's *Solutions sociales* into English in 1886 (New York: J. W. Lovell Co., 1886).

48. Cesare Lombroso, *Genio e follia*, 4th ed. (Milan: Hoepli, 1887); idem, *L'Homme de génie* (Paris: F. Alcan, 1889); trans., *The Man of Genius* (London: Walter Scott and New York: C. Scribner's Sons, 1891).

49. Peter Strasser, "Cesare Lombroso: L'Homme délinquant ou la bête sauvage au naturel," in *L'Âme au corps*, 352–59. See also *Wunderblock: Eine Geschichte der modernen Seele*, ed. Jean Clair, Cathrin Pichler, and Wolfgang Pircher, exhib. cat., *Sonderausstellung des Historischen Museums der Stadt Wien* (Vienna: Löcker, 1989).

50. Adolphe-Lambert-Jacques Quételet, *Sur l'homme et le développement de ses facultés, ou Essai de physique sociale* (Paris: Bachelier, 1835); Adolphe Quételet, *A Treatise on Man and the Development of His Faculties* (Edinburgh: William and Robert Chambers, 1842); facsimile of trans. (Gainesville, Fla.: Scholars' Facsimiles and Reprints, 1969).

51. Quételet, *Treatise on Man*, 96–103; idem, *Physique sociale, ou Essai sur le développement des facultés de l'homme* (1869; reprinted, Brussels: Académie royale de Belgique, 1997). See also Philippe Comar, "Les chaînes de l'art," in *L'Âme au corps*, 394–404.

52. See especially Adolphe Quételet, *Anthropométrie, ou Mesure des différentes facultés de l'homme* (Brussels: C. Muquardt, 1870).

53. Marta Braun, *Picturing Time: The Work of Etienne-Jules Marey (1830–1904)* (Chicago: University of Chicago Press, 1992).

54. Dr. Paul Richer, *Anatomie artistique: Description des formes extérieures du corps humain au repos et dans les principaux mouvements* (Paris: E. Plon, Nourrit et Cie, 1890); facsimile editions (Paris: Inter-livres, 1988) and (Paris: Bibliothèque de l'image, 1996); idem, *Canon des proportions du corps humain* (Paris: C. Delagrave, 1893); idem, *Physiologie artistique de l'homme en mouvement* (Paris: O. Doin, 1895); idem, *Introduction à l'étude de la figure humaine* (Paris: Gaultier, Magnier et Cie, 1902).

55. Giovanni Morelli, *Della pittura italiana, studii storico-critici: Le Gallerie Borghese e Doria-Pamphili in Roma*, ed. Jaynie Anderson (1897; reprinted, Milan: Adelphi, 1991).

56. Oskar Schlemmer, László Moholy-Nagy, and Farkas Molnar, *Die Bühne im Bauhaus* (1924; reprinted, Mainz: Kupferberg, 1965). See also Oskar Schlemmer, *Man: Teaching Notes from the Bauhaus*, ed. Heimo Kuchling, trans. Janet Seligman (London: Lund Humphries, 1971).

57. Juillerat and Bonnier, *République française...Rapport...sur les enquêtes effectuées;* idem, *République française...Rapport...sur les recherches effectuées.*

58. Roger-Henri Guerrand, *Le Logement populaire en France: Sources documentaires et bibliographie, 1800–1960* (Paris: École nationale supérieure des Beaux-Arts, 1979), 97.

59. Paul Weindling, *Health, Race and German Politics between National Unification and Nazism, 1870–1945* (Cambridge: Cambridge University Press, 1989).

60. Wilhelm Heinrich von Riehl, *Die Naturgeschichte des Volkes als Grundlage einer deutschen Social-Politik*, 3 vols. (Stuttgart, Tübingen, and Augsburg: J. G. Cotta, 1854–56).

61. Wilhelm Heinrich Riehl, *The Natural History of the German People*, ed. and trans. David J. Diephouse (Lewistown, N.Y.: Edwin Melten Press, 1990), 324.

62. Ibid., 306–09.

63. Ibid., 312.

64. "Man müsse ein Haus von innen nach außen bauen": Heinrich Tessenow, *Hausbau und dergleichen* (1916; reprinted, Braunschweig and Wiesbaden: Vieweg & Sohn, 1986), 19; idem, "Housebuildings and Such Things," trans. Wilfried Wang, *9H* 8 (1989): 9–33.

65. Von Riehl, *Natural History*, 318–23.

66. Friedrich [Anton Heller] von Hellwald, *Kulturgeschichte in ihrer natürlichen Entwicklung bis zur Gegenwart*, 2 vols. (Augsburg: Lampart & Co., 1876–77); (reprinted, Leipzig: Friesenhahn, 1896).

67. About Haeckel's work, see Ernst Haeckel, *Kunstformen der Natur* (Leipzig and Wien: Verlag des Bibliographischen Instituts, 1899–1904); trans., *Art Forms in Nature: The Prints of Ernst Haeckel* (Munich and New York: Prestel, 1998). On Haeckel's influence, see Christoph Kockerbeck, *Ernst Haeckels "Kunstformen der Natur" und ihr Einfluß auf die deutsche bildende Kunst der Jahrhundertwende: Studie zum Verhältnis von Kunst und Naturwissenschaften im Wilhelminischen Zeitalter* (Frankfurt am Main and New York: P. Lang, 1986), and Daniel Gasman, *Haeckel's Monism and the Birth of Fascist Ideology* (New York: P. Lang, 1998).

68. Von Hellwald, *Kulturgeschichte*.

69. Friedrich von Hellwald, *Haus und Hof in ihrer Entwicklung mit Bezug auf die Wohnsitten der Völker* (Leipzig: Schmidt, 1888).

70. Wilhelm Baer, *Der vorgeschichtliche Mensch: Ursprung und Entwicklung Menschengeschlechtes*, 2 vols. (Leipzig: O. Spamer, 1874).

71. Quoted by L. Poliakov, 273. See Ludwig Büchner [Louis Büchner], *Force et matière, études populaires d'histoire et de philosophie naturelles*, 2nd ed., trans. A. Gros-Claude (Paris: C. Reinwald, 1865); idem, *Conférence sur la théorie darwinienne de la transmutation des espèces et de l'apparition du monde organique* (Leipzig: T. Thomas, 1869); Ludwig Büchner, *Lumière et vie: Trois leçons populaires d'histoire naturelle sur le soleil dans ses rapports avec la vie, sur la circulation des forces et la fin du monde, sur la philosophie de la génération*, trans. Ch. Letourneau (Paris: C. Reinwald, 1883); idem, *Darwinismus und Sozialismus, oder der Kampf um das Dasein und die moderne Gesellschaft* (Leipzig: E. Günther, 1894).

72. August Meitzen, *Siedelung und Agrarwesen der Westgermanen und Ostgermanen, der Kelten, Römer, Finnen und Slaven*, 4 vols. (Berlin: W. Hertz, 1895). Both works by Friedrich von Hellwald and August Meitzen are rebuked by Jacques Flach, professor at the Collège de France; see his "Etude sur les origines et les vicissitudes historiques de l'habitation en France," in *Enquête sur les conditions de l'habitation en France: Les Maisons-types* (Paris: E. Leroux, 1899), 2: 1–97, esp. 7, 17.

73. Lawrence A. Joseph, *Henri Cazalis: Sa vie, son oeuvre, son amitié avec Mallarmé* (Paris: A. G. Nizet, 1972). He published his first poem in 1859, and his main literary work was *L'Illusion* (1875), which was republished five times during his lifetime. Henri Cazalis, *L'Illusion* (Paris: Alphonse Lemerre, 1875). Some of his verses were put to music by the composer Camille Saint-Saëns (1835–1921). He exchanged many letters with his friend Stéphane Mallarmé and translated works from the German, Italian, and English. Cazalis appears in Marcel Proust's *Recherche* as a doctor—and poet—named Legrandin. Marcel Proust, *A la recherche du temps perdu* (Paris: Bibliothèque de la Pléiade, 1954), 1: 67.

74. Cazalis was the doctor and confidant of Guy de Maupassant (it was Cazalis who brought the writer to a clinic after his suicide attempt). Cazalis's pseudonym, Lahor, which fascinated Henry James, referred in a mysterious and anagrammatic way to "Le Horla," a famous short story by de Maupassant in which, in a dream, the furniture of a house starts to move, acquiring a ghostly life of its own. *The Notebooks of Henry James*, ed. F. O. Matthiesen and Kenneth B. Murdock (New York: Oxford University Press, 1955), 213, and Joseph, *Henri Cazalis*, 195–203. See also Guy de Maupassant, "Le Horla" (1887), *Contes et nouvelles* (Paris: Gallimard, N.R.F., Bibliothèque de la Pléiade, 1979), 2 : 913–38.

75. Henri Cazalis [Jean Lahor], *W. Morris et le mouvement nouveau de l'art décoratif*, conference held in Geneva, 13 January 1897 (Geneva: C. Eggimann, 1897). See also his previously published "William Morris et l'art décoratif en Angleterre," *Revue encyclopédique*, 15 August 1894: 349–59.

76. Gabriel de Tarde, *Les Lois de l'imitation*, 2nd ed. (1895; reprinted, Paris and Geneva: Resources, Slatkine, 1979), 409; trans., *The Laws of Imitation*, trans. Elsie Clews Parson (New York: H. Holt & Co., 1903).

77. Lahor, *W. Morris*, 59. See also Jean Lahor, *L'Art nouveau, son histoire, l'art nouveau étranger à l'Exposition, l'art nouveau au point de vue social* (Paris: Lemerre, 1901).

78. Lahor, *L'Art nouveau*, not paginated.

79. Edward William Beeson, *Port Sunlight: The Model Village of England* (New York: Architectural Book Pub., 1911); Thomas Raffles Davison, *Port Sunlight: A Record of Its Artistic and Pictorial Aspect* (London: L. B. T. Batsford, 1916).

80. Ibid.

81. Gustave Le Bon, *Les Civilisations de l'Inde* (Paris: Firmin-Didot, 1887); idem, *Psychologie des foules*, 4th ed. (Paris: F. Alcan, 1889); trans., *The Crowd: A Study of the Popular Mind* (New York: Macmillan Co.,

1896), 139; idem, The Crowd (New Brunswick, N.J.: Transaction Pub., 1995).

82. Le Bon, The Crowd (1896), 134. Le Bon is quoted, for instance, in Georges Sorel, Les Illusions du progrès, 2nd ed. (Paris: Marcel Rivière, 1911), 332. See also idem, Reflections on Violence (1908; reprinted, New York: Collier Books, 1974).

83. Le Bon, The Crowd (1896), 143–45.

84. Ruth Schwartz Cowan, Sir Francis Galton and the Study of Heredity in the Nineteenth Century (New York: Garland Pub., 1985).

85. Poliakov, Aryan Myth, 273–74.

86. His book was reprinted in Germany in 1939. Georges Vacher de Lapouge, L'Aryen. Son rôle social. Cours libre de science politique professé à l'Université de Montpelliers, 1889–1890 (Paris: Albert Fontemoing Editeur, 1899); trans., Der Arier und seine Bedeutung für die Gemeinschaft: Freier Kursus in Staatskunde, gehalten an der Universität Montpellier, 1889–1890 (Frankfurt am Main: M. Diesterweg, 1939). Many volumes were written to refute Vacher's thesis on the "dolichocephalic blond race," including Emile Houzé, L'Aryen et l'anthroposociologie: Etude critique (Bruxelles and Leipzig: Misch & Thron, and Paris: Marcel Rivière, 1907). See also Georges Vacher de Lapouge, Race et milieu social: Essais d'anthroposociologie (Paris: M. Rivière, 1909).

87. It is interesting to note that these same categories, under the ironic wording of dolicho-blond (for dolichocephalic blond), would be used in the same year by the American sociologist Thorstein Veblen in his Theory of the Leisure Classes (1899; reprinted, New York: Penguin Books, 1994), 134. See also Richard Hofstadter, Social Darwinism in American Thought, 1860–1915 (Philadelphia: University of Pennsylvania Press, 1945), and Mark H. Haller, Eugenics: Hereditarian Attitudes in American Thought (New Brunswick, N.J.: Rutgers University Press, 1963).

88. Linda L. Clark, Social Darwinism in France (Tuscaloosa: University of Alabama Press, 1984), 133–36; Jean-Marc Bernardini, Le Darwinisme social en France, 1859–1918 (Paris: CNRS Editions, 1997); Mike Hawkins, Social Darwinism in European and American Thought, 1860–1945 (Cambridge and New York: Cambridge University Press, 1997).

89. Lahor, L'Art nouveau.

90. Ibid.

91. Henri Cazalis, La Science et le mariage, étude médicale (Paris: O. Doin, 1900), Bibliothèque nationale de France, Paris [Don 80–1863 (2571)], "Envoi autographe de l'auteur à Maurice Barrès"; see Maurice Barrès, Les Déracinés (Paris: Fasquelle, 1897). See also Robert Soucy, Fascism in France: The Case of Maurice Barrès (Berkeley: University of California Press, 1972); and Zeev Sternhell, Maurice Barrès et le nationalisme français (Paris: A. Colin, 1972).

92. Jean Lahor, L'Art pour le peuple: À défaut de l'art par le peuple (Paris: Larousse, 1902).

93. Henri Cazalis, La Science et le mariage, and idem, Conférence...à propos des risques pathologiques du mariage, des hérédités morbides, et d'un examen médical avant le mariage (Brussels: Imprimerie Van de Weghe, 1902); idem, Quelques mesures très simples protectrices de la santé et de la race (Paris: Doin, 1904).

94. Jean Lahor, Les Habitations à bon marché et un art nouveau pour le peuple (Paris: Larousse, 1903).

95. Ibid., 3rd ed. (Paris: Larousse, 1905), 37–38.

96. See Exposition universelle de 1900, section française, groupe XII, classe 69. Meubles de luxe et à bon marché M. Léon Benouville for the comité d'admission (Paris: Librairies-Imprimeries Réunies, 1899).

97. Lahor, Les Habitations à bon marché, 89.

98. Lahor, L'Art pour le peuple, 25. On Cazalis's [Lahor's] orientalism, see René Petitbon, Les Sources orientales de Jean Lahor (Paris: A. G. Nizet, 1962).

99. F. Müller-Lyer, *History of Social Development*, 349. See also Walter Gropius, "Die soziologischen Grundlagen der Minimalwohnung für die städtische Industrielbevölkerung," *Die Justiz* 5 (1929); trans., "La Ration raisonné d'habitat, une sociologie du logement de Gropius," trans. S. Deleule, *Amphion, études d'historie des techniques* 2 (Paris: Picard, 1987), 59–68.

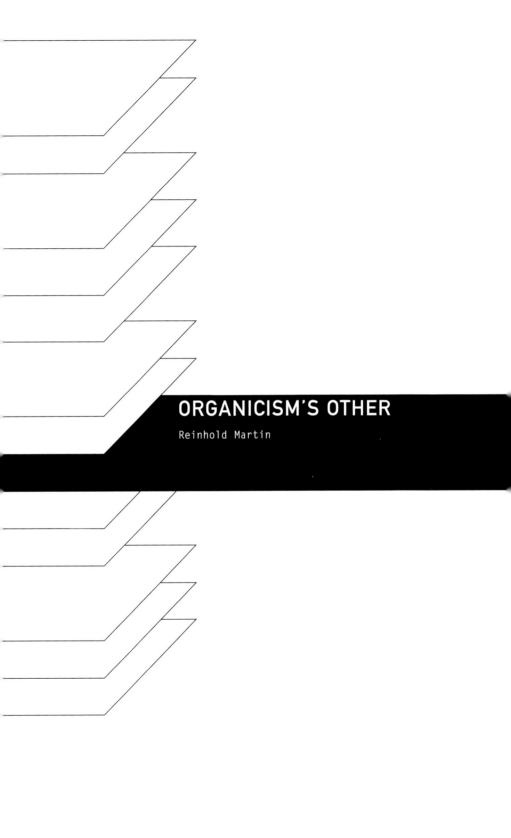

ORGANICISM'S OTHER

Reinhold Martin

If what follows appears mainly to be concerned with art, and perhaps marginally with science, that is only because it is written primarily with reference to architecture—from the outside looking in, as it were. I emphasize this since the disciplinary topologies involved in such an effort are very much at issue in the material under consideration, the formally architectural dimensions of which emerge only via an itinerary that, unfortunately, must begin at the end. The end in question is marked by a single event: the publication in 1972 of an essay by Robert Smithson entitled "The Spiral Jetty" in *Arts of the Environment*, the last volume of the Vision + Value book series published by George Braziller and edited by artist and writer Gyorgy Kepes.[1] Smithson's essay begins with a straightforward description of his interest in red-tinted salt lakes, and his eventual decision to locate a work of ambiguous nature in the Great Salt Lake in Utah. Along the shores of that lake he encounters wreckage sunken into the salt flats, and a field of oil seeps with rusted pumps and a ruined hut, a site that "gave evidence of a succession of man-made systems mired in abandoned hopes."[2] One mile to the north is Rozel Point, which Smithson selects as a site for the work he is planning. As he describes his choice, his text begins its rapid acceleration into the spinning series of disjunctive cross-references that links its structure to the logic of its subject.[3] This series ultimately doubles back on itself with the insertion of Smithson's spiraling piece of land art, completed in 1970, into a mediatic spiral instigated by the filming of the construction process ("a film is a spiral made up of frames"),[4] in which that footage is combined with images of prehistory: "The movieola becomes a 'time-machine' that transforms trucks [seen carting the Jetty's boulders] into dinosaurs" (fig. 1).[5]

By Smithson's account, from the outset—on location, that is—the process of producing the *Spiral Jetty* thus set off a certain disorientation: "My dialectics of site and nonsite whirled into an indeterminate state, where solid and liquid lost themselves in each other."[6] And perhaps in his textual imagination more than in the actual film (relatively sober and documentary by comparison), the spatiotemporal collapse thus precipitated was reduplicated in cinematic form:

> The movie recapitulates the scale of the Spiral Jetty. Disparate elements assume a coherence. Unlikely places and things were stuck between sections of film that show a stretch of dirt road rushing to and from the actual site in Utah. A road that goes forward and backward between things and places that are elsewhere. You might even say that the road is nowhere in particular. The disjunction operating between reality and film drives one into a sense of cosmic rupture. Nevertheless, all the improbabilities would accommodate themselves to my cinematic universe. Adrift amid scraps of film, one is unable to infuse into them any meaning, they seem worn-out, ossified views, degraded and pointless, yet they are powerful enough to hurl one into a lucid vertigo.[7]

(fig. 1)

Robert Smithson, still from The *Spiral Jetty*, 1970 ©Estate of Smithithson/ VAGA, NY, NY

REINHOLD MARTIN

I begin, then, with this disorientation. It is an affirmative disorientation, a "lucid vertigo" that is founded on a series of reversals or interchangeabilities (i.e., "The mainland oscillated with waves and pulsations, and the lake remained rock still") and a telescopic confusion of scales (i.e., "The shore of the lake became the edge of the sun, a boiling curve").[8] But it stages such dualities in an effort to freeze—or, more precisely, to exhaust—their dialectical interplay. More even than a Benjaminian "dialectics at a standstill" that admits the messianic through the flash of a reanimated "now" (Jetztzeit), Smithson's exhausted dialectic seeks to kill off the biological time of historical evolution, or modernist progress, by emptying Benjamin's "empty time" still further into an absolute exteriority, an outside—the other side of time itself. According to Smithson, in the Jetty, "fragments of a timeless geology laugh without mirth at the time-filled hopes of ecology."[9]

I begin here because this is also where Kepes begins his introductory essay to Arts of the Environment, entitled "Art and Ecological Consciousness," as he had previously begun many other essays in his thirty-year career. He warns of the dangers of "a wildly proliferating man-made environment" that has blunted the senses and "relentlessly expanded noise and complexity."[10] For Kepes, the "ecological consciousness" of his title entails a renewed sense of connectedness, a reorientation within what he calls a "new, higher gestalt," a dynamic assemblage of human and environment in which "the increasing magnitude and complexity of interacting lives must make us realize that our future depends upon an understanding and control of our common system—a self-regulating, interdependent, dynamic pattern that moves from yesterday into today and from today into tomorrow."[11] He also sees, as he has seen many times before, instructive parallels for art in the scientific insights and technological innovations of the age: the human body as a self-regulating system figured as a model for "environmental homeostasis on a global scale"; "computer game theory, theories of the servo-mechanism, systems approaches" as a means of confident confrontation with overwhelming complexity, lacking though they are in social conscience; and the nervous system itself, growing and developing in response to environmental stimuli, as a site of "control and communication" in precarious tension with a "world of ghettos, criminal wars, urban violence, and inner erosion that coexists with bioengineering, genetic engineering, the pill, distant sensors, cyborgs, and an ever-increasing communications network"—all telescoped together in what Kepes terms a "new dynamic scale."[12]

But again, this is merely the end of the story. There is a letter from Kepes to Smithson, dated 25 May 1971, written on the letterhead of the Center for Advanced Visual Studies (CAVS), the art and technology laboratory that Kepes had founded at the Massachusetts Institute of Technology in 1967. In that letter, Kepes apologizes to Smithson for his inability to offer funding for a large-scale project at MIT, while reiterating an earlier invitation for Smithson to come to the center as a visiting fellow for several weeks that fall.[13] Kepes was responding here to a letter that he had received from Smithson sometime in the previous two weeks proposing what he calls "an expedition" that would involve the construction of such a project, and going on to suggest that "a film could be made of the project and put together at the Center." He also suggests that the project could involve the collaboration of several schools, and he asks whether MIT has any scientific study stations in remote areas, noting that "the artist could cooperate with the field scientist and move between the station and the Center. As you pointed out in your perceptive essay, 'Individual artistic imagination is not self-sustained, it is part of the larger social field.' Film is a good bridge between the disciplines."[14]

The essay Smithson is referring to is one that Kepes had probably sent to him on 29 April 1971 describing the mission of the CAVS, with the letter in which he first formally invited Smithson to consider a fellowship at the center. If he wasn't aware of it already, Smithson would thus have understood the center's commitment to experimental film and multimedia as a means of establishing communicative links among art, science, and technology. By this point, the filming of the *Spiral Jetty* construction process was complete, so we can also assume that Smithson saw the CAVS as a potential site for further exploration of the multimedia disorientation that began on location at the Jetty site and was reduplicated in the editing of the film. For his part, in his initial fellowship offer Kepes went into some detail regarding the center's funding scenario, pointing out to Smithson his interest in fostering what he calls a "more dynamic relationship" with visiting artists. An exploratory visit to Cambridge was also proposed.[15]

These invitations from Kepes—which, it seems, were never consummated—themselves ensued from another abortive encounter. On 1 April of the same year (1971), Kepes had invited Smithson to participate in a symposium on civic art at MIT. As he informed Smithson, his aspirations for the symposium were essentially this: interdisciplinarity, communication, and feedback, all in the interest of environmental self-regulation. Smithson, it appears, received the invitation after the fact and was unable to attend.[16]

Kepes's subsequent persistence in soliciting Smithson's involvement with the CAVS should not be surprising in the context of the center's commitment to artworks in the civic arena. The earthworks that Smithson and others had begun constructing in the late 1960s would certainly seem to fit in this category. But as it turns out, the exchange is far more overdetermined, far more symptomatic. The first hint in the correspondence comes six months before the symposium invitation. On 6 October 1970, Kepes wrote to Smithson to acknowledge receipt of the manuscript for the "Spiral Jetty" essay. He had one request, however. Kepes asked whether, given the "very wide range of public" from which the readership of the Vision + Value series was drawn, "you could make some minor adjustments in your paper, taking into account that many of your readers will be unfamiliar with the latest stages of art activities in this country and that their basic interest is in finding common denominators of significance in this complex troubled world."[17] Judging from the text as published, it does not seem that Smithson complied,[18] possibly because he recognized that what was being advanced in Kepes's polite but firm request, expressed at the level of a benevolent interdisciplinarity, was the very organicism, an organicism of dynamic patterns and self-regulating systems, to which Kepes had dedicated most of his career.

The original title of *Arts of the Environment*, as given by publisher George Braziller in his letter of 22 October 1969 inviting Smithson to contribute to the volume, was *The Art and Science of the Environment*.[19] That it was Braziller and not Kepes writing to Smithson this time may be of little significance. But it is tempting to note the switch, since just a few months before, Kepes and Smithson had had an epistolary exchange far more heated than the rather tentative encounters we have witnessed thus far. The chain indicated in the original title, art-science-environment, had become a kind of signature for Kepes, a shorthand summary for his project of mobilizing one (art) to regulate the effects of the other (science) by, elliptically, projecting the principles of one (science) onto the other (art), within a determined yet dynamic totality called "environment." An example of these loops—which must, strictly speaking, be described as *feedback* loops—in action was to be found on the occasion that began Kepes's correspondence with Smithson in 1969.

As organizer of the United States' contribution to the 1969 São Paulo Biennial, Kepes had invited Smithson to participate in the exhibition. He also requested, however, that participating artists give up a degree of autonomy and allow their work to be arranged so as to emphasize continuity with the others, based on what Kepes saw as a shared interest in the conjunction of art and science. Here he is writing to Smithson for the first time, on 30 May 1969: "We do not intend to display the individual artist's achievements as isolated entities, but to create, to borrow a phrase, a synergetic system of all the artwork involved without sacrificing their individual quality and identity. The emphasis is on an interdependence; and environmental community."[20] The term "synergetic system" (borrowed, as Kepes indicates, from Buckminster Fuller) is underlined by hand in Smithson's copy of the letter.

However, political repression and censorship of the arts in Brazil, the events of 1968, and the United States' role in the Vietnam War ultimately caused a number of the American artists to withdraw from the event in protest in solidarity with many of their peers from other countries who had done likewise. Smithson was not the first to do so, having been preceded by at least five others. In all, nine of the twenty-three artists who were invited withdrew, including Hans Haacke, Robert Morris, and Smithson, causing Kepes—who also objected to the political situation but continued to favor what he called participatory "communication" with the Brazilian public—to call off the exhibition.[21] Yet Smithson's objections pointed to something more than merely a disagreement as to the appropriate means of political protest. In a letter dated 3 July 1969 informing Kepes of his decision, he called Kepes's optimism toward science and technology "a sad parody of NASA. . . . As rockets go to the moon the darkness around the Earth grows deeper and darker." Smithson also rejected the notion of continuity between works: "The 'team spirit' of the exhibition could be seen as an endorsement of NASA's Mission Operations Control Room with all its crew-cut teamwork. . . . If one wants teamwork he should join the army. A panel called 'What's Wrong with Technological Art' might help."[22]

Kepes was dismayed. On 16 July 1969 he responded, noting that in telephone conversations Smithson had commented favorably on his writings, which had led Kepes to assume Smithson's sympathy with his project.[23] In other words, what Kepes expected from Smithson was what he himself took to be self-evident, something that existed, for him, outside or above both ideology and political praxis. In short, Kepes expected an organicism.

REINHOLD MARTIN

Parenthetically, I want to note that *organicism*, as I am using it in this context, is a decidedly imprecise term. Nevertheless, I am not using it here *despite* its imprecision, but rather *because* of it. It is a term that lends itself to numerous levels of articulation, each of which, in an organicist regime, would resonate with and condition the other. Which is to say that the susceptibility of vast regions of modernist discourse to the designation "organicist" is what renders the term nearly useless or meaningless but also supplies it with the potency of indexing that which is taken to be self-evident. Thus, in acknowledging the term's flexibility, I seek to inhabit for the moment the paranoid linkages—of everything to everything else—unique to the systems organicism practiced by Kepes and his colleagues, in the interest of disarming the presumed self-evidence of its assumptions if not its methods. Here, for example, we would also find—in the tradition of the modern avant-gardes—the technobiologically inflected hypothesis of aesthetic and social change as developmental, or, more precisely, evolutionary. In the case of Kepes, following his mentor László Moholy-Nagy, this would mean a second-order evolutionism indebted in part to the so-called evolutionary humanism of biologist Julian Huxley, which announced, as Kepes pointed out in his introduction to *Arts of the Environment* with reference to Huxley, the advent of a "self-conscious evolution," an epochal shift in which humanity begins "to understand that, through social communication, it is within our intellectual and emotional power to shape a sounder evolutionary future."[24] In other words, human intervention—through rational action—in evolution itself. In Huxley's case, in 1930s Great Britain, this meant eugenics.[25]

But back now to the itinerary we have been following. The overtures made by Kepes in the correspondence must be read in the terms with which we began this excursus—as efforts to construct a common ground for communication with Smithson, in whom he misrecognized (or perhaps, in the end, correctly recognized) traces of his own project. In that sense, these overtures were, like all of Kepes's editorial endeavors, instruments of a self-regulating organizational imperative, a regime in which science and art were forced together into a feedback loop of mutual reorientation. However, lodged as they were between the São Paulo incident (mid-1969) and the apparent Kepes-Smithson rapprochement (mid-1970), the *Spiral Jetty* and the essay of the same name—in their vertiginous disorientation—actively interrupted the "team spirit" of an art-science collaboration toward which Kepes wanted to steer them, *despite* Smithson's rather transparent, opportunistic efforts one year later to secure MIT support for another project of comparable magnitude by appealing to Kepes's own rhetoric.

Still, there are many reasons to believe that, as Kepes implies, not only might Smithson have already been acquainted with his work; he might have actively engaged it. For example, in a brief, undated, and unpublished text preserved in his archive entitled "Modular Properties in Structural Art," Smithson reiterates the minimalist preoccupation with "primary structures," or modules, by copying descriptions of the six primary crystal systems from Alan Holden and Phylis Singer's *Crystals and Crystal Growing* (1960), an entry in Doubleday's Order in Nature series (fig. 2). The text was to be illustrated with Smithson's own "tracings" of the accompanying diagrams, which he encourages the reader to color in with colored pencils.[26] Indeed, Smithson's deadpan literalness with respect to the crystal and its technical representation suggests that this text was a direct, critical response to Kepes's project in the Vision + Value series. Among the seven titles in that series, published in two sets of three in 1965 and 1966 and one (*Arts of the Environment*) in 1972, was a volume entitled *Structure in Art and Science* (1965) and another entitled *Module, Proportion, Symmetry, Rhythm* (1966). Smithson owned a copy of the latter, on the front cover of which he wrote, in red block letters, REVIEWED.[27] To suggest, then, that his "Modular Properties in Structural Art" was actually a "review" of Kepes's book if not the entire Vision + Value project is to mark the difference in the manner that each drew on the imagery of science.

First, the Vision + Value series must be understood as a self-conscious intervention into human evolution along the lines of Huxley. It was itself the result of a series of interdisciplinary seminars Kepes had convened at the

(fig. 2)

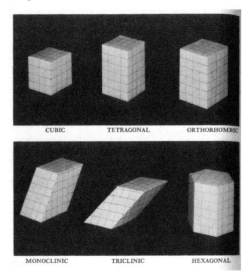

Diagrams of the six primary crystal systems, from Alan Holden and Phylis Singer, *Crystals and Crystal Growing* (1960)

School of Architecture at MIT during the late 1950s and early 1960s that registered an epistemological project with demonstrable debts to postwar efforts
to counter the dangers and abuses of isolated specialization associated with
the emergent military-industrial complex. Wartime collaborations between
science, industry, and the military, such as the Manhattan Project, had become
for many intellectuals the very model for the atomization of scientific knowledge; their explicit proscriptions against intercommunication among specialists working in segregated units were intended as much to keep the scientists
unaware of the uses to which their work would be put as they were to prevent leaks. Such—justifiable—suspicion, that isolated academic research could
be linked covertly to the escalation of the arms race, predisposed many, like
Kepes and a variety of his scientist colleagues, toward an investment in systems models of transparent communication among disparate agents.

But this merely elevated to the level of representation the logic of
the communications network that had already penetrated research universities through capillary back channels like specialized research centers. In the
dispersed coordinates of the Manhattan Project and other wartime research
initiatives, the isolation of the scientist as a cultural agent formed the back-
drop for the consolidation of overwrought academic microcommunities,
which were effectively turned inside out after the war to explore collabora-
tively what was termed the "endless frontier" of science in a space that itself
extended beyond the physical confines of the laboratory into such net-
worked channels as ARPANET.[28] Another way of putting this is that the postwar military-industrial complex produced—at many levels—the *effect* of a
disoriented alienation that activated a desire for communication coincident
with the interests of state and corporate power without being directly
informed by them. Kepes's own version of the ideology of teamwork sought
to overcome this alienation effect through a communicative aesthetics. In
doing so, however, Kepes bound himself more tightly to the logic of control and communication that organized the complex in the first place. This
is what Smithson recognized in his critique of Kepes's curatorial agenda at
São Paulo. Mobilized against an alienation effect that actually served to *integrate* further the subject of postwar technoscience into an invisible, dispersed
communications network, Kepes's project merely re-presented the organicist logic of the military-industrial complex in the form of visible networks
reweaving cultural agents into a base of what he called "human values." This

was why he asked Smithson to address his "Spiral Jetty" essay to a non-art public, a public of nonspecialist intellectuals.

Thus also the presence of *vision* in the center's name and in the Vision + Value series title. An outgrowth of Kepes's earlier preoccupation with gestalt-oriented theories of visual perception, the network-as-organism (a notion borrowed from cybernetics) found its first full articulation in his work in *The New Landscape in Art and Science* of 1956, a book in which Kepes compared the organized patterns revealed in scientific photographs of natural structures to the products of modern art and architecture.[29] According to Kepes, these images all exhibited traces of a universal system of natural order—a system of recurring patterns telescoping up and down in scale. This was essentially the same notion of organizational continuity—from the intergalactic to the sub-atomic levels—that was expressed somewhat later by Kepes's friends Charles and Ray Eames in their film *Powers of Ten* of 1968. And in both cases—the Eameses and Kepes—its function was also the same. We are speaking, during the atomic age and the space race, of the scaleless reinscription of the human into a technoscientific milieu that described the universe as a "system of systems." This was a humanity that (mis)recognized itself as precisely that— "human," that is—only through a technologically mediated ability literally to *incorporate* itself into hidden organizational patterns. It was a humanity that pre-supposed technological mediation—a humanity that came *after* technology, not before it.

In this regard—approaching the disciplinary horizon of architecture, to be sure, but again looking inside from without—we might consider the following. In a special issue of *Daedalus* entitled "The Visual Arts Today" that he guest-edited in 1960, Kepes complained,

> A beautiful crystalline structure in America's greatest city (itself a symbol of the finest thinking in contemporary architecture and at the same time, like the *torre* of medieval Tuscany, a boastful symbol of wealth and power) displays, in surroundings that state an absolute control of contemporary materials and techniques and a perfect mastery of the new beauty of architectural space, images of the torn and broken man. In its offices and corridors are paintings and sculptures shaped with idioms in tune with the twilight spirit that created them: surfaces that are moldy, broken, corroded, ragged, dripping; brush strokes executed with the sloppy brutality of cornered men.[30]

His target is abstract expressionism, and his architectural reference is probably the Seagram Building. But we should not be misled by Kepes's description of that building as a "beautiful crystalline structure" into automatically diagnosing a nostalgia for the crystalline expressionism of Paul Scheerbart, Bruno Taut, and the early Bauhaus. His reference to crystals must be understood instead in the context of the images of microscopic crystalline lattices and other such figures he collected in *The New Landscape* and thereafter. The crystal was for Kepes a module, an abstract integer, a cipher that encrypted order at all scales. This is what joins Kepes's work to that of his friend Buckminster Fuller, a contributor to one of the volumes of Vision + Value and a vigorous theorist of the crystalline organization of tetrahedra from microcosm (as a molecular basis for structural efficiency in nature) to macrocosm (as a template for the remapping of the Earth as a field of intensity and of flow) (fig. 3). With respect to Smithson, then, we must again mark a difference. Fuller's "synergetics" was resolutely mobilized against entropic disorder. And, as Smithson put it, "Unlike Buckminster Fuller, I'm interested in collaborating with entropy."[31]

As is well known, the figure of the crystal, which we have already encountered in his unofficial "review" of Kepes's book, is also ubiquitous in Smithson's work and writings, including his reflections on architecture. It is there in the form of the "empty 'box' or 'lattice'" in his readings of minimalist sculpture in "Entropy and the New Monuments" of 1966, announcing a "new kind of monumentality" that registers an "inactive history" (Dan Flavin) articulated with the formula "As action decreases, the clarity of such surface structures increases."[32] In the same text, the crystal's stasis in turn sponsors Smithson's readings of the "sadistic geometry" of Paul Thek's simulated pieces

(fig. 3)

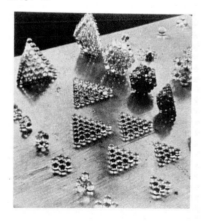

R. Buckminster Fuller, crystalline solids, from Fuller, "Conceptuality of Fundamental Structures," in *Structure in Art and Science*, ed. Gyorgy Kepes (1965)

of torn flesh encased in glass vitrines, works that achieve a "putrid finesse" reminiscent of William Burroughs. So, too, for the "lumpy sexuality" of Craig Kauffman's vacuum-formed plastic reliefs where, for Smithson, "the slippery bubbling ooze from the movie *The Blob* creeps into one's mind. Both Thek and Kauffman have arrested the movement of blob-type matter."[33] It is precisely this winding down of temporality, the arrest of the animate and its reduplication in a crystalline mirror, that is registered in Smithson's collaborations with entropy. And already in 1966 he identified film as an accessory to such an unwinding. Describing the moviegoing habits of his friends, Smithson notes that "'the blood and guts' of horror movies provides for their 'organic needs,' while the 'cold steel' of Sci-fic movies provides for their 'inorganic needs.'"[34] But it would be insufficient to read this organic-inorganic duality as the setup for even an open-ended dialectic that develops a critique of organicism through a negative turn toward the crystal—and not only because the crystal has for centuries exhibited a mobility of its own with respect to such polarities. Merely to allow such a dialectic to pulsate (even interminably and nonteleologically) would be to stop short of the crisis of temporality—a peremptory exhaustion of the biological time of historical movement, of "animate" history—staged by Smithson.

Retroactively reading a work of his own in 1970, Smithson writes of his triangulated spiral sculpture *Gyrostasis* (1968) (fig. 4):

> When I made the sculpture I was thinking of mapping procedures that refer to the planet Earth. One would consider it as a crystallized fragment of a gyroscopic rotation, or as an abstract three-dimensional map that points to the SPIRAL JETTY, 1970 in the Great Salt Lake, Utah.[35]

Smithson had been looking at Fuller's Dymaxion projections, maps that resolved the spherical geometry of the globe into a triangular lattice correlated

(fig. 4)

REINHOLD MARTIN

with the molecular geometry of crystalline solids. He was also making maps of his own, including one sketched during an interview conducted in 1969—signed in 1970 as *A Surd View for an Afternoon*—that charted the vertiginous routes connecting space and time in his work.[36] Shown there, at the terminus of *Gyrostasis*, was his unrealized *Island of Broken Glass*, a proposal to pour one hundred tons of tinted glass on a small islet off of Vancouver that drew fierce resistance from local environmentalists. The coincidence of this piece and others like it, including his maps of hypothetical glass continents as well as the Map of Glass (*Atlantis*) realized on Loveladies Island in New Jersey in 1969, with the formlessness of his "pours," including the *Glue Pour* (1969) realized in Vancouver during the same visit in which he pursued his island proposal, marks the intersection of a glassy, crystalline solid—a kind of broken-glass architecture—with a liquid *informe* in an entropics that promises to run its own dialectical premises into the ground.[37]

Consider, then, Smithson's treatment of the salt crystal in the "Spiral Jetty" essay (fig. 5):

> One's downward gaze pitches from side to side, picking out random depositions of salt crystals on the inner and outer edges, while the entire mass echoes the irregular horizons. And each cubic salt crystal echoes the Spiral Jetty in terms of the crystal's molecular lattice. Growth in a crystal advances around a dislocation point, in the manner of a screw. The Spiral Jetty could be considered one layer within the spiraling crystal lattice, magnified trillions of times.[38]

Kepes should indeed have recognized himself in this image: the fractalization of the crystalline module feeding back crystalline patterns into itself at all scales. But is not the disorientation and confusion of scales toward which Smithson's essay—and his project—tends (rather than from which it withdraws, as does Kepes), is this not clear evidence of—at minimum—a reversal

(fig. 5)

Robert Smithson, still from The *Spiral Jetty* (salt crystals), 1970 © Estate of Robert Smithson/VAGA, NY, NY

of the terms, if not their entropic collapse? Is not his recognition (and rejection) of the logic of military-industrial control and communication in Kepes's curatorial strategy at São Paulo an opening onto an outside, the other of the organism? Is not the crystal, displaced by Smithson from its vitalist origins onto the "crystal land" of post-industrial New Jersey, where "fragmentation, corrosion, decomposition, disintegration, rock creep, debris slides, mud flow, avalanche were everywhere in evidence,"[39] or onto what he called the "evolution in reverse" of the "cold glass boxes" of Park Avenue,[40] is this not the very antithesis of the "evolutionary humanism" driving Kepes, agent of an organizational regime? Does not Smithson's spiral run this film backward, into the irreversible entropy of a counterorganic (and not merely inorganic) ersatz future—a rejoinder to the *Gemeinschaft*, or organic community, Kepes envisioned artists creating out of the systems think tanks of the Cold War?

Yes, and no. Yes, since what is ultimately at stake in Kepes's encounters with Smithson—and vice versa—is a certain alterity. But also no, not only because Smithson showed himself to be more than willing to explore joining Kepes's organic community if the price was right. The issue is this: Smithson, in reversing the terms already formulated by a post-Bauhaus, postwar systems organicism in order to play out his exhausted dialectic, found himself, too, caught in the web of what we can call an "organizational complex."

In "Entropy and the New Monuments," Smithson describes the recently completed Union Carbide skyscraper on Park Avenue by Gordon Bunshaft of Skidmore, Owings & Merrill as the very model of what he calls "architectural entropy" (figs. 6, 7).[41] In the lobby was an educational exhibit called "The Future" by designer Will Burtin, who had just published an article entitled "Design and Communication" in the 1965 *Education of Vision* volume of Kepes's series (fig. 8).[42] The exhibit included a section on "Atomic Energy in Action," with a room-size model of a uranium atom. Smithson observed dryly, "If there ever was an example of action in entropy, this is it. The action is frozen into an array of plastic and neon, enhanced by the sound of Muzak playing faintly in the background." As he also noted, underground director Ron Rice set parts of his 1963 film *Queen of Sheba Meets the Atom Man* in this exhibit, with actor Taylor Mead creeping around the hall like a "loony sleepwalker... lick[ing] the plastic models depicting 'chain–reaction'" (fig. 9).[43]

In an undated draft that contains fragments of the "New Monuments" essay entitled "Interstellar Flit," Smithson makes his context

(fig. 6)

Gordon Bunshaft of Skidmore, Owings & Merrill, Union Carbide Building, exterior. 1960. Photograph by Ezra Stoller

(fig. 7)

Gordon Bunshaft of Skidmore, Owings & Merrill, Union Carbide Building, lobby, 1960. Photograph by Ezra Stoller

ORGANICISM'S OTHER

clear: "The chilly blue interior of a model nuclear reactor reminds one of Norbert Wiener's ruminations in his book *The Human Use of Human Beings*. This arctic of neon and plastic has an infernal beauty. Not just cool, but like ice" (which is to say, crystalline).[44] Likewise, referring to the Union Carbide Building in the "New Monuments" essay itself: "This kind of architecture without 'value of qualities [sic],' is, if anything, a fact. . . . As the cloying effect of such 'values' wears off, one perceives the 'facts' of the outer edge, the flat surface, the banal, the empty, the cool, blank after blank; in other words, that infinitesimal condition known as entropy."[45]

The fact that Smithson goes on from here to further identify his architectural entropics with the suburbs and urban sprawl acquires a certain resonance in the light of an unpublished outline entitled "Two Attitudes toward the City" (with a footnote, "In terms of art"), in which he distinguishes what he calls the "old city," the "city as an organism" conditioned by "metaphors of biology" and "natural architecture" (the architecture of Frank Lloyd Wright), from the "new city," the "city as a crystalline structure" conditioned by "the metaphors of physical science."[46] It is possible that this distinction correlates with Smithson's encounter with George Kubler's *The Shape of Time* (1962), in which the art historian argued for the rejection of biological metaphors to describe the historicity of inanimate objects, in favor of something approaching an electrodynamics of circular causality.[47] What is more, in the annotations to his outline Smithson adds a third city, what he calls a "technological apparatus" identified with kinetic art.[48] His exchanges with Kepes underscore Smithson's aversion to the systems organicism of this technological city—in favor, it would seem, of the entropics of the "new," crystalline one. But what he does not recognize, possibly because he is not reading Norbert Wiener closely enough, are the hidden affinities between his first two models as indexed in the third—in other words, the *organicism* of the crystalline city of "blank after blank," a city of new monuments, of Union Carbide buildings marching up and down Park Avenue and spiraling up and down in scale in the crystalline modularity of the *Jetty*.

This was the organicism of integrated, modular systems, in which corporations like Union Carbide both organized and represented themselves as social models able to maintain dynamic equilibrium via the mechanism of so-called "flexibility" (fig. 10). In the words of Gordon Bunshaft, architect of the Union Carbide skyscraper, "what emerged over the years . . . was the word flexibility...non-specialized space."[49] This was a principle extended into a set of architectural techniques that covertly reenchanted an architectural object—the postwar office building—that Smithson took to be "without value of qualities." Its organicism was invisible to Smithson, who sought refuge from the ideology of teamwork he associated with military-industrial think tanks and technological art alike in the entropic abstraction of its own instruments, which, like the Union Carbide Building, radiated the alienation effect—which must be understood as a technologically orchestrated *special* effect—that I have already suggested served a deeper and more violent level of integration. For Smithson, it still seemed possible, therefore, to move outside of the "system" by attenuating its dynamics. This was the premise of the *Spiral Jetty* and of the essay of the same name. For Smithson, the effect of the *Jetty* as recorded in the film, with its collapse of a remote, inaccessible past

(fig. 8)

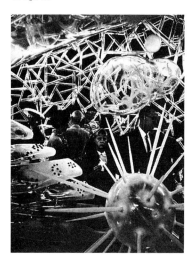

Will Burtin, "Structural Model of a Basic Cell," educational display, from Will Burtin, "Design and Communication," in *Education of Vision*, ed. Gyorgy Kepes (1965)

(fig. 9)

Taylor Mead in *Queen of Sheba Meets the Atom Man*, directed by Ron Rice, 1963 Distributed by Film-maker's Cooperative

onto an equally distant, "ersatz" future and of microcosm onto macrocosm, was to stage a chaotic interchangeability of scale that unhinged the organic order figured in the spiral itself. Even so, the crystal, the very same scaleless module around which the entire process spun, had already been prepared—in architecture—as an instrument of reorientation and reintegration. This is what Kepes recognized in Smithson.

Thus the confusions and compromises that descend upon all efforts such as Smithson's to stage organicism's other, its outside, are and remain inevitable since organicism's other is itself, in two ways. First, in the sense that organicism repeatedly appears, uncannily, outside itself, as when Smithson misrecognizes the covertly organicist Union Carbide Building as an entropic tomb for modernist progress. And second, organicism's other appears as an impossible identity, an outside within, as when Kepes, mimicking the logic of military-industrial control and communication, attempts to bridge the unbridgeable gap between art and science with a homeostatic feedback loop, in his books and in the environments (such as that proposed at São Paulo) in which he sought to materialize this fearful union. Thus the "environment"—including architecture—that hovers just outside the work of these two figures, but also deep within, harbors an alterity gone underground, under cover. Its spaces both exhibit and mask a difference, a becoming-other of the very humanity that sought refuge, in these years, from itself and from its technologies in an interdiscursive region renaturalized by the instruments of war: crystalline spirals and spiraling crystals—digits, messages, feedback. This humanity, produced by science rather than producing it, was itself now on the outside looking in. But if, with Smithson, the entropic flattening of the evolutionary, organic time (progress, again) so dear to Kepes was registered on

(fig. 10)

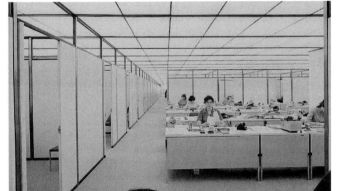

Gordon Bunshaft of Skidmore, Owings & Merrill, Union Carbide Building, office interiors. 1960. Photograph by Ezra Stoller

the face of each crystal and in each frame of the film, within a cybernetically inflected organizational matrix this flatness was submitted to the ultimate modulation of ones and zeroes, which—far from displacing the subject of technoscience into a schizo-delirium of disorientation—may have turned out to be yet another turn in the spiral, reinscribing the "human" in ever more monstrous forms.

NOTES

1. Robert Smithson, "The Spiral Jetty," in *Arts of the Environment*, ed. Gyorgy Kepes (New York: George Braziller, 1972), 222–32.

2. Smithson, "The Spiral Jetty," 223.

3. On the textuality of *The Spiral Jetty*, see Craig Owens, "Earthwords," *October* 10 (fall 1979): 127–28.

4. Smithson, "The Spiral Jetty," 226.

5. Ibid., 228.

6. Ibid., 223. In an endnote, Smithson describes his site-nonsite "dialectic" with a list of paired terms he considers to be in constant tension in his work, including open limits/closed limits, scattered information/contained information, and edge/center (231 n. 1). Smithson's use of the term *dialectic* is somewhat idiosyncratic, since it is a dialectic without a synthesis.

7. Ibid., 230.

8. Ibid., 223.

9. Ibid., 231.

10. Gyorgy Kepes, "Art and Ecological Consciousness," in *Arts of the Environment*, 1.

11. Ibid., 4–5.

12. Ibid., 6–9.

13. Gyorgy Kepes to Robert Smithson, 25 May 1971, Robert Smithson Papers, Archives of American Art (hereinafter RS AAA), Reel 3833.

14. Smithson to Kepes, handwritten draft, undated, RS AAA, Reel 3833.

15. Kepes to Smithson, 29 April 1971, RS AAA, Reel 3833.

16. Kepes to Smithson, 1 April 1971, RS AAA, Reel 3833.

17. Kepes to Smithson, 6 October 1970, RS AAA, Reel 3833.

18. Likewise, only a very few small changes were made between the undated draft of "The Spiral Jetty" in Smithson's archive, RS AAA, Reel 3835, and the text as published.

19. George Braziller to Smithson, 22 October 1969, RS AAA, Reel 3832.

20. Kepes to Smithson, 30 May 1969, RS AAA, Reel 3832.

21. Kepes proposed including Smithson's *Mirror Ladder* in the 1969 São Paulo Biennial. A dossier in the Robert Smithson Papers details the debates surrounding the exhibition, including responses from artists internationally. "Brazil 1969: Partial Dossier of the Cultural Repression," n.d., RS AAA, Reel 3832.

22. Smithson to Kepes, 3 July 1969, RS AAA, Reel 3832.

23. Kepes to Smithson, 16 July 1969, RS AAA, Reel 3832.

24. Kepes, "Art and Ecological Consciousness," 4. See also Julian Huxley, *Evolution in Action* (New

York: New American Library, 1953), 132 ff.

25. See, for example, H. G. Wells, with Julian Huxley and G. P. Wells, *The Science of Life* (New York: Doubleday, 1934), 1468–72; and C. Kenneth Waters and Albert Van Helden, eds., *Julian Huxley: Biologist and Statesman of Science* (Houston: Rice University Press, 1992).

26. Robert Smithson, "Modular Properties in Structural Art," undated typescript, RS AAA, Reel 3834.

27. A copy of Gyorgy Kepes, ed., *Module, Proportion, Symmetry, Rhythm* (New York: George Braziller, 1966) was included in Smithson's library, with "REVIEWED" handwritten on the front of the dust jacket, RS AAA, Box 7. The other volumes in the Vision + Value series, all edited by Kepes and published by Braziller, included *Education of Vision* (1965), *Structure in Art and Science* (1965), *The Nature and Art of Motion* (1965), *The Man-Made Object* (1966), *Sign, Image, Symbol* (1966), and *Arts of the Environment* (1972).

28. *Science—The Endless Frontier* (Washington: U.S. Government Printing Office, 1945) was the title of an influential report authored by Vannevar Bush that set an agenda for postwar government policy on science and technology. ARPANET, or Advanced Research Programs Agency Network, was the communications network set up between key research laboratories, beginning in 1969 with connections between laboratories at UCLA, the University of California at Santa Barbara, the Stanford Research Institute, and the University of Utah.

29. Gyorgy Kepes, *The New Landscape in Art and Science* (Chicago: Paul Theobald, 1956).

30. Gyorgy Kepes, introduction to "The Visual Arts Today," *Daedalus* (winter 1960): 10.

31. Robert Smithson, "...The Earth, Subject to Cataclysms, Is a Cruel Master," interview with Gregoire Miller, in *Robert Smithson: The Collected Writings*, ed. Jack Flam (Berkeley and Los Angeles: University of California Press, 1996), 256.

32. Robert Smithson, "Entropy and the New Monuments," *Artforum* 4 (June 1966): 26, 27.

33. Ibid., 29.

34. Ibid.

35. Robert Smithson, "Gyrostasis" (1970), in *Robert Smithson: The Collected Writings*, 136. Originally published in *Hirshhorn Museum and Sculpture Garden Catalogue* (1974).

36. "Four Conversations between Dennis Wheeler and Robert Smithson," ed. Eva Schmidt, in *Robert Smithson: Collected Writings*.

37. See Yve-Alain Bois and Rosalind E. Krauss, *Formless: A User's Guide* (New York: Zone Books, 1997), and in particular Bois, "Liquid Words," 124–29.

38. Smithson, "The Spiral Jetty," 225.

39. Robert Smithson, "The Crystal Land," in *Robert Smithson: Collected Writings*, 9. Originally published in *Harper's Bazaar*, May 1966.

40. Smithson, "Entropy and the New Monuments," 27.

41. Ibid.

42. Will Burtin, "Design and Communication," in *Education of Vision*, ed. Gyorgy Kepes (New York: George Braziller, 1965), 78–96. Burtin's illustrated text describes in detail his large-scale demonstration models of a "basic cell," an "audio-visual experience," and the "metabolic process," commissioned by the Upjohn Company.

43. Smithson, "Entropy and the New Monuments," 27.

44. Robert Smithson, "Interstellar Flit," undated typescript, RS AAA, Reel 3834.

45. Smithson, "Entropy and the New Monuments," 27.

46. Robert Smithson, "Two Attitudes toward the City," undated annotated typescript, RS AAA, Reel 3834.

47. See Pamela M. Lee, "'Ultramoderne': Or, How George Kubler Stole the Time in Sixties Art," *Grey Room* 02 (2001): 46–77.

48. Smithson, "Two Attitudes toward the City."

49. Gordon Bunshaft, in an audiotaped interview with Arthur Drexler, 1980, in the Gordon Bunshaft Architectural Drawings and Papers, the Avery Architectural and Fine Arts Library and Archives, Columbia University, Box 14.

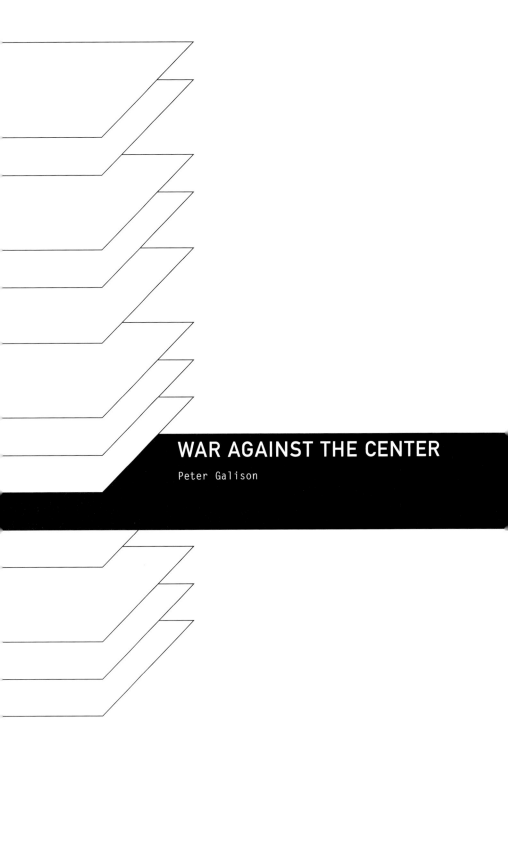

WAR AGAINST THE CENTER

Peter Galison

DISPERSIONS

In the 1980s, we learned to view postmodernist architecture as a form of decentering, a dispersion of form and function away from the critical node. For half a century, the Empire State Building had stood for modernism, pinpointing not only the symbolic dead center of New York City, but even focusing its own central axis around its needlelike antenna. When postmodern theorists like Fredric Jameson sought to contest that centripetal force of modernism, they gestured to the Westin Bonaventure Hotel with its repetitious cylindrical structures iterating elevators and escalators so numbingly that visitors wandered disoriented, unable to find the same place twice. For David Harvey and other late-twentieth-century theorists of urban design, the postmodern celebrated "dispersed, decentralized, and deconcentrated urban forms" that had become "technically possible" only in the previous decade.

The modernist trope of concentration became that postmodernist dispersal, cohesion shifted to fragmentation, and metropolis to counterurbanization.[1] A city-world more like William Gibson's Sprawl seemed in the offing for the early twenty-first century, rather than the compact star of Walter Benjamin's Paris, radiating from its heart, capital of the nineteenth century. Our vision of the late twentieth century: an urban geography of Deleuzian rhizomes burrowing every which way without beginning or end—no tracking back to an ultimate origin, center, or peak; no hierarchy; in short, an end to the modernist, arboreal dream organizing all around a rooted center predicated on located cities, centered societies, and integral psyches.

Among the many meanings of postmodernism (historical quotation, stylistic pastiche, multiple coding, depthless meaning), the removal of hierarchy was crucial for the move toward counterurbanization, easily adapting itself to the 1990s salvational narrative in which the Internet starred as postmodern, democratic, and liberatory. (Even the briefest of Web searches yields hundreds of sites with titles like "Internet = Postmodernism" or "The Internet as Post-Modern Culture.")[2] How did we lurch from the centered modernism to this aesthetic, architectural, economic, and, according to some, metaphysical placelessness? For Harvey and Jameson, the underlying transformation in the disposition of buildings and cityscapes lay in the ever widening gyrations of multinational corporations: the cultural logic, as Jameson put it, of late capitalism. Others, like Charles Jencks, mapped the decentering back to a cultural context of literary theory and philosophy. More recent work by Peter Rowe and others importantly attends to the

(fig. 1)

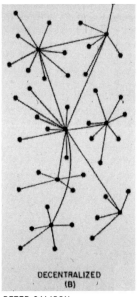

Decentralized network, from Paul Baran, "On Distributed Communications: I. Introduction to Distributed Communications Network," RAND Corporation memorandum RM-3420-PR, August 1964

PETER GALISON

remarkable juxtaposition that has characterized suburban growth—on the one hand pulling toward technical, rational planning, and on the other toward an arcadian imaginary.[3]

Here I would like to point toward an architectural dispersion rather less abstract than that celebrated by a generalized zeitgeist, by a shift in an economic base "reflected" in the cultural superstructure, by an epochal postwar taste change toward suburban life, or by an entropic flow away from an ordered city core. No doubt, such intellectual, pragmatic, aesthetic, and stochastic drives did contribute to the pressure driving dense city cores outward. But this essay begins elsewhere. Not in 1973 with the oil crisis and subsequent economic upheaval, nor with the social upheavals or deconstructivist literary-theoretical work of the 1960s. Nor, for that matter, with the Internet.

Instead it will address bombs: the bombs of the long war that, in a certain sense, began in the 1930s, accelerated after the Nazi seizure of power, continued across the end of World War II, through the Cold War, and even past the fall of the Soviet Union into the present unsettled moment. But we need to step back two decades before the 1960s.

As British and American planners began designing their strategies for the massive bombing campaign of the war, the targeters joined the elite civilian sectors of law, business, academic social science, and economics. Together they composed the Army Air Force's Committee of Operations Analysts. "Operations analysis" was essentially a methodical theoretical reconstruction of the interconnections that held together the German economy and war machine and that asked how it could be blown apart. Where, they asked, were its nodal points, the linchpins that, when pulled, would topple the economy, forcing the Nazi war machine to a halt? Analyzing this whole process—that is, the effects of the bombing effort—was the task of the United States Strategic Bombing Survey, founded in 1944 while Flying Fortresses were still leaving each day for German targets from the airfields of East Anglia. The Survey was an immense affair, employing well over a thousand people, including, as "directors," specific, mostly industrial, experts on their topics. For example, the head of a major mining firm directed work on munitions, the executive vice president and general manager of Standard Oil directed the petroleum division, and a former vice president of the Curtiss-Wright Corporation ran the aircraft division. Appropriately enough, Franklin d'Olier, president of Prudential Insurance, ran the whole of the Survey—the greatest damage-assessment program in history. Among the major figures running other divisions were John Kenneth Galbraith (overall economic effects), George Ball (transportation), and Paul Nitze (equipment and utilities).[4] Starting on the lower rungs of the ladder were Marxist economist Paul Baran and poet W. H. Auden.[5]

One of the first targets was the Luftwaffe itself, a task in destruction that the Army Air Force aimed to complete by pulverizing airframe factories. This proved vastly more difficult than the Allies had expected. After dismissing the Versailles agreement forbidding the construction of air power, the Nazi regime hammered into place a German air force proofed, as far as possible, against enemy attack. Emphasizing protection for their factories against air raids, the Luftwaffe planners sited new plants away from frontiers, in suburban or country districts, concealing structures, deploying camouflage, separating buildings within the plants, and providing on-site air-raid shelters for workers. The Reich pooled patents and structured the airframe "complex" so that spatially separated plants could stamp out replaceable segments of their completed product. It was an efficient, powerful apparatus that, as the Survey promptly conceded, continued to produce an abundance of fighters and bombers even under the years-long rain of explosives.[6]

Responding to some fourteen attacks on the German aircraft industry between July and December 1943, the Germans dispersed their factories as rapidly as they could. For example, initial American and British attacks against the Focke-Wulf plant at Bremen and the Heinkel plant at Rostock were not very successful; worse for the Allies, the bombing runs led the German authorities to splinter Focke-Wulf production from the heartland in Bremen into East Prussia and Poland. Not only did this dispersal open new forced-labor supplies to the Nazis, but it would also, the Germans believed, put the plants out of harm's range. Large-scale dispersion began during the Allied assault of the second half of 1943, and compulsory dispersion took hold in February 1944.[7] To realize these goals, Albert Speer's assistant, Karl-Otto Saur, created a vast "fighter staff" from which one member was dispatched, permanently, to every airframe factory in the Reich even as the fighter staff partitioned the factories into hundreds of sites, many of which stood in forest clearings.[8] Acknowledging the success of the dispersal program, the Strategic Bombing Survey allowed that Nazi airframe production actually *increased* during 1944. They concluded that Germany lost control of

(fig. 2)

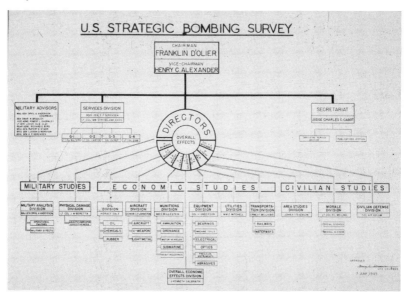

Organization chart, U.S. Strategic Bombing Survey, from Overall Report
(*European War*), 30 September 1945

(fig. 3)

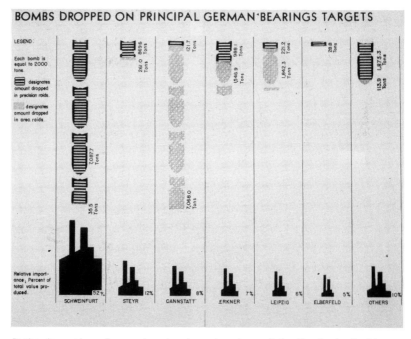

Bombs dropped on German bearing targets, from U.S. Strategic Bombing
Survey

the air not by a lack of planes, but by the shortage of well-trained pilots and aviation fuel.

But the operations analysts selecting targets were not just after particular pieces of munitions factories; their goal was to precipitate a collapse of the German economy as a whole. To that end, they directed a series of studies designed to locate just those plants where destruction would cause shortages to ripple through the entire system. Operations followed. Army Air Force general Henry ("Hap") Arnold, for example, tempted Harry Hopkins with the notion that blasting the German ball-bearing industry "would probably wreck all German industry."[9] At the top of the Allies' bombing priority list stood ball bearings, without which, they reckoned, German machinery would, quite literally, grind to a halt. As the authors of the Strategic Bombing Survey put it,

> On the afternoon of the 17th of August 1943 some 200 Flying Fortresses, flying from their bases in England deep into Bavaria and unescorted after reaching the German border, struck the first great blow aimed at the complete destruction of an entire and essential segment of the German war economy.[10]

(fig. 4)

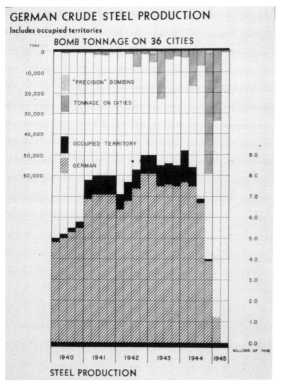

German crude steel production, from U.S. Strategic Bombing Survey

Some 52 percent of German bearing production lay in an enormous factory complex at Schweinfurt. U.S. Army Air Force planes hit the city with some 400 tons of bombs, while the Germans struck down thirty-six of the attackers. The raids continued, with some 11,000 tons of bombs dropped, the most destructive of which took place on 14 October 1943. Again, over two hundred planes descended on the plant, letting loose 450 tons of high explosives and incendiaries, destroying 10 percent of the machinery, 20 percent of the stock, and 350,000 square feet of plant. German antiaircraft batteries and fighters shot down an even greater number of planes than on the earlier big raid, killing some six hundred airmen. As a direct result of that attack, Speer, near panic, put his closest associate, Philip Kessler, in charge of protecting and dispersing the bearing industry. By August 1944, when the Allies flew an eight-hundred-plane raid against Schweinfurt, half the factory was elsewhere.[11] Having faced this barrage, the Germans bragged at war's end, "Es ist kein Geraet zurueck geblieben weil Waelzlager fehlten" (No equipment was left behind because bearings were lacking). American analysts ought to take the lesson to heart, the authors of the Strategic Bombing Survey insisted, "even in the case of a very concentrated industry very heavy and continuous attack must be made, since otherwise the enemy, if he can survive the initial shock, will be able to take successful countermeasures."[12]

These target categories, airframes and bearings, were supposed to have choked the German war-making capacity. Both, after a frantic dispersal, lost the vulnerability that the Americans expected. Consequently, starting in spring 1944, Allied strategy broadened, in large measure because, by then, they had air superiority over the entirety of Germany. Planners began to plot two new "bottlenecks" to squeeze shut. First, the operations analysts began directing airplanes against the synthetic oil industry—that is, oil produced with the massive coal deposits of the Ruhr. They hit the steel industry hard and drove massive missions against chemical plants. By doing so, they aimed simultaneously to damage the German home economy and to cripple rolling armor at the front.

While reporting successful "bottleneck" attacks, such as the campaign against oil, the report itself was, in essence, doing its own reconstruction of the German economy—and its authors did not hesitate to point out where the original planners had failed to find a vulnerable point. For example, they lamented that the combined Allied air forces let loose only 0.5 percent of their bomb load on the electrical industry even though the Germans them-selves (as Speer later asserted) were terrified of an engulfing Allied drive against German generating stations. Power plants were concentrated in a limited num-ber of locations, generators could not stockpile their electrical product, and the Germans had a terrible time repairing damaged power stations. Perusing cap-tured documents, the Strategic Bombing Survey authors reported,

> The secret minutes of the central planning committee, studying the power shortage, make this weakness clear. The difficulties of adding capacity, the limitations of the so-called grid system, the relationship of curtailment and shortage of electric energy to production losses in industry, and their fears that their extreme vulnerability would be discovered, are all paraded open-ly in these minutes made by the Germans in the midst of the war.[13]

Hitting forty-five plants would have been dangerous for Germany as a whole—a result they justified by testimony from Speer himself. And these plants, unlike much else, could not be dispersed. Similarly, "a major oppor-tunity in the Allied air offensive against oil was unexploited" in that the pro-duction of ethyl fluid was crucial for aviation fuel, and ethyl fluid required tetraethyl lead. There were only two tetraethyl lead plants in Germany. These, the report insisted, should have been hit.[14] Or again, "concentration on the few synthetic rubber plants as a primary bombing target early in the war would have proven profitable."[15]

Again and again, the bomb analysts repeated their message: aerial warfare worked when it hit concentrated, centralized production standing at a functional node, upstream of many other industries. Bombing failed when the Germans effectively dispersed their factories. Separation in space worked exceedingly well in other sectors. Beginning in 1934, the Nazis had already scattered their explosives and propellant plants, but only in 1944 had they launched (rather unsuccessful) attempts to decentralize plants producing nitrogen (needed for gunpowder) and methanol (crucial for high explo-sives).[16] Similarly, Speer and his most valued lieutenant, Edmund Geilenberg, scrambled desperately in the final months of the war to disperse J-2 jet fuel for their last-ditch attempt to stem air losses with their new wonder weapon, the jet fighter.

THE BOMBSIGHT MIRROR

While they were assessing the air war against Nazi Germany, the Strategic Bombing Survey analysts had under way a massive inquiry into the assault on Japan. Without reviewing the bulk of their study of conventional bombing, I want to turn to the report they filed on the atomic attacks on Hiroshima and Nagasaki. That text chronicles the horrific effects of the blasts, separately and methodically outlining their effects on buildings and bodies due to pressure, heat, and radiation. Taking the testimony of hundreds of survivors, the analysts asked about morale and inquired about feelings of rebellion toward the government and about attitudes toward the United States. The bomb surveyors even, if briefly, explored the effect of the nuclear devastation on internal, high-level Japanese deliberations about the future of the war.

Suddenly, in the concluding section of the report, the authors took a different tack, and the tone changed. Gone was the absolute distance the surveyors had managed to maintain toward industrial targets, cities, and military objectives. All at once the weapons dropped on an enemy just months before began to appear in an inverted vision in which those same weapons appeared turned against the United States:

> The Survey's investigators, as they proceeded about their study, found an insistent question framing itself in their minds: "What if the target for the bomb had been an American city?" True, the primary mission of the Survey was to ascertain the facts just summarized. But conclusions as to the meaning of those facts, for citizens of the United States, forced themselves almost inescapably on the men who examined thoughtfully the remains of Hiroshima and Nagasaki.[17]

Sifting the rubble, interviewing the wounded survivors, the Bombing Survey investigators began to see similarities between Japanese buildings and American ones, between surviving structures at Hiroshima and possible shelters in the United States. They made it clear in print that they thought the two nuclear-devastated sites were the best argument against war itself, but they also began to speculate on how Americans might survive the kinds of attacks they themselves had just visited on the Japanese:

The fate of industries in both cities again illustrates the value of decentralization. All major factories in Hiroshima were on the periphery of the city—and escaped serious damage; at Nagasaki, plants and dockyards at the southern end of the city were merely intact, but those in the valley where the bomb exploded were seriously damaged.[18]

Medical facilities, typically located in the central parts of the cities, lay in smoldering ruins. So it had been in Hamburg, where survivors of the raids had lain in shock, without assistance, in their hours of greatest need.

Looking at Hiroshima, Nagasaki, and Hamburg, Survey personnel began to see their own large cities. Already, in 1946, they pressed for a dramatic shift in the way those cities were conceived:

> The similar peril of American cities and the extent to which wise zoning has diminished it differ from city to city. Though a reshaping and partial dispersal of the national centers of activity are drastic and difficult measures, they represent a social and military ideal toward which very practical steps can be taken once the policy has been laid down.[19]

Efforts toward decentralization remained desultory during 1947. But already, Congress had ordered the National Security Resources Board to begin exploring

(fig. 5)

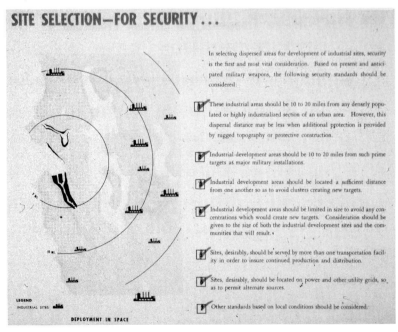

Site selection for security, from Industrial Dispersion, National Security Resources Board, *Is Your Plant a Target?* (1951)

industrial relocation. Abruptly, in the summer of 1949, the laissez-faire mood ended. For it was in August that the Russians detonated their first atomic bomb, named, by the West, Joe 1. Despite nearly four years of warning that the Russians would probably have nuclear weapons within five years of the Trinity test, American policy experts, politicians, military officers, and atomic scientists reacted with an alarm bordering on panic. Called to offer a response to the Russian bomb, in October 1949 the General Advisory Committee (GAC) under J. Robert Oppenheimer convened, only to harden their resistance to further escalation of the arms race. In a surprising and unanimous vote, the GAC recommended *against* building the hydrogen bomb, on moral grounds. A weapon of genocide, they asserted, an "evil under light." It was that anti-H-bomb decision, soon ratified by the Atomic Energy Commissioners, that sent a fissure straight down the center of a community of scientists grown close-knit during the war.

The GAC's H-bomb report catalyzed a swift, hard struggle between opponents and proponents of this new category of weapon. Lobbying began in secret—and then burst into the public arena after a congressional leak. Editorials in newspapers, magazines, and television erupted on both sides, with debate continuing all the way up to President Harry S. Truman's decision in January 1950: the country would, in fact, build the hydrogen bomb. In June 1950, the Korean War began—mobilization, industrial and military, heightened as never before, and the government inaugurated a still continuing national commitment to a huge military establishment.

It was in this context that, in August 1951, the president announced a national policy for industrial dispersion, and the National Security Resources Board quickly followed with a booklet entitled *Is Your Plant a Target?* that proclaimed, "The risk of an all-out atomic attack on the United States grows greater each day, since we are no longer the sole possessor of the secret of the atomic bomb. This means that no industrial area in the Nation can be considered safe from attack."[20] To guarantee survival, the National Security Resources Board insisted, would require that productive capacity be protected: "The dispersion (or deployment in space) of *new* plant development for war-supporting industries can make American production less vulnerable to attack." Space could protect men at the battlefield, the authors continued, and space, by multiplying targets, would diminish "the vulnerability of any one concentration."

Behind this national program lay four principles: first, the dispersion would be of new industries rather than old; second, "no region of the country [was] to be built up at the expense of another"; third, the dispersion would take place within so-called "marketing areas"; and fourth, state and local governments with private industry would initiate the change, and the federal government would encourage and provide technical guidance.

To tempt industrialists, the Feds advertised additional benefits that would accrue to those industries that dispersed: better working and living conditions for workers, greater production by avoiding urban congestion, a healthier, more stable economy. Adding further, quite material sweeteners to the mix, the federal government promised to allocate "certificates of necessity," critical materials, emergency loans, and defense contracts to those industries that escaped the confines of urban concentration. Reading the booklet, the industrialist and the civic leader could begin asking themselves these questions:

> The handy cow pasture on the edge of town may look like a good site, but does it measure up to the all-important security standards? Is it strategically located in relation to labor supply, fuel, transportation, and other requirements for efficient and economical production? Is the site properly located in relation to future homes, shops, schools, and other community developments? Has full consideration been given to... efficient wartime production and long-term benefits to industry and community?... When you have answered these questions, you are on the way to developing a sound industrial dispersion program.[21]

Industrialists swarmed toward Washington to assess the new plans.

Gathered under the auspices of the Executive Office of the President, the National Security Resources Board assembled the key players on 7 September 1951 in the Executive Office Building in Washington, D.C.

Jack Small, chairman of the Munitions Board, told the assembled that he was more scared now than when he came down to Washington some nine months earlier:

> In the intervening time that God has given us we have made progress in the production of weapons, getting new weapons made and creating a force

PETER GALISON

strength, but we are not yet ready and we are in really desperate danger in the event that our enemy attacks. . . . For God's sake, don't get the idea that this thing is over or that the danger has finished or that these fanatic enemies of ours have changed their plans or objectives one iota. They have not. . . . We will have achieved by next year a posture of more strength. . . but still it will not be enough strength to prevent aggression.

The "all-out" could come at any moment, Small insisted to the industrialists, and it could come by intention or by accident. There was only one hope: "Space is the one thing that really works."[22]

Soon, however, the discussion turned away from plutonium and toward profits. How, queried the representatives from Alabama and Louisiana, might this dispersion bring industry to their areas and away from the Northeast, which already had such access to the federal silver spoon? Industrialists wondered aloud how much federal force-feeding there would be, and the officials reassured them that they intended in no way to damage business interests, lower productivity, or threaten a loss of labor supply. This was to be dispersion within a marketing area—not wholesale relocation to distant states.

Small and his colleagues in dispersion left the audience with somewhat vague injunctions. But the national policy did vastly more; it aimed to make citizens of every community into target analysts of their own region. As the Bureau of Commerce patiently explained, "materials and methods for identifying the potential target areas are described on the following pages."[23] Those "potential target areas" were the cities and towns of the United States.

Here is how the Commerce Department directed every community, but especially the top 168 metropolitan areas, to proceed. First, check the list of industrial classifications and identify all those plants employing more than one hundred workers per peak shift. These ran from industrial inorganic chemicals, coke, and by-products to steel mills, engines, aircraft, scientific instruments, photographic equipment, and ordnance. Then identify those locations on a map (naturally not disclosing the precise role of any single plant to unwanted eyes). Combine this information with outlines of heavily populated sections, following the information of the Census Bureau. Lay out two large maps (one inch equals one mile) showing political subdivisions, arterial highways, railroads, ports, and harbors alongside industrial areas.

(figs. 5-10) Self-targeting. From U.S. Department of Commerce, Industrial
Dispersion Guidebook for Communities (1952)

Step I: Take the list of government
designated defense-related industries
and plot their location and employment.
This is the first task toward the construction of areas known as the highly
industrialized sections.

Step II: To complete the construction
of the perimeter of the highly industrialized sections, draw circles of a
four-mile radius and connect centers of
circles containing more than 16,000
workers.

Step III: Label populations from census
tracts.

II. CONCEPTUAL FRAMEWORKS

PETER GALISON

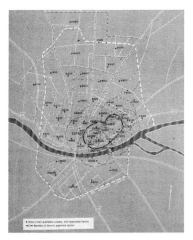

Step IV: To complete the construction of densely populated sections, draw circles of a four-mile radius and connect the centers of circles with more than 200,000 inhabitants.

Step V: Now superimpose the highly industrialized area on the densely populated area. Taken together they form the potential A-bomb target zone.

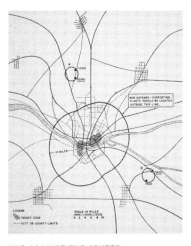

Step VI: Drawing the potential A-bomb target zone on a regional map, planners should now construct a safety margin of ten miles from the outside of the endangered area. All new industrial plants should be dispersed outside this ten-mile radius.

Next draw a series of 4-inch (4-mile) circles on transparent overlays—these correspond to the area destroyed by an atomic bomb.

Now you are ready to identify your region's target zones, "those areas that contain sufficient concentrations of industry or population so as to constitute attractive atom-bomb targets."[24] Just "attractive atom-bomb targets," not sites "likely to be targeted by the Russians"—the reified shorthand compresses all those years of wartime and then postwar targeting. Your goal in what follows is to use these circles to form a target out of the city as a whole by transecting the four-mile-diameter circles once they are judiciously located. In particular, the full target will contain both valuable defense-related industries (employing 16,000 workers in toto) or a residential population of 200,000 people.

Here is the schematic procedure:

This region, outlined by the dark line, encloses the "highly industrialized section" as defined by the National Industrial Dispersion Program. Next, each community is to plot the census tracts on the second set of working maps. At the center of each tract goes a dot and the population. Again you overlay a four-mile transparent circle, moving it until it circles a population of 200,000. When you connect the centers of these 200,000-person circles you have formed a "densely populated section." Next, join the two maps in such a way as to form a combined area embracing the high density of regions of both industry and population. This joint region, the Commerce Department declared, would be known as a *potential A-bomb target zone*. From that zone, measure 10 inches (10 miles) out to form the dispersal limit line. There is your goal: locate all future critical industry and its associated populations past the line of safety, taking care not to create inadvertently a secondary potential A-bomb target zone.

These maps were not designed just to scare; they would form, with a factory proposal, an application for a "certificate of necessity" (granting accelerated tax amortization), facilitating the approval of defense loans, and securing defense contracts.

Bombing the Axis economy and dispersing the American one were reflections of one another. When Charles E. Wilson, director of the Office of Defense Mobilization, came before the National Security Resources Board of the president's Executive Office, he needed an expert on how to disperse industry. To the captains of industry assembled for a 1951 hearing, Wilson sought to justify his strictures about splitting plants by 10 or 20 miles. "Mr. Gorrie brought me a real expert on that. I call him a real expert because he was one of the men who had done bombing in the industrial arena of Germany, and certainly he convinced me that 10 or 20 miles provides reasonable safety."[25] Bombers braced for bombs.

In 1952, Project East River (Associated Universities contracted to the federal government) reported on how Washington could drive industry outside the expanding urban areas, "leapfrogging" away from urban cores. One role was to create "public understanding" of the need for "satellite town" planning and its defense use. More materially, the East River gang reported, the federal government should provide aid to assist in the construction of urban arteries to the satellite towns, provide rent subsidies to small businesses, send appropriations to match metropolitan planning units, offer tax assistance for new construction in outlying areas, demand dispersal to qualify for federal defense insurance, and promote federal loans and grants for the construction of outlying schools, streets, water, and sewers. The government should subsidize ring roads around cities—like Route 128 around Boston—and strive to locate defense industry on it. Above all, the fast-increasing population, office buildings, and industry heading into cities had to be reversed. There must be constant vigilance against the re-creation of new centers.[26]

Eponymously, the report took as its "area study" the imagined case of a Hiroshima-scale nuclear weapon detonated several thousand feet above a 260-acre rectangle in Manhattan adjacent to the East River. With detailed information about the age, structure, and flammability of individual buildings—and recent census data—this not-so-typical piece of America could then be tracked as it shattered and burned under the assault of nuclear attack. How many of the 35,000 people residing between 59th and 72nd Streets (between Third Avenue and the river) would become casualties if a weapon were to be exploded at 2 A.M.? How many minutes' warning would they have to take shelter? How much radiation would they receive? Would a firestorm erupt? Based principally on the results of the U.S. Strategic Bombing Survey on Hiroshima and Nagasaki, this report was, in a sense, a dully terrifying answer to the question the Bombing Survey had posed seven years earlier. What would the bombs that were let loose over Hiroshima have looked like were they to have been dropped back home?[27]

Under the guidance of these various boards and the lucrative draw of taxes, loans, and contracts, one by one, key industrial and civic leaders learned to see themselves through the reflection of a bombsight. One by one, they began plotting their own dispersion. In September 1955, for example, the *Chemical and Engineering News* reported on atomic vulnerability in the chemical process industry. Nuclear weapons, jet airplanes, and the concept of total war combined, wrote Neil P. Hurley, S.J., to blur the distinction between military force and industrial potential. The role of an industry—its functional interdependence on other industries—fixed the likelihood of its plants becoming targets. Chemical-process industries were vulnerable on two fronts: geographic concentration and functional criticality. The conclusion was as inevitable as it was fearsome: "Three well-directed H-bombs on these key target areas would have serious consequences for the industrial chemical producing complex."[28] Two thirds of workers making industrial chemicals lived in ten states.

American chemical dispersion in 1955 was directly and explicitly linked to German chemical dispersion in 1945. Over and over again, Hurley cited the Strategic Bombing Survey: "It is worth noting that antifriction bearings represented an Achilles heel in the German economy in World War II. The Strategic Bombing Survey indicated a paralysis of German industry following Allied air force bombings of Schweinfurt where more than 50 percent of German antifriction bearings were produced." Four H-bombs, for example, could wipe out half the United States' capacity to produce instruments and related products. "Unfortunately, the U.S. has many Schweinfurts. In the Great Lakes region . . . are to be found 47 percent of the nonelectrical machinery production." A saturation attack on that region—and saturation would not take many bombs—would, Hurley noted, destroy a vast array of industries, including that of chemicals.[29]

Throughout the 1950s, the Strategic Bombing Survey remained central to thinking about nuclear warfare and the dispersion of industry. Hurley, for example, in constructing his report on American chemical priorities, reproduced the Survey's list of the ten most vital chemicals for the German war effort, from nitrogen, methanol, and calcium carbide down to caustic soda, chlorine, and sodium carbonate. He recapitulated the Survey's conclusions about the shortages of nitric acid on the manufacture of explosives, the reduction of methanol that cut into the making of high explosives,

(fig. 7)

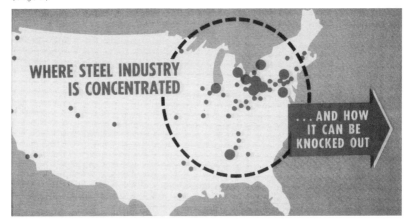

Where the steel industry is concentrated, from Admiral Ben Moreell, "What the H-Bomb Can Do to U.S. Industries," *U.S. News and World Report*, 7 May 1954

(fig. 8)

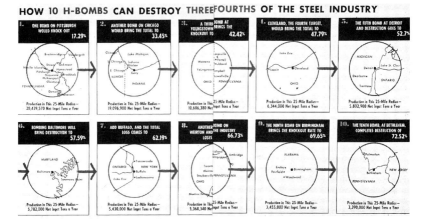

Destroying steel, from Moreell, "What the H-Bomb Can Do to U.S. Industries"

(fig. 9)

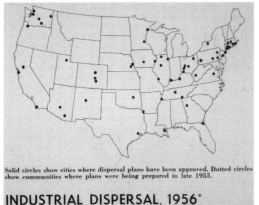

Industrial dispersal, 1956. Solid circles show cities where dispersal plans were approved by late 1955; dotted circles indicate communities where plans were under preparation. From Theodore K. Pasma, "Industrial Dispersal, 1956," *Industrial Development: The National Magazine of Area Analysis and Business Site Selection*, January–February 1956

and the Germans' vain, last-ditch efforts to create underground factories. In this new narrative, Americans played the role previously performed by Germans; Russians took over the bombing role from the Allies. Those who had used their knowledge of American industry had planned the strategic bombing of the Axis; now they became the potential bombing victims readying plans to disperse. Here is Hurley:

> To avoid a repetition in this country of the unfortunate experiences of the Germans during World War II, necessary moves must be made before any outbreak of hostilities. The Germans enjoyed the luxury of learning from their mistakes. It is highly doubtful whether in the atomic age any nation will have the same opportunity—one mistake may well be the last.[30]

Dispersal could aid in reconstruction and also prevention—a stronger nation "protected in space" (as the phrase went) would deter any attacker.

Admiral Ben Moreell, retired from the Navy and in the mid-1950s chairman of Jones & Laughlin Steel Corporation, had just presented to the Secretary of Commerce the manifesto of the purposes of the Iron and Steel Advisory Council. The council had urged a mobilization plan for steel in light of the threat presented by high-speed jet airplanes, long-range missiles, and nuclear weapons that "our prospective enemy" might, at any time, hurl without warning. Big steel needed a complete control center, one linked by telegraph and radio to the steelmaking plants. Admiral Moreell and his fellow advisers emphasized the proximate danger of Russians with H-bombs, and, in fact, as Moreell noted, the Russians had one just a few days after his committee laid out its report at Commerce. Worriedly, the admiral allowed that 75 percent of American steelmaking capacity could be destroyed by a mere ten hydrogen bombs. The council's recommendation: disperse 25 percent of the capacity in such a way that the resulting plants would be split up into numerous single-function plants, providing each plant with at least three alternative modes for transporting its products. It was time, Moreell intoned, to take similar measures in a host of other industries, including rubber, copper, glass, aluminum, textiles, automobiles, and electrical products. Prepare for real costs: for steel alone, the dispersion bill would run to some $10 billion. He continued:

PETER GALISON

Perhaps I have overemphasized the hazard under which we now live. I do not believe so. The facts which are coming out with respect to the tactics and policies of the Communist enemy in China and Korea, added to what we already know about them, justify the conclusion that we are facing a ruthless adversary who will permit no humane consideration to influence his decisions, who will strike without prior warning, and whose ambition is to rule the world.[31]

Dispersion might help, the admiral concluded. Like so much of this literature, issues of profitability and patriotism stood side by side, and he concluded, under the flag, gesturing to the Founding Father, "In time of peace, prepare for war."

Preparations advanced. In 1956, *Industrial Development*, a national magazine dedicated to "area analysis and business site selection," reported that the Office of Area Development had reviewed and approved some fifty-eight of the self-prepared urban area surveys. Money talked. By mid-June 1955, projects valued at $30 billion had qualified for tax abatements under the program.

Take Milwaukee. In December 1953, the city's mayor, Frank Zeidler, traveled to the White House, where the president addressed some two hundred large-city mayors in stark terms: "For the first time in history, cities have become principal targets for an enemy seeking to conquer our nation. The city has moved from a position of support in the rear. It has moved out . . . into the front line." Immediately, Zeidler arranged to meet with the Wisconsin governor and the mayors of Racine, Madison, and Green. Joining the chorus of civil-defense authorities, the mayors agreed that in the short term they would need plans for rapid evacuation in the event of a nuclear attack; at the same time, they needed to begin longer-term planning for the dispersal of the city. By May 1954, Milwaukee had its report: "New building in the core of an urban target [ought to] be prohibited except when it replaces existing structures. This is intended to halt the pouring of greater target values into areas which are already richly rewarding as targets." Spreading industry wasn't all that the report advocated. The new region would need new school districts, novel tax structures, and alternative types of local governments. Zoning would force dispersal from the center, institute bands of open space, and deliver industrial plants to hinterlands deliberately bypassed by major radial or circumferential roads in order to avoid creating secondary concentrations. "There is little doubt," the report's author reckoned, "that some of [these] measures would have to be fought through the Supreme Court before they were accepted by all."[32] Pressed by national codes, taxes, defense spending, and imprecations by the president on down, local and federal authorities competed to outdo the other in the rush away from the targeted center.

America was not alone in declaring war on the urban center. Canada, in the midst of a major effort to plan urban growth in 1956, also began defensive dispersal. The Office of the Civil Defense Coordinator, in collaboration with the Defense Research Board and McGill University, prepared a *Guide to Urban Dispersal*. "Dispersal is the characteristic of present day urban growth," the authors asserted. Satellite towns and villages made urban regions the right scale on which to rethink patterns of communication, government, and demography. "Defense is critical. In modern warfare the initial blow is struck at the civilian population, to destroy at a stroke the ability to resist. The greatest vulnerability lies in urban concentration—the greatest security would be achieved by urban dispersal." That dispersal would follow a survey of a ring located an H-bomb radius away from the regional center. That is where the *Guide* came in. Based in part on a real area and in part on generic characteristics, the book was a how-to manual for planning the scattering of the urban into the regional. Slope of the land, location of water, avenues of communication, and transport needs all had to be reckoned. The *Guide* instructed local leaders and planners how to diagram all this for their future. Satellite towns would perch outside the ring of safety—towns that under no circumstances ought to attract more than 40,000 inhabitants. Ultimately, government-propelled "urban regions" would replace the "amorphous form" of current metropolitan development, alleviating social and economic problems while securing spatial defense against thermonuclear attack.[33] City by city, country by country, the bomb helped drive dispersion. Indeed, coming full circle, the Germans, already all too familiar with aerial bombardment, began preparing for a rain of hydrogen bombs. Hannover, Bremen, and Düsseldorf issued the first three analyses, and others would follow. Their comprehensive treatments covered the status of police, fire, hospital, postal service, and road service following a nuclear attack.[34]

Preparation for atomic war was certainly on President Dwight D. Eisenhower's mind as he strove to resuscitate the long-debated federal highway system. Franklin D. Roosevelt had pushed the idea in the 1930s, not least for its promise of providing jobs. Reports rolled in. The Bureau of Public Roads undertook one in 1938, and the chairman of that organization presided over another, called Interregional Highways, dated 1943. Other reports and standards marched on through the war, with some actually leading to road building—in 1947, crews began cutting the first miles of interstate highway. Still, by the time Eisenhower came into office in January 1953, there were but 6,000 or so miles of road improvements actually on the ground (at a cost of nearly $1 billion).

Eisenhower liked highways. He had struggled across the country in a motorized convoy back in 1919, an unpleasant sixty-two days of slipping on ice, sticking in mud, breaking into wooden bridges, and freezing under snow. The contrast with Germany was stark. As Supreme Commander, General Eisenhower had been astonished by the autobahns, taking particular note of the advantages that road system afforded as he had to move masses of men and matériel across the conquered Reich: "Germany...made me see the wisdom of broader ribbons across the land." On 12 July 1954, Vice President Richard Nixon, facing the conference of state governors at Lake George, New York, read from Eisenhower's prepared speech, and the message was clear: the obsolete network had to go; its antiquated byways were clogging the roads and courts while leaving a death toll on the citizenry comparable to "a bloody war." But Eisenhower's final jab at the current system was stark, holding up for public contemplation its "appalling inadequacies to meet the demands of catastrophe or defense, should an atomic war come."[35] Radial roads would afford clear routes for city evacuation. Circumferential roads, Project East River had recommended back in 1952, should be encouraged wherever possible to drain industry and population from the dense city centers.[36] In fact, highway designers consulted with federal civil-defense agencies, and military planners aimed for interstate highways that would bypass urban areas to avoid "route[s] that had suffered a direct A-bomb hit."[37] It took two years of political wrangling, and it goes without saying that economic, housing, and nonnuclear forces for the interstate were surely among its powerful motors. By the end of 1956, the Interstate and Defense Highway System had funding—some $25 billion of federal support.[38]

DISTRIBUTED KNOWLEDGE

By 1960, the Air Force began dreaming worse nightmares than nuke-laden bombers bullying their way past fighter defense: atomic strikes against the continental United States could be launched with missiles for which range of flight was no longer an issue. The RAND Corporation made its mark with contracts to think about this thermonuclear threat; from the new think tank issued shelves of studies, including the famous (and famously parodied) volume by Herman Kahn, *On Thermonuclear War*. Just as Kahn stepped into the limelight, the much less well-known Paul Baran, an electrical engineer coming from Hughes Aircraft Company's systems group, joined RAND. His job was to develop a scheme that would ensure the survival of the United States telecommunications infrastructure through a Russian first strike—a vital link not only for domestic communication but also for command and control. His response, in a series of papers launched in 1960, was a plan to remove, completely, critical nodes from the telephone system. Like the three highways many wanted from each dispersed defense plant, Baran's vision aimed for safety in redundantly connected, spatially distributed minicenters.

Baran put it this way in one of his first papers:

The cloud-of-doom attitude that nuclear war spells the end of the earth is slowly lifting from the minds of the many. Better quantitative estimates of post-attack destruction together with a less emotional discussion of the alternatives may mark the end of the "what the hell—what's the use?" era. A new view emerges: the possibility of a war exists but there is much that can be done to minimize the consequences.

(fig. 10)

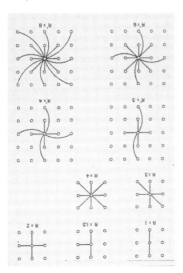

Definition of redundancy, from Baran, "On Distributed Communications"

Survivable atomic war—the goal of the fifteen-year struggle since the Survey crew picked through the still radioactive rubble at Hiroshima. Baran again:

> If war does not mean the end of the earth in a black and white manner, then it follows that we should do those things that make the shade of gray as light as possible: to plan now to minimize potential destruction and to do all those things necessary to permit the survivors of the holocaust to shuck their ashes and reconstruct the economy swiftly.[39]

That reconstruction demanded the elimination of the hierarchical center, alternately referred to over these first decades of the Cold War as the linchpin, the bottleneck, and the node.

The problem, as Baran formulated it, involved new equipment to label, digitally, each packet of information with a "to" and "from" and then to route these fragments over diverse paths toward their eventual reassembly on arrival. But before anything could be built, moved, digitized, or reinforced, the conceptual problem required attention. That reconceptualization now took, as it had not before, a mathematical form: if nodes were replaced with redundant links, how could he exploit the information-theoretic approach of Claude Shannon to count the surviving paths between points in the array? Baran reasoned:

> Let us consider the synthesis of a communication network which will allow several hundred major communications stations to talk with one another after an enemy attack. As a criterion of survivability we elect to use the percentage of stations both surviving the physical attack and remaining in electrical connection with the largest single group of surviving stations. This criterion is chosen as a conservative measure of the ability of the surviving stations to operate together as a coherent entity after the attack.[40]

(fig. 11)

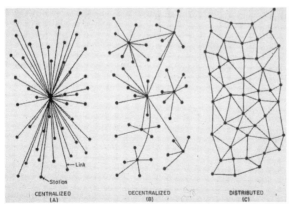

Centralized, decentralized, and distributed networks, from Baran, "On Distributed Communications"

With the result that a redundancy of at least R = 3 would ensure a likely survival rate of nearly 75 percent, Baran could now sketch the distributed system that would vouchsafe communication after nuclear war.

Worst, obviously, was the centralized node that represented the single, critical target. This was the situation with concentrated steel, electricity, or oil plants; it was the structure of the hubbed railway system. It was, in short, the bombing planner's dream and the bombing victim's nightmare. Decentralized nodes that maintained a local hierarchical structure were clearly better; a complete grid structure was best of all. To a certain extent, such grids stood for the defensive ideal of dispersion more generally. By increasing the number of targets, one decreased the likelihood of incapacitation. Halting, abortive, and awkward though it was, Baran's scheme (along with a similar one developed in England) slowly wended its way through different incarnations in the ARPANET and MILNET. But the elusive goal all through these decades of distributed communication was a distributed grid or mesh, a thrust in the first instance aimed at removing the critical node. Though in the garb of nuclear survivability the grid may not appear as the redemptive Internet of our dreams, that technology grew directly out of fifteen years of longing for a world still standing after thermonuclear war.[41]

WE ARE BECOME TARGETS

During the years of World War II, American and British planners and analysts learned to see through a bombsight. Not in a single glimpse, but in the routine killings and losses that accompanied ever more frequently repeated raids. Twenty-four hours a day, day after day, month after month, year after year, the planners and analysts studied and restudied the interdependencies of the German economy, circled targets, blasted factories, leveled cities, analyzed the damage, and struck again. Chemicals: nitric acid, methanol. Basic materials: rubber, steel, oil, aviation gas. Transport systems, electrical generators. And population centers: area bombing by the combined American and British forces killed some 600,000 Germans. In a war that the Nazis rendered ever more vicious even as their defeat seemed inevitable, the Americans' early dreams of precision bombing went by the way. Two hundred planes over Schweinfurt, then four hundred; but also Hamburg, Lübeck, Münster, Berlin, Dresden, Regensburg, year after year. Measuring bomb loads, accuracies, reconstruction time: three-fifths ton of bombs per acre to induce damage of

8 percent; delay time for reconstruction: two and a half months. A calculus of fractions, probabilities, delays.

A new category of analyst had come into existence, more often than not social scientists and industrialists but also humanists, diplomats, mathematicians, and natural scientists. Piecing together fragments of intelligence, examining reconnaissance photographs, they painted an elaborate portrait of a wartime foe. By war's end, the Survey analysts had come to see German and Japanese cities through what one might call a "destructive functionalism": dependencies leading backward, they kept hoping, to the ever elusive linchpin that, when pulled, would topple the structure. Schweinfurt with its all-important bearing factories was supposed to be one such point. And after Schweinfurt there were other "bottlenecks" to be targeted, other cities, other plants, other trans-shipment points.

Perhaps before Hiroshima the bombsight eye had already begun to reflect back. I didn't know. But in the atomic rubble, as the analysts interviewed hundreds of blast survivors and canvassed the broken structures, as they methodically noted which kinds of concrete walls still stood at various radii of destruction, they began, quite explicitly, to see themselves, to see America, through the bombardier's eye. They began to wonder what an American city would look like after the bomb had fallen. Returning to the United States and publishing their Strategic Bombing Survey, things began to look different. They began to see themselves, their towns and factories, on the crosshairs of radial targeting maps. Far from a technological determinism, the all-too-material technologies and concepts of self were fully imbricated.

One thinks here of the origins of cybernetics, launched when Norbert Wiener began to think of the enemy bomber pilot as a kind of feedback machine that could be mimicked electronically; from there, it was a short step to thinking of the Allied gunner in the same way. Then human physiology began to appear as a cybernetic system, then the human mind, then life, then even the world system as a whole.[42] Somewhere in the midst of total war, a technocratic vision of a technical Enemy Other rose to become a vision of ourselves. It was but a heartbeat before cybernetics saturated the writings of Gregory Bateson and Margaret Mead, not to speak of philosophers, planners, and architects.

But the consequence was this: three years before the Russians had the bomb, in fact before, on just about anyone's account, the Cold War had begun, American analysts were already advocating a massive dispersion of factories and populations against atomic aerial attack.

As the Cold War arms race accelerated, the search for "defense in space" grew more desperate: jet bombers, atomic bombs, hydrogen bombs, intercontinental ballistic missiles. With each step, more frantic urging to spread the cities into their "marketing areas." Highway systems, dispersed factories, gridded telephone links. If nuclear war could not be won, it could, perhaps, be survived—if the nodal points of the society could be broken up and scattered, redundantly, through space. Meshed satellite communities joined by an interstate and defense highway system; grids of phone nodes joined by an array of cables and radio links.

Throughout the transformation of these architectures of infrastructure, computation, highways, and factories lay the remarkable practice of training Americans to see themselves as targets. I have laid particular stress on the step-by-step procedures of laying out regulation maps, identifying critical plants, consulting the Census Bureau's assessment of population, and then circling, outlining, and tracing the perimeters of destruction. The reason is that it is a crucial part of these events that each community, each industry, each factory was pressed into service this way, pressed to *see itself this way*, rather than simply receiving a designated perimeter line drawn by the federal government. This was an enlistment, an attempt to draw localities into a frame of mind, a form of moral-cartographic vision. Factory owners who wanted the tax advantages had to attach these targeting maps to their proposals, and only by doing so would they garner the certificate of necessity they needed. An atomic imaginary joined itself to the most mundane aspects of electrical and phone lines, highway construction, and emergency preparation. A state of vigilance both proximately apocalyptic (at any moment the "all-out" could come) and yet full of the banalities of everyday business: profit margins for the long term, plans for market regions and economic tributaries.

Here stands a new, bizarre, and yet pervasive species of Lacanian mirroring. Having gone through the bomb-planning and bomb-evaluating process so many times for enemy maps of Schweinfurt, Leuna, Berlin, Hamburg, Hiroshima, Tokyo, and Nagasaki, now the familiar maps of Gary, Pittsburgh, New York City, Chicago, and Wichita began to look like them: radii around impact sites joined centers to form "attractive," "remunerative," and "profitable" ground zeros. How many H-bombs to wipe out 60 percent of the chemical or steel industry? How many bombs to sever the connectivity of 30 percent of the telephone system? The microtechnology of targeting and dispersing became everyday reasoning. Duck and cover, so to speak, for the Fortune 500 and for the one hundred largest American cities. Safety in space meant avoiding concentration at all costs.

Now, as the politicians, planners, military, and industrial captains never tired of saying, there were other reasons to disperse away from squalid city centers. It is surely so that other forces were already driving dispersal: postwar housing shortages for returning servicemen and their families, real estate prices, racial tensions, access to transport. But the obsession with protection in space labeled and levered the process of dispersion, validated deurbanization as a patriotic duty, certified decentering national life as a bulwark of national survival, linked it with the Office of Defense Mobilization, published it through industrial journals, tied it to the metropolitan planning processes, and paid for it with billions of dollars of tax rebates and zoning shortcuts.

Finally, it would be absurd to hunt in the 1940s and 1950s for all that came to characterize the architectural scene's fascination for dispersal in the last quarter of the twentieth century: absurd because it is always possible to find antecedents for this or that cultural fragment. And yet, whatever American postmodernism came to mean at the height of the Cold War in the 1980s and 1990s, it included the architectures of dispersion, counterurbanization, and nonhierarchical grids. That dispersion had a legitimating logic—if one can dignify it by that term—in the pounding, repetitive process of planning, delivering, and analyzing strategic air strikes along with the destructive functionalism of economic life that accompanied it. It has been a long, mirrored war against the center.

NOTES

1. See, for example, Fredric Jameson, *Postmodernism or the Cultural Logic of Late Capitalism* (Durham, N.C.: Duke University Press, 1991), 38–44; David Harvey, *The Condition of Postmodernity* (1980; reprinted, Oxford: Blackwell, 1989), 76 and table 4.1, 340–41; Charles Jencks, *The Language of Post-Modern Architecture* (1977; reprinted, New York: Rizzoli, 1984); and Andreas Papadakis, ed., *Postmodernism on Trial* (London: Academy Editions, 1990).

2. See, for example, www.heise.de/tp/deutsch/special/eco/6191/4.html; and http://www.usyd.edu.au/su/social/papers/liska.html.

3. Peter G. Rowe, *Making a Middle Landscape* (Cambridge, Mass.: MIT Press, 1991), which also contains extensive references to the vast field of work (cultural, sociological, historical) on suburbanization.

4. David MacIsaac, *Strategic Bombing in World War II* (New York and London: Garland, 1976), 54–56.

5. Michael S. Sherry, *The Rise of American Air Power: The Creation of Armageddon* (New Haven, Conn.: Yale University Press, 1987), 194–95.

6. U.S. Strategic Bombing Survey, *Overall Report (European War)*, 30 September 1945, reprinted with an introduction by David MacIsaac (New York: Garland, 1976), I: 11.

7. Ibid., 16.

8. Alan J. Levine, *The Strategic Bombing of Germany, 1940–1945* (Westport, Conn.: Praeger, 1992), 124–25.

9. Sherry, *Rise of American Air Power*, 150.

10. U.S. Strategic Bombing Survey, *Overall Report (European War)*, I: 26.

11. Ibid., 29; and Levine, *Strategic Bombing of Germany*, 106.

12. U.S. Strategic Bombing Survey, *Overall Report (European War)*, I: 29.

13. Ibid., 83–84, quotation p. 84.

14. Ibid., 45.

15. Ibid., 49.

16. Ibid., 53.

17. U.S. Strategic Bombing Survey, *The Effects of the Atomic Bombings of Hiroshima and Nagasaki*, Chairman's Office, 19 June 1946, 44. Available on-line at http://www.whistlestop.org/study_collections/bomb/large/strategic_bombing/text/bmd1-2tx.htm.

18. Ibid., 48.

19. Ibid.

20. Industrial Dispersion, National Security Resources Board, *Is Your Plant a Target?* (Washington, D.C.: National Security Resources Board, 1951). Based on an Industrial Dispersion Task Force representing the Seattle Chamber of Commerce and the City and County Planning Commissions, under the chairmanship of Ethan Allen Peyser.

21. Ibid., 13.

22. Executive Office of the President, National Security Resources Board, *Conference of Industrial Development Executives*, 7 September 1951, 49–50.

23. U.S. Department of Commerce, *Industrial Dispersion Guidebook for Communities*, Domestic Commerce Series no. 31 (Washington, D.C.: U.S. Government Printing Office, 1952), 3.

24. U.S. Department of Commerce, *Industrial Dispersion Guidebook for Communities*, 4.

25. Ibid., 13.

26. Project East River, *Reduction of Urban Vulnerability*, part V (New York: Associated Universities, July 1952), esp. part II, 17–45.

27. Ibid. Reliance on the USSBS was reported in part V(a), sections 1.3 and 3.2.

28. Neil P. Hurley, S.J., "Atomic Vulnerability in the Chemical Process Industry," *Chemical and Engineering News*, 5 September 1955: 3655–60, quotation p. 3655.

29. Ibid., 3655.

30. Ibid., 3658.

31. Admiral Ben Moreell, "What the H-Bomb Can Do to U.S. Industries," *U.S. News and World Report*, 7 May 1954, 62.

32. All quotations from Oscar Sutermeister, *Reduction of Vulnerability in the Milwaukee Area: An Exploratory Study*, 17 May 1954 (n.p.).

33. H. Spence-Sales, *A Guide to Urban Dispersal* CD-3 (Montreal: McGill University and Canada Defense Research, Committee on Physical Planning, October 1956).

34. See, for example, Dr.-Ing. Alfred Müller, *Hannover, Städtebauliche Luftschut-zuntersuchung* (Hannover: Gebr. Höltje, 1957).

35. Address of Vice President Richard Nixon to the Governors Conference, Lake George, New York, 12 July 1954. Typescript courtesy of Richard Weingroff, Federal Highway Administration.

36. Project East River, *Reduction of Urban Vulnerability*, part V, 37–39.

37. Tom Lewis, *Divided Highways* (New York: Viking Penguin, 1997), 108.

38. Richard F. Weingroff, Federal-Aid Highway Act of 1956: Creating the Interstate System, available online at http://www.tfhrc.gov/pubrds/summer96/p96su10.htm.

39. Paul Baran, "Reliable Digital Communications Systems Using Unreliable Network Repeater Notes," RAND Corporation memorandum P-1995, 27 May 1960, quoted in Adam Walter Bellack, "Behind the Wizards' Curtain: The Origins of Wide-Area Packet-Switched Computer Networks" (honors thesis, Department of the History of Science, Harvard University, 1999), 29.

40. Paul Baran, introduction to "On Distributed Communications: I. Introduction to Distributed Communications Network," RAND Corporation memorandum RM3420-PR, August 1964, originally from c. 1961. Available online at http://www.rand.org/publications/RM/RM3420/RM3420.chapter1.html.

41. Ibid.

42. Peter Galison, "The Ontology of the Enemy: Norbert Wiener and the Cybernetic Vision," *Critical Inquiry* 21, no. 1 (1994): 228–66.

WHY ALL THESE BIRDS?
BIRDS IN THE SKY, BIRDS IN THE H

Catherine Ingraham

Why all these birds?

—Claude Lévi Strauss, *Totemism*

It has been argued, somewhat whimsically, that while representational precision in drawings of animals does not arrive until the late fourteenth century, when it does appear, "it appears chiefly in the representation of birds."[1] Birds were of particular interest to the medieval mind because "they were free, decorative and...unencumbered by symbolic associations. They were simply objects of delight."[2]

We can now (so sensitive is our collective radar) immediately read the signs of how this line of thought goes awry. Precision in drawing or sculpting animals that, at any given moment, "occupy man's curiosity"[3] is rarely a precision that is about the animal itself—or even about attributes of the animal. An attribute of the bird, such as its ability to fly, may constitute part of its attraction as a representational object, but the desire of representation is to fix its object, to stop the bird in flight; this is the primary force that draws the bird into the representational field.[4] As we also now know, almost too well, this "fixing of the object" took a particularly interesting turn in the Renaissance with the invention of "accurate" perspectival representation. An accurately constructed perspective appears to capture objects preexisting in homogeneous space, but it would be equally accurate to say, as many discussions of perspective have suggested, that perspectival representation aggressively subordinates objects and space to its own very picky requirements; that it subordinates everything, first, to the symbolic visual and, second, to the ideality of a homogeneous spatial continuum whose outer conceptual reach is the concept of infinity.[5] "It is not for nothing," Rosalind Krauss writes famously in The Optical Unconscious, "that this geometry turns around the almost unimaginable limit of 'infinity,' a point that is literally reduced to nothing." "Far from nothing coming from nothing," Krauss continues,

> [T]he truth that arises from this Euclidean meeting of parallel lines at that point beyond the limit of imagining is the solidity of the construction's basis in geometrical law. And the infinite smallness of this point in the eye from which the entire architecture is suspended is, as well, an infinite rapidity.[6]

Krauss's use of King Lear's words to Cordelia—"nothing will come of nothing"—constructs the cosmic order of the two motions of perspective, one toward the infinitesimal smallness and nothingness of the vanishing point, and the other toward the solid vastness of the whole world over which perspective casts its net.[7] In a remarkably economical gesture, a bird in flight is thus simultaneously constructed and ensnared by the lines drawn to represent it. The fact that birds are among the most skittish and rapid of possible art objects might make their capture in art particularly noteworthy.

By the end of the Renaissance (the beginning of the age of representation, as Manfredo Tafuri calls it), this is a double capture: first, to get the animal—the bird, for example—to sit still,[8] then to capture it in the lines of perspective representation. By the end of the eighteenth century, this is a triple capture: to get the bird to sit still, to capture it in the cage of the drawing,

CATHERINE INGRAHAM

and to identify it within its genus and species by means of the classification sciences, not necessarily in that order. Perhaps one identifies the animal first and then draws it. Birds thus might be seen as a peculiar testing ground for the artistic science of perspective and the scientific art of classification.

Not incidentally, and in ways that will eventually pertain to all these discussions, birds are also from the sky. Birds inhabit the milieu of the infinite, an oxymoron. They are dark, moving points in the sky that belong, at least in part, to the "infinite rapidity" that maintains the theoretical vanishing point in the perspectival construction. Like Piet Mondrian's *Plus and Minus* paintings—*Pier and Ocean* (1914–15) and *Composition in Lines* (1916–17)—which, as Krauss states, started "from the expanse of sea and sky" and throw the "net" of an "abstract grid" over "the whole of the external world in order to enter it into consciousness,"[9] birds mark an expansive context with the dark plus sign of their wings, which is not, as Mondrian showed, a mark of presence (figs. 1, 2).

The sky is that problematic field of space against which buildings are stamped in perspectival drawings. The unrepresentable amorphous field of "sky" was an interesting problem in Brunelleschi's original experiments in drawing perspectives[10] and continued to represent a problem, representational and otherwise, throughout subsequent epochs of architecture. Sciences of the sky—astrophysics and meteorology, for example—are where crucial revisions in paradigms of matter and space are formulated. Recent work in

(fig. 1)

Birds in the sky

WHY ALL THESE BIRDS?

dynamical systems theory routinely uses bird flocks (and fish schools) as examples of complex systems, where sky (and water) are understood to be relatively open fields of operation. Birds are both occupants of and emissaries from the troubled and turbulent domain of the sky.

But it is a long way from the condition of birds in the sky, and the representational puzzles suggested by that condition, to architecture, specifically the problem of movement, life, and animation in architecture, which is the subject of this essay and the larger work from which it comes.[11] At the very least, this is a two-pronged problem, with those prongs converging rather than diverging from each other. First is the problem of life inside architectural structures and space and how that life moves between outside and inside, implicating the membrane—the structure itself—in the process. Second is the problem of the movement of architectural structures, also oscillating between inside and outside, implicating the occupant in the process. The structure as well as its occupant are, in some sense, in motion and alive, but there is a taxonomy to this motion and aliveness. It is not the same from all vantage points. From a historical standpoint, the discipline of "life," biology, and the discipline of the space of life (the milieu), architecture, come into being at the same moment. But architecture and life have histories that move at different speeds. Architecture acquires a formal distinctness as early as Vitruvius, long before human or animal life are classified as discrete entities with specific attributes. When life is formalized, architecture is already prepared to receive it.

To speak of "birds in the sky" (free animals, individual and collective) and "birds in the hand" (art, science) is a fertile, although perhaps too artful, way of presenting the problem of movement with respect to objects—specifically architectural objects—that submit specific attributes of aliveness (relative freedom of movement, for example) to the requirements of form. While birds are acting metaphorically here, they may also be acting as classical animal "helpers"[12]—animals whose metaphoric role is to act out single strands of human behavior, benevolent or malevolent, inside their own skins. The animal qua animal is inert with respect to these attributes. However, some aspect of the existential status of the animal—which I only allude to generally here by opposing what is "free" to what is "caught"—remains as a necessary, formal, signifier of the nonhuman, a signifier of a paradise, or purgatory, lost or foregone.[13] This existential residue of the animal is important to any account of architecture's relation to life.

(fig. 2)

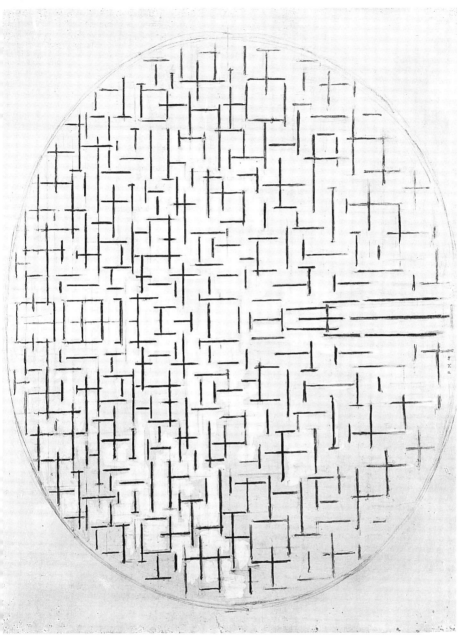

Birds in the Hand. Piet Mondrian (1872-1944), *Pier and Ocean*. 1914-15. Charcoal and white watercolor on buff paper. The Museum of Modern Art, New York. Mrs. Simon Guggenheim Fund. Photograph ©2002 The Museum of Modern Art, New York

But here we again need art theory. Does it make any sense to speak of a kind of artistic production that sublimates yet maintains a formal reference to some aspect of aliveness that informs the artistic material? Would such a class follow the familiar lines of difference between figurative art and abstract art, for example, the difference between portraiture[14] and Frank Stella's *Hyena Stomp*, or between the exaggerated verisimilitude of Leonardo's horses and the huddled abstract bulk of Henry Moore's sheep (fig. 3)? And does it matter if we are speaking of painting or sculpture or architecture? Formal references to "life" in art, whatever that might mean at different moments in time, use the usual paths of representation—in contemporary art, verisimilitude, mimesis, abstract movement; in ancient art, what Panofsky calls the "antique authorities"[15]—many of which are almost completely absent from architectural objects. Architecture uses, relies on, its isomorphism with life—the self-evidence of life—to advance its symbolic relation with life; but what form this takes remains to be seen. Nowhere are architecture's references to life understood to refer to anything other than human life. The use of animal motifs in architectural ornaments is relatively common up to the twentieth century, but architectural ornaments routinely assimilate other worlds, the animal world for example, into the human world of structure, order, symbolic and spiritual life.

Clement Greenberg, again in Krauss's *The Optical Unconscious*, wrote of modern painting:

(fig. 3)

Leonardo da Vinci (1452-1519), *Study of Horses*

The heightened sensitivity of the picture plane may no longer permit sculptural illusion, or *trompe l'oeil*, but it does and must permit optical illusion. The first mark made on a surface destroys its visual flatness, and the configurations of a Mondrian still suggest a kind of illusion of a kind of third dimension. Only now it is a strictly pictorial, strictly optical third dimension.[16]

Greenberg's optical illusion of a third dimension that belongs to modernist painting "into which one can look, can travel through, only with the eye"[17] is an observation that Krauss will find extremely objectionable on the grounds of its transcendentality (for example, the transcendental idea of the pure immediacy of seeing). The idea of a "strictly optical third dimension" was also an important idea in modern architecture, although architecture is complicated, corrupted perhaps, by already being three-dimensional space, which in turn produces the necessity of moving the whole (problematic) body through space in order to grasp the paradox of the "architectural object." The apparent purity of seeing that erases the body in front of the modern painting is never fully possible in architecture, and, indeed, Krauss radically addresses the impossibility of this kind of seeing in modernist painting as well. In this she might be said, in part, to be substituting the dimensioning, moving, gaze of/onto architecture for the static gaze of/onto painting or, in her more precise words, substituting the optical unconscious for optical immediacy. But Krauss would not agree with this attempt to draw her into an architectural reading. Architecture—particularly its literal relation to space[18]—is the very thing art theory, and art itself, contests. The unconscious rarely can find housing for its desires in the literal space of architecture, although an unhoused unconscious is the very definition of madness. Architecture inspires what Walter Benjamin first articulated as a *stop start stop start* kind of seeing that accumulates over a certain interval in which space and time are traversed and fit together.[19] But architecture also eludes optical summation because the seeing is corrupted by movement and the movement is corrupted by seeing. Architecture never gets beyond this jerky seeing/movement, although the computer now is attempting to bring seeing and movement into a kind of reconciliation. In any case, this architectural optical dimension determines the existential status of everything within its grasp.

Why revisit this subject, which has been so well treated by others that one can only repeat the mantras? Questions remain. Nothing has produced more turns of the screw in art and architecture than discussions of the subject and object: the mobile eye/I as it scrutinizes and is, in turn, scrutinized by, its environment; the wonderful persuasiveness and self-evidence of homogeneous space. To be an object, by definition, means to have extinguished the subjectivity that is a defining attribute of life. But multiple conditions of objectivity continue to invoke and provoke the subjectivity implicit in the object's production, perception, usage, and display. There is no pure object. But neither is there pure perception.[20] The object and its reception in the field of life, the eye and its grasp of the object, the "gray matter" that is the milieu of the eye,[21] the life that is the milieu of the gray matter—all are in active negotiation. But the question here is not just the fact of subjectivity that objects call out, nor the production of the object by the subject, nor the notorious counterconstructions of eye/I and world, but the specific kinds of subjectivity that the history of life has claimed and how architecture fits into that history. Are all aspects of the architecture/life question answered by the child's game: *Animal? Vegetable? Mineral?* Or, say, the other, Lacanian, game: *"I"? "Object A"? "You"?*[22]

BIRDS IN THE SKY: LIFE

Almost all definitions of life since Aristotle have wrestled in some form with the problem of separating the living from the nonliving, the vital subject from the dead object. Georges Canguilhem reviews this history in *A Vital Rationalist* as a history of similarity and difference between and among "life forms" that are themselves differentiated, vis-à-vis Aristotle, from nonliving forms by being "identified with animation . . . the life-soul is the form, or act, of which the living natural body is the content":

> All the medical philosophies that held, down to the beginning of the nineteenth century, that life was either a unique principle or somehow associated with the soul, essentially different from matter and an exception to its laws, were directly or indirectly indebted to that part of Aristotle's system which can equally well be called biology or psychology.[23]

Or tautology. Living beings exhibit life. Life is different from nonlife because it is infused with a life principle. Because Aristotle, particularly in his *Parts of Animals*, regarded the classification of "parts"—organs, actions, functions, modes of life—as a way of directly recording the effects of this soul or life force,[24] subsequent attempts at systematizing the world were able, more or less, to sidestep the direct question of life in favor of increasingly refined classification systems. As Canguilhem remarks, "Buffon and Carolus Linnaeus could describe and classify life forms without ever defining what they meant by 'alive.'"[25]

It is therefore a moment of shock when Xavier Bichat begins his *Recherches physiologiques sur la vie et la mort* (1800) with the statement "Life is the collection of functions that resist death."[26] Bichat defines life, as Canguilhem writes, "in terms of a conflict between, on the one hand, a body composed of tissues of specific structure and properties (elasticity, contractility, sensitivity) and, on the other, an environment, or milieu, as August Comte would later call it, governed by laws indifferent to the intrinsic needs of living things."[27] This statement was issued one year before the term *biology* is used in Germany by Gottfried Reinhold Treviranus and in France by Jean-Baptiste Lamarck.[28] The definition of life includes here, and henceforth, the milieu, which, "governed by laws indifferent to...living things," forces the question of the milieu to comport itself, in spite of its indifference, inside the question of life. Biology instantiates itself as the science of studying life—not merely its parts and manifestation but also, implicitly, its essence—at a moment when life itself is being defined as that which resists, but nevertheless is part of, the milieu within which it resides.

BIRDS IN THE HANDS: ARCHITECTURE

How are we to understand the architectural milieu in relation to the biological milieu of Bichat, specifically the human biological milieu, but also the animal? Architecture in the eighteenth and nineteenth centuries, to follow Foucault and others, is increasingly concerned with the civic and secular realm in which reformations are under way in institutional organization, systems of knowledge, medical technologies, and urban planning. Architecture attempts to organize, in some form, a clear set of directions for the construction of appropriate modern spaces while maintaining various connections with classicism and primitive symbolic realms newly theorized.[29] The increased desire of architecture to make itself clear—as a discipline and practice—increasingly enlightens the category of space itself so that it eventually becomes a revealed, exteriorized, orderly, and "principled"[30] space against which the, by now increasingly named and categorized, activity of life can take place. This activity of life, in turn, defines itself against an external milieu that it is dependent on and to which it is simultaneously in danger of losing its life. Life is process. As Georges Cuvier argues:

> It is a mistake to look upon [life] as a mere bond holding together the various elements of a living body, when it is actually a spring that keeps those elements in constant motion and shifts them about.... [T]he state or composition of the living body changes from moment to moment.... [T]he instant of absolute rest, which is called total death, is but the precursor of further moments of putrefaction.[31]

Life is driven by its need to change and adapt, which, in turn, enlivens its environment. The diverse environments in which life resides, however, are not wholly dedicated to the organisms that inhabit them but also to the maintenance of their own orderliness and integrity. An organism might be said, as Schrödinger says in *What Is Life*, to "suck its orderliness from its surroundings."[32] Schrödinger's statement represents both a tempting and tricky idea when we speak of architecture, because architectural "surroundings" are designed by the organism itself. The organism in architecture sucks its orderliness from ideas of orderliness—the inside from the outside from the inside. Architecture is a container put in place by the contained, just as the head is defined and understood by the brain. Neither can speak to the other, by definition. And from this, other varieties of circularity implicit in the question of architecture and life emanate: How have we inhabited, for example, the orderly exterior spaces of modernity as a biological being that responds to an internal order? Does the "design" of space contain or repress the internal springlike adjudication of life processes to external structures? In what sense is architecture isomorphic with human life processes? Or, opening to the next discussion, if human life is process and architecture is the ubiquitous nonnatural milieu occupied by humans, how are we to situate the problem of movement and animation in architecture?

What, in other words, do we mean by motion, aliveness, inertness, stillness? There are, of course, multiple manifestations and definitions of movement and aliveness, some literal and others metaphoric. At one moment aliveness means adaptability and plasticity;[33] at another, life means resistance to death. Cuvier's definition of life includes death.[34] "Motion," at any given time, might refer to the relation of forces between occupant (alive) and building (not alive); to the movement of the building itself that from the moment of its completion, as Aldo Rossi once characterized it, enters into a continuous trend toward disintegration and collapse; to the movement implied by representation, which necessitates a gap between orders of being and is a precondition for the existence of space itself; to the animation of space, or the production of space, by means of physical forces such as gravity, electricity, connections to urban grids (light, sewer, gas lines), shear, wind loads, or circulation; to the counterfeit movement produced by computers and film; and finally, to the movement of the culture, history, and discourse within which buildings and architecture reside over time.

The definition of movement/life, diverse as it is, is classically framed and limited by its opposing terms, inertness/death. In our so-called "postclassical age," however, an age "dominated by images and models of flux—not simple mutability but complex and usually in(de)terminable dynamics,"[35] classical philosophical oppositions such as life/death, motion/stillness still make sense but no longer describe opposing states of being. Motion and flux characterize death as well as life.

Inertness—an inability "to move or act," where no "chemical activity" is exhibited, a totally unreactive state[36]—thus might be better understood in architecture, as Deleuze knew, through mechanics and the principle of inertia, particularly if we want to explore Rossi's instincts about moving forces latent in static material.[37] Inertia is classically defined as "inactivity and indifference." Georges Canguilhem writes, "Life is the opposite of indifference to one's surroundings."[38] So initially, "indifference"—which suggests not an outright refusal but a lack of interest—delicately maintains the oppositional tension between life and death. But inertia is also the tendency, in a resting body, to resist movement, or a tendency in a moving body to resist deviation; in general, it is resistance to a change of state. Thus inertia is a stillness or movement that is fabricated inside the potential for movement or stillness. Inertia acknowledges movement even as it resists it.[39] Part of the argument that links life with death or movement with stillness is reasoned in just this way, as an argument about potentials. The moving mechanical realm of architecture is endowed with these potentials, as is the stasis of a material building itself. The question of the *content* of the indifference that life and a milieu exchange between themselves remains open.

At the same time, inertness is in an asymmetrical relationship to movement, as is death to life, because whereas movement is an indisputable sign of life, and life is indisputably multiple, regenerative, and hermeneutical, inertness is almost always either a rehearsal for death, or death itself, an irreversible state, the endpoint of the arrow of biological time. The asymmetry results from the overestimation of the value of life—which is the overestimation of movement— inherent to the opposition. "To live is to attach value to life's purposes and experiences."[40] The very "postulate that [human knowledge] exists—which is the first condition of its possibility—lies in the systematic negation, in any object to which it is applied, of the reality of the qualities which humans, knowing what life means to them, identify with life."[41] The concepts of symmetry and asymmetry are pivotal in this discussion, partly for the significant role these concepts have played in architecture and partly for the role they have played in classical modes of argumentation. In Darwin, the organism "always has the first word" to which the environment reacts, a proposition that the geneticist Richard Lewontin later vehemently contests on the grounds that "reaction" between organism and milieu is multivalent and consequential, in evolutionary terms, for both.

Architecture is the art/science that has continuously contended with the oscillation between, and coexistence of, the "bird in the sky/bird in the hand" problem since that problem was inaugurated in the Renaissance. Architecture does not gesture, through some kind of representational life-likeness, to an animate past, as portraiture in painting might, because life is always contemporaneous with the enactment of architecture, even when we are talking about the ruin or the unoccupied building whose former life has apparently been extinguished. Architecture, in this sense, is never historically positioned with respect to life, only with respect to itself.

Brunelleschi was, as we never tire of reminding ourselves, an architect. To note again how the intersection of perspectival representation and architecture was significant to the development of both, was significant to the invention of "open space," we can summarize the central premises of the perspectival system. The presentation of a building as an object where inside and outside are equally accessible, and accessible by means of the same instrument, creates the illusion, and a certain attitude toward reality, that all interiors, no matter how hidden, could be opened to light. The invention of modern space was indebted to the idea that space is coterminous with itself,

CATHERINE INGRAHAM

that it is continuous and infinite. The opening of the interior and the homogeneity of space led us directly to the present, where space is a fully open architectural category, apparently free for the taking.[42]

This question of space—which we have seen above is connected with the possibility of bringing birds out of an unrepresentable domain of the sky into the representational domain of the picture plane and the cage—has everything to do with how we are able to get into architectural space and talk about the inside, and the movement both of and inside that space. Representation—as it arises by means of the perspectival model, which is primarily a visual model—and the critique of representation are not the whole story, but they are an exceptionally interesting part of the story. The birth of the idea of space and the invention of ways of encaging space—as well as of decaging space,[43] and, more recently, of creating digital and wire-framed architectures—enable all the familiar denotations of passage that populate our everyday usage of, and reference to, architecture: threshold, room, passageway, corridor, and so forth.

But there is yet another piece to this, mainly the history neither of specularity and optics, nor of movement as a mechanical or philosophical phenomenon, nor of space as a cage, but of the (by now almost fully vetted) "humanist subject" that was born in the Renaissance, eventually to become the subject of what we now call architectural humanism.[44]

The history of perspectival space coincides, through the humanist subject, with architecture and another aspect of the "problem of birds," that is, the history of the animal. The definition of the humanist subject only makes sense, biologically, as a radical, but eventually scientifically endorsed, partitioning of the human away from its animal beginnings.

As part of the larger discussion about architecture and questions of animation (which unfolds in different ways in the book from which this essay is an excerpt), I want to think for a minute about this human/animal history. This includes an analysis of the "animal," not for itself, but as a surrogate form of life for architecture, where we are meant to hear simultaneously, in this word *surrogate*, the (largely French) ideas of substitution and supplement. Surrogacy is not primarily a symbolic construction in which one thing is made to stand for another, unlike other forms of material substitution such as fetishism. Surrogacy is not primarily an analogy, although there are analogical aspects to it. Animals do not stand, for example, as metaphors for deeper or more superficial human beings in architecture. We would never be convinced by such a metaphor.[45] Nor do animals stand for a pure morphological presence. Except in exceptional cases, we would never confuse the shape of a fish or the horned head of a beast with the shape or head of a human being. Surrogacy, in the usual paradoxical construction characteristic of transfers of responsibility from one place to another, is a "real substitution," in the same way ersatz coffee is real[46] or surrogate mothers are real. But the specificity of the substitution is important. Not all non-coffee substances are ersatz; only those that attempt to simulate coffee in texture, taste, or color. Surrogate formations rest on the exercise of specific functions in a way that other analogical transfers of meaning do not. By definition, surrogates are almost always deeply flawed when compared with the "original." Ersatz coffee may function in every way but one like "real" coffee, but the absence of caffeine continuously returns us to a longing for the original. Surrogate mothers—which can mean the birth mother or the substitute mother—cultivate a relation between real and surrogate based on specific acts and functions that supplement what is missing from each side. Surrogacy implies an incomplete transfer, a lack. This lack, which is again, as usual, the evidence of the workings of desire, is not eliminated by the "real" but merely repressed. If the animal is a surrogate architectural subject/object and, in other ways, impinges on the question of form in architecture, it carries within itself the complex traces of its attachment to the human. But we come to know about this animal only through its displacement into form and space, the way it is formed in its milieu. This is, since Darwin, the same way we know the animal "in the wild," as a function of an exterior set of environmental pressures. Later, as I mention above, geneticists argue for the hegemony of genes, internal forces, over these external pressures, but Darwin's theories of adaptation are still with us. Darwin did not at first apply his theories of evolution to humans, partly to avoid theological quagmires; but, as the historian Maurice Mandelbaum argues, he was aware of "the applicability of his fundamental concepts to questions concerning man's mental and social life."[47] Darwin's theory of the origin of species brought human genealogy to a point of explicit intersection with animal genealogy. Humans emerged from a "non-human ancestry."[48] The architectural milieu is not external to human life in exactly the same way the natural world is external to organic life. And the question of what is "inside" the milieu in architecture is different from the biological

CATHERINE INGRAHAM

interior of an organism. But I think the types of surrogacy that have characterized the relationship of architecture to "life" through much of its history depends on the tactic existence of this link between humans and animals and between the inside and the outside (not even thinking, for the moment, in any strict terms about the "natural" or the "organic" in architecture) where adjustments are continually under way between the fabricated and the natural, the container and the contained. The relationship between architecture and the human detours through the animal. This relationship is never about the animal itself, as some kind of being free of symbolism and wild, but instead about the existential contribution of the animal, the importation into architecture of a particular kind of aliveness[49] characteristic of animals. It is this "humanized" animal that slips back into the human enclave at the moment of its most extreme exclusion in the eighteenth century.

The humanized animal is neither fully human nor fully animal. It is "post-animal" in the sense that it emerges from an "all animal" world in two senses: first, it emerges from a world where living beings exist coextensively with each other; and second, it emerges from a world where the animal is, for all practical purposes, dead. Before going to the animal part of this transfer, there is one more thing to say about surrogacy, about why this particular kind of transfer is important. One temptation opened up by a mechanism such as surrogacy is the facility with which one can move back and forth across the divide. Metaphors—linguistic transfers of meaning—alter reality irretrievably; they indicate the metaphoricity of reality. But the surrogate relation is more protective of the, albeit transitory, "real." It is thus, in a sense, appropriate that architecture—a discipline that historically has seen itself as protecting reality—should use the animal in a surrogate, rather than a more extreme metaphoric, way. While I have said that architecture detours through the animal on the way to the human, I would have to say also that architecture detours through the human on the way to the animal. Surrogacy, in other words, is primarily a way of stating that life, from an architectural point of view, whether human or animal, is understood to be displacement—the disruption, in architectural terms, of place and of the realities connected to place. This displacement is mechanistic in the sense that it moves bodies and forms around, just as architecture does. Having said this, I want to leave the oscillatory aspects of surrogacy in the rhetorical domain in order to consider what I am calling the animal side of things.

François Jacob, in his dense and extremely interesting book *The Logic of Life*, characterizes the natural world before the Renaissance as follows: prior to the beginning of modern science in the seventeenth century (from antiquity through the Renaissance), "each mundane object, each plant and each animal can be described as a particular combination of matter and form. Matter always consists of the same four elements" (earth, air, water, fire) and matter is indestructible; otherwise everything would have already been used up. Jacob remarks that an object, during this time, "is thus characterized by form alone.... The hand that confers form on matter to create stars, stones or living beings is that of Nature... [which is] an executive agent, an operative principle working under God's guidance."[50] Thus "reading nature," prior to the Renaissance, is a matter of deciphering clues about relationships, similitudes, that might reveal this divine intention. Resemblances between things, for example, are particularly interesting because they argue for the overarching existence of a "design" and a divine system of symbolic relation. "The resemblance of a plant to the eye," Jacob writes, is "the sign that it should be used for treating diseases of the eyes. The very nature of things is hidden behind the similitudes."[51]

In this period, "form ... distinguishes one animal, or being, or thing, from the next, [but] form does not fix this being in one place." Jacob explains:

> When Aldrovandus deals with the horse, he describes its shape and appearance in four pages, but he needs nearly three hundred pages to relate in detail the horse's names, its breeding, habitat, temperament, docility, memory, affection, gratitude, fidelity, generosity, ardor for victory, speed, agility, prolific power, sympathies, diseases and their treatment; after that the monstrous horses appear, the prodigious horses, fabulous horses, celebrated horses, with the descriptions of the places where they won glory, the role of horses in equitation, harness, war, hunting games, farming, processions, the importance of the horse in history, mythology, literature, proverbs, paintings, sculpture, medals.[52]

Because of the vast, diverse, and interrelated place occupied by each being, the world cannot be hierarchized or arranged according to form, as happens later with the invention of species: "It is difficult to decide where one domain begins and ends."[53] Various Aristotelian distinctions among plants, animals, and man that persist during this period refer not to distinctions between forms but to distinctions between the kinds of souls invested in them by a divine being. And while the separation, on mostly metaphysical or theological grounds, between humans and beasts is discernible, beasts themselves are more than mixed up with plants and minerals. Monsters and hybrid beings have access to the human enclave by means of this system of diverse associationism, by means of resemblances, dissimulations, and visual and formal likenesses.[54]

Subsequently, in the seventeenth and eighteenth centuries, living bodies are "scraped clean" (as Jacob puts it) of their encrusted sets of relations, and, through systems and techniques of classifying differences (species), the continuum of things merging into things and things into space is cut into so that beings hold a place uniquely their own. Speciation arises out of various developments in locational technologies (such as mapping) and through applied mathematical principles. It also arises, however, from a different view of objects in the world. "The analysis of objects," Jacob says,

> Now...requires that...objects...be represented by a system of signs. The sign is no longer the stigma placed on things by the Creator to enable man to divine his intentions. It becomes an integral part of human understanding, both a product elaborated by thought for the purpose of analysis and a tool necessary for exercising memory, imagination, or reflection. Among the sign systems, mathematics is evidently supreme. By means of mathematical symbols it is possible to divide up the continuum of things, to analyze them and rearrange them in various combinations.[55]

Newtonian science organizes the world in terms of algebraic analysis that expresses universal laws; and the universality of these laws suggests that "living beings were machines in which only shapes, sizes and movements were significant."[56] As Jacob says, "that [identification with machines] was not a metaphor....It was an exact identification."[57] Mathematical speciation parallels linguistic speciation, the language of classification which is the language of language itself.

So the formation of the humanist subject is, first, an act of freeing the subject from fantastic and multiple relations and, second, later on, an act of granting the subject scientific status as a mechanical force, a mathematical entity that acts according to universal laws, subject to gravity.[58] But still, until the end of the eighteenth century, "there is no clear boundary between beings and things. The living extended without a break into the inanimate. . . . Everything was still continuous in the world and, said Buffon, 'one can descend by imperceptible degrees from the most perfect creature to the most shapeless matter, from the best organized animal to the roughest mineral.' There was as yet no fundamental division between the living and the non-living."[59] Not incidentally, the focus on laws and movement—that is, finding the laws that unified the forces governing the world—privileged things that move, animate life.[60] This gradual separation between living and nonliving eventually brings the human being into a fully separate place with respect to its surroundings, to the architectures that house it, and to the animal. This place is not only biologically separate, it is also technically and economically separate. This will prove to be, ultimately, a false separation, as genetic research and the computer now show us; but under its heading, architecture entered into the scientific age.

It is not exactly right, perhaps, to say that from the invention of perspective onward the animal is capable of being not only metaphorically caged but literally caged as well, but it may be almost right to say that it was in the Renaissance that human beings, architecture, cagelike space, and animals in spaces of capture, began to exhibit coordinated histories. The interesting emergence of new systems for distinguishing beings from each other—the classification sciences—by necessity, then, involved the Renaissance invention of space as a homogeneous medium and the seventeenth- and eighteenth-century carving up of space into niches that could be occupied by one body at a time with a distinct and measurable boundary around it.

Perspectival representation organized the cage as a space of infinite but controlled variation within a frame, and this also had interesting reverberations for theories of the evolution and generation of living beings that unfolded in subsequent eras. Darwin's theory of evolution, for example, depends on forces of adaptation and morphological variation that operate inside a stream of possibilities out of which a moment of "fit" between organism and milieu arises. This idea would have been impossible without an idea of space that could simultaneously fix a location—geographical, regional—as a space of identification and place a living body firmly inside that location. "Firmly inside" does not mean, however, that space anticipates its precise

CATHERINE INGRAHAM

occupants, or vice versa. Perspectival space, particularly in architecture, has a certain proleptic feel to it. We represent spaces using perspective, design them, with an occupant in mind that generally governs the dimensions of the space. In designing perspectival space, the space cage, we imagine only those animals that can be caged. And we imagine this space as neutral, not so much an environment as a transparent organizing principle. But the adaptive and reproductive pressure from the side of the organism turns even philosophical or heuristic cages into environments. This happens routinely with architecture—the diagram, plan, elevation, becomes, in effect, a biological environment. The particular spaces occupied by living bodies, in Darwin's theory of evolution, are not set in advance as appropriate to that organism. Particular species accumulate in particular places over a period of time because there is, for however long it lasts, reproductive success in that location. "With Darwin . . . the formation of an organism precedes its adaptation. Nature only favors what already exists. . . . [V]ariation occurs at random . . . without any relation between cause and result. Only after a new being has emerged is it confronted by the conditions of existence."[61] In Darwin, the organism is born and then buys a house, in which it finds reproductive happiness or not. Again, Lewontin argues the question of fit between organism and environment differently. In his scheme, the organism and the house are, in a sense, reproductive partners. Darwin's is the classical view of the house; Lewontin's, the post-animal, and later, postclassical view of the house.

The localization of space and its encagement through identification and coordinate systems is not, paradoxically, a system of reference to what lies outside of it. This spatial construct is hermetic and self-sufficient in spite of the fact that this space has to be specifically produced. Insofar as organisms exist as individuals, they exist in this nonreferential space; they are captured. But insofar as organisms exist as part of an evolutionary process that is off-stage—a history of generation congealed in the individual but taking place somewhere else in time and space—they are not captured, they are loose; wild cards. Darwin, as a traveler, studied networks of interactions between living beings and geographically distinct places.[62] On the Galapagos Islands, the diversity of bird species does not suggest evolutionary diversity so much as a community of descent: "All the species of this family are thus linked together, writes Darwin, by 'indirect lines of affinity of various lengths going back into the past through a large number of predecessors.'"[63] François Jacob suggests that these island birds are formative for Darwin's theory. Birds—because they are unlike other vertebrates in that "a large number of forms connecting... [bird] ancestors to those of other forms have vanished"[64]—seem to prove Darwin's theory of a "hidden bond" between all species.

"All true classification is genealogical," writes Darwin. "Community of descent is the hidden bond which naturalists have been unconsciously seeking, and not some unknown plan of creation, or the enunciation of general propositions, and the mere putting together and separating objects more or less alike."[65] He continues:

> Each island has its own birds, as it were.... But all these birds have a family likeness with each other.... It is as if the differences stood out on a background of resemblances, as if these various species of birds were all derived from a common ancestor, and their individual characteristics were only the result of their isolation in their geographical territories.[66]

The distinctness of species is due not to multiple origins for living beings but to a "tree" of divergences whereby a small number of ancestors eventually branch into a large number of adaptive offspring. Difference is a matter of degree of difference in the sense that clear-cut distinctions "are due to the extinction of intermediate forms."[67] Within this sense of continuum, there is also, however, "contingency." No overarching plan governs the picture:

> There is no sudden appearance of new organs which seem to have been specially created for some purpose.... There is no longer a simple, unique and continuous impulse to produce new forms in the course of time. The emergence of organisms represents the consequence of a long struggle between opposing actions, the resultant of contending forces, the outcome of a conflict between the organism and its environment.[68]

The idea of shaping the world, which in antiquity suggested that the whole world had been constructed according to a grand plan that had to be discerned here and there by means of the signs of Nature, breaks into parts with the invention of perspective and, two centuries later, the discoveries/inventions of natural history and science. So it is no surprise that architecture as a historical discipline—a discipline with an orderly past, a series of comparative types, species of form—models itself after the natural sciences. The entanglement of the animal with the human, and the consequences of this entanglement for architecture, is only evident when perspectival representation begins to give human beings and animals a place to stand that can be "named," coordinated, such that he/she can be disentangled in and from space—from the space of other living and nonliving beings—and, simultaneously, recaged by means of similarities and differences. This is not to dismiss the diversity of architectural types, particularly those that depart from, or critique, the episteme of the spacebox, nor is it to ignore the different interpretations of what it means for an organism to "inhabit" a milieu. It is only to say that some part of the genealogy of architectural space—a history and genealogy we have been studying intensively throughout the twentieth century as if the category of space itself were so startlingly new, or so stunningly coalesced, that we could not get enough of it—begins with these representational and locational strategies, and animal-surrogacy, issues.

NOTES

I am very grateful to Paulette Singley for her generous reading of this and other chapters. Some of her excellent recommendations were pivotal to my thinking on this subject matter. (C.I.)

1. Kenneth Clark, *Animals and Men: Their Relationship as Reflected in Western Art from Prehistory to the Present Day* (New York: William Morrow and Co., 1977).

2. Ibid. Clark writes: "[Birds] had an inexhaustible fascination for the medieval mind and eye.... [They] abound in the margins of fourteenth-century MSS., the most beautiful being in the Sherborne Missal; and among the source-books which were circulated to the various scriptoria were drawings of the various birds and beasts that might be thought appropriate to the margin of a book, or on a piece of *opus Anglicanum* embroidery.... They were probably not done from life, but were derived from life drawings done with great accuracy and power of observation" (26). And later in the same book, under the heading "Animals Observed": "The way back to Nature was only fully opened by the Italian Renaissance, when the physical work became an object of passionate study for its own sake" (108).

3. Ibid., 26.

4. It is interesting in this regard, as discussed in n. 3 above, that medieval artists worked from models of life rather than life itself. In reproducing these models, the problem of flight (of flightiness in an artistic object) would have already been resolved.

5. The three most pertinent discussions of perspective—Erwin Panofsky, *Perspective as Symbolic Form*, trans. Christopher S. Wood (New York: Zone Books, 1991); Hubert Damisch, *The Origin of Perspective*, trans. John Goodman (Cambridge, Mass.: MIT Press, 1994); and Robin Evans, *The Projective Cast* (Cambridge, Mass.: MIT Press, 1995)—all speak to the larger field of meaning embraced by perspective, not simply the mathematical construction.

6. Rosalind Krauss, *The Optical Unconscious* (Cambridge, Mass.: MIT Press, 1993), 213. She continues: "If, in the art historian's perspective diagrams, the eye is always pictured open and fixated, staring into the pyramid's tunnel, that's because it is an eye that sees with such dazzling quickness that it has no need to blink. It sees in a twinkling, before the blink. And this twinkling, this infinite brevity or immediacy of the gaze, is the analogue to the picture's own condition in the all-at-once, for painting's ontological truth as pure simultaneity."

7. This is not Lear's world, however, where every object and subject faces the crisis of losing its form, where nothing threatens to come of nothing, a monstrous inheritance. See Catherine Ingraham, *Architecture and the Burdens of Linearity* (New Haven: Yale University Press, 1998), esp. chap. 1.

8. "[H]ow did he ever persuade a hare to sit still long enough for him to record all that detail?" Clark asks, speaking of Albrecht Dürer. Clark, *Animals and Men*, 28.

9. Krauss, *Optical Unconscious*, 12. Krauss continues: "The whole of the external world. That, I can imagine the social historians saying, is a bit of an exaggeration. It's sea and sky, or dunes, sea, and sky, that have been segmented off from the rest of the world, from everything political, or economic, or historic, and themselves made into an abstraction of that world. . . . And they would be right, of course. The sea and sky are a way of packaging 'the world' as a totalized image, as a picture of completeness, as a field constituted by the logic of its own frame. But its frame is a frame of exclusions and its field is the world of ideological construction."

10. Damisch, *Origin of Perspective*, 89–90. Damisch quotes Antonio di Tuccio Manetti, *The Life of Brunelleschi*, trans. Catherine Enggass (University Park: Pennsylvania State University Press, 1970), 42–44: "And insofar as he had to show the sky, that is, where the painted walls stamped themselves against the air, he used silver burnished in such a way that natural air and sky were reflected in it, and even clouds that one saw pass by in this silver pushed by the wind, when it was blowing" (89). The sky in the drawing mirrors the actual sky.

11. This essay is a slightly adapted chapter from the author's *The Discipline of the Milieu: Architecture and Post-Animal Life*, manuscript in progress.

12. Harriet Ritvo, *The Animal Estate* (Cambridge, Mass.: Harvard University Press, 1987). Ritvo discusses the "animal helper" in children's fiction as a hybrid creature whose role is to carry human virtues in animal form.

13. The existential status of animals in what I call a "post-animal world" is characterized as a "non-psychological living form." The animal is also speechless. Catherine Ingraham, *The Discipline of the Milieu: Architecture and Post-Animal Life*, manuscript in progress.

14. Portraiture is an interesting case. "It is no accident," Walter Benjamin writes in "The Work of Art in the Age of Mechanical Reproduction," "that the portrait was the focal point of early photography. The cult of remembrance of loved ones, absent or dead, offers a last refuge for the cult value of the picture. For the last time the aura emanates from the early photographs in the fleeting expression of a human face." But gradually, as the exhibition value of photography gains hegemony, and film becomes the art of the twentieth century, "man [the film actor] has to operate with a whole living person, yet foregoing its aura." In Hannah Arendt, ed., *Illuminations*, trans. Harry Zohn (New York: Schocken Books, 1969), 225–29.

15. Panofsky, *Perspective as Symbolic Form*, 63.

16. Krauss, *Optical Unconscious*, 7.

17. Ibid.

18. Mark Linder discussed this question of the literal in his public lecture "Literal 1967: How *Art*

Forum Stole Architecture," presented at Pratt Institute, Brooklyn, New York, January 31, 2002. See also Linder's book on the same subject, *Nothing Less Than Literal: Architecture After Minimalism* (Cambridge, Mass.: MIT Press, forthcoming).

19. This movement is somewhat like that created by early optical instruments such as the zootrope, in which the progression of openings and closings counterfeits the intervals between different positions of a bird's wings as it flies and thus is able to counterfeit the movement of flight. See images of the zootrope from *La Nature* (1888) in Krauss, *Optical Unconscious*, 206–10.

20. "Now I don't know what perception is and I don't believe anything like perception exists," writes Jacques Derrida at the end of "Structure, Sign and Play," in *The Structuralist Controversy*, ed. Richard Macksey (Baltimore: Johns Hopkins University Press, 1969), 20.

21. Krauss elaborates: "If the Renaissance had diagrammed the punctuality of [the infinite vanishing point], it was modernism that insisted on it, underscored it, made the issue of this indivisible instant of seeing serve as a fundamental principle in the doctrine of its aesthetic truth." *Optical Unconscious*, 213. The counterargument—the "antivision" argument—pits the "gray matter" (Duchamps) against the "retinal" (Greenberg).

22. Krauss, *Optical Unconscious*. "[Lacan] sees that identity in all its power and resonance comes from being able to break into this circuit of impersonal rules and to join it by saying, and meaning, 'I.' But he also believes—and here is the slippage between deictic and deixic—that the pointing gesture, the 'this,' which initially singled out the subject as unique and instituted it as the one who can identify itself as 'I,' this gesture comes from outside the subject. It is a primary pointing to the infant by someone or something else, a pointing constituted for example by the look of the mother, a look that names the child to itself, for itself" (23–24).

23. Georges Canguilhem, *A Vital Rationalist*, ed. Francois Delaporte, trans. Arthur Goldhammer (New York: Zone Books, 1994), 67.

24. See Aristotle, *Parts of Animals, Movement of Animals, Progression of Animals*, trans. E. S. Forster (Cambridge, Mass.: Harvard University Press, 1993), 53–73. Aristotle writes:

> We must [also] decide whether we are to discuss the processes by which each animal comes to be formed . . . or rather the animal as it actually is. . . . [W]e ought first to take the phenomena that are observed in each group, and then go on to state their causes. . . . [T]he process is for the sake of the actual thing, the thing is not for the sake of the process. . . . [W]e need not concern ourselves with Soul in its entirety; because it is not Soul in its entirety that is an animal's 'nature,' but some part or parts of it (61).

25. Canguilhem, *Vital Rationalist*, 68.

26. Ibid., 69.

27. Ibid., 68. The italics are the author's. That the definition of life includes here, and henceforth, the milieu, which is "governed by laws indifferent to the intrinsic needs of living things," forces the question of the milieu in the midst of the question of life.

28. Ibid., 69.

29. Anthony Vidler, *The Writing of the Walls* (Princeton, N.J.: Princeton Architectural Press, 1987). "The careful collations of ancient and modern examples of primitive life . . . had the effect, important for the history and theory of architecture, of establishing a belief in the intimate, if not instrumental, relationship between social customs and the forms of dwelling, between religious rituals and the iconography of monuments" (12).

30. Anthony Vidler, *Writing of the Walls*, 12–21. The word principled recurs throughout Vidler's discussion but particularly with respect to the example of Robinson Crusoe as the exemplary eighteenth-century settler, "a paradigm of economic man, mercantile and colonialist ... in no way a 'natural man'.... Defoe's materialist account of architectural origins [in *Robinson Crusoe*] ... was both progressive and principled, embodying the simple and fundamental precepts of all good building, joined inextricably to economic and social development" (14).

31. Quoted in Canguilhem, *Vital Rationalist*, 70.

32. Quoted in Evelyn Fox Keller, *Refiguring Life: Metaphors of Twentieth-Century Biology* (New York: Columbia University Press, 1995), 68.

33. Canguilhem, *Vital Rationalist*, 17.

34. See, in particular, ibid., 74–75.

35. Barbara Herrnstein Smith and Arkady Plotnitsky, eds., *Mathematics, Science and Postclassical Theory*, special issue of *The South Atlantic Quarterly* 94, no. 2 (spring 1995): 379.

36. *American Heritage Dictionary*, 2nd College ed., s.v. "inert."

37. Gilles Deleuze and Félix Guattari, *Nomadology: The War Machine*, trans. Brian Massumi (New York: Semiotext(e), 1986), 36–37.

38. Quoted in Canguilhem, *Vital Rationalist*, 72–73.

39. Ibid., 73–74. "It may be paradoxical to attempt to explain a power such as life in terms of concepts and laws based on the negation of that power" (73).

40. Ibid., 74.

41. Ibid., 72.

42. The question of space has always been connected with issues of representation, even before the Renaissance. Vidler's work on Daniel Libeskind's Holocaust Museum, in which he remarks on how that museum puts space itself on stage by means of a void housed in an "orphaned architecture," is suggestive of how architecture might involute, on its own exhibitionist behalf, the problem of space and representation. Anthony Vidler, lecture presented at the Graduate School of Architecture and Planning, Columbia University, New York, New York, 2001.

43. Everyone noticed, already by the fifteenth century, that the space cage could be spoofed by using mirrors, enfilades, and bent perspectives.

44. The "Renaissance man" was a figure of specific learned accomplishments. Humanism was also the beginning of the secularization of culture.

45. A student at a lecture asked, "Do you mean that when I get to be an architect, I will be designing for animals?" I answered, "Yes, but you will know how to do it." My point was that the architectural conception of the human as animal is already built into the process of designing and conceptualizing buildings.

46. The French word for "surrogacy" is *ersatz*.

47. Maurice Mandelbaum, *History, Man, and Reason* (Baltimore: Johns Hopkins University Press, 1971), 77. "[I]t was not until 1871, when he published *The Descent of Man*, that Darwin made public his own views on these questions."

48. Mandelbaum, *History, Man, and Reason*, 78.

49. As Canguilhem points out in *A Vital Rationalist*, there was no definition of the condition of being "alive" in the eighteenth century. The term *biology* first came into use in 1802, which, in a sense, is the beginning of the discipline of aliveness (68–69).

50. François Jacob, *The Logic of Life: A History of Heredity*, trans. Betty E. Spillman (New York: Pantheon

Books, 1974).

51. Ibid., 21.

52. Ibid., 22.

53. Ibid., 22.

54. Ibid., 26.

55. Ibid., 31.

56. Ibid., 33.

57. Ibid.

58. Ibid., 32–33.

59. Ibid., 33.

60. Jacob, *Logic of Life*. "The passage from objects to Beings is, among other things, an increase in complexity" (33–35).

61. Ibid. "Only once they exist are candidates put to the test of reproduction" (174).

62. Ibid. "Geographical inquiry reached the same conclusions as investigation of 'paleontological archives': in the course of time, a small number of similar organisms produces a large number of different descendants" (163).

63. Ibid., 165.

64. Ibid., 163. Jacob is quoting Darwin, *The Origin of the Species* (1859).

65. Darwin, *The Origin of the Species*, quoted in Jacob, *Logic of Life*, 165.

66. Jacob, *Logic of Life*, 163.

67. Ibid., 166–67.

68. Ibid.

I. PLACES AND SITES

II. CONCEPTUAL FRAMEWORKS

III. TOOLS AND METAPHORS

ENCOUNTERS WITH *THE FACE OF AMERICA*

Felicity D. Scott

It is surprising how few nations thought of laughter as a means of communication.

—Bernard Rudofsky, "On Exhibition Design"

On 20 April 1957, Howard S. Cullman, the U.S. commissioner general of the 1958 Brussels World's Fair, appointed Bernard Rudofsky and Peter G. Harnden as architects for the exhibitions to be displayed in the U.S. pavilion. The fair's theme was "'A New Humanism'—an era of man's greater understanding of his world and his opportunities for a fuller life." Within this expansive framework, Rudofsky and Harnden were commissioned to tell "the American story."[1] Harnden, an American architect trained at Yale, with offices in both Washington, D.C., and Paris, had served previously as designer and producer for thirty-five U.S. exhibitions in national and international trade fairs and oversaw the Brussels project from Europe. Rudofsky's background was more complex, his qualifications to represent America perhaps less assured. Trained at Vienna's Technische Hochschule in the 1920s, he had subsequently practiced as a modern architect in both southern Italy and Brazil before arriving in the U.S. in 1941 as "Bernardo Rudofsky," a South American prize winner in the Museum of Modern Art's Organic Design in Home Furnishings competition. Since his arrival in New York he had worked in numerous capacities: architectural editor at *Interiors* magazine, costume designer for Broadway plays, graphic designer, shoemaker, and author, as well as exhibition designer and curator, notably for MoMA's *Are Clothes Modern?* exhibit of 1944 (fig. 1). In 1955 Rudofsky published *Behind the Picture Window*, billed on the cover as "an unconventional book on the conventional modern house and the inscrutable ways of its inmates."[2] In 1956, a year before the Brussels appointment, he returned to MoMA to design the installation for *Textiles USA*, a spectacular display that turned expectations regarding the aesthetics and utility of textiles on their head. Unlike Harnden, Rudofsky remained in New York to work on the Brussels project, coordinating the overall organization of the numerous exhibits and designing a few specific sections.[3] During the final installation phase, he moved to Europe, but he left for Tokyo immediately prior to the opening of the fair in April 1958 in order to write a book on Japan as a "rear-view mirror of the American way of life."[4]

(fig. 1)

Bernard Rudofsky, dressed in a laboratory coat, installing his exhibition *Are Clothes Modern?* at the Museum of Modern Art, New York, November 1944

The U.S. pavilion in which the exhibits were housed was designed by Edward Durell Stone (fig. 2). Stone had recently enjoyed popular success for his design of the U.S. Embassy in New Delhi (1957–59), models of which Rudofsky had seen displayed alongside the work of Eero Saarinen, Ludwig Mies van der Rohe, Minoru Yamasaki, and Skidmore, Owings & Merrill in Arthur Drexler's 1957 MoMA exhibition Buildings for Business and Government.[5] With its slender, almost classicizing colonnade and punctured screen wall, the embassy was widely hailed as an aesthetic counterpoint to the modular curtain wall, which had proliferated in the 1950s.[6] In his U.S. pavilion Stone applied his embassy aesthetic to a gigantic circular structure measuring 341 feet in diameter. Flags from the forty-eight states and three territories adorned the facade.[7]

Registering his own disdain for Stone's aesthetic, Rudofsky noted in his 1958 lecture "On Exhibition Design" that the Belgians called the pavilion "la bonbonnière."[8] Stone's work, however, was generally well received by both the press and the public as a suitable tribute to American culture, an impressive mix of monumentality and scintillation.[9] Rudofsky's installations enjoyed no such favor, provoking such front-page headlines as "Brussels Exhibit Irks Eisenhower."[10] On entering the U.S. Pavilion, visitors found themselves under a large overhead map of the country. Suspended at a height of a little more than fourteen feet, the map itself was not the explicit content of this exhibit, which was rather contained in a series of displays related to states, regions, and the nation. Housed in vitrines, suspended on vertical boards, and set atop pedestals, a collection of ordinary artifacts offered—according to Rudofsky—an anthropological portrait of the country (fig. 3). If his colossal map of the U.S. initially seemed to extend Stone's celebration

(fig. 2)

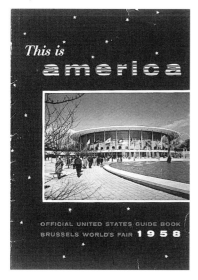

Edward Durell Stone, United States Pavilion, Brussels World's Fair, 1958, featured on the cover of This Is America, published by the Office of the U.S. Commissioner General, Brussels World's Fair, in the same year

of nationalist imagery, upon closer inspection it very soon became apparent that something had gone awry.

In June 1958, one concerned American visitor felt an urgent need to write to President Eisenhower in order to "give an idea of the confusing impression of the heterogeneous exhibits," in particular "those on the main floor right near the front entrance," which included:

> Football outfit under glass; shoe exhibit—Notre Dame knitted booties; space shoes with springs on soles, molded shoes, Indian beaded moccasins; shorts, eyelet embroidered; dark glasses, extremely fancy; shells; fossil fish; Hawaiian Chief's feather cape; Idaho potatoes; Mickey Mouse comic strip; mineral rocks, small; election buttons; Old Windsor chair (with sign "used with modification in schools"); old theater bills, restaurant menus; old fashion porcupine thresher; small statuettes in uniforms; cross section of redwood tree; Indian corn; old fire engine; collection of state license plates; old clay pottery; and Spanish penitent cart used in New Mexico.[11]

As reported in The New York Times, "the complaint heard most frequently [from visiting Americans] is that the exhibits are superficial and give an inadequate

(fig. 3)

Rudofsky, installation of The Face of America, U.S. Pavilion, Brussels World's Fair, 1958

or distorted image of the American scene and character." Stone's pavilion, however, was "specifically excluded from the attacks."[12]

Entitled *The Face of America*, Rudofsky's installation was intended to produce "an indirect, a sort of reflected portrait" of the nation through the presentation of a collection of everyday objects.[13] In contrast to familiar representations, from the soldier to the tourist, Rudofsky set out to present the American's "native environment, especially the man-made kind: his house and the objects he accumulates in the pursuit of happiness; his likes and dislikes as reflected in his surroundings."[14] Like remnants from a strange museum, these artifacts were offered up to the spectator not as evidence of advanced cultural practices but rather as barely familiar traces of that "native environment."

The main complaint regarding *The Face of America* was that Rudofsky's exhibits failed in both their ideological and their visual content to represent the U.S. adequately. They were too exceptional, too heterogeneous, and too poorly captioned to communicate their national, or even regional, significance. As yet another citizen complained to President Eisenhower, "the titles of the exhibits do not tie the different exhibits together and almost none explain why that particular exhibit is shown."[15] The varied exhibits simply failed to provide a comprehensive or unifying image, as might be expected of a national portrait.

Rudofsky's exhibits were in fact considered so confusing to Americans, and so lacking in clarity, that private companies funded an "official guidebook" entitled *This Is America*. Following from the "central complaint" that the exhibitions did not "represent the United States or 'tell the American story,'" the supplementary guidebook aimed to "close some of the gaps" in the representation of America.[16] It opened with a familiar icon, the Statue of Liberty, and presented basic facts, for instance, that "most Americans live in houses or apartments which have electric lighting, hot and cold running water and central heating"—information not necessarily evident from Rudofsky's display of domestic objects.[17]

With its presentation strategies situated somewhere between the techniques of the natural history museum and those of the department store, *The Face of America* seemed to imply the collapse of these two realms. Its relics harbored a natural or historical specificity, and occasionally an irreplaceability, that was at odds with the increasingly exchangeable figures of representation within commodity culture and the mass media. Yet beyond this form of interruption of exchange, Rudofsky's selection of objects aimed to confound normative and familiar representations of the United States through transforming institutionalized codes of visual presentation and the signifying regimes within which they participated. Under the purview of a cultural fair themed around the topic of "A New Humanism," *The Face of America* posed a challenge to what Rudofsky understood as the universalizing logic of certain cultural and scientific imperatives in the United States and the normative forces through which they operated.

This exhibition is not, however, to be counted among those advancing avant-garde strategies of negation; rather, it is for the manner in which Rudofsky set out to engage habitual modes of perception within a fully commodified milieu that this installation emerges as an interesting object of study. Founded on an amateur reading of anthropology, the exhibit presents a symptomatic analysis, by an architect, of the intersection of the realms of culture and science within an increasingly spectacular postwar historical condition.

A SOCIETY IN FERMENT

Prior to appointing designers for the cultural exhibits, Deputy Commissioner James S. Plaut approached the State Department and the U.S. Information Agency (USIA) "to ask for assistance in preparing a theme . . . that might subsequently be translated into the visual terms of the exhibit."[18] In December 1956 and January 1957, the USIA interviewed "more than thirty prominent Americans in all fields of activity" to determine which aspects of America were to be emphasized.[19] The USIA task force decided, however, that the initial suggestions were too heavily weighted toward the "cultural side of American life,"[20] and together they consulted with members of the humanities department at the Massachusetts Institute of Technology to discuss how they might extend this focus. Plaut wrote to Dean John Burchard of MIT on behalf of the U.S. commission, "We wish to present science and technology as the setting in which the new humanism may be developed and considered."[21] In April 1957 a conference was held at MIT's Endicott House that brought the commission staff together with a group of prominent scientists to discuss the impact of science and technology on creating "the American way of life."[22] Following their appointments, Rudofsky and

Harnden were faced with the task of bringing their design expertise to this discussion.

As announced in a "Progress Report" on the fair published in the September 1957 issue of the magazine *Interiors*, the MIT conference established that, with regard to American culture, "oddly enough, there [were] many positive facets which neither Hollywood nor the detergent advertisements [had] revealed to [Europeans], and the unknown truths happen[ed] to be astonishing as revelations of the positive cultural effects of material progress."[23] According to the report, among the "influential realities" informing daily life in America and requiring an integrated cultural and scientific explanation for the European audience, were:

1. the enormous amount of electrical energy at the command of the average individual
2. the amount of leisure time made available to each individual by machines both as implements of production and as household servants
3. the collapse of distance resulting from rapid transportation
4. immediate communication
5. increased average longevity [24]

American culture was to be understood as arising out of the benefits of advanced industrial society—electrical power, automation, communication, and transportation—technological forces leading to a long and leisured life.

"A Society in Ferment" was the theme chosen by the commission to express the dispersed yet connected mode of organization operating within this technological milieu. As Deputy Commissioner Plaut reported in the platitudinous language of the 1950s,

> The idea was expressed at the MIT conference that what we are dealing with is the phenomenon of continuous revolution; that the American people are dynamic, energetic, impatient and restless for changes; and that because of the vastness of our country, the diversity of our origins, and the free conditions pertaining to American enterprise, we are committed to a constant, unremitting search for an improved way of life. We have reached the conclusion that the entire contents of the American pavilion can be keyed to the theme of our ever-changing society, and that the "controlled

chaos" of the American way of life will be manifest in the diversity of the exhibits themselves....Moreover, it would be well to emphasize that the process is more important to Americans than the *product*; in other words, that the challenge of creation and achievement is still the central excitement in the American way of life.[25]

Although put forward as a notion of diversity and experimental creation, this figuration of a force of change was also, of course, a vivid description of the condition of late capitalism. And while presented as a form of subjective agency—dynamism, energy, impatience—this "controlled chaos" of constant technological change operated through a feedback loop of commercial, technological, and political imperatives.

Among the participants of the MIT conference was design professor Gyorgy Kepes, who "noted with satisfaction" that the designers were among the event's "most vocal participants."[26] To him this meant that "the design team was thus protected against the danger of receiving an incompletely digested set of instructions, of being expected to translate incorrectly understood concepts."[27] Following Kepes's long-standing program of integrating aesthetic and scientific discourses, the conference had, according to the progress report, successfully "welded policy-makers and those who had to carry out that policy into a single mind."[28] Closer inspection reveals, however, that this integration would not be sustained by Rudofsky's activities. It was not, however, that he had incorrectly understood the conceptualization of the project; rather, he set out to articulate a more dystopic analysis of the impact of such a systematic integration of commercial, technological, and political forces (fig. 4).

The "Progress Report" noted that Rudofsky and Harnden had forced the commission to recognize that "the sheer mass of American wealth and the sheer power of American industry have been dinned into European ears *ad nauseum*" and that "another repetition of production statistics could be counted on to arouse boredom, perhaps irritation, certainly envy."[29] That their assessment was correct was confirmed in subsequent reports.[30] "Foreigners," wrote Walter Waggoner for *The New York Times*, "do not seem to share the American dissatisfaction with the interior exhibits." The effect of the exhibition, however, was not simply to fulfill European preconceptions. Although the unfamiliarity of the objects on display did not arouse the same level of anxiety experienced by American visitors, the exhibits seemed to

FELICITY D. SCOTT

cause a peculiar shift in perception. "My European friends, by and large, like our Pavilion very much," explained one American observer,

> But every one of them said something oddly repetitious—that it somehow doesn't seem like the United States to them as they have thought of it (Of course they always thought our food was bad, and the Brass Rail [restaurant] amply fulfilled this image). It's not very useful to speculate on the many versions of the United States that people all over the world carry around with them. What is important is that these stereotypes must have been subjected to some modification as a result of our Pavilion, certainly for the better.[31]

Judging from such responses, it seems evident that Rudofsky had not simply refused to present America's scientific, technical, and commercial advancement, as required by the U.S. Commission. Rather, as American visitors observed, he had presented them in a manner that did not, strictly speaking, *represent* them. His intervention was directed precisely at those normative images that people carry around with them. Arising out of a wry assessment of the impact of science, technology, and commerce and a reading of the complex determination of culture by such forces, Rudofsky's

(fig. 4)

Interior view of U.S. Pavilion, Brussels World's Fair, 1958

installation set out to mobilize perceptual responses other than those he understood to be perpetuated through mass culture. What, then, would be the experience of an archive such as that on display as "the face of America"?

IMPRESSIONS OF THE UNITED STATES

In December 1958, only a few months after leaving Brussels and arriving in Japan to begin a two-year residence as a Fulbright scholar, Rudofsky gave his lecture "On Exhibition Design" at Tokyo's International House. A large portion of the lecture, preserved in manuscript form, is dedicated to his work in Brussels, including its techniques of visual communication.[32] Produced without "censorship" or "compromise,"[33] *The Face of America* held a special status among his installations at the fair. He provided some clues as to its aims. "How does one go about portraying 48 states without using all the clichés of travel bureaus and chambers of commerce?" he asked the Tokyo audience rhetorically. "How does one pick objects that are interesting, unfamiliar, unique, yet significant, revealing; that possibly tell a story or throw light on things known or remembered?"[34] In an earlier description he similarly offered a few clues. "The entrance sector"

> consists of objects and groups of objects that bring to one's mind places, states or sections of the United States of America, all adding up to the vast panorama of the country. This, however, must not be taken literally—we will not identify a state by the state flower or license plate. Nevertheless, the objects in this section are representative of a state or region. They are unfamiliar objects, or objects known from pictures only, their cumulative effect leading up to a kind of Treasure Island, or rather Treasure Continent which, in a sense, the United States is to many Europeans. Thus, the idea of a pictorial map is transposed into a display, real and not painted.[35]

If Rudofsky's collection of artifacts "added up" to a panorama, it did not give the viewer any sense of an overview or articulate even a provisional totality such as that implied by the overhead map. And although it was important to him that the objects were "real and not painted," the transposition from a pictorial map into "real" objects did not necessarily render their message more accessible to the spectator. Indeed, most visitors experienced a level of estrangement when confronted with his choice of objects. Rather than familiar icons for each state or region, the artifacts presented

interrupted the expected terms of such a display. Rudofsky never fully articulated how this not-identifying-but-nevertheless-representative quality operated within his exhibits; he just noted that the objects would prompt some
sort of identification other than the literal one. What, then, would trigger
this operation?

Positing that one could make a "parlor game" out of the selection
of objects for The Face of America, Rudofsky queried, "What should be chosen
to stand for New York State? New York's skyscrapers? The Statue of Liberty?"
Noting that there had been dozens of stereotypes to avoid, he picked
the Sunday edition of The New York Times. While taken for granted by New
Yorkers, at five hundred pages, "to a foreigner, [it is] nothing short of
fabulous, indeed monstrous"; it "looked to Europeans," he claimed, "more
like an encyclopedia than a morning paper."[36] All 480 pages of The New York
Times from Sunday, 24 November 1957, were mounted on a large, faceted
plywood structure (fig. 5). Each double page occupied its own indentation,
and these were spread out, or unfolded, into five tiers. Taken together, the
whole edition formed a visually complex wall of images, texts, and advertisements that enveloped the viewer and engaged a habitual mode of perception for the postwar subject—the panoramic gaze at the urban billboard. The
display took one technical substrate of the news media—the newspaper—
and recast it as a distinct form. Confronted with an outdated and rather ordinary day's news and advertisements now rendered monumental, the viewer
would be called upon to address the distorted presentation of the newspaper's information.

Other exhibits were less grand in scale. Alaska, the nation's largest
state, had the smallest exhibit—the canceled check for the Alaska purchase in

Rudofsky, installation
of *The New York Times*
exhibit, *The Face of
America*, 1958

the amount of $7.2 million. Rudofsky recalled that his request to present the check "only a few hundred feet from the Russian pavilion," while initially entertained, was later refused by the State Department and that only after much negotiation had he obtained permission to have a facsimile produced by a forger (then doing time in prison).[37] The National Archives had at one point sent a photograph for consideration. This reproduction was rejected by Robert Warner, a government coordinator sympathetic to Rudofsky's project, as "absolutely worthless"; "It looks like a photograph," he remarked.[38] The State Department indeed found Rudofsky's request to present the original check to be quite a challenge, leading them to plan elaborate security measures.[39] "Here is a really tough one for you," wrote Warner to Gerson H. Lush in the office of the U.S. Commissioner, making further requests for the original document. "After all," he wrote, "what other country has the audacity to go buy continents?"[40] The expansion of U.S. territory as a product of economic power was thus presented as a simple transaction, one amounting to "half the cost of our Brussels Pavilion," as Rudofsky pointed out in "On Exhibition Design." Its political significance was not, however, missed. Recuperated from the archive, this artifact—or at least a one-off facsimile—was mobilized by Rudofsky to circulate toward other ends. He noted in particular that the proximity to the Russian pavilion would "add piquancy to the document."[41] Confronting the observer with a modest (reproduced) artifact, but one standing in for an event of great historical magnitude, Rudofsky's exhibit did not offer contours of a legible physiognomy but pointed to relations of power.

Other artifacts followed different trajectories. The exhibit for California was a 16-foot-diameter slab of redwood weighing 2,500 pounds

(fig. 6)

Rudofsky, installation of a California redwood, *The Face of America*, 1958

(fig. 6). "It is only of medium size as redwood trees go," Rudofsky noted, "yet it had been growing since prehistoric times."[42] Distinct from the presentation of technologically advanced products, here was a piece of America's natural history, a slice through time. For Hawaii, Rudofsky presented "a man-made object. Not a hula-skirt, but the cape of a native chief."[43] He recalled that there had been "a charming, most cultured mistake" in its reception. Collapsing the formal attributes of an "anthropological" specimen with a modern one (Rudofsky's favorite pseudomorphic technique), "some people," he noted, "mistook it, at first glance, for one of the vestments that Matisse had designed for the chapel of Vence."[44] About an exhibit of tumble-weeds, Rudofsky recounted with glee, "One correspondent wrote with disbelief: 'Our tumble weed seems to be attracting as much attention as the Russian sputniks.'"[45]

To further this view of the heterogeneous nature of Rudofsky's selection, we might point also to his displays of Edison's first electric light bulb, opera playbills from the Wild West, Walt Disney's first sketches of Mickey Mouse, Spanish moss from Louisiana, the first gold nugget found in California in 1849 (which, he claimed, started the gold rush and led to the rapid settlement of the West), Kansas wheat, a rattlesnake (Eastern variety), New England patchwork quilts, a Pennsylvania Amish costume, rural mailboxes, automobile license plates, a Franklin stove, cowboy gear, seashells from a beach in Georgia (fig. 7), three ears of corn harvested one thousand years before Columbus, a 1903 Model A Ford,[46] and a collection of American clothing, including a pair of Dr. Murray's molded plastic shoes that had previously been shown in *Are Clothes Modern?* Incidentally, these shoes (whose inventor had fantasized the return of the foot to its natural splayed condition)

(fig. 7)

Rudofsky, installation of seashells from Georgia, *The Face of America*, 1958

were joined by equally peculiar "space shoes" produced by the Murray Space Shoe Corporation.

Although grouped under the map of the United States, which loomed overhead like a giant organizational device, these dislocated, hetero-geneous artifacts failed to produce a coherent picture for American visitors.[47] Unlike the unifying, identifying, and classifying functions of a traditional archive, and unlike the story of man presented in natural history museums, Rudofsky's collection did not produce what Jacques Derrida has referred to as "a system of a synchrony in which all the elements articulate the unity of an ideal configuration."[48] Nor did the objects evoke historical memory. For even if most could be recognized or in some manner decoded, they were not familiar national symbols. And what, Rudofsky might have asked, would be the function of memory and of tradition in a society based solely on progress, one less than two hundred years old, a "society in ferment"? What would it mean to enshrine the products of such a society?[49]

Unlike Rudofsky's other installations at Brussels—which operated through and upon modern, if not entirely contemporary, media such as film, photography, and commercial graphics—*The Face of America* presented objects of seemingly little value, objects that were, furthermore, often technologically and semantically outdated. They were not objects currently circulating in contemporary media such as television or magazines, and their lack of familiarity seemed counter to the presentation of "daily life." Thus, to many it seemed as if Rudofsky was presenting the wrong archive, not that of an advanced industrial culture but of his own private selection. "As [James S.] Plaut put it," Rudofsky recalled with some satisfaction, "it is, for better or worse, a One Man's America."[50] Standing at odds with America's self-image as progressive, and operating outside of familiar codes of repre-sentation, *The Face of America* provoked responses from observers ranging from outbursts of laughter to outpourings of angry letters to senators and con-gressmen. The public space of the World's Fair thus became the site of a pri-vate encounter.

As Derrida has argued in *Archive Fever*, the archival object is without immediacy, being reliant upon an external substrate or prosthetic to elicit memory, yet it still produces an "impression." Such an impression gives rise to an indeterminate quality that sets it against the supposedly more stable notion of the concept. "Archive" itself, he writes, is a notion entailing "the unstable feeling of a shifting figure... an in-finite or indefinite process."[51] The indeterminacy of that impression opens it up to the future, to a promise.

While we cannot attribute Derrida's formulation to Rudofsky, we might note that, in distinction to offering familiar icons, he repeatedly claimed that he was offering the visitor to the fair an impression of the country, one that would refuse preformed, and in particular, nationalist concepts. He proposed, for instance, that through visiting *The Face of America* "the American continent" could "be tasted in a few precious samples, the way a wine taster *feels* the sun, the soil, and the air of his country with every sip."[52] Contrasting his work to an academic treatment (which would formulate concepts), Rudofsky tried, furthermore, "to give the visitor a vivid but accurate impression of the immeasurable vastness of the United States, of an ever-changing society, ambitious, restless and enterprising."[53] Offering an "experience rather than an exhibition,"[54] his installation attempted to move away from the conventional transmission of information toward a space of encounter with artifacts, a space that posed a challenge to the viewer's preconceptions. If many Europeans responded with pleasure to this experience, most American visitors adamantly refused to be propelled down this alternative trajectory of signification.

NATURAL HISTORY

The objects in *The Face of America* had the appearance of belonging to a particular type of archive—that of an anthropology or natural history museum—and it was indeed with such collections that Rudofsky frequently associated his research and exhibition work. As early as 1946, in an article entitled "The Art of Display," he had pointed to commonalities between commercial and museological techniques of display.[55] Central to his reading of the latter were installations of non-Western artifacts in two New York institutions, the Museum of Modern Art and the American Museum of Natural History. For Rudofsky, both institutions deployed techniques of salesmanship; "Good showmanship," he asserted, "is as worthwhile in educational as in commercial display."[56] Moreover, he observed the manner in which older modes of presentation had ceased to elicit visual satisfaction, pointing, for instance, to the "miles of unimaginative glass cases crammed with an indigestible mass of small specimens [which] kept the public from many parts of the New York Museum of Natural History even while the famous wildlife zoological groups were educating droves of small boys and other citizens who were not in search of scientific information."[57] The *Kunstkammer*-type collections of multiple objects in vitrines had given way to the seductive power of the habitat groups of flora and fauna. While the habitat groups entertained, they failed to convey important information. For the anthropologist this led to the dilemma of how to balance the seductive power they held (in contrast to the dusty vitrines) against their scientific and educational content. Following the arrival of a new director, Albert Parr, the Museum of Natural History's architectural department addressed this problem, as Rudofsky noted, by "experimenting with illusion effects—mirrors, periscopes, magnifiers, and similar instruments."[58] The architect would himself deploy the aid of such effects in Brussels, as we shall see.

In "The Art of Display," after noting the importance of a certain group of ethnological displays at the Museum of Natural History ("the American (North) Indian life groups, and the striking collection of the arts of the Incas, Aztecs and other South and Central American Indians"), Rudofsky went on to unfavorably compare changes made upon Parr's arrival to another exhibition then on display at MoMA, René d'Harnoncourt's *Arts of the South Seas*.[59] Rudofsky repeated the comparison many times, noting that while both were "ethnological," *Arts of the South Seas* produced an "exhilarating experience."[60] While he never articulated what was producing the latter's success, it appeared to revolve around the apparently seamless visual connections produced through the organization of the exhibition space.

The superior showmanship of *Arts of the South Seas* was also commented on by anthropologist Gregory Bateson. If Bateson pointed to the inadequacy of the installation's scientific content, he was provoked to question why it was so visually compelling. "The writer and in general those who have seen the exhibit," he posited, "agree on two expressions of emotion: 'It makes sense' and 'it is very exciting.'"[61] Noting that the exhibition itself was a work of art, Bateson set out to "define more precisely this excitement and sort of coherence which is implicit in the sequence and lighting...to look for what is touched off by this arrangement of alien items in an occidental syntax."[62] What Bateson had recognized as the very "occidental syntax" of d'Harnoncourt's technique was a form of decontextu-

III. TOOLS AND METAPHORS

alization that enabled ahistorical and pseudomorphic connections across distinct cultures.

Such pseudomorphisms were also common to Rudofsky's work. Increasingly, however, what came to disturb him about this universalizing manner of connection—the assumption that all human cultures can be reduced to commonalities—was the logic of functional integration upon which it was implicitly based. Throughout the 1950s and into the 1960s, his exhibition work set out to disarticulate such connections that for him had become tantamount to forced integration.[63] As with Edward Steichen's famous exhibition *The Family of Man*, first exhibited at MoMA in 1955, the ultimate object of such supposedly abstract universals was the eradication of difference. "Steichen's *Family of Man*," Rudofsky lamented at one point to Harnden with regard to the aims of the Brussels commission, "has paralyzed their thinking."[64]

Beyond Steichen's high-modernist sensibility, Paul Rudolph's seamless installation of this spurious photographic narrative of a "family of Man" might have confirmed for Rudofsky the universalizing logic of its model of humanism, as famously noted by Roland Barthes in his 1957 essay "The Great Family of Man." Having projected an image of Babel across the world, Barthes explained, "from this pluralism, a type of unity is magically produced: man is born, works, laughs and dies everywhere in the same way."[65] Such a projection of the American nuclear family across the globe would not, to Rudofsky's thinking, have been an adequate response to the Brussels theme of "A New Humanism." Either this new humanism was simply a problematic expansion of an earlier incarnation, now more extensively articulated through the mediation of communication technology, or, if the qualification "new" was to mark the opening up of a space of radical difference, then the seamlessness of such a model of integration would foreclose its very possibility. While it is beyond the scope of this essay to trace the development of Rudofsky's exhibition work in detail, it is important to note that from the time of his remarks on display from the 1940s to his rethinking of display techniques in the 1950s, his attitude underwent a transformation. After attempting to embrace the "functional" mode of display (in opposition to the chaotic), in the 1950s he began to explore the breakdown of functionalist logic in favor of other modes of (dis)organization that for him served to open up spaces of differentiation.

In his essay "Museum Matters," Gyan Prakash explains that "appropriation of alterity is an integral part of the humanist and historicist representations of difference encountered in ethnographic museums."[66] Reframing dislocated objects produced the illusion of cultural wholeness. Rudofsky's display of "exotic" (but American) objects participated in such an appropriation insofar as it made visual reference to displays of "authentic" cultural, anthropological, and natural history specimens. Yet unlike the systems of cultural organization produced through such techniques, the arrangement of The Face of America did not presuppose an integrated cultural whole or functional integrity such as would typically be found in a museum (or Family) of Man.[67] The exhibit was, rather, staged as the site of a massive piling up of fragments held together only through Rudofsky's overhead map. His presentation thus implied a structural failure of the logic of totalization. Rudofsky's "specimens" were opposed not only to the commodified status of iconic images but to the ordering, classification, and metonymic function of representative samples operating in scientific techniques of anthropological display. His specimens refused any such legibility and organizational coherence, in spite of the map. While gathered together as an assemblage of archival objects, they had been reframed without a master narrative; they were not properly reassembled. Moreover, the (neo)colonizer of the 1950s was here recast through cultural specimens; here were "exotic" artifacts from a culture that did not consider itself so.

This estrangement effect is problematic, of course, both for the manner in which it suggests—in a negative fashion—that America might not be subject to the same logic as other anthropological exhibits (the implied ethnocentrism of a simple inversion in which the West is finally offered up as ethnographic, but not quite) and for the elision of any historical memory of the violence effected in the production of a unified America (that is, the suppression of this history of conflict and domination of native peoples). But insofar as this confrontation with alterity produced for many a massive disintegration of the "face" of America, one that at least provisionally refused a stable image of "advanced" culture, it offered the beginnings of a rethinking of how that unified history was constructed in the first instance. It provided fissures in that surface.

How, then, to characterize the connection Rudofsky forged between his own discipline—architecture—and anthropology as a scientific discourse?

If initially it seems that this engagement took the form of metaphor or perhaps affinity, it is more properly understood through other rhetorical tropes—irony and humor, both of which continue to suggest a level of precision in the overturning of institutionalized codes of signification. And here we might locate a critical vocation for this project. Rudofsky's operation as a designer of specific installations of archival objects seems to have taken the form of irony. In *Proust and Signs*, Gilles Deleuze argues that "the Socratic demon, irony, consists in anticipating the encounters. In Socrates, the intelligence still comes before the encounters; it provokes them, it instigates and organizes them."[68] Yet beyond this, the provocation of many exhibits—that of opening the subject up to the violence of such an encounter (one that left familiar objects radically strange)—would be closer to the experience of humor, in which, as Deleuze explains of Proust, the intelligence comes after, for the subject is forced to think beyond the habitual reception of a pre-formed concept.

COMMUNICATION

What, then, was to be read on *The Face of America*? In typically evasive terms, Rudofsky later explained at a conference on "Total Architecture" that the "face of a country (and that is after all what we are concerned with when we talk about total architecture)—the face of a country is not the result of a design program or some pious resolutions. It is, for better or worse, the reflection of a way of life."[69] Rudofsky's "indirect" or "reflected portrait" of America from the late 1950s also rejected such forms of "official" codification—design programs and resolutions as well as national symbols and propaganda—in favor of presenting a symptomatic analysis of those forces impacting daily life in America—precisely those forces giving rise to "a society in ferment." But the forces impacting the "American way of life"—as identified at the MIT conference—were not presented directly to the audience. Rather, the dispersed yet connected mode of organization that informed the "controlled chaos" of late capitalism became the very problem upon which Rudofsky operated. His first concern was to confound expectations of how America should be portrayed, and the second was to find other modes of occupying this new territorial arrangement—modes of reception that figured a rather utopian disarticulation of this totalizing system.

On the one hand, Rudofsky offered an image of a provisional totality in the form of an overhead map. Yet the artifacts found below, presented as specimens of America's natural, cultural, social, technical, political, and economic history, failed to cohere into a legible or unified image and thus implicitly questioned the desirability of a signifying system that would achieve such a mode of consensus, even one in a constant state of transformation. Rather than adopting a unifying or coherent structure—such as that he attributed to the commercial system, which for him simply produced imperatives to consume and conform—Rudofsky searched for potential moments of differentiation in the reception of objects on display.

The mode of communication figured in *The Face of America* was not that of a seamless transmission of information (messages) but a process of exchange between viewer and installation and hence, in a mediated form, between installation designer and viewer. Rudofsky hoped that this process of exchange would not be determined by the designer but would arise out of the viewers' somewhat random participation and their unforeseen interaction with his exhibits. It is in this moment of naive optimism that his utopian project is most clearly revealed, as are its limits. He premised his intervention on the hope that, by eliciting other (fetishistic) relations to objects on display, the viewing subject could be disarticulated from the signifying modalities of dominant visual paradigms. The exhibit presumed a subject with some capacity for resisting spectacular arrangements; it presumed that the subject would be open to such an encounter; and it presupposed in addition that such a provisional mode of critical distance would be able to withstand immediate recuperation into that "controlled chaos" against which it operated.

NEGOTIATIONS

As reported in *The New York Times* under the headline, "Brussels Exhibit Irks Eisenhower," Rudofsky's installations were considered so disturbing to American visitors that President Eisenhower eventually sent an envoy to investigate. "A 'very irritated' President Eisenhower undertook today to find out whether the United States' exhibit at the Brussels fair was as bad as some critics were saying. . . . He ordered George V. Allen, Director of the USIA, to make a flying inspection trip to the fair and give him a personal

FELICITY D. SCOTT

report."[70] Allen, as Rudofsky was told, "was the dramatist's dream investigator—tightlipped, serious, full of the importance of his mission."[71] What had particularly "irked" Eisenhower was a three-and-a-half-page letter from Senator Styles Bridges of New Hampshire. The senator was passing on the comments of an aggravated constituent. After having visited the fair with a party of twenty-three American tourists, predominantly from Ohio and Illinois, the anonymous individual became infuriated: "To every American I met, including everyone in our tour party, the exhibit was bewildering and completely unlike the America we know," he wrote. Bridges recounted,

> [H]e reported "as you enter the main doorway there is a thick plate-glass baffle about four feet high on which is etched in black a picture of a man on a beach talking to a woman bare to the waist with what seems to be an Indian headdress." In the background, he added, "her tribesmen are roasting the lower half of a human body on a spit." Immediately behind this was a chair used in a school in the 1700's and the card beneath it "conveys the idea in three languages that children today use the same chair," he said. "A group I saw read the card and burst into laughter."[72]

Following his visit, Allen reported to the President that certain exhibits were "too sophisticated and impressionistic for the average visitor." With particular regard to Rudofsky's *The Face of America*, he suggested the "elimination of puzzling things such as mailboxes, sun glasses, odd shoes, football uniforms etc." and the expansion and enlargement of "captions and explanations."[73] While many changes were made to another exhibit by Rudofsky, *Islands of Living*, few were made to this one, and both the press and the general public continued to be full of complaints. Two displays in particular were frequently singled out: the football uniform and the Idaho potatoes, both of which were illustrative of Rudofsky's peculiar operations.

Writing for the *Herald Tribune*, critic Emily Genauer registered her annoyance at "a football uniform laid out in a glass case like the effigy of an armored knight carved on a medieval tomb."[74] Writing for *Arts and Architecture*, June Wayne, however, noted the exhibit's humor: "I found people staring fascinated at a magnificent glass case containing a football suit complete with padding, helmet and paraphernalia, laid out with the loving care and straightforward sobriety with which a costume museum composes its rarest Coronation robe."[75] Rudofsky's installation of the football uniform registered strong reactions. And yet, as its creator explained, pointing to the mass-produced quality of the artifacts, "you may find every single piece of this outfit in the show window of Abercrombie and Fitch, or any other sports shop, and you would probably never give it more than a glance." It was not, of course, just the artifacts causing the response but Rudofsky's recuperation and recoding of their cultural significance. As he acknowledged, "all the pieces put together...as done here, revealed a new aspect of a player, of a sport, and, like everything new, filled visitors with new emotions."[76] In another context, he confirmed the implied relation to European heroes. With respect to the effigy he explained:

> This was the equivalent of the medieval knight.... Nothing is more characteristic of the U.S. to me than this modern knight in football padding and it is something totally unknown in Europe. So I took this padding and stretched it out a little, you know, so he might have been almost seven feet in the box and showed him as the medieval knights are, sleeping in the old European cathedrals.[77]

(fig. 8)

Rudofsky, installation of Idaho potatoes, *The Face of America*, 1958

Transposing the aura of the modern football player into that of the medieval knight (and vice versa), Rudofsky captured the image it produced within a distinct but equally efficacious signifying regime, one that highlighted the cultic status and decorative excess of such "modern" artifacts. While Rudofsky resisted further commentary in his Tokyo lecture, noting that "this is not the time and the place to go into these matters," his concluding remarks on the uniform point to the crux of this installation. "This could be the cue to a lecture on the psychology of seeing things, and of crowd reactions in particular."[78]

His exhibit of Idaho potatoes would deploy a similar technique but would ultimately take the potato's signifying capacity, or lack thereof, in another direction. "Five big Idaho potatoes," Le Soir announced, "are sleeping in a small prismatic glass-box."[79] Rudofsky explained that for small objects he did not want to use "conventional showcases." "When you look at an ordinary square case," he explained, "you see, mainly, your own reflections. A vertical sheet of glass acts as a mirror."[80] Yet it was not reflections that he aimed to exclude; rather, he designed his own steel-and-Plexiglas vitrines specifically "to avoid unwanted reflections, [and] to obtain an unobstructed view downwards" (figs. 8, 9).[81] This set up a dual or two-stage reception. From a distance his showcase looked "like an oversized crystal; it multiplies

(fig. 9)

Rudofsky testing designs for his vitrines, circa 1957

the objects and gives a kaleidoscopic image of them."[82] Reflected upon the faceted glass surface, the amorphous and indistinct objects would seem to float in midair. This peculiar quality, he suggested, would attract people who could not determine the contents; it was an example of what he called his "now-you-see-it, now-you-don't principle," a principle according to which the vitrines would motivate the viewer and raise his curiosity.[83] "From a distance, these cases looked more or less like solid chunks of glass," he remarked. "One could not see what they contained, and they made people come close."[84]

It was only when observers finally reached a position from which they could look directly down into the vitrine that a second image was revealed, the reflections giving way to provide a clear view of the Idaho potatoes resting on a bed of scarlet velvet. The exhibit was thus transformed from spectacular fragmented image to the mute presentation of an organic thing. Rudofsky recounted that part of its estrangement effect turned around the potato's ubiquity. Although "all Americans are fond of them," he stated, people "are used to seeing them in grocery stores only"; they were "shocked to find them in a showcase."[85]

Bringing together two forms of vitrine—those for commercial goods and for museum or scientific exhibits—Rudofsky's installations for both the football uniform and the Idaho potatoes confused one form of viewing with another. In *Are Clothes Modern?* he had effected a similar collapse. "The very same garments and accessories which we are accustomed to see displayed for sale in windows and stores," he posited, "assume quite a strange aspect when we see them arranged as in the way of an ethnological exhibit." He went on to explain this effect: "At first sight they look as amusing as any exotic costumes. At second sight, however, the merely aesthetic impression disappears and gives way to a sensation of a different nature: the visitor will suddenly lose or loosen his conventional attitude of taking present-day sartorial questions for granted."[86] For Rudofsky, both regimes of vision—commercial and ethnological—were subject to normative codes that functioned through recognition. Brought together, however, one destabilized the other, producing an encounter that provoked the subject to think.[87] If Idaho potatoes are in and of themselves recognizable objects, Rudofsky's installation made them the subject of such an encounter.

FELICITY D. SCOTT

What might such a group of potatoes signify? Despite the widespread popularity of the Idaho potato, the exhibit of irradiated specimens (donated by Brookhaven Laboratories, Long Island, New York) pushed the question of the presentable itself. The exalted presentation of the lowly potato invited the observer to abstract from its base materiality, one akin to that produced by the kaleidoscopic reflection on the surfaces of its diamond-shaped vitrine. Yet, at the same time, the Idaho varietal had a representative capacity that already seemed to carry with it an idealism. Could this endow it, however, with the capacity to function as a state symbol? As indicated by visitors' responses, the potatoes' appearance defied this idealist operation, especially as their irradiation treatment came to the end of its ability to prevent them from rotting.[88] This disjunction produced an absurd gesture. On the one hand, certain aspects of the exhibit called into play the heightened status of the potato as a state symbol: for instance, its label, its metonymic association with the state as well as the jewel-like reflection produced on the sides of Rudofsky's specially constructed vitrine. On the other hand, the exhibit revealed the formless object's inability to be recuperated into a signifying regime of signs, at the level of both concept and form. In this operation I would like to argue that we find Rudofsky at work to produce a second mode of dissolution, a further disruption of legibility; beyond the project of disarticulating a cohesive or totalizing system of representation in the overall organization of his exhibit, here we find him also operating to overcome the cohesiveness of the object itself.

Perhaps surprisingly, Rudofsky was not the only modern architect to have reflected on the status of the potato. Mies van der Rohe also invoked the lowly tuber. Demarcating a hierarchy of use value, a hierarchy through which the expression of function or purpose should be decided, Mies situated the potato as an object without "spiritual" value:

> A thing may have a practical value, an economical value or a spiritual value. The value of a thing is in its use. A walking stick, a practical thing, should not be compared to the Parthenon—this has a spiritual value. Accordingly, a powerhouse is not a cathedral, and if a transgression is attempted the result would not be architecture. While both are based on the same natural principles, we ask of a rose only that it be a rose; we ask of a potato only that it be a potato. Philosophically speaking, only then do they exist. In architecture there are, also, roses and potatoes.[89]

Unlike Mies's designation of the potato's resolute lowness, Rudofsky, it might be said, maintained a shimmering dialectic of the potato. This produced a back-and-forth movement "from refuse to ideal" akin to Georges Bataille's reading of the status of the big toe in an essay of that name that Rudofsky, as I have argued elsewhere, had paraphrased in the 1940s.[90]

Pointing to the resilient idealism behind most materialist enterprises, Bataille had insisted on the "conformity of dead matter to the idea of science," since both answered the "question of the essence of things, precisely of the idea by which things become intelligible."[91] It was science, according to Bataille, that maintained this idealism in relation to form. If science—even that which investigated complexities and instabilities—sets out to codify functions, constants, and laws, and to semiotize the otherwise chaotic and heterogeneous field of events, Rudofsky's project refused to do so.[92] His base potatoes posed a challenge to scientific ideals, one exacerbated by their presentation as specimens. In contrast to the project of both the natural and human sciences to codify knowledge of form and organization, Rudofsky's installation of potatoes attempted an escape from the straitjacket of such codification, whether it be scientific or nationalistic. Outside of the symbolic register, escaping its dictates, the incongruous potatoes were supposed to function at a presignifying, indeterminate level.[93]

When faced with "those vacant lots, those suburbs and factories, whose appearance expresses the nature of industrial societies," Bataille argued, "we cannot deny that present-day humanity has lost the secret, kept until the current age, of giving itself a face in which it might recognize the splendor that is proper to it."[94] Rudofsky, too, understood that the production of a legible physiognomy was not available to advanced industrial cultures such as the postwar U.S. What, then, was the designer to do? Unlike many of his contemporaries in the 1950s, he did not search out prospects for renewing organic society.[95] He pursued quite the reverse, seeing any such organicism not as a reflection of a cultural milieu but rather as the insidious phantasm of a unified community. For him such an image was merely the workings of a fully technological milieu operating through totalizing networks of organization to capture the subject's desires within the commodity system. Presented in *The Face of America*, however, was a barely perceptible reflection of a way of life. The objects must be understood as archival, as the last remnants, or even the ruins, of a way of life no longer fully available to the subject but perhaps able, nevertheless, to produce an impression.

Challenging an already receding capacity of cultural memory—and refusing to allow the congealing of familiar modes of signification—Rudofsky produced a rather derisive disorganization of national identity. Flying in the face of that "occidental syntax" noted by Bateson, his own collection of artifacts was experienced as a massive deterritorialization of America's face.

Laughter at—or perhaps in—*The Face of America* was what had irked Eisenhower so much as to prompt an investigation into Rudofsky's exhibits. Toward the end of his Tokyo lecture, Rudofsky lamented that "Americans saw our participation in Brussels as little more than an episode in the Cold War, a contest with Russia."[96] In his mind, the presentation had not engaged in this oppositional logic:

> All we did, or tried to do, was to prove that, for once, we could do without self-praise, without self-advertisement. To put it into vulgar language: *We did not try to sell ourselves.* Instead, we tried to relax, to make fun; above all, to make fun of ourselves. Our great luxury was *laughter.* It is surprising how few nations thought of laughter as a means of communication.[97]

Laughter, wrote Bataille, "most often decomposes without consequence, and sometimes with a virulence that is so pernicious that it even puts in question composition itself, and the wholes across which it functions."[98] Less a form of communication than of communication breakdown, laughter erupts when a subject is faced with the unknown, when assurances are overthrown or positioned as unstable or deceptive.[99] Following Bataille, Michel Foucault would also experience an unstoppable laughter when faced with an unfamiliar order of things. Reading Borges's quotations from a "certain Chinese Encyclopedia," one that detailed a wondrous taxonomy in which animals are divided into such classes as "belonging to the Emperor," "frenzied," or "drawn with a fine camel-hair brush," Foucault recalled that it provoked in him a laughter that "shattered all the familiar landmarks of my thought—the thought that bears the stamp of our age and our geography."[100] The Chinese taxonomy had "disturb[ed] and threaten[ed] with collapse our age-old distinction between the Same and the Other"; it had revealed to him the constructedness of Western knowledge, including that which classifies and orders concepts and artifacts within the human sciences. As testified to by numerous visitors to the Brussels World's Fair, Rudofsky's *Face of America* also shattered such familiar landmarks of thought.

NOTES

1. This was reported in the press release: "News from the Office of the United States Commissioner General to the Brussels World's Fair—1958/Public Affairs Division/U.S. Department of State/45 Broadway, New York 6, NY. Whitehall 3–8000 Extension 109/for release: April 21, 1957." The press release also announced that Rudofsky would work in association with Harnden, National Archives at College Park, Maryland. Record Group 43.12.16, Records relating to U.S. participation in the Brussels Universal and International Exhibition of 1958 (hereafter, National Archives).

2. Bernard Rudofsky, *Behind the Picture Window* (New York: Oxford University Press, 1955).

3. I have not found any official document detailing the arrangement between Harnden Associates and Rudofsky, nor any specifying who was responsible for which part of the overall design process. Archival documents including initial proposals and extensive correspondence between Rudofsky in New York and Harnden in Paris give a reasonably clear indication that Rudofsky undertook a large part of the conceptual design work of the overall organization of the exhibits as well as the specific design for a number of sections. Harnden's office in Paris did the documentation and design-development work and provided the technical expertise for this scale of exhibition work. Rudofsky was also the main contact person with the commission in New York during the development phases of the project, although the initial connection was clearly through Harnden's extensive work with the United States Information Agency and other State Department officials. Publications from the period vary with regard to attribution, with *Architectural Design* 27, no. 8 (August 1958), citing Rudofsky (only) as "display designer" (330). Most other publications referred to Peter Harnden Associates as responsible for the American exhibits and cited Rudofsky as the designer of the specific installations for which he was in charge. In his future biographical notes, Rudofsky referred to himself as "Chief Design Architect."

4. Bernard Rudofsky to Serge Chermayeff, 13 November 1960, archives of Berta Rudofsky, Nerja, Spain.

5. Exhibition #615, *Buildings for Business and Government*, was on show at MoMA from 27 February through 28 April 1957. Rudofsky recounted viewing Stone's design and commiserating with René d'Harnoncourt.

6. Supposedly operating as a palliative to the expansion of the serial organization of the curtain wall, the decorative screen (itself equally applicable to embassy, house, pavilion, or office) offered a populist and thus more palatable veil through which to perpetuate this globalizing trend.

7. See J. M. Richards, "Special Issue: The Brussels Exhibition," *The Architectural Review* 124, no. 739 (August 1958).

8. Bernard Rudofsky, unpublished manuscript of lecture, "On Exhibition Design," given at International House, Tokyo, 5 December 1958, 23, Bernard Rudofsky Papers, Accession #920004, Getty Research Institute, Research Library.

9. Stone's work did not enjoy as favorable a reception among modernist historians as in the popular press. On the "crisis in taste and discrimination" of Stone's work, John Jacobus wrote, "Embodied in the exhibition pavilion in Brussels, its qualities of commercial styling and the flair with which it smugly displayed the affluent society made this perforated screen idiom acceptable." *Twentieth-Century Architecture, 1940–65* (London: Thames and Hudson, 1966), 152.

10. John D. Morris, "Brussels Exhibit Irks Eisenhower," *The New York Times*, 18 June 1958.

11. Wyllys P. Ames, Upper Montclair, N.J., to Dwight D. Eisenhower, President of the United States,

23 June 1958, National Archives.

12. Walter H. Waggoner, "Americans Score U.S. Fair Exhibits," *The New York Times*, 24 April 1958.

13. Rudofsky, "On Exhibition Design," 13. The term *indirect* was crossed out on his manuscript.

14. "Brussels '58: The United States Speaks to the World, Progress Report," *Interiors* 117 (September 1957): 139 (hereafter referred to as "Progress Report"). Emphasis in the original.

15. Jacqueline H. Hume to President Dwight D. Eisenhower, 23 September 1958, National Archives.

16. Walter H. Waggoner, "Guidebook to Aid U.S. Fair Exhibit," *The New York Times*, 11 May 1958.

17. Ibid.

18. "Progress Report," 134.

19. A report explained that "interviews with recognized authorities in the fields of mass information media, the arts, sciences and the humanities continued from January 1957, until the M.I.T. conference, and afterward." Working document entitled "The American Theme," National Archives. No author noted.

20. "Progress Report," 134. Rudofsky often complained of the constitutive inability of the American officials to comprehend that the Brussels exposition was a cultural rather than a trade fair.

21. "Progress Report," 135. The report noted that MIT had been selected "both because of its outstanding achievements in the technological field and because of its integration of the humanities into its technological curriculum" (135).

22. As reported in *Interiors*, this group included "Dean John H. Burchard of MIT; Associate Professor of Political Science De Sola Pool; Professor of Electrical Engineering Weisner; Professor of History Rostow; Professor of Physics Weiskopf; Professor of Education Siepman . . . M IT design Professor Gyorgy Kepes." "Progress Report," 134–35.

23. Ibid., 136.

24. Ibid., 135–36.

25. Ibid., 136.

26. Ibid., 135.

27. Ibid. Kepes knew Rudofsky already, since the latter had taught at MIT the previous year.

28. Ibid., 135.

29. Ibid.

30. Waggonner, "Americans Score U.S. Fair Exhibits," 2. With comic faithfulness to this report, a letter to the editor of *The New York Times* responded to the adverse criticism of Rudofsky with a "European view of Fair." Characterizing the American visitor as "competition-minded," he explained that "the Brussels exhibit is neither a trade fair nor a competition. A mere display of power and wealth does not fit its high moral ambitions. Besides, the European is repelled by bigness and mass." H. Grunstein, "Letter to the Times: European View of Fair," *The New York Times*, 7 July 1958.

31. June Wayne, "Brussels Conclusion," *Arts and Architecture* 76, no. 1 (January 1959): 31.

32. Rudofsky's lecture also addressed his installation design for the MoMA exhibition *Textiles USA*, along with the overall organization of the Brussels exhibits and three other sections for which he was primarily responsible: *Islands of Living, Streetscape*, and a series of loop films.

33. Rudofsky writes:

> At one point when it seemed that the pavilion would contain little more than commonplace exhibits, I requested the use of the entrance area on the ground floor for a

special exhibition, that I would think up and assemble myself, without benefit of a commission or committee; with no strings attached, no censorship, no compromise. To my surprise this was granted and I was given free hand. It was to become the notorious exhibit, called *The Face of America*, that raised the temperature of American visitors. "On Exhibition Design," 25.

34. Ibid., 26.

35. "Progress Report," 139.

36. Rudofsky, "On Exhibition Design," 26.

37. Ibid., 27.

38. Robert Warner, coordinator, U.S. Building Exhibits, to Gerson ("Lefty") H. Lush, Office of the U.S. Commissioner, Brussels World's Fair, 14 January 1958, National Archives.

39. The letter discussed security for the check in detail:

> The check could be placed in a ship's safe in care of the captain in transit, and on arrival at Le Havre could be met by the Embassy Security Officer plus one of our top officials plus anyone else the National Archives want to assure the check's safe arrival. Here it would be kept in the Embassy safe until placed in the pavilion. In the pavilion it would be placed behind heavy bullet-proof glass and, of course, would be made as burglar-proof as possible. We would have a guard in the area at all times even during those hours when the Fair was not in operation.

Ibid.

40. Ibid. The subsequent process was blocked by the director of the Smithsonian.

41. Rudofsky, "On Exhibition Design," 27.

42. Ibid., 28.

43. Ibid.

44. Ibid. This is presumably a reference to the Matisse vestments in the collection of MoMA's architecture and design department. These were first displayed in the exhibition *Matisse Chasubles*, on view in New York between 20 December 1955 and 15 January 1956. Rudofsky had actually visited the church in Vence in the late 1940s: "Went to Vence, but Matisse was sick and away; talked to the Vicar at Vence and may see Perret (who works with Matisse on the Vence church) in Paris." Bernard Rudofsky to Douglas Haskell, 29 July 1949, archives of Berta Rudofsky.

45. Rudofsky, "On Exhibition Design," 31.

46. After noting that "the European is repelled by bigness and mass," a European observer explained, "That's why the display of the first Ford model is so exquisite; it has the prestige of ancestry and uniqueness and reminds the visitor that the United States is the homeland of this formidable invention. The 1958 Ford runs all over the world; why show it at the fair?" Grunstein, "European View of Fair." A mass-produced, standardized object, the car made reference to the increasing mobility of the American population. Not yet subject to the pseudodifferentiation of midcentury commodities, for Rudofsky it might also have stood for a technical invention not yet coopted by capital.

47. In this sense it was an anomaly. With regard to the typical workings of a display, Susan Stewart asserts:

> Any collection promises totality. The appearance of that totality is made possible by the face-to-face experience of display, the all-at-onceness under which the collection might be apprehended by the observer. This display, of course, marks the defeat of

time, the triumph over the particularity of contexts in which the collected objects first appeared.

"Death and Life, in That Order, in the Works of Charles Willson Peale," in *Visual Display: Culture beyond Appearances*, ed. Lynne Cooke and Peter Wollen (Seattle: Bay Press, 1995), 31.

48. Jacques Derrida, *Archive Fever: A Freudian Impression*, trans. Eric Prenowitz (Chicago: University of Chicago Press, 1995), 3.

49. Rudofsky notes in 1967:

> A civilization where practically everything is disposable, including civilization itself, has no room for relics. Things old and durable are looked upon with suspicion, if not with contempt. Even such a venerable institution as the house—the sort we frivolously called home—fails to engage our affection. The thought that a building constructed centuries ago might still serve its original purpose is heresy to those who believe that progress is unavoidable, indeed irremediable. Today, when technological obsolescence has become the prime mover and prerequisite of progress, our buildings are wrecked long before they have outlived their usefulness. . . . And though conventional sentiment does tolerate the cult of ruins (no doubt because there are almost none in our country), the continued use and care of superannuated architecture abroad—not just of grandiose buildings but of humble houses as well—strikes us as absurd. Their very longevity is felt as a drag on the advancement of mankind.

Bernard Rudofsky, "Troglodytes," *Horizon* 9, no. 2 (Spring 1967): 30.

50. Bernard Rudofsky to Israel Shenker, 17 September 1958, archives of Berta Rudofsky. Reading an archive is, in any case, a private affair. "Private story telling," as Alice Yaeger Kaplan argues, "dominates all stages of work in the archives." "Working in the Archives," *Yale French Studies* 77 (1990): 103.

51. Derrida, *Archive Fever*, 29.

52. Bernard Rudofsky, "First Draft of an informal report on the exhibits proposed for the American pavilion at the Brussels Exhibition, 1958," sent as a memorandum to James Plaut, 5 June 1957, 5, archives of Berta Rudofsky. Emphasis in the original.

53. Rudofsky, "On Exhibition Design," 12.

54. Ibid.

55. Bernard Rudofsky, "The Art of Display," *Interiors* CV, no. 9 (April 1946): 89.

56. Ibid., 142.

57. Ibid., 112.

58. Rudofsky, "Art of Display," 144. On the installation techniques, and in particular Albert Parr's background and refitting of the American Museum of Natural History during this period, see Ann Reynolds, "Visual Stories," in *Visual Display: Culture beyond Appearances*, 82–109. With respect to the habitat groups, she explains:

> These groups present life-scale, three-dimensional reproductions of particular places or events in enclosed showcases. The museum's artists achieved a high degree of illusionism in the groups through the use of sophisticated techniques for accurately transferring specific landscape views and individual specimens or casts of plants, rock formations, and indigenous wildlife from 'the field' to the museum.

Reynolds also explains that, following Parr's arrival in 1942, the habitat groups came under criticism for being 95 percent art and 5 percent science, that they were "expensive, pretty, three-dimensional pictures." She traces how Parr came up with the notion of visual diagrams that presented the museum's collection through his ecological, not evolutionary, model. Rudofsky met with Margaret Mead during his research on the collections of the museum, and also befriended Parr, who would subsequently act as a reference for his application for research funding for his work on vernacular architecture.

59. Exhibition #306, *Arts of the South Seas*, was on view at MoMA from 29 January through 19 May 1946.

60. Rudofsky, "Art of Display," 144.

61. Gregory Bateson, "Arts of the South Seas," *Art Bulletin* 28, no. 2 (June 1946): 119.

62. Ibid.

63. On this, see my essay "Bernard Rudofsky: Allegories of Nomadism and Dwelling," in *Anxious Modernisms: Experimentation in Postwar Architectural Culture*, ed. Sarah Williams Goldhagen and Réjean Legault (Cambridge, Mass.: MIT Press, and Montreal: CCA, 2000), 215–38.

64. Bernard Rudofsky to Peter G. Harnden, 9 March 1957, archives of Berta Rudofsky.

65. Roland Barthes, "The Great Family of Man" (1957), in *Mythologies*, trans. Annette Lavers (New York: Hill and Wang, 1972), 100.

66. Gyan Prakash, "Museum Matters," in *The End(s) of the Museum: Symposium*, ed. Thomas Keenan (Barcelona: Fundacio Antonio Tápies, 1995), 53–66.

67. Prakash argues:

> [I]f fragments are gathered up to constitute a whole, they are also marked by the stamp of authenticity. Exotic artifacts are positioned as authentic residues of myths, practices, values, and forms of organization that are thought to underlie the wholeness and integrity of other cultures. Such projections of authenticity and wholeness project the exhibition of exotic cultures as entirely separate from and unaffected by the structure that gathers and stages them. Thus, ethnographic displays represent their exhibits as objects saved from the inevitable decay of time, protected from the certain fate of impurity that awaits them. Rescued from history and authorized as authentic remains, they become collections-in-order that represent other cultures as integrated wholes, unaffected by the structure of power that collects and exhibits them. They are wrenched from the history of unequal relations within which they have entered the museum and placed in the frozen time of tradition. Encased and exhibited in separate halls devoted to a slice of time or to a part of the history of Man, discrepant histories are entombed as tradition, continuity, essence.

"Museum Matters," 56. Prakash goes on to figure the West as the absent center of all such ethnographic techniques, citing James Clifford to the effect that "the orders of the West were everywhere present in the Musée de l'Homme, except on display" (57).

68. Gilles Deleuze, *Proust and Signs*, trans. Richard Howard (New York: Braziller, 1972), 167.

69. Bernard Rudofsky, "The Human Side of Architecture," unpublished lecture, delivered in Seattle, 1966, archives of Berta Rudofsky.

70. Morris, "Brussels Exhibit Irks Eisenhower."

71. Israel Shenker to Bernard Rudofsky, 23 September 1958, archives of Berta Rudofsky. Shenker, who worked in the Central European bureau of Time-Life International, was responding to a letter from Rudofsky inquiring about writing a review of the fair.

72. Morris, "Brussels Exhibit Irks Eisenhower."

73. "Text of the Report to the President by George V. Allen, Director of the United States Information Agency, White House Press Release for June 29, 1958, 2, National Archives. See also "Allen Files Report on Brussels Fair," *The New York Times*, 29 June 1958. Having received news about the Brussels fiasco, Rudofsky wrote to Israel Shenker: "What American publication would risk printing a piece written by me on the Pavilion, more especially on *The Face of America* (which was after all my own idea and was handled, from the choice of every object to the most minute detail of installation, by me . . .)[?]" He explained that he did not wish to pursue a "defense" but rather an "attack," since, as he explained, "there is a great deal to be said about such topics as: the limitations of the design-er as an artist; government censorship; mob mind; etc. . . . I 'd be happy to have a say in this quar-rel about America's Face, to write a short epilog on the United States' participation." Bernard Rudofsky to Israel Shenker, 17 September 1958, archives of Berta Rudofsky. According to Rudofsky, that participation had reflected an American populace mired in uncritical mass consumption, unwilling or unable to think of America except through unified, normative representations, and a government deploying censorship to assure such a homogeneous picture. In "On Exhibition Design," he referred to the "allegorical figure of the presidential investigator," noting that "his pro-nouncements, his silences, his every move, made headlines at home and abroad." He maintained that "the presence of an American Grand Inquisitor did not fit the European's picture of the United States as a mature and free country." Rudofsky, "On Exhibition Design," 35.

74. Emily Genauer, "US Art Show at Brussels Fair," *New York Herald Tribune*, clipping from archives of Berta Rudofsky (n.d.). This clipping must be from around September 1958, since Genauer men-tions that the fair has four months remaining. Thus the football uniform must have survived Allen's editing, despite his recommendation that it be removed. Genauer called for a further "res-cue operation" and asked for "responsible outside authorities [to] force a reexamination of the thinking behind our pavilion."

75. June Wayne, "Brussels Conclusion," *Arts and Architecture* 76, no. 1 (January 1959): 30.

76. Rudofsky, "On Exhibition Design," 34–35.

77. Bernard Rudofsky, quoted in Barbara Flanagan, "Designer Is a Versatile Idea Man," *Minneapolis Morning Tribune*, 25 January 1962.

78. Rudofsky, "On Exhibition Design," 35.

79. "A Visit to the U.S. Pavilion: From the Potato to the Isotope," *Le Soir*, 23 April 1958, trans. Hughes Vehenne, National Archives.

80. Rudofsky, "On Exhibition Design," 31.

81. Ibid., emphasis added.

82. Ibid., 32.

83. Ibid.

84. Ibid.

85. Ibid.

86. Bernard Rudofsky, "The Argument," one-page typescript from the exhibition files for *Are Clothes Modern?* Office of the Registrar, Museum of Modern Art, New York.

87. In *Proust and Signs*, Gilles Deleuze notes that there are in fact two kinds of things in the world. Following Plato, he distinguishes between those that leave the mind inactive and those that "force us to think":

> The first are objects of recognition; all of the faculties are upon these objects, but in a contingent exercise, which makes us say "that is a finger," that is an apple, that is a

house, and so on. On the contrary, there are other things which force us to think: no longer *recognizable* objects, but things which do violence, *encountered* signs.

Deleuze, *Proust and Signs*, 166. Emphasis in the original.

88. Despite their having been irradiated, one visitor observed, "some of them were in bad condition." Hume to President Eisenhower, 23 September 1958.

89. Ludwig Mies van der Rohe, quoted in Peter Carter, "Mies van der Rohe, An Appreciation on the Occasion, this Month, of His 70th Birthday," *Architectural Design* 31 (March 1961): 115.

90. See my article "Underneath Aesthetics and Utility: The Untransposable Fetish of Bernard Rudofsky," *Assemblage* 38 (April 1999): 58–89. As evident from his notebooks, Rudofsky would continue to read Bataille until the 1970s. While there is no direct trace of Bataille's writings in Rudofsky's musing on *The Face of America*, the dissident librarian and philospher's thought remains resonant with this project. Georges Bataille, "The Big Toe," (1929), trans. Allan Stoekl, in *Visions of Excess: Selected Writings, 1927–1939*, ed. Allan Stoekl (Minneapolis: University of Minnesota Press, 1985), 20-23.

91. Georges Bataille, "Materialism" (1929), trans. Allan Stoekl, in *Visions of Excess*, 15.

92. See Jean-François Lyotard, *The Postmodern Condition: A Report on Knowledge*, trans. Geoff Bennington and Brian Massumi (Minneapolis: University of Minnesota Press, 1984).

93. Caught between these two poles—idealism and materialism—the potato posed a challenge to the semiotic reading that would normally be called forth. Precisely through being aberrant, Rudofsky's exhibit raises questions regarding the functioning of what Gilles Deleuze and Félix Guattari refer to as the "signifying regime of signs." In this sense Rudofsky's *Face of America* can be understood as a turn away from a signifying regime of signs toward a complex assemblage of other semiotic systems: presignifying, countersignifying, postsignifying regimes of signs. Within this formulation, Rudofsky's project articulates a passional betrayal, the production of a line of flight from what he regarded as a despotic signifying regime. See Gilles Deleuze and Félix Guattari, "587 B.C.–A.D. 79: On Several Regimes of Signs," in *A Thousand Plateaus: Capitalism and Schizophrenia*, trans. Brian Massumi (Minneapolis: University of Minnesota Press, 1987), 111–48. Deleuze and Guattari are careful to insist that it is not that any particular cultural or historical formation operates through a particular regime of signs but rather that they all operate through differing degrees of each of them. Indeed, capitalism, which we are dealing with here, operates according to a particular machinic assemblage (of forces and matter) within which each of these regimes of signs will be mobilized by, or in relation to, the official, state apparatus.

94. Georges Bataille, *The Accursed Share*, trans. Robert Hurley (New York: Zone Books, 1988), 1: 131.

95. See, for instance, Walter Gropius, *Scope of Total Architecture: A New Way of Life*, ed. Ruth Nanda Anshen (New York: Harper and Brothers, 1955).

96. Rudofsky, "On Exhibition Design," 36.

97. Ibid., 37. Emphasis in the original.

98. Georges Bataille, "The Labyrinth" (1935–36), trans. Allan Stoekl, in *Visions of Excess*, 176.

99. "In sum," writes Bataille,

> it makes us laugh to pass very abruptly, all of a sudden, from a world in which each thing is well qualified, in which each thing is given in its stability, generally in a stable order, to a world in which our assurance is suddenly overthrown, in which we perceive that this assurance is deceptive, and where we believed that everything was strictly anticipated, an unforeseeable and upsetting element appeared unexpectedly

FELICITY D. SCOTT

from the unforeseeable, that reveals to us in sum a final truth: that superficial appearances conceal a perfect lack of response to our anticipation.

"Nonknowledge, Laughter, and Tears," trans. Michelle Kendall and Stuart Kendall, in *The Unfinished System of Nonknowledge*, ed. Stuart Kendall (Minneapolis: University of Minnesota Press, 2001), 135.

100. Michel Foucault, *The Order of Things* (New York: Random House, 1970), xv–xvi.

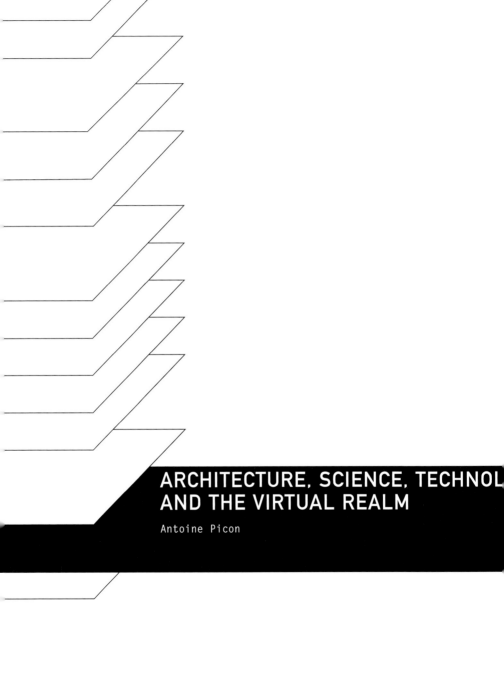

ARCHITECTURE, SCIENCE, TECHNOLOGY AND THE VIRTUAL REALM

Antoine Picon

In recent years, a growing number of images and metaphors taken from mathematics, physics, and molecular biology have spread among architects. A large number of these images and metaphors are linked to the development of digital architecture and to the growing importance given to the virtual dimension in the architectural discipline. It seems worthwhile to reflect on their possible significance. Is the abundant use of references such as topology, fractals, chaos theory, or DNA sequencing a mere rhetorical habit, or is it dictated by more profound reasons? In other words, at what level do scientific references function in contemporary architecture? The question has become unavoidable, given the multiplication of these references.

The use of scientific images and metaphors within the architectural discipline is, of course, no recent phenomenon. Throughout the nineteenth century, architects made frequent reference to the rapidly developing biological sciences. Similarly, the main protagonists of the modern movement invoked scientific notions such as Einstein's theory of relativity. But these episodes are not equal in status or importance to those of today.

The greater or lesser degree of importance of the scientific references made by architects can be assessed through the extent of their contribution to the architectural culture. In the architectural field, borrowings from science have sometimes led to the production of new concepts and notions that have proved seminal for architectural practice. What would nineteenth-century architecture have been without the notion of structure? This notion resulted from a series of exchanges between architecture and the study of living beings. Actually, the French word *structure* was first used to designate the internal organization of the body and its various organs before it was applied to buildings.[1]

Some scientific references have proved more superficial than others. Such was the case with relativity and the modern movement. For an architect like Le Corbusier, relativity remained a prestigious but remote and somewhat obscure theory. What are the conditions that, at certain times, make the relations between science and architecture truly productive? This question, again, is difficult to escape, given the contemporary state of affairs in the architectural domain.

At this point, we may consider a possible answer. The productive character of certain episodes in the history of relations between science and architecture is perhaps attributable to the existence of similarities between the operations upon which science and architecture are based. We know, indeed, that concepts and notions do not develop in an ethereal intellectual sphere. They are inseparable from practice, from concrete instruments and operations. Geometric constructions and surveying techniques were, for example, common to the European scientific and architectural practices of the fifteenth, sixteenth, and seventeenth centuries. Nineteenth-century biological sciences and architecture shared the practice of dissection. As Martin

ANTOINE PICON

Bressani has shown in his dissertation on Viollet-le-Duc, dissection was as fundamental for the nineteenth-century rationalist archaeologist and architect as for the scientist studying living beings.[2]

These similarities would present no meaning if they were not imbued with a sensorial dimension. In other words, science and architecture meet when they both contribute to the cultural construction of perception. As Michael Baxandall puts it in *Patterns of Intention*, to live in culture is synonymous with a specific education of the senses.[3] Vision is especially important in dealing with architecture. Science and architecture often meet in their common attempt to shape or reshape the categories of visual perception.

These categories are in their turn inseparable from the construction of the subject who looks at the world. From the Renaissance on, major shifts in vision have also been shifts in the definition of the human subject. What science and architecture share is not only the ambition to interpret and transform the world but above all to populate the world with subjects different from one period to another.

ARCHITECTURE AND THE VIRTUAL DIMENSION

Let me deal now with the question of the virtual. How is "virtual reality" to be defined? Etymologically, virtual means full of virtue, virtue being taken here as a capacity to act. According to the old philosophical distinction between capacity and act, virtual reality is nothing but a potential awaiting its full actualization. Virtual reality is by no means unreal, but its full effect is not yet in evidence. Reality is not the problem; it is its full development or presence that is partly lacking. Virtual reality can be interpreted as a germ, as the starting point of a dynamic evolution.

The distinction between what was only potential and what was fully realized played a fundamental role in medieval theology and philosophy. In the seventeenth century, it remained fundamental for philosophers such as Leibniz, hence the recurring interest taken by Deleuze in Leibniz's philosophy. Among contemporary philosophers, Deleuze is the one who has dealt most extensively with the theme of the virtual.

From its philosophical origin, let us remember this fundamental feature of virtual reality: it is a reality, but a potential one. Virtual reality might very well represent the potency, the tension, the fold or indefinite series of folds, if we want to use Deleuze's vocabulary,[4] that makes the ordinary reality possible.

In such a perspective, architecture presents a strong virtual content, for architecture is to be reduced neither to a collection of remarkable buildings nor to the aesthetic, utilitarian, and constructive rules that make these buildings remarkable. Architecture is neither a collection of things nor a set of rules. It has more to do with a creative principle enabling the constant exchange between the built reality and the domain of knowledge, precepts, and rules. Architecture might very well be grounded in virtual reality.

This virtual character can be viewed from various angles. The notions of project and design correspond clearly to one of the most fundamental viewpoints. The distinction between the building and the intention that gives birth to it is essential indeed to the modern definition of the architectural discipline. This definition began to appear at the Renaissance with the emergence of the Italian notion of *disegno*, meaning both the intention and its spatial expression. The French word *dessein* and the English *design* had comparable meanings at the time.

From the start, design was a compound of numerous things. In addition to covering both the general intention and its spatial translation, design also comprised a technological dimension. Brunelleschi's famous cupola for the cathedral of Florence was among the very first examples of this technological dimension. It is well known that Brunelleschi designed not only a structure but also the machines and the process that enabled its realization.[5] His inheritors did not always follow his path, but this comprehensive conception of design has remained an ideal ever since that time. In many respects, Jean Prouvé's *idée constructive*, or constructive idea, is a new formulation of this old ideal.[6]

What is the reality of an architectural design? It is precisely a virtual reality. Through the maze of its determinations, design makes the actualization of an intention possible. Design is among the virtual dimensions of architecture.

The importance of this virtual dimension has grown almost continuously from the Renaissance on. After the founding episode of Brunelleschi's cupola, Alberti put the stress on the intellectual nature of architectural design in his *De re aedificatoria*. But until the late eighteenth century, this humanist conception was constantly challenged by a more down-to-earth vision giving

ANTOINE PICON

precedence to practical rules founded on the observation of existing models as well as to technical rules. This attitude was especially pronounced in France, where the professional figures of the architect and the master mason remained close to one another for a very long time, many architects being actual master masons. By the end of the eighteenth century, however, a radical turn toward a more liberal definition of the architect took place. This turn was accompanied by a new emphasis on the intellectual content of architecture. "What is architecture?" asked Etienne-Louis Boullée in his *Essai sur l'art*, written circa 1780:

> Am I to define it, with Vitruvius, as the art of building? No. Vitruvius's definition contains a flagrant error; he mistakes the effect for the cause. To execute, you must first conceive. Our earliest forefathers did not build their huts until they had first conceived the image of them. That production of the mind, that creation, constitutes architecture.[7]

By the end of the eighteenth century, Boullée was not the only architect to consider design as synonymous with the production of a mental image. At a time when architecture was trying to distinguish itself from engineering, imagination was given precedence over other intellectual qualities such as pure reason. The importance given to imagination, interpreted as man's ultimate creative faculty, reinforced the virtual dimension of architectural design. Simultaneously, architects became concerned about its social role in a changing world. As Manfredo Tafuri stated many times in his books, this preoccupation gave birth to a new relationship between the architectural project and social utopia.[8] Such a connection was to reach its climax with the modern movement. For the moderns, architecture and urban design were filled with a potential that would not only reshape the building industry but also transform the entire world. Nothing was to escape the power of the actualization of modern architecture and urban design.

Leaving now the question of design, let me turn to order and proportion. For centuries, these two notions were synonymous with another virtual dimension at work in architecture. In the frame of thought provided by the Vitruvian tradition, order and proportion were not something static such as a set of rules tacked onto the building. Extending beyond the architectural realm, they were at the core of the universe. The French seventeenth-century theologian and philosopher Jacques Bénigne Bossuet was very explicit about their importance when he stated that God had created the world by providing it with order and proportion.[9] At a more modest scale, the architect was in a sense replicating God's fundamental course of action when making use of the architectural orders and proportions.

Although treatises like François Blondel's or Charles D'Aviler's courses of architecture gave indications about what the correct proportions of architecture should be, order and proportion could not be encapsulated in a single set of formulas. They were variable, oscillatory, hence the importance given to problems such as optical correction. Order and proportion were among the virtues of architecture. Through their use, architecture expressed its dynamism, its living essence.

Just like order and proportion, the traditional status of ornament also began to be challenged by the end of the eighteenth century. Until then, ornament had been another expression of the potency at work in architecture. Contrary to our contemporary vision, ornament had no connotation of gratuity. It was not something added to construction; it sprang from necessity, as Vitruvius or Alberti stated it. Like order and proportion, ornament expressed the fundamental regularity of the universe and, above all, its fecundity. Ornament, in general, gave evidence of the creativity and the beauty of the cosmic order, just as the fruits and flowers that it often imitated were the product and the finery of nature. Its reduction to an agreeable but inessential part of the project was synonymous with an impoverishment of the virtual reality at work in architecture.

In the process leading to this reduction and impoverishment, Piranesi occupies a key position. In his work, ornament is already partially gratuitous; but its proliferation enables it to regain part of its former importance. As an isolated motif, Piranesi's ornament is somewhat arbitrary; it remains essential, however, as the mark of an indefinite process of ornamentation.[10] Almost a century after Piranesi, Gottfried Semper also explored this path in his theoretical work, the ornamental impulse playing a fundamental role. From the elementary plait to the richest embroidery, Semper saw this impulse at work in the art of textile production, which he associated with the origin of architecture.[11]

Order, proportion, and ornament—these traditional virtues of architecture have become far less powerful since the decline of the Vitruvian tradition that began in the late seventeenth century. In the past two centuries, other traditions have appeared that have become even stronger.

Structure is among these traditions. Structure is often misinterpreted when it is seen as a purely static organization. The writings of Viollet-le-Duc or Auguste Choisy may help us correct this view. For these proponents of nineteenth-century structural rationalism, structure was the consequence of a seminal principle, a "means to a product rather than a production."[12] In his *Entretiens sur l'architecture*, Viollet-le-Duc explained, for instance, that structure was, in his eyes, the result of a founding tension between the social needs and the technological culture of a period.[13] According to him, the resulting structure always bore the mark of this fundamental tension.

Another way to understand the dynamic nature of structure is to pay attention to the fact that we actually never "see" a structure, in the ordinary sense. We only perceive its result, an assemblage of parts and materials. Structure is what makes this assemblage possible. Structure is a potency.

At the beginning of the twentieth century, the dynamic character of structure was further enhanced with the appearance of *On Growth and Form* by D'Arcy Wentworth Thompson. In this important book, which influenced generations of architects and engineers, structure became synonymous with the process of growth and development.[14] The virtual character of structure was thus reinforced. With Thompson, we are not so far from our contemporary notion of program. Structure becomes synonymous with program.

This brief review of the virtual dimensions at work in architecture would not be complete without a mention of space—architectural space as it was defined by the moderns. Architectural space was neither the Cartesian geometric space nor the space of sensorial perception: the first was too abstract; the second, too concrete. Geometric space did not take into account phenomena such as human scale or the perception of light and texture. Space as sensorial perception was too rich and complex to allow for any kind of design. Regarding space, the ultimate ambition of modern architecture was to find a compromise between these two extreme conceptions of space in order to stimulate thought as well as sensation.

The importance given by the moderns to movement and its icons, such as the automobile, was part of this general ambition. In their eyes, movement appeared precisely at the intersection of the abstract and the concrete, of geometrical measurement and sensorial experience. Le Corbusier's famous definition of architecture as a machine for producing feelings was perhaps the best expression of the founding tension between rigor and emotion that gave birth to architectural space.[15]

Like other key dimensions of architecture, space was not a thing but an operator enabling a constant oscillation between the abstract and the tangible, the mobile and the motionless. Such an oscillation allowed the architect to design spaces that were both specific and imbued with universal meaning; in other words, it enabled architects to reconcile place and space.

Design, order and proportion, ornament, structure, and space—the potencies of architecture that I have been reviewing—may help us understand the medium's strong virtual content. Architecture is not something stable. It appears through a series of productive tensions or potentials. Design, order and proportion, ornament, structure, and space are among these tensions or potentials that have made and still make works of architecture and, above all, architectural expression possible.

THE VIRTUAL AS A MATRIX OF EXCHANGE

At this stage, let me return to the general problem of the relations between architecture and science. Like architecture, science is permeated by the virtual. Indeed, science is reducible to neither a set of theoretical results nor to a collection of experimental data. In its development, science appears as the productive tension between theory and experiment or, to put it differently, between abstract knowledge and practice. Science studies have shown convincingly that science is not to be assimilated with pure knowledge.[16] It is no more satisfactory, however, to consider only its practical side. Envisaged as a dynamic, science appears as the potency, the tension or the fold linking these two terms.

The virtual dimension at work in both architecture and science might very well account for the constant circulation of images and metaphors between the two fields. I should note in passing that such a circulation is by no means unidirectional. Throughout its history, science has repeatedly made use of architectural notions. In their quest for the regularities of the universe, sixteenth- and seventeenth-century scientists, for instance, often referred to the architectural principles of order and proportion. Peter Galison has shown how early-twentieth-century German science was obsessed with the notion of *Aufbau*, which was clearly imbued with an architectural meaning.[17]

ANTOINE PICON

From order and proportion to space, the various expressions of the virtual dimension at work in architecture appear to have played a major role in its recourse to scientific images and metaphors. These expressions proved all the more influential for being linked to instruments and operations shared by architects and scientists. As previously discussed, from the Renaissance to the end of the seventeenth century, the reference made by architects to order and proportion was linked to the use of geometrical constructions as well as to surveying techniques that were also used by scientists. Hence, the capacity of order and proportion to provide a base for convincing exchanges between the two domains.

These expressions were also inseparable from a cultural shaping of the senses—of vision in particular. Such a relation is evident in the case of order and proportion, which presupposed a specific education of the eye. But it is also true of structure and space. If we do not actually "see" structures, we perceive them through the combination of visual and muscular intuition. The Spanish engineer Eduardo Torroja had this combination in mind when he stated that structural design required an understanding "to the backbone" of the mechanical principles of inner equilibrium.[18] Combining the eye's power of appreciation with kinesthetic sensations, this type of understanding is a cultural construction.

Through this kind of sensory construction, architecture, just as science or technology, contributes to the respective definitions of man and his nonhuman environment; it contributes to the structuring of their interface. As a cultural production, architecture is more than a mere combination of solidity, commodity and beauty; it is as much about what man is as what he is not, about the relations between the subject and his environment. As Nelson Goodman has said, architecture, like science, is about the way we "make" worlds, worlds populated with subjects and objects the definitions of which are always historically determined.[19]

Today, the computer is symptomatic of a profound change in the way we make worlds. Through the generalization of notions such as information, code, and program, it affects both the way we construct the subject and the interpretation we give the subject's environment. In between these extremes, society is changing also. We live in a new type of society, an information-based society that is the basis for the process of globalization we are experiencing. Many of today's sociologists and historians are tempted to assume that this society preceded the invention of the computer. Whether this is true or not, one thing is certain: the possession of information, such as a file of potential clients, has become often more vital than the possession of physical goods.

How could architecture remain untouched in such a context? To the various critics who tend to play down the impact of the computer on architecture, there is this response: the computer is only the tip of the iceberg. It is not that the computer in itself has changed architecture; it is that, because both nature and society have changed, architecture is confronted with new challenges. Its intensive use of scientific metaphors appears as a consequence of such a situation.

A NEW VIRTUAL REALITY

For architecture, the virtual reality so often invoked today corresponds in fact to the emergence of a new virtual dimension. To understand its most salient features, those that explain to a large extent the connections with science that are claimed by contemporary architects, one must pay attention to its historical origins.

The origins of computer-based reality can be traced back to the end of World War II and the development of the Cold War. At this time, a new space was emerging, a space of phenomena that could be visualized only through the use of screens, maps, and diagrams. These phenomena could be almost anything: attacks by bombers or armies, the state of military supplies, economic trends. They were sometimes "real," sometimes mere hypotheses. They were studied using radar, strategic maps, and charts in places such as control or war rooms. In such a context, the effective and the simulated were in constant interaction one with another. To the strategist, what mattered were events and scenarios, either realized or simply possible.

There was surely something paradoxical in the importance given to events and scenarios whose realization could not be predicted; the new strategic space of the Cold War was, to a large extent, the result of calculation. From predicting financial markets to political voting, we have become so used to this strange coexistence of calculation and chance that we no longer pay attention to it. It does not mean, however, that the paradox has disappeared.

Historians such as Paul Edwards have shown how such a context was to shape the subsequent development of the computer and the emer-

ANTOINE PICON

gence of cyberspace.[20] From its beginning, architects and engineers were intrigued by virtual reality. They were also well aware of its military connotation. In an enlightening article, Mark Wigley has shown the influence of virtual reality on Buckminster Fuller and his "World Game," a proposal for a global simulation that was clearly inspired by the key principles of the war room as well as by the perspectives opened up by electronic calculators.[21] Transposed by NASA, these principles were also present in Archigram's theoretical projects.[22]

Although the military connotation has become less evident today, the virtual dimension that computers help to produce retains some of its original features, such as the preeminence of events and scenarios over static entities. From an architectural standpoint, the major consequence of this preeminence is the destabilization of form, a destabilization all the more paradoxical since it is the operations of the designer and the calculations of the computer that simultaneously, and rigorously, define form.

Architectural form used to appear as the ultimate result of a process of research. Its beauty was the beauty of the end, of the point of equilibrium. The equilibrium was often dynamic, but the form was supposed to dominate the movement, to encapsulate it. The beauty of architecture could be somewhat analogous to the pleasure derived from the spectacle of a dance or a flow. But it was the underlying structure of the dance or the flow, the choreography or the mechanics, that was made visible through the architectural medium.

A computer-generated architectural form can no longer pretend to achieve this status. Even if it appears as the most satisfying configuration for its designer, it remains the result of an arbitrary stop in an endless process of geometric transformation, the type of process that Greg Lynn calls "animation" (fig. 1).[23] Architectural form becomes similar to a cross-section in a continuous geometrical flow. Whereas the traditional status of architectural form suggested a comparison with the human body, its new status renders it closer to the snapshot or the videogram.

New problems arise from this situation. There is certainly a problem of aesthetics. How are we to judge the beauty of the blobs and all the other creatures that appear on our computer screens? Even when the projects are supposed to be realized in the physical world, even when they are actually built, this problem remains.

Part of the problem is linked to an impression of arbitrariness. Why has the designer stopped the process of geometrical transformation at one stage and not the other? Justifications are not always visually evident.

When the process is haulted, architectural form becomes similar to an event, although design is more and more comparable to the writing of a scenario. The architectural form literally appears on the screen, while its production from carefully selected parameters looks like the layout of a plot. The similarity between form and event is probably one of the most important effects computers have had on architecture. From the elementary bit to the geometrical transformation made visible on their screens, computers are machines that produce sequences of events. But this link between architecture and the computer is rooted in something more profound, namely the fact that information is nothing but a production of events. That fact was made clear as early as 1949, in Claude Shannon's *Mathematical Theory of Communication*, which played a seminal role in the construction of the modern notion of information. Indeed, for Shannon, information was linked to the problem of the selection of a given message in a set of possible ones. Selection, choice: the notion of information has definitely something to do with the production of events.[24] From the elementary bit to the determination of the final form of a project, selection and choice remain the fundamental issue in our computerized architectural world.

The fascination exerted by scientific metaphors on so many young contemporary architects is probably a consequence of this new status of architectural form. In particular it explains the interest taken in the nonlinear dynamic systems that have invaded entire fields of scientific research. The latter systems are often described as chaotic. The atmosphere and the weather are paradigmatic of this chaotic nature.[25] What happens in these systems cannot be predicted because of their high sensitivity to initial conditions. Does it mean that the ultimate justification of the architectural form is that it happens just like rain?

Until now, one of the functions of virtual reality was to anchor architectural production to some kind of necessity. Design was synonymous with the quest for the necessary form. Order and proportion, structure, and, above all, space were supposed to be essential and thus imparted with an internal necessity. One of the most disconcerting features of virtual reality is

ANTOINE PICON

that it seems to be synonymous with a high degree of arbitrariness. In other words, nothing can now guarantee the designer that his project is the result of the best possible choice.

The recent fascination for diagram—a fascination again rooted in the observation of scientific practices and an attempt to imitate some features of science—might very well stem from this situation of uncertainty and doubt, with diagram acting as a possible antidote.[26] Apart from its various philosophical justifications, borrowed from thinkers such as Michel Foucault and Gilles Deleuze, one of the major interests of the diagrammatic approach is to re-create an internal necessity in the design process. According to its proponents, diagram appears as an abstract machine or as a program whose unfolding is synonymous with a new rigor.

More specifically, the two partners of UN Studio, Ben van Berkel and Caroline Bos, have related the use of diagrams to what they call "deep planning" [fig. 2].[27] In their projects, like the Arhem station, they aim at depth by integrating as many data as possible. Technical and functional data must, of course, be taken into account, but the ambition is to master other fac-

[fig. 1]

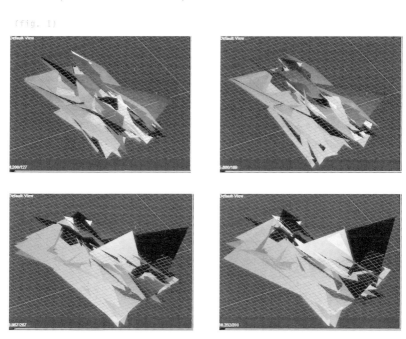

Greg Lynn, "House Prototype"

ARCHITECTURE, SCIENCE, TECHNOLOGY, AND THE VIRTUAL REALM

tors—economic and even political factors. From this perspective, the use of diagrams is meant to avoid any preconceived idea of what urbanism and architecture should be about as well as to stave off any premature recourse to form. Urban and architectural design is supposed to be generated through the analysis made possible by diagrams. Thorough analysis, however, is not the only dimension that is mobilized, for diagrams are also supposed to encapsulate a specific dynamism at the intersection of social rhythms and their programmatic translation. For van Berkel and Bos, understanding and orienting this dynamism toward the completion of the project is far more important than any formal recipe. MVRDV has a similar ambition with its so-called datascapes. Measurements and statistics are supposed to allow form to appear without any prejudice, in the same way that scientific laws are supposed to emerge from the gathering of experimental data.[28]

There is a certain degree of naiveté involved in this quest for objectivity. Science studies have shown that, in science itself, results are always "constructed" rather than the purely logical outcome of observed facts. But the naiveté is only partial, for there is more at work in the use of diagrams than the mere desire to imitate scientific procedures.

In addition to these procedures, marketing techniques are also a reference. The aim is to shape the project in the way products and services are

(fig. 2)

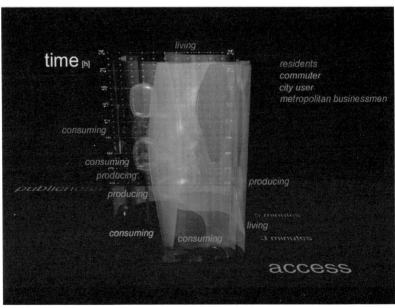

UN Studio, Ben van Berkel and Caroline Bos, "Three Diagrams"

ANTOINE PICON

defined, produced, and commercialized. Deep planning and datascapes claim to be in profound accordance with market forces. Such a claim has become quite general among young designers. What seems to be at play is a trend toward a new realism. The aim of the architect is no longer to propose an alternative, and allegedly better, world but to take the world as it is, to contribute to the further actualization of its potential rather than bring about the advent of a remote utopia. Another way to put it is to ask, as Sanford Kwinter has, for an architectural discipline taking "the flow of historical conditions as its privileged materiality."[29] Rem Koolhaas and OMA have been pioneers of this new attitude.

Among the criticisms raised by the acceptance of market forces, there is the accusation that true generosity is missing; a realistic architecture runs the risk of being cynical. Massimiliano Fuksas may have wished to exorcize the risk by choosing the theme "less aesthetics, more ethics" for the 2000 International Architecture Exhibition of Venice.[30] Jesse Reiser also addressed this issue in his *Solid-State Architecture*, in which, following Deleuze, he contrasted power and potential (fig. 3).[31] According to this distinction, the aim of the architect is not to exert power but to express the creative potential of the existing world, a potential that might prove emancipating in the end.

Faith in the emancipating power of the present is often rooted in a strange, vitalistic conception of the world, a notion that verges on pantheism, with its belief in the auto-organizing power of the universe, which man must divert and master for his own purposes. Here, again, we find all the rhetorical figures that are borrowed from dynamic systems and their capacity of auto-organization. The use of that type of metaphor by architects often approaches the ideological agenda at work in the creation and development of the Internet. Just as with the Internet, the realistic architecture of our time claims to be both compatible with the invisible hand of the market and capable of revealing a potential for generosity and altruism.

All these assumptions are questionable. But even if we take them for granted, other problems related to contemporary virtual reality remain. The problem of scale is especially striking. In many computer-produced projects, scale is not absolutely evident. One might be facing molecules, spaceships, planets, or constellations. Whereas man used to be the measure of architecture, such is no longer the case, at least on computer screens.

At this stage, it is interesting to note that the question of scale is quite general nowadays. We live in a world in which scale has become highly problematic because of the shift of our visual and perceptive categories. On the one hand, with satellites or computer-generated global models, we see at a much broader scale than our immediate ancestors did. On the other hand, we are able to look at microstructures as if they were right under our eyes. We have difficulty dealing with our environment at a traditional distance.

Science and the often computer-generated images that illustrate it play a role in this crisis of scale. Scientific notions and representations shape our vision of the world. Among them, information plays a key role. Contrary to the traditional notion of structure, information ignores the distinction between the large, the medium, and the small, between the macro and the micro. Hence the suggestive power of fractal geometry to describe a world where complexity is to be found at every level.[32]

The blurring of the very big and the very small, and the crisis of scale that is its main consequence, tends also to reflect the fundamental evolution of our society. Specialists often say that globalization is characterized by the suppression of the intermediaries between the global and the local, between worldwide organizations and individuals. It is fascinating to observe how the categories of vision are evolving in a similar direction.

(fig. 3)

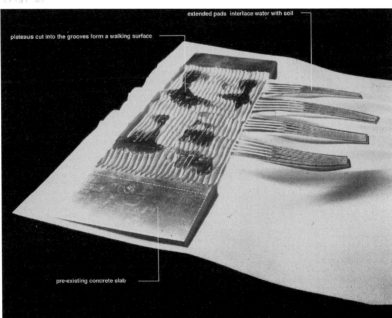

extended pads interface water with soil

plateaus cut into the grooves form a walking surface

pre-existing concrete slab

Reiser+Umemoto, "Water Garden"

ANTOINE PICON

Digital architectural forms truly belong to this context of globalization. What is their real size? Are they big as mountain chains or small as pebbles? Indeed, they evoke two apparently contradictory terms: landscape on the one hand, texture on the other.

Critics have already commented abundantly on the recent impact of landscape on the theory and practice of architecture. Let us here discuss the strategic importance of the notion of texture. Texture is the level on which abstract information and tangible sensation meet today. Computer images are based upon textures. But texture is also a fundamental feature of materials. Texture seems to abolish the distinction between the abstract and the concrete. In the field of digital architecture, the importance given to texture, to the play between grain and light, goes hand in hand with the desire to reconcile the immaterial and the material, the conceptual and the tangible.

In the modern creed formulated by architects like Le Corbuier, reconciliation between the conceptual and the tangible was realized by architectural space. The new interest in textures is part of the crisis of the notion of architectural space as the moderns defined it. Jean Nouvel gave this crisis striking expression some years ago when he announced the definitive abandonment of Albertian perspective for a two-dimensional universe of mobile textures and lights.[33] The announcement of the death of Albertian perspective has proved a little premature, but we have indeed entered a world full of textures and lights.

Texture implies a new attitude toward reality, as if things were seen at much broader or, on the contrary, much closer range. Their reality becomes both problematic—since nothing is more abstract than a surface seen from very far or very near—and more intense. *Hyperrealism* is an apt term for this suspension of the traditional scale of perception and the specific intensity that it generates. We live in a hyperreal world of surfaces and textures in which we can see either entire worlds or only small particles.

Seen from very far or very near, the universe seems always on the verge of breaking open to allow glimpses on another world. Hypertext is very similar; it is possible with a click to open up parallel or derivative textual contents. As with the World Wide Web, the reality that surrounds us is in a state of constant multiplication; it is populated with thresholds that can be assimilated to events. The most meager computer screen appears as a door open on alternative spaces. Computer-generated architecture is about the unstable reality of infinite connections.

As already mentioned, this new version of Blaise Pascal's two infinities surely has something to do with the major economic and social trends of our time. In a context of globalization, the acceptance of the invisible forces of the market is part of hyperrealism, and the interplay of these invisible forces is part of the intensification of our perception of the reality of the world.

In such a world, the contemplative distance of the past is becoming more and more difficult to locate. We are either too far or too near. This difficulty might very well be the symptom of a radical destabilization of the subject/object polarity. Who is producing architecture? Above all, for whom is architecture being produced? The modern movement had postulated a posthumanist subject, as K. Michael Hays has shown it in one of his books.[34] The posthumanist subject is perhaps no longer the one that computer-based architecture has in view. Indeed, digital architecture is contemporary with a shift from the anonymous individual of the early technological age to the self-developed personality of the Internet civilization. In our competitive society, self-development and assertiveness have become a rule of life.

Are we back to the humanist subject of the Renaissance? Certainly not, if we pay attention to the disconcerting importance technology is now playing in the very definition of the subject. The early-third-millennium individual is defined to a large extent by his or her capacity to be hooked up to giant networks. A recent essay of mine hypothesized that one of the easiest ways to conceive this new individual is in reference to the figure of the cyborg.[35] This compound of flesh and technology has been haunting science-fiction literature and film for quite a long time. More recently, it has begun to influence anthropology and history, from books and articles on feminism by Donna Haraway to the study of the Cold War by historians such as Paul Edwards.[36] The cyborg's shadow is now beginning to appear in the background of many architectural projects.

Two characteristics of the cyborg are especially remarkable from this perspective. The first is his full acceptance of the world as it is; the cyborg is not a utopian figure but the result of the full use of existing technologies. The second is that technology enables it to see things differently, at very con-

ANTOINE PICON

trasted scales and with an intensity that traditional vision does not possess. Hyperreality is meant for cyborgs.

The cyborg is, of course, a fiction, but the humanist subject, the ideal man of the Renaissance, was also one. Architecture's virtual dimension is ultimately about the constant invention of the subject. Design, order and proportion, ornament, structure, and space were already about the possible definition of the subject. Computer-based design has perhaps to do with a new emerging definition in a rapidly changing world.

In addition to this aspect, digital architecture represents also an opportunity for architecture to reestablish strong links with contemporary science and art. These links are synonymous with the even greater importance of experimentation and the experimental attitude in the architectural field. Digital architecture is often accused of being based only on formal manipulations. The very notion of manipulation, however, goes hand in hand with experimentation. What, for instance, is MVRDV's Data Town if not an experiment comparable, to a certain extent, to what is going on in science?

The possibility to experiment is further enhanced by the flexibility of computer programs that can be diverted from their original purposes to be used by architects. The latter are not alone in this process of diversion. Artists can also benefit from applications developed in domains like industry or medicine. Often their use produces surprising designs. New relations between architecture and art based on the extensive use of the computer are also emerging.

The reestablishment of strong links between contemporary science and art does not mean that architecture will regain its former status as an all-encompassing discipline. The architect can no longer appear as both a scientist and an artist, as Vitruvius wanted him to be. William Mitchell's ambition to transform the architect into the chief planner of cyberspace is perhaps unrealistic as well.[37] Rather, the new virtual dimension of architecture is synonymous with the possibility to participate fully in the development of the world, with modesty and determination. Beyond utopia, there is still a lot to do for a practice that Diderot and d'Alembert once placed under the aegis of imagination.[38]

NOTES

1. Such, for instance, is the meaning of the word in Claude Perrault's writings. See Antoine Picon, *Claude Perrault 1613–1688, ou la curiosité d'un classique* (Paris: Picard, 1988).

2. Martin Bressani, "Science, histoire et archéologie: Sources et généalogie de la pensée organiciste de Viollet-le-Duc" (doctoral diss., Université de Paris IV, 1997). See also Caroline van Eck, *Organicism in Nineteenth-Century Architecture: An Inquiry into Its Theoretical and Philosophical Background* (Amsterdam: Architectura & Natura Press, 1994).

3. Michael Baxandall, *Formes de l'intention. Sur l'explication historique des tableaux* (Nîmes: Jacqueline Chambon, 1991), 176; originally published as *Patterns of Intention* (New Haven: Yale University Press, 1985).

4. Gilles Deleuze, *Le pli: Leibniz et le baroque* (Paris: Minuit, 1988).

5. See, for instance, Paolo Galluzzi, ed., *Renaissance Engineers from Brunelleschi to Leonardo da Vinci* (Florence: Istituto e Museo di Storia della Scienza, 1996).

6. Dominique Clayssen, *Jean Prouvé: l'Idée constructive* (Paris: Dunod, 1983).

7. Etienne-Louis Boullée, *Architecture: Essai sur l'art*, ed. J.-M. Pérouse de Montclos (Paris: Hermann, 1968), 46.

8. See, for instance, Manfredo Tafuri, *Architecture and Utopia: Design and Capitalist Development*, trans. Barbara Juigia La Penta (Cambridge, Mass.: MIT Press, 1976).

9. J.-B. Bossuet, *Introduction à la philosophie, ou de la connaissance de Dieu, et de soi-mesme* (Paris: R.-M. d'Espilly, 1722), 37–38.

10. See Didier Laroque, *Le discours de Piranèse: L'Ornement sublime et le suspens de l'architecture* (Paris: Les Editions de la Passion, 1999).

11. On Semper's theory, see Wolfgang Herrmann, *Gottfried Semper: In Search of Architecture* (Cambridge, Mass., and London: MIT Press, 1984); Harry Mallgrave, introduction to Gottfried Semper, *The Four Elements of Architecture and Other Writings* (Cambridge: Cambridge University Press, 1989), 1–44; Kenneth Frampton, *Studies in Tectonic Culture: The Poetics of Construction in Nineteenth and Twentieth Century Architecture* (Cambridge, Mass.: MIT Press, 1995).

12. Eugène-Emmanuel Viollet-le-Duc, *À Monsieur Adolphe Lance, rédacteur du journal L'Encyclopédie d'architecture*, extracted from *L'Encyclopédie d'architecture*, January 1856 (Paris: Bance, 1856), col. 11.

13. Eugène-Emmanuel Viollet-le-Duc, *Entretiens sur l'architecture*, 2 vols. (Paris: A. Morel et Cie., 1863–72).

14. D'Arcy Wentworth Thompson, *On Growth and Form*, rev. ed. (Cambridge: Cambridge University Press, 1942).

15. On the scope and meaning of the reference to the machine in Le Corbusier's work, see, for instance, Alexander Tzonis, *Le Corbusier: Poétique, machines et symboles* (Paris: Hazan, 2001).

16. See Dominique Pestre, "Pour une histoire sociale et culturelle des sciences: Nouvelles définitions, nouveaux objets, nouvelles pratiques," *Annales histoire sciences sociales* 50, no. 3 (May–June 1995): 487–522.

17. Peter Galison, "Aufbau/Bauhaus: Logical Positivism and Architectural Modernism," *Critical Inquiry* 16 (1990): 709–52.

18. Eduardo Torroja, *Les structures architecturales: Leur conception, leur réalisation* (Paris: Eyrolles, 1971), 28.

19. Nelson Goodman, *Ways of World Making* (Indianapolis: Hackett Pub. Co., 1978).

20. Paul Edwards, *The Closed World: Computers and the Politics of Discourse in Cold War America* (Cambridge, Mass.: MIT Press, 1996).

21. Mark Wigley, "Planetary Homeboy," *Any Magazine* 17 (1997): 16–23.

22. See *Archigram* (Paris: Editions du Centre Georges Pompidou, 1994).

23. Greg Lynn, *Animate Form* (New York: Princeton Architectural Press, 1998).

24. "[A] bit is neither a particle of matter, nor an elementary idea, it is an atomic occurrence." Pierre Levy, *La Machine univers: Création, cognition et culture informatique* (Paris: La Découverte, 1987), 124.

25. James Gleick, *Chaos: Making a New Science* (New York: Viking, 1987); Jean Louis Chabert, Karin Chemla, and Amy Dahan-Dalmedico, eds., *Chaos et déterminisme* (Paris: Le Seuil, 1992).

26. On diagrams, see, for instance, "Diagram Works," *Any Magazine* 23 (1998).

27. Ben van Berkel and Caroline Bos, *Move. I: Imagination, II: Techniques, III: Effects* (Amsterdam: UN Studio & Goose Press, 1999).

28. Winy Maas and Jacob van Rijs, eds., with Richard Koek, *Farmax: Excursions on Density* (Rotterdam: 010 publishers, 1994).

29. Sandford Kwinter, contribution to *Flying the Bullet, or When Did the Future Begin?* (New York: Princeton Architectural Press, 1996).

30. Massimiliano Fuksas, ed., *Less Aesthetics More Ethics* (Venice: Marsilio, 2000).

31. Jesse Reiser, *Solid-State Architecture* (Academy Editions, dist. New York: John Wylie, 1998).

32. Benoît Mandelbrot, *Les Objets fractals: Forme, hasard et dimension*, 3rd rev. ed. (Paris: Flammarion, 1989).

33. Jean Nouvel, "A Venir," *L'Architecture d'aujourd'hui* 296 (1994): 50.

34. K. Michael Hays, *Modernism and the Posthumanist Subject: The Architecture of Hannes Meyer and Ludwig Hilberseimer* (Cambridge, Mass.: MIT Press, 1992).

35. Antoine Picon, *La Ville territoire des cyborgs* (Besançon: Les Editions de l'Imprimeur, 1998).

36. Donna Haraway, "Manifesto for Cyborgs: Science, Technology, and Socialist Feminism in the 1980s," *Socialist Review* 15, no. 2 (1985): 65–107; idem, *Simians, Cyborgs and Women: The Reinvention of Nature* (New York: Routledge, 1991); Edwards, *Closed World*.

37. William J. Mitchell, *City of Bits: Space, Place and the Infobahn* (Cambridge, Mass.: MIT Press, 1995).

38. Denis Diderot and Jean Le Rond d'Alembert, "Système figuré des connoissances humaines," in *Encyclopédie, ou dictionnaire raisonné des sciences, des arts et des métiers*, 17 vols. (Paris: Briasson, 1751–72); see vol. 1.

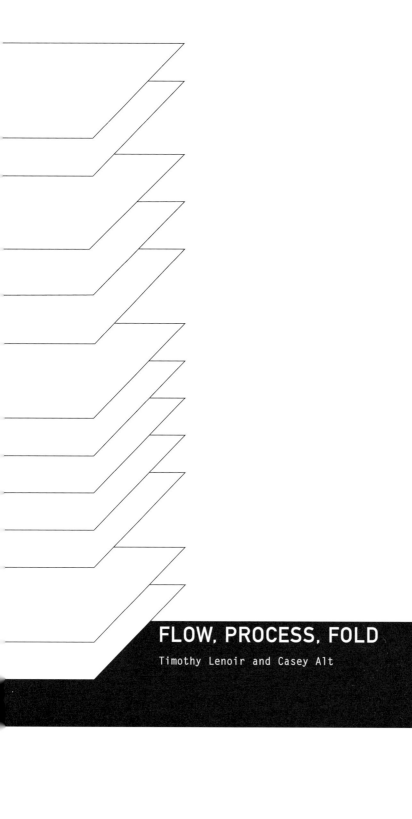

FLOW, PROCESS, FOLD

Timothy Lenoir and Casey Alt

A growing repertoire of computer-based media for creating, distributing, and interacting with digitized versions of the world pervades contemporary life. Computer-mediated communication has already become significant in biology and medicine, and several developments—not all of them integrally connected—in fields of bioinformatics, biomedical imaging, and surgery, have become significant for other areas in which computers mediate processes of work and creativity. Oft noted features of the growth of computer-mediated forms of work and communication—particularly evident in the biomedical areas—are the acceleration of nearly every aspect of design and production, along with the high degree of both modularity and adaptability of processes. Information technology workers have responded to the explosion of data created by digital technology by generating dynamic systems for facilitating the flow of information, replacing static forms with fluid architectures for extracting meaning.

Of particular concern here is the architect's engagement with information technology (IT). Some architects are using IT to address critical contemporary issues of philosophical, ethical, and social concern. Many have found resonance in the philosophical writings of Gilles Deleuze and Félix Guattari, particularly in their efforts to displace key modernist notions of difference, such as other, lack, or negative, with difference as a positive source. Equally powerful are Deleuze and Guattari's rejections of positions stressing reductionism and organic unity; in place of totalizing unity, they advocate locality, situatedness, rhizomic strategies, "bodies without organs," and machinic assemblages.[1]

The architects explored here have engaged with computer technology on many planes. They have sought to engage the digital communications revolution in the material expression of the buildings they construct. They have also embraced computer-mediated design and production as an opening for a new critical discourse, a new line of flight, at once a new critical language and phenomenology.

BIOINFORMATICS: A NEW BIOLOGY FOR THE INFORMATION AGE

One of the most interesting developments in recent biology is an inexorable shift—almost in spite of the rhetoric of the practitioners themselves—toward a disunified model of science. It is not that biological scientists have given up their search for laws of nature. Hardly. In the past two decades, however, a new biology has arisen: a highly context-specific yet mathematically exact form of local science that might be described as a science of the particular. Similar trends can be seen in areas of medicine such as surgery, where surgical planning and simulation are being tailored to the specific patient as opposed to a generic subject selected from a medical atlas.

TIMOTHY LENOIR AND CASEY ALT

Similarly, the goal of pharmacogenetics, a new postgenomic field, is to target drug design for the individual.

It is computing technology, particularly broadband Web and simulation technology, that has made these developments possible. Work on protein structure provides an example. Rather than telling the familiar story of François Jacob and Jacques Monod's theoretical work and how it propelled biology into the information age, a media-sensitive account would look at the contributions of information technology itself. About the same time as Jacob and Monod's work, new developments in computer architectures and algorithms for generating models of chemical structure and simulations of chemical interactions allowed computational experiments to interact with and draw together theory and laboratory experiment in completely novel ways.

Notions of theorizing have radically shifted in many areas of science, not least biology. For decades many biologists aspired to theoretical constructs modeled along the lines of the physical sciences. Like physicists, they have searched for the holy grail of a grand unifying theory, preferably reducible to fundamental laws of physics and chemistry. For those wanting to view molecular biology as an extension of physics and chemistry, a key step was provided by the work of Christian B. Anfinsen, whose Nobel Prize–winning work on protein folding established that all the information required to fold proteins into their final (native) state is contained in the linear sequence of amino acids themselves.[2] But how is the tertiary structure, the final folded state of molecules, encoded in that primary sequence? Biologists have needed to determine this structural code in order to understand the genetic message.

Anfinsen's work suggested that it is reasonable to suppose that the native fold of a protein can be predicted computationally using information about its chemical composition alone and that finding the global minimum of a protein's potential energy function should be tantamount to identifying the protein's native fold.[3] Unfortunately, the task of finding the global minimum of one of these functions has not proven easy, because the potential energy surface of a protein contains many local minima. Some computational biologists have argued that even more is possibly at stake here than just the computational complexity of the task. It may be impossible in principle to fold proteins without the assistance of "chaperones," or the rapid formation of local interactions, which then determine the further folding of the peptide.

This suggests local amino acid sequences, possibly the result of evolutionary adaptation, that form stable interactions and serve as nucleation points in the folding process. Indeed, Cyrus Levinthal, the author of this hypothesis (known as Levinthal's Paradox), argued that the conformation space—the set of all possible configurations a molecule can assume in folding from its starting uncoiled state to its native fold—for even the average-size protein molecule is exponentially large. For example, each bond connecting amino acids can have several possible states (three for this example), so that a protein of 101 amino acids could exist in $3^{100} = 5 \times 10^{47}$ configurations. Even if the protein is able to sample new configurations at the rate of 10^{13} per second, or 3×10^{20} per year, it will take 10^{27} years to try them all. Proteins actually fold in a time scale of seconds or less. Levinthal concluded that random searches are not the way proteins fold.[4]

Computer modeling and the introduction of tools from artificial intelligence (AI) and expert systems in biochemistry during the 1960s and 1970s seemed to offer a way out of the dark woods of protein folding and at the same time promised the theoretical unification of biology. What has actually emerged is something quite different, however, perhaps best described as a disunified but more effective biology.

Models, whether physical or virtual, have always played crucial roles in understanding the structure of biological molecules. For James Watson and Francis Crick's discovery of DNA, making a physical model was the key step, for example. In biology, as in architecture, geometry is everything, because the functional properties of a molecule depend not only on the interlinkage of its chemical constituents but also on the way in which the molecule is configured and folded in three dimensions. Much of biochemistry has focused on understanding the relationship between biological function and molecular conformational structure. Model building is the sine qua non of this enterprise.

A milestone in the making of physical three-dimensional models of molecules was John Kendrew's construction of myoglobin. An attempt to build a physical model from a Fourier map of the electron densities derived from X-ray crystallographic sources, Kendrew's model was a room-filling forest of brass rods and wires. It was obvious that such 3-D representations would become truly useful only when it was possible to manipulate them at will—to size and scale them arbitrarily from actual X-ray crystallographic

TIMOTHY LENOIR AND CASEY ALT

and electron density map data. Proponents of the field of computer graphics and computer-aided design—newly minted at the Massachusetts Institute of Technology in Ivan Sutherland's 1963 dissertation—argued that computer representations of molecular structure would allow these manipulations.

Computer modeling, requiring the specification of codes to produce these models from known data, was embraced at first because it promised molecular biologists, particularly the biophysicists among them, a unified theory; it would move the field toward such a goal by providing a framework from which would emerge a fully mathematized and thus fully scientific theoretical biology.[5]

Levinthal first illustrated the method for representing molecular structure in computer graphics by adapting Sutherland's computer-aided design (CAD) program to biochemistry. Levinthal reasoned that since protein chains are formed by linking molecules of a single class (amino acids), it should be relatively easy to specify the linkage process in a form mathematically suitable for a digital computer.[6]

But there was a hitch: in an ideal world dominated by a powerful central theory, one would like, for example, to use the inputs of xyz coordinates of the atoms, the types of bond, and so on to calculate the pairwise interaction of atoms in the amino acid chain, predict the conformation of the protein molecule, and check this prediction against its corresponding X-ray crystallographic image. However, as we have noted above in our discussion of Levinthal's Paradox, the parameters used as input in the computer program do not provide much limitation on the number of molecular conformations. Other sorts of input are needed to filter the myriad possible structures. Perhaps the most important of these is energy minimization: the basic physical hypothesis that, like water running downhill, a large protein molecular string will fold to reach the lowest energy level. Such minimization calculations could not be done, as Levinthal noted, because the necessary formula could not, in the state of molecular biological theory of 1965, be written down and manipulated with a finite amount of labor.

Levinthal's solution to the problem of filtering possible molecular conformations was to create a computer visualization generated in real-time interaction between human and machine. The computer became in effect both a microscope for examining molecules and a laboratory for quantitative experiment, all in the service of producing a general theory of protein folding.

Levinthal emphasized that interactivity facilitated through visualization was a crucial component of his model-building program, CHEMGRAF,[7] where the user could *observe* the result of the calculations and be able to halt the minimization process at any step, either to terminate it completely or to alter the conformation and then resume it.[8] CHEMGRAF was thus a first step toward decentering the importance of theorizing in biology and elevating the emphasis on visualization, haptic interaction, and experimental tinkering as a method of investigation. It would take an explosion in molecular biological data to complete the redefinition of biology as information science.

The measures taken by Levinthal to avoid computationally intensive techniques illustrate the wide variety of simplifications that have typically been introduced into molecular dynamics computations, such as constructing models that hold fixed certain parameters or ignore others deemed not to be essential for purposes of approximation. Other approaches have used time averaging or ensemble averaging to calculate properties such as the global free energy of the protein. Another approach has been to construct simulations using randomized Monte Carlo methods for generating successive configurations and averaging over all samples that are generated. While both molecular dynamics and Monte Carlo methods are theoretically capable of treating the protein-folding problem, they too require very large amounts of computation time for molecules with many degrees of freedom.

Characteristic of the trend in contemporary science away from reductionist theories is the tendency to draw upon strategies and methods

(fig. 1)

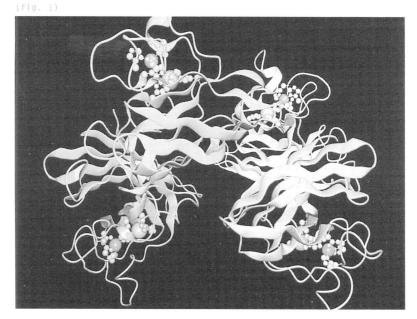

A vector-ribbon diagram of the molecule superoxide dimutase, from the Brookhaven Protein Databank

from completely different domains, in effect to cut the Gordian knot in one area by adapting tools from another. One such approach to protein folding that will prove relevant to our architectural concerns is the use of algorithms based on robot-motion planning by Jean-Claude Latombe, Douglas Brutlag, and colleagues in order to improve the speed and efficiency of protein-folding simulation methods.[9] In this context, similar to the elements of a robot navigating a local terrain, Latombe et al. model molecules as sequences of vectors (fig. 1), in which each vector is an element of secondary structure, such as an alpha-helix or beta-sheet. The set of all its 3-D placements is the molecule's conformational space, over which the energy field is defined (fig. 2). Instead of inducing the motion of the robot through actuators, Latombe et al. examine the possible motions of the robot induced by the energy landscape of its immediate environment and generate a network of pathways called a probabilistic conformational road map, a graph whose nodes and edges are, respectively, low-energy conformations and short-weighted pathways. The weight of a pathway measures the difficulty for the molecule in moving along it. The power of a probabilistic conformational road map derives from its ability to encode compactly a huge number of energetically favorable folding pathways, each defined as a sequence of contiguous local pathways. Instead of simulating the entire set of potential fold configurations, the motion-planning technique guesses several possible intermediate configurations of the protein and obtains a distribution of energetically favorable intermediate configurations to which a "difficulty weight" is assigned representing the energy barriers along the path.

(fig. 2)

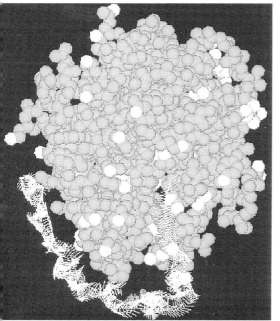

Brutlag and Latombe's time-lapse image of plausible binding motions for a flexible ligand (in white) and a protein structure (in gray), as mapped according to their conformational-probabilistic-road map technique

A PARADIGM SHIFT IN BIOLOGY

The type of modeling represented by Levinthal's work, as well as the recent work on motion planning, depends crucially on high-quality crystallographic data, and these have proved difficult to obtain in the quantity desired to drive the field rapidly forward.[10] Simultaneously, however, another stream of work flooded the biological knowledge base. The development of restriction enzymes, recombinant DNA techniques, gene-cloning techniques, and PCR (polymeraze chain reaction) produced a deluge of data on DNA, RNA, and protein sequences.[11] Since the mid-1980s, sequence data have been growing at an exponential rate, doubling over fifteen months, reaching a figure of ten million base pairs a day. Such an explosion of data encouraged the development of a second approach to determining protein structure and function, namely prediction from sequence data alone.

The field of bioinformatics has taken an approach to this problem different from the "bottom-up," brute-force energetics approaches. Rather than deriving structure and function directly from the physical properties of amino acids and the first principles of protein-folding dynamics, the bioinformatics approach involves comparing new sequences with preexisting ones and discovering structure and function by homology to known structures. The approach is eclectic, heterogeneous, and multiple; rather than proceeding linearly from genetic information to molecular structure to function, in the spirit of the old "central dogma" ("DNA produces RNA, produces protein, produces function"), bioinformatics draws on bits and pieces of pattern in one domain and maps them comparatively in another domain through sophisticated probabilistic methods of data analysis, pattern matching, machine learning, and robotics. This is not to suggest that scientists in the field of bioinformatics reject energetic or thermodynamic accounts of protein folding; far from it. But in their search for methods that save computing cycles, they have followed a bootstrapping approach in which the statistical and knowledge-base methods of bioinformatics have assisted in refining the structures input into large all-atom energetics calculations for ab initio structure prediction.[12] In the new paradigm, both approaches inform one another.

The "bioinformatics" approach identifies the function and structure of unknown proteins by applying search algorithms to existing protein libraries in order to determine sequence similarity, percentages of matching residues, and the statistical significance of each database sequence. A database of proteins for which structural and sequence information is available is used to predict structural features for proteins of neighboring sequences. From proteins of known structures, a comparison of sequence and 3-D geometry makes it possible to derive rules or parameters that will subsequently permit the determination of the probability for a given fragment to arrange into a particular regular structure. As for tertiary structures, they also allow the researcher to define sequence templates for families of protein structures that adopt a common fold. If a sequence of an unknown structure can be matched with a template, a model of the fold can be built by analogy. Schematically, for predicting structures of unknown proteins, model building in bioinformatics proceeds through three main alternative approaches:

1. starting from the sequence knowledge
2. assembling fragments from different, known homologous structures
3. carrying out limited structural changes from a known neighboring protein.

ELEMENTS OF PROTEIN STRUCTURE

To elucidate the structure and function of proteins, bioinformatics focuses its computational tools on secondary and tertiary structure. Secondary structure consists of local folding regularities maintained by hydrogen bonds and is traditionally divided into three major classes: alpha-helices, beta-sheets, and coils representing all the rest. In alpha-helices, backbone hydrogen bonds link residues i and i + 4, whereas in beta-sheets, hydrogen bonds link two sequence segments in either parallel or antiparallel fashion. The secondary structure can be sensitive to single amino acid changes and depends on both local and long-range interactions. A key tool used in elucidating structure-function relationships is a search for sequences that correspond to small, conserved regions of proteins—modular structures known as motifs. Motifs are key patterns of amino acids that form the building blocks in the secondary structure of proteins. The sequence patterns defined by motifs are powerful probes for searching databases of known structure and function to determine the structure and function of an unknown gene or protein. Several different kinds of motifs are related to secondary structure and to tertiary structure, the final folded structure of protein. Secondary structure consists of patterns of repeating polypeptide structure within an alpha-helix, a beta-sheet, and reverse turns. At the next level, supersecondary structure refers to a few common motifs of interconnected elements of secondary structure. Segments of alpha-helix and beta-strand often combine in specific larger structural motifs. One example is the alpha-helix–turn-helix motif found in DNA-binding proteins. This motif contains twenty-two amino acids in lengths that enable it to bind to DNA. Another motif at the supersecondary level is known as the Rossmann fold, in which three alpha-helices alternate with three parallel beta-strands. This has turned out to be a general fold for binding mono- or dinucleotides and is the most common fold observed in globular proteins.

In addition to searching for motifs, another principal strategy for determining structure-function relations uses various sequence-alignment methods. Among these are consensus sequences, weight matrices, and profiles, all of which employ a battery of different probabilistic methods for teasing out structure similarity.

In order to keep pace with the flood of data emerging from automated sequencing since the 1990s, genome researchers have looked increasingly to artificial intelligence, machine learning, and, as noted above, even robotics in developing automated methods for discovering protein motifs and folding patterns from sequence data. The power of these methods is their ability both to represent structural features rather than strictly evolutionary steps and to discover motifs from sequences automatically. Indeed, a central axiom of the field is that massively automated methods are the only ways to get at the structure of large genomes and make sense of medically relevant sequence information. The methods developed in the field of machine learning, such as perceptrons, genetic algorithms, neural networks, Bayesian networks, hidden Markov models, minimal-length encoding, and context-free grammars, have been used singly and in combination to extract conserved residues, discover pairs of correlated residues, and find higher-order relationships between residues.[13]

FLOW AND FOLD

The results of automated sequencing of genes and proteins, combined with the necessity of devising novel informatics techniques for extracting meaning from these data, have radically transformed the theoretical enterprise of biology. The "central dogma" emerging from the work of

Watson, Crick, Monod, and Jacob in the late 1960s may be schematized as follows:

DNA ◊ RNA ◊ protein ◊ function

The fundamental dogma of this new biology reformulates the central dogma of Jacob and Monod in terms of "information flow":[14]

genetic information | molecular structure | biochemical function | biologic behavior

Genomics, computational biology, and bioinformatics have restructured the playing field of biology, bringing a substantially modified tool kit to the repertoire of molecular biology skills developed in the 1970s. The new biology is a data-bound, rather than observational, science. To understand the data, the tools of information science have not become mere handmaidens to theory; they have fundamentally changed the picture of biological theory itself. As a result, disciplinarily, biology has become an information science, while institutionally it has become Big Science. Along with biochemistry components, new skills are now required to sift through the data, including machine learning, robotics, databases, statistics and probability, artificial intelligence, information theory, algorithms, and graph theory.[15]

A 1985 report by the National Institutes of Health (NIH) sums up the difference between a unified biology and the information-technology-infused, heterogeneous, multiple, data-driven, and enfolded state of biology. Contrasting this biology with theoretical physics, "which consists of a small number of postulates and the procedures and apparatus for deriving predictions from those postulates," NIH writers view contemporary biology as an interconnected assemblage of different strata, from DNA to protein to organismic and behavioral biology, each with its own unique set of laws and processes.[16] Rather than through a unified theory, the field's critical questions can often be answered only by relating one biological level to another through the techniques of informatics.[17]

SHARED METAPHORS

Biology as it was once practiced has been remade by the steady introduction of computational tools, computer-mediated forms of communication, and an entire material infrastructure of genetic and cellular tagging, labeling, sequencing, and processing that has turned the world of biological flows and folds into digital information. As a result, the practitioners of biology *in silico* have a relationship to their research objects that is different from that possessed by their predecessors. The first generation of computational biologists looked to computers as tools for data storage and retrieval and for assistance in carrying out lengthy, redundant computations, but not as the site for experiment and design work. Genomics researchers, by contrast, find themselves immersed in increasingly automated computational environments for the identification, manipulation, and design of their research objects. In a certain sense, the ontology of the domain has shifted.

A number of architects have been similarly affected by engagement with computers, and they have looked to computational biology for metaphors to articulate the new directions in which they want to take architectural practice. The term *postarchitects* seems fitting for this group, who all share an interest in engaging with the computer in their architectural practice, not just as a useful tool for implementing designs or as a new medium for expression, but as a new material agency that can challenge the foundations of traditional design practice and propel architecture in a new direction, a new line of flight. In addition to their interest in computers and computational biology, what characterizes postarchitects in our account is their agreement on what they take to be the limitations of "postmodern architecture" and on a new program that can move beyond those limitations. For postarchitects, the writings of Gilles Deleuze are particularly salient. Architectural computing, fused with metaphors from computational biology, commingle with the philosophical positions articulated by Deleuze to inspire a new architecture.

Peter Eisenman has provided one of the clearest statements of the motivation postarchitects share for engaging computational media. In a recent essay entitled "Visions Unfolding: Architecture in the Age of Electronic Media," Eisenman points to a crisis in the current state of his art: "During the fifty years since the Second World War, a paradigm shift has taken place that should have profoundly affected architecture: this was the shift from the mechanical paradigm to the electronic one."[18] Updating Walter Benjamin's 1935 "The Work of Art in the Age of Mechanical Reproduction," Eisenman argues for a necessary distinction between the mechanically repro-

TIMOTHY LENOIR AND CASEY ALT

duced and the electronically mediated. Mechanical reproduction has always required a human subject to mediate and interpret the process of reproduction itself; photographs, for instance, are differentially printed according to the specific visual characteristics desired by the photographer. In this way, Eisenman contends, "the photograph can be said to remain in the control of human vision."[19]

Electronic media, on the other hand, are not subject to human intervention or interpretation because they are not produced according to a visible mechanical logic. Rather, electronic media are themselves *processes of mediation* that are hidden from the user and controlled by the internal wirings of an entirely other logic—that of the digital. Eisenman asserts that electronic media's elision of the human discursive function in the process of production places it outside the control of human vision. By vision, Eisenman means the process linking "seeing to thinking, the eye to the mind" that perpetually aligns the production of content with the desires of an anthropomorphizing subject.[20] Electronic media, because they do not pass through the intermediary of human vision, are capable of disrupting how we experience reality itself, since "reality always demanded that our vision be interpretive."[21]

Eisenman wonders how, when every other cultural practice has been fundamentally transformed by the shift to electronic media, architecture has remained largely unchanged. As we have argued, the field of biology no longer exists as it was once envisioned: bioinformatics is the electronic mediation of biology, remaking the field right down to the central dogma of molecular biology. Why has architecture resisted such a transformation? Eisenman posits that architecture has remained stolidly rooted in the mechanical paradigm because "architecture was the visible manifestation of the overcoming of natural forces such as gravity and weather by mechanical means."[22] As a result, architecture has not only centered on designing structures that shelter, but in doing so has produced designs intended *to look as though* they will securely shelter—that is, the mechanics of their design is immediately interpretable by human vision. Such continuing recourse to the "mechanics of vision" in architecture has resisted an ability to *think architecture* in ways more commensurate with the new paradigm of electronic mediation.

Realizing the limitations inherent in an architecture dominated by the mechanics of vision, architects such as Neil Denari and Greg Lynn, in addition to Peter Eisenman, have discarded the eye-mind connection in favor of the transformative powers of electronic media and openness toward the systems of metaphor that such media enable, encourage, and engender. Denari foregrounds such an openness when he wonders:

> [W]ould it be possible today to describe certain architectural propositions without the lush and open-ended (technical) language of the life sciences? It seems that almost no architect is completely immune to the models offered by the soft systems of molecular biology, especially as they are transposed through forms of communication (media-based languages, etc.) that are themselves compounding the possible theoretical positions for architecture. [My] works ... while less indebted to the formal models of biological systems, do nonetheless employ the conceptual and abstract terminologies of such systems. After more than a decade ... of rapid absorption into the discourse of architecture, concepts and fields such as entropy, cybernetics, self-organizing systems, neural networks, and complexity have helped construct new formations of meaning, geometry, and space.[23]

Lynn extends this sentiment in pointing to the further transformative potential for a merger of new media, the tools of computational biology, and architecture:

> In their search for systems that can simulate the appearance of life, the special effects and animation industry has developed a useful set of tools for these investigations; as contemporary animation software utilizes a combination of deformable surfaces and physical forces. The convergence of computer aided technological processes and biological models of growth, development and transformation can be investigated using animation rather than conventional architectural design software. Rather than being designed as stationary inert forms, space is highly plastic, flexible, and mutable in its dynamic evolution through motion and transformation. In animation simulations, form is not only defined by its internal parameters, as it is also effected by a mosaic of other fluctuating external, invisible forces and gradients including: gravity, wind, turbulence, magnetism and swarms of moving particles. These gradient field effects are used as abstract

TIMOTHY LENOIR AND CASEY ALT

analogies for pedestrian and automotive movement, environmental forces such as wind and sun, urban views and alignments, and intensities of use and occupation in time.[24]

NEW ARCHITECTURE AND COMPUTER-AIDED DESIGN

The strongest buttress of the eye-mind complex has been architectural theory itself, especially as espoused by modernism. In its search for unity, harmony, and simplicity in design, modernism aspired to remake every site in the image of man, a monument to human ingenuity and Western ideals of beauty, proportion, and progress. Modernism encompassed each site within its totalizing logic, viewing local particularities as obstacles to the realization of the architect's vision. One way to dismantle the eye-mind link is to reject such generalized theories in favor of increased attention to the indigenous differences in each site. Just as the new biology has moved away from sweeping—but unuseful—theoretical generalizations, architects have begun to discard the totalizing tenets of modernism and embrace more context-specific practices of building.

Such a shift in focus is not, however, an entirely recent phenomenon. Inspired by the poststructuralist writings of Jacques Derrida, architectural deconstruction, or deconstructivism, emerged in the 1970s and 1980s as a postmodern antidote to the hegemonic narratives of modernism. Intending to subvert the homogenizing anthropocentrism of modernism, deconstructivist architects sought to expose the contradictions and flaws inherent in the process of building itself.[25] As a common technique, deconstructivist architects disrupted traditional architectural regimes by identifying "repressed" styles within the local context of a site, then forcefully combining the repressed motifs in a single building without any concern for overall unity or design. Exemplary of deconstructivist architecture is the Frank Gehry House in Los Angeles, which, according to Lynn, represents

> materials already present within, yet repressed by, the suburban neighborhood: sheds, chain-link fences, exposed plywood, trailers, boats and recreational vehicles. . . . The house is seen to provoke conflict within the neighborhood due to its public representation of hidden aspects of its context. The Gehry House violates the neighborhood from within.[26]

Deconstructivism engaged in dispersed guerrilla warfare against the modernist tradition of architecture by tactically dismantling localized contexts from within. In order to expose the inherent superficiality of modernism, deconstructivist architects deracinated the modernist motifs, styles, and materials from their underlying semiotic regimes and recombined them in a free-floating currency of signs.

By the early 1990s, however, many architects had begun to feel that postmodernism had trapped itself as a negative reaction against modernism.[27] Rather than freeing architects from the self-aggrandizing styles and forms of traditional modernism, deconstructivism appeared to be a superficial reshuffling of styles permanently bound within the same rhetoric it struggled to resist. Eisenman diagnosed this persistent problem in postmodernism: "[D]espite repeated changes in style from Renaissance through Post Modernism and despite many attempts to the contrary, the seeing human subject—monocular and anthropocentric—remains the primary discursive term of architecture."[28] Architecture, according to Eisenman, still had to move outside its self-inscribed circle of discourse. His remedy for the problem was to form a new collaboration, a human-machine assemblage that would decenter the architectural design process.

Eisenman, of course, was not the only former devotee of postmodernism to turn to computers for new approaches to design.[29] Gehry also turned to computer-aided design in search of new directions. Gehry's buildings of the 1990s, especially the Experience Music Project in Seattle, the Guggenheim Bilbao, and the planned Disney L.A. Opera House are rife with imagery of flow, folds, and biological metaphor. But in our view, Gehry's work does not represent the embrace of the machinic assemblages and decentering practices of postarchitecture. Computers, as we will show below, do not in and of themselves enable the architect to break free of traditional assumptions. If anything, they can reify those assumptions in software code and firmware in ways difficult to escape.

To appreciate the ways in which the group we are calling post architects have used computers in attempting to break free of traditional constraints, let us consider briefly the history of computer-aided design. Computer-aided design entered our story at the very beginning of the field. Sketchpad, the first CAD program, was the basis of Levinthal's early molecular design program, CHEMGRAF. Architects were no less receptive to CAD

TIMOTHY LENOIR AND CASEY ALT

than early molecular biologists were to molecular graphics and computational modeling. Indeed, the reactions of the two groups often paralleled each other. As initially conceived, architectural CAD programs were used mainly as tools to augment the existing design techniques of architecture.[30] Architects did not design using CAD programs; rather, they used the traditional drafting tools of architecture to design buildings as they always had. After completing original designs, architects tended to use CAD programs to produce slick, full-color design layouts to entice clients and to store their designs digitally. Similarly, the word in the lab corridors among molecular biologists was that molecular graphics produced pretty pictures rather than aiding discovery.[31] Though CAD programs were electronic media from the start, architects used them more as high-tech additions to an older tool kit for mechanical reproduction.

Part of the initial resistance to designing in CAD stemmed from the fact that initial CAD programs were not immersive design environments. In fact, only recently did CAD programs such as AutoCAD become truly three-dimensional in a real-time volume-rendering sense. Early PC CAD programs were actually two-dimensional graphing systems that automatically extended shapes to a single fixed vanishing point, then projected a vertical "thickness" to the 2-D forms in order to approximate solid volumes. This 2-D approach, as it is called, created the semblance of geometric solids; however, the perspective of the solid was mapped only to the vanishing point from the position at which the shape was originally drawn. Therefore, if you rotated the 2-D shape around its vertical axis, the shape would appear to recede in reference to the original vanishing point, even though the rotation of the object should also rotate the vanishing point and change the perspectival projection in 3-D space. Only recently have most architectural CAD programs been completely overhauled to provide true 3-D volumetric rendering that plots solids dynamically in real time from an underlying data-tree representation of the object, an innovation coded into bioinformatics media from the beginning.

The design tools presented in CAD also limited the extent of potential collaboration between the designer and the medium. Since early CAD programs were used to reproduce traditional design processes, architectural CAD programs were coded to integrate the same traditional rectilinear drafting techniques into a set of computer tools: the protractor, compass, straightedge, T square, and French curve were all automated as tool options within the program's own architecture. As such, early CAD programs provided no real advantage over traditional drafting techniques; in fact, they were often less intuitive. It is important to understand the precise capabilities and limitations of early architectural CAD programs because, as William J. Mitchell observes, "architects tend to draw what they can build, and build what they can draw."[32] Rather than providing a means for interactive collaboration as in CHEMGRAF, CAD programs reified a system of traditional design processes and significantly limited the ability to think outside of them. Coloring outside the lines is not only stylistically unadvisable in CAD programs, it is technologically impossible, because there is no tool to allow it. Again, as Mitchell notes, "by greatly enhancing the efficiency of traditional drafting practices, these systems further marginalized alternative practices."[33] In architectural CAD programs, the template for an ideal conventionalized architecture—the traditional paradigm of the mechanics of vision—is coded into the program itself. Subsequent releases and offshoots of these early programs preserved or exaggerated these initial limitations.

In the 1990s, computer-aided design linked with computer-aided manufacturing and a new repertoire of malleable building materials encouraged many architects to express fascination with the soft, anexact forms of bioinformatics; but this appreciation at times masked the radical potential of the technology underpinning these capabilities. In his article for the celebration of the Guggenheim Bilbao, for instance, Mitchell focuses on Gehry's building process as a means of generating soft, pliant forms and circumventing the built-in limitations of CAD. According to Mitchell, Gehry's process begins by freely sculpting a physical model of his desired design. Gehry then inputs the three-dimensional structure of his physical models into the robust CATIA program (the CAD/CAM environment used by Boeing to design the 777, the first airplane to be entirely designed in CAD/CAM) (fig. 3). Mitchell describes this process as follows:

> In Gehry's office, the process begins with the use of a very accurate three-dimensional digitizer to capture vertex, edge, and surface coordinates from a large-scale physical model. Using CATIA, mathematical curves and sur-

(fig. 3)

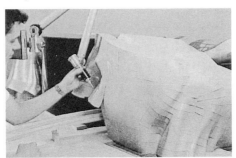

faces are then fitted as closely as possible to these digitized points. Rapid-prototyping devices, such as computer-controlled three-dimensional deposition printers and multi-axis milling machines, are then used to "build back" physical models for visual inspection and comparison with the original. The process iterates, with adjustments as necessary to the digital model, until the design team is satisfied.[34]

In this way, Mitchell views Gehry's iterative multimedia process as "far more revolutionary" in its ability to transcend the limitations of traditional CAD functionality alone.[35]

However, despite Gehry's apparent ability to both utilize and transcend the functionality of CATIA, he is in fact doing nothing revolutionary with CAD. To be sure, he begins with 3-D rather than 2-D models. Nevertheless, as with previous CAD architectural implementations, Gehry has recourse to a metaphysics of presence in privileging *real* materials. His high valuation of the "direct tactility of the physical model and the speed, freshness, and energy of the freehand gesture"[36] smacks of a Pollock-esque modernism in which the artist spills his singular genius onto canvas. Professor of digital architecture Dennis Dollens argues that Gehry's design process combines the "warps and wefts of one experiment with the [vector lines] and lofts of another and arrives at a third transformative structure,"[37] a work process paralleling that of the postarchitects. With due respect to Dollens, however, Gehry does not engage in a transformative repetition of form through CATIA; rather, he subjects each CATIA prototype to a process of "visual inspection and comparison with the original" and thus privileges the original physical form. He produces no "third transformative structure" but only a progressive digital approximation of the physical model, a form that for all its anexact smoothness stems directly from the anthropomorphic ideals of Gehry himself. Gehry uses CATIA solely to prototype rapidly and apply his design to an automated process of highly specific mechanical production,[38] not to draw upon the powers of its electronic mediation to decenter his interpretive function as architect. Dollens reports that Gehry's approach

Three photographs depicting Frank Gehry's design process for the 1995–2000 Experience Music Project. In the first image, the physical model is being digitally scanned into CATIA. The final image is a view of the completed building in Seattle.

enables his initial drawings and models to "be enhanced digitally, allowing him to take such advantage of electronic production while not being seduced by technology."[39] Such a fear of the "seductive" powers of technology reveals Gehry's unwillingness to subject his artistic genius to an equally powerful process of electronic mediation, an attitude binding him to the modernist architects he intends to oppose.

An alternative approach—that of postarchitects Eisenman, Lynn, and Denari—is to use electronic media to interact with anexact forms on their own terms and within an equally mediated space. If traditional CAD software is circumscribed within the mechanics of vision, why not change the software to the types of robust, high-powered programs of bioinformatics? Peter Eisenman observes, "What we need is the kind of software that the people who model complex biological and physical data in complex research institutions employ that can be used as models for architecture."[40] Through the increasing use of rigorous modeling applications such as Alias|Wavefront's Maya, Discreet's 3D Studio Max, and SOFTIMAGE|3D, architects are beginning to acquire such media. Utilizing Non-Uniform Rational Bézier Spline (NURBS) based strategies for generating vectorial topologies, these new modeling programs enable new ways of thinking about form and space. According to Lynn, the newer media offer "perhaps the first opportunity for architects to draw and sketch using calculus...by supplanting the traditional tools of exactitude and stasis with tools of gradients, flexible envelopes, temporal flows and forces."[41] Architects can now work on a level similar to that of bioinformaticists, a level where complex algorithms can model the affective space of each site, thereby allowing them to think architecture in the language of Deleuze through a process of collaboration with the electronic media. Eisenman has endorsed such a process of collaboration:

> I am certain of the need to reassess architecture within a digitized process, i.e. that there is no beginning, there is no truth, there is no origin, and there is no a priori given. In other words, there is no longer the necessity to begin from a rectangle, a circle, or a square. The notions of the Cartesian absolute as a priori truth already invested with beauty and goodness no longer exist or no longer are taken as truthful or necessarily beautiful, or the only necessarily youthful and beautiful. If this is the case, then one has to find other matrices of form-making. And the human hand/

mind relationship is not able to conceptualize this because all it can do is draw from the inventory of what it is possible to do with the human hand. That inventory of the possible is limited through knowledge and experience; the computer is not limited by the same knowledge and experience. The computer has no experience or knowledge of the images that it makes.[42]

In fostering a collaboration in which electronic media present their own reciprocal subjectivity, architects have succeeded in displacing their own discursive function. The result of this folding together of the desire of the architect with the computational/graphical power of electronic media is a cyborg assemblage that allows for an expanded opening onto greater degrees of creative freedom.

FINDING THE FOLD: REBSTOCK PARK

One of the first to articulate the postarchitectural style was Eisenman. In 1992 Eisenman submitted a proposal for the redevelopment of Rebstock Park, a 250-acre site on the perimeter of Frankfurt. First developed in the mid-nineteenth century by Ernst May, the original architecture of Rebstock Park employed the once fashionable suburban solution of the *Siedlung*: mass-produced blocks of housing and commercial areas repetitively and densely staggered across large peripheries of development without interpenetrating streets or alleyways. *Siedlungen* were simple, cost-efficient, and immediate solutions to the problems of urban expansion at the time, but as the larger urban fabric of Frankfurt developed, the unvascularized space between the cellular series of buildings gradually degenerated into a necrotic zone of stagnant urbanism. In Eisenman's words, "Now all the open space was in a sense left over; the 'ground' became a wasteland."[43]

Rebstock Park posed an interesting challenge to Eisenman in that the carefully gridded homogeneity of the site left little to deconstruct. Ironically, it was the mechanical regularity of the grid itself—the interstitial spaces of difference *between* the cloned buildings—that became the strongest element of Rebstock Park, with the potential to infect and subvert the architectural plan as a whole. In many ways, the site had already been deconstructed by the urban framework itself, its most apparent flaws laid bare in its development within its surrounding context.

In contrast to his earlier attempts to draw inspiration from the works of Derrida, Eisenman, now disenchanted with deconstructivism, found resonance for his new direction in the works of Gilles Deleuze, a contemporary French philosopher whose works escaped the standard bounds of philosophy, just as architects tried to move beyond the traditional trappings of architecture. Rather than seeing the semiotic slippages opened up by deconstruction as unbridgeable lacks or absences (différance), Deleuze views differences as positive elements, as lines of flight capable of cutting across disciplines and opening new possibilities. Difference for Deleuze is expressed as diffuse and dispersed leaks from outside the perimeters of traditional thought; difference can erupt inward, propagate, and transform the entire process of thinking. For some architects, Deleuze offers a means for thinking architecture as a positive program centered on and generated by just such an unfolding of difference: the inhuman, irrational element capable of decentering or deterritorializing the anthropomorphic subject. Lynn describes this new disciplinary shift: "Where complexity and contradiction arose previously from inherent contextual conflicts, attempts are presently being made to fold specific locations, materials and programs into architecture smoothly while maintaining their individual identity."[44] As with bioinformatics, a new fold of architects—the postarchitects—filters out redundant patterns of data within a specific locus in order to isolate the unpredictable variants in accordance with the basic tenet of informatics: an increase in information can grow only out of an increase in difference.

Eisenman's approach to Rebstock Park was Deleuzean. Rather than erase or cover up the corrupted grid, he decided to push it to its limits, to nurture it through a process of repetition until it erupted into a new singularity that transformed the totality of the site.

Eisenman's desire to subvert the stability of the grid led him to the work of René Thom, a French mathematician who had studied the dynamics of unexpected events within stable mathematical systems.[45] Thom's work, commonly known as catastrophe theory, is often demonstrated by a series of mathematical diagrams known as the "butterfly cusp," in which, according to Eisenman,

> a catastrophe begins with a stable condition, moves through the radical moment of change, and then returns to a stable condition. Isolated in their

TIMOTHY LENOIR AND CASEY ALT

original sequence these figures are the residual inscriptions of a condition that is impossible to represent in a single frame of time or space.[46]

Intrigued by the notion that the highly mechanical grid held within it the potential for a momentary buckling of traditional form, Eisenman used Thom's "ideas of 'event' and 'catastrophe' [to] circumscribe the project for Rebstock and formalize, as indices of a mathematical process, the urban context of Frankfurt"[47]—a city traditionally known for its well-regulated financial stability yet nonetheless caught in the two largest cultural disruptions of the twentieth century.

In order to trigger a new shape for Rebstock, Eisenman first mapped the local geography of the site using a 7 x 7 orthogonal grid, choosing the number seven arbitrarily, simply to represent the seven drawings of Thom's butterfly cusp series. Eisenman then overlaid and shaped this grid to the Rebstock ground plain "in an attempt to establish both spatial and temporal modulation."[48] As a second step, Eisenman superimposed another unmodulated 7 x 7 orthogonal grid over the modulated landscape grid and connected the translated vertices between the two "to produce a warped surface which first appears to separate the two grids rather than connect them."[49] In a second study of the two grids, Eisenman again connected each vertex of the orthogonal grid to its corresponding vertex of the landscape grid as well as to the vertex directly below it (fig. 4). The result of this second translation was that "another warped, netlike structure/surface appears which suggests not an oppositional relationship between the two figures, but rather a construct of perpetual mediation—the fold."[50] The topology of the fold became the primary logic for Eisenman's new plan for Rebstock. The architect then orthogonally projected the original *Siedlung* footprint onto the disrupted, multidimensional surface of the fold in such a way that the uniformly repeated blocks of the *Siedlung* were distorted in accordance with their position in the fold, each building disrupted and disrupting within the productive transformation of the grid (fig. 5).

By focusing on and iterating the wasted space of the grid, which threatened to overwhelm the rational plan of the *Siedlung*, Eisenman provoked a catastrophe—an intrusion of external forces in the unexpected form of the fold—that transformed Rebstock Park from the *outside* according to a new and other logic—what Eisenman calls an "ur-logic"—that operates outside that of the subject. In *The Fold: Leibniz and the Baroque*, Deleuze develops Leibniz's notion of the fold as resembling "a sheet of paper divided into infinite folds or separated into bending movements, each one determined by the consistent or conspiring surroundings."[51] Deleuze's "consistent or conspiring surroundings" are the possibilities of the outside—the potentials for change inherent in the local particularities of the environment—that intrude upon and influence the anthropomorphic form of the grid. Eisenman himself borrows the metaphor of folded paper in comparing the fold to origami: "Deleuze's idea of folding is more radical than origami, because it contains no narrative, linear sequence; rather, in terms of traditional vision, it contains a quality of the unseen."[52] The grid is therefore inflected by what cannot be seen by the subject: the virtual field of possibilities indigenous to each site.

INCORPORATING THE AFFECTIVE

Although such talk of the *unseen*, the *virtual*, and the *outside* might suggest a revitalized form of mysticism, neither Deleuze nor Eisenman intends such a connotation. Rather, they imply quite the opposite: that the outside, in its multiplicity of possibilities, completely flouts the human ability to know, see, or imagine, and that that is precisely its power. The outside is not so much mystical as rigorously computational. In explaining his notion of probabilistic conformational roadmaps in robot motion planning and ligand folding, Jean-Claude Latombe describes a similar phenomenon:

> The traditional framework of robot motion planning is based on manipulating a robot through a workspace while avoiding collisions with the obstacles in this space. Our application of motion planning, on the other hand, is aimed at determining potential paths that a robot (or ligand) may naturally take based on the energy distribution of its workspace. Hence, instead of inducing the motion of the robot through actuators, we examine *the possible motions of the robot induced by the energy landscape of its immediate environment.*[53]

Latombe's distinction between the two approaches to motion planning is an important one in that it foregrounds Deleuze's distinction between *effective* and *affective* space. Effective space is rational space functioning according to a

(fig. 4)

Diagram of Peter Eisenman's creation of the Rebstock Park fold, displaying how the fold emerged when each vertex of the seven-sqaure butterfly cusp grid was attached to the corresponding and adjacent vertices of the modulated ground-plain grid

discernible logic, as in the first method for motion planning. It is negotiated by a binary logical process, such as colliding/not colliding with obstacles. In effective space, actions are directed from the inside out: the subject is able to adapt by exerting itself within the space. As a result, interactions within effective space are *extensive*, concerned with conditions of quantity rather than quality.

Affective space, on the other hand, does not operate according to a knowable or predictable logic and can only be inferred in excess of its effective conditions. Rather than allowing an extensive, outward response to the space, affective space induces an *affect* within the subject: an *intensive*, outside-in inflection in response to specific forces inherent in the site. Subjects do not logically adapt to an affective space; rather, they are qualitatively changed and adapted by the space. In the case of ligand binding, the second method of motion planning not only takes into account the navigation of the effective space of the molecular environment but also considers the affective space, whether or not the energetic forces in the environment reconfigure the structure of the ligand into a different molecular conformation.[54] The probabilistic conformational road map can therefore be considered an extrapolated mapping of the affective space in regard to energy minimization.

An understanding of effective and affective space allows us to revisit Eisenman's development of the Rebstock fold within the larger history of architecture. The unifying figure of traditional modernism was that of the anthropomorphic, rectilinear grid, often the nine-square grid of the skyscraper that acted as the basic diagram for the ultimate monument to modernism. In modernist building, the grid was imposed on a site: the ground was cleared as a tabula rasa and the architecture was extended upward with a will toward overcoming its environmental conditions. Modernism therefore viewed spaces as only effective, conceiving of contextual conditions as physical, knowable, and mechanical phenomena to be rationally overcome.

Deconstructivism aimed to disrupt the grid through its conception of the diagonal, a transgressive cutting across that mimicked its dismantling of modernism. The diagonal subverted the effective space of modernism by revealing the hidden or suppressed directionals (the diagonals) inherent in all grids and all modernist agendas. The slant drove a critical wedge into modernism by exposing its hidden attempts to surmount the

TIMOTHY LENOIR AND CASEY ALT

(fig. 5)

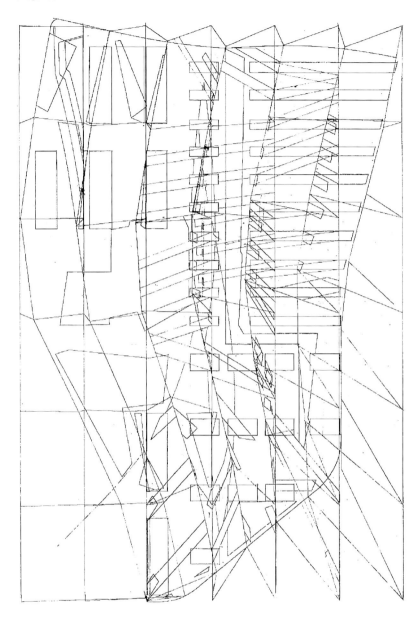

Eisenman's projection of the original *Siedlung* footprint onto the east-west orientation of the fold

effective space of local context, but it could not bring affective spaces to bear upon architecture.

With Rebstock, however, the grid became the object of affective space. Eisenman allowed the differential forces at play in the site to inflect his seven-square grid to produce the fold. In this way, differences within the site could be incorporated within the grid to produce a context-specific architecture. Lynn, Eisenman's colleague and former student, achieved a similar result in his Stranded Sears Tower project. As with most modernist skyscrapers, the Sears Tower is constructed along the guidelines of the nine-square grid and consists of nine interconnected structural tubes that mutually reinforce one another in a unified overcoming of gravity. In his project, Lynn played with the possibility of undoing the unity of the nine tubes in order to allow each tube to be differentially inflected by the affective space of its surrounding environment. Lynn described his project:

> The Stranded Sears Tower attempts to generate a multiplicitous urban monument that internalizes influences by external forces while maintaining an interior structure that is provisional rather than essential. . . . The iconic status of the existing Sears Tower arises from its disassociation from its context. The building establishes itself as a discrete and unified object within a continuous and homogeneous urban fabric. My project, by contrast, affiliates the structure of the tower with the heterogeneous particularities of its site while preserving aspects of its monumentality: laying the structure into its context and entangling its monolithic mass with local contextual forces allows a new monumentality to emerge from the old forms.[55]

Denari also employs techniques of folding to produce what he calls a "localized worldsheet," consisting of "a single curving sheet . . . that bends into itself, creating invelopes or internal surfaces that merge seamlessly with the exterior" (fig. 6).[56] In projects such as Vertical Smoothouse of 1997, Denari used his localized worldsheets to transgress traditional binarisms of architecture such as inner/outer. In all three projects, the final architectural form was produced by the interaction of outside forces with more traditional forms of modernism in the affective space of the site, thereby displacing the architect subject as the anthropomorphic interpreter of form. Eisenman describes this process of decentering: "When the environment is

TIMOTHY LENOIR AND CASEY ALT

inscribed or folded in such a way, the individual no longer remains the discursive function; the individual is no longer required to understand or interpret space."[57]

One should note that the architectures developed within such affective spaces are not only products of affect but are also integrated within the affective space itself as yet another external force. In other words, affectively produced architectures are affective spaces themselves that displace their spectators' subjectivity. Since the smooth surfaces of folded architecture are not reducible to generalized concepts or idealized forms, they resist their viewers' interpretation: they are forms in and of themselves rather than microcosms of a grander vision. In this way, affective architecture resists subjugation by the optical—that is, the mind-eye reading of the observer. Eisenman describes this power of the fold to resist the optical whole:

> Once the environment becomes affective, inscribed within another logic or an ur-logic, one which is no longer translatable into the vision of the mind, then reason becomes detached from vision. . . . This begins to

(fig. 6)

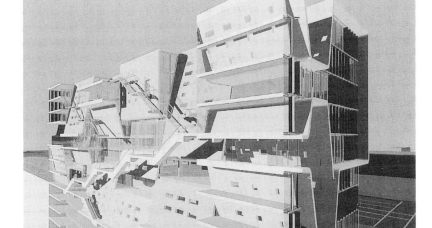

Longitudinal sectional perspective of Neil Denari's Multisection Office Block project, 1998. The "laminar structure" of Denari's localized worldsheets serves as a single continuously folded structure that mediates between previous binaries such as "inside/outside" and "vertical/horizontal."

produce an environment that "looks back"—that is, the environment seems to have an order that we can perceive, even though it does not seem to mean anything.[58]

Such an ability to "look back," or what Eisenman calls *reciprocal subjectivity*, endows architecture with a new power to deterritorialize the viewer—a *haptic*, as opposed to *optic*, ability to induce an affective change rather than effect an interpretation for rapid visual consumption. The fold is therefore one strategy for moving beyond the mechanics of vision in favor of a new relationship to built space: a performative encounter with the other, the outside. Taken as a larger field of movement, the fold represents a dramatic turn away from traditional forms and theories of architecture toward a Deleuzean ontology as a positive building program.

FURTHER VECTORS FOR MOVEMENT

While the above-mentioned three projects—Eisenman's Rebstock Park, Lynn's Stranded Sears Tower, and Denari's Virtual Smoothouse—index a similar move away from previous practices of building, they all nonetheless retain connections to modernism in their use of modernist forms as initial objects of inflection and in their relatively static methods of determining local forces. Though Eisenman's development of the Rebstock fold as the "in-between" of the gridded ground plain and the seven-square grid allows an unpredictable form to emerge from the outside, the "forces" it seeks to internalize in the grid are not so much dynamic forces as static geographies. Similarly, Lynn's Stranded Sears Tower maps each independent tube to relatively static influences, such as "adjacent buildings, landforms, sidewalks, bridges, tunnels, roads and river's edge."[59] What is missing from both Eisenman's and Lynn's experiments is an ability to generate new form, rather than merely inflect older modernist diagrams, within a context of temporally and spatially dynamic forces, instead of local static geometries.

As his own answer to this challenge, Lynn has developed a new theory and practice of architecture known as *animate design*. In animate design, Lynn considers that "force is an initial condition, the cause of both motion and the particular inflections of a form . . . so that architecture can be modeled as a participant immersed within dynamic flows."[60] To implement such

III. TOOLS AND METAPHORS   TIMOTHY LENOIR AND CASEY ALT

a system, Lynn maps the flows of local forces over time—wind and weather patterns, traffic flows, information and energy channels, animal migration patterns—in order to model the affective space of the site. Lynn then inserts a form to the force-field model of the space that represents the internal constraints of the desired building—such as five differently sized spheres for the number and types of rooms required—and allows them to be inflected and arranged in response to the tensions within the space (fig. 7). Once the forms have reached a stable pattern, Lynn will usually then envelope the forms within a single membrane, or blob, that is itself inflected by each of the forms. The resulting "folded, pliant, and supple" surface complies with and mediates between each of the forms "in order to incorporate their contexts with minimal resistance."[61]

In order to move beyond the inert lines and points of Euclidean geometry, Lynn has adopted a topological or NURBS approach in which surfaces are defined as vector flows whose paths are inflected by the distributed forces within the space. These splines literally seek the path of least resistance among the network of forces in order to establish a distributed field of equilibrium in a manner analogous to Latombe's probabilistic conformational road maps. Just as bioinformaticists use polymeraze chain reactions to map the energetics vectors within a space in order to predict the folding patterns

(fig. 7)

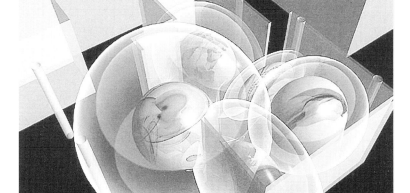

Generation of blob surface from the five project nodes for Greg Lynn's Artists Space installation, 1995. In order to generate a continuous surface between the five different projects to be displayed, Lynn allowed five globular spheres to interact within the local forces of the gallery space, then joined the five spaces by generating a topological surface that flowed among the surface of each node.

of proteins or ligands induced by the space, Lynn submits the forms of his internal building constraints to the vectorial forces inherent in each site in order to produce a new form that complies with the affective space while still retaining its identity.

To many observers, Lynn's desire for his architecture to accommodate the dynamic forces of its environment is a fool's quest, since architecture is innately static—at least, any architecture that is intended to serve as a permanent protective shelter.[62] Though it may be possible to create a computer model in which a pliant surface dynamically adapts itself to a flux of forces, it is much more difficult to build such structures with physical materials. Lynn's only option, according to his critics, is to take his structures from a single frozen image within a larger simulation; such an architecture, they say, is no more animate than more traditional modes of building.

However, it is problematic to assume that a fixed form can derive only from a fixed image. A single fixed form can evolve from a composite of multiple possible configurations of the same form over time. In order to dismiss reductive readings of his process, Lynn describes such a composite form in the shape of a boat hull:

> Although the form of a boat hull is designed to anticipate motion, there is no expectation that its shape will change. An ethics of motion neither implies nor precludes literal motion. Form can be shaped by the collaboration between an envelope and the active context in which it is situated. While physical form can be defined in terms of static coordinates, the virtual force of the environment in which it is designed contributes to its shape. The particular form of a hull stores multiple vectors of motion and flow from the space in which it was designed. A boat hull does not change its shape when it changes its direction, obviously, but variable points of sail are incorporated into its surface. In this way, topology allows for not just the incorporation of a single moment but rather a multiplicity of vectors, and therefore, a multiplicity of times, in a single continuous surface.[63]

As with the boat hull, the resultant forms of Lynn's architecture are fashioned in response to a virtual multiplicity of forces, thereby enabling Lynn to successfully generate new forms from the active fluctuation of forces within a given locus. Architectural forms cannot physically fold once they have been built; however, they can index a virtual process of continuous folding. As an affective space, Lynn's animate forms operate according to what Eisenman calls an "excessive condition"[64]—the field of possibilities in the process of folding are indexed in their excess in the actualized physical form.

An early example of Lynn's use of animate design is his March 1995 entry in the competition to design a protective roof and lighting scheme for the underside of the bus ramps leading into the New York City Port Authority Bus Terminal (fig. 8). Lynn summarized his design process for the Port Authority Gateway as follows:

> The site was modeled using forces that simulate the movement and flow of pedestrians, cars, and buses across the site, each with differing speeds and intensities of movement along Ninth Avenue, 42nd and 43rd streets, and the four elevated bus ramps emerging from below the Hudson River. These various forces of movement established a gradient field of attraction across the site. To discover the shape of this invisible field of attraction, we introduced geometric particles that change their position and shape according to the influence of the forces. From the particles studies, we captured a series of phase portraits of the cycles of movement over a period of time. These phase portraits are swept with a secondary structure of tubular

(fig. 8)

Particle phase portrait study for Greg Lynn's submission to the New York City Port Authority Gateway competition, 1995. In this study, Lynn used an animation sweep technique to capture the movements of geometric particles introduced to an invisible field of local forces.

FLOW, PROCESS, FOLD

frames linking the ramps, existing buildings and the Port Authority Bus Terminal. Eleven tensile surfaces are stretched across these tubes as an enclosure and projection surface.[65]

Lynn's modeling practices recall the techniques used by environmental scientists in generating dynamic visualizations of massive flows of weather data; there are close parallels, however, to modeling practices in bioinformatics as well. For instance, Lynn's "gradient field of attraction" bears a striking resemblance to the mapping of molecular energy landscapes. Equally analogous is the means by which Lynn's possible vector flows of particles cross through the field of attraction, just as bioinformaticists "represent the protein as a sequence of vectors, each representing an SSE [secondary structure element]"[66] that folds in accordance with its particular molecular energy landscape. Increasingly, at the outer limits of experimental explorations in each field, architecture and bioinformatics have begun to fold back upon each other.

THE DIGITAL OUTSIDE

Biology had to take a leap into molecular biology; dispersed life had to regroup in the genetic code. Dispersed work had to regroup in third-generation machines, cybernetics, and information technology. What would be the forces in play with which the forces within man would then enter into a relation? It would no longer involve raising to infinity or finitude but to an unlimited finity, thereby evoking every situation of force in which a finite number of components yield a practically unlimited diversity of combinations. It would be neither the fold nor the unfold that would constitute the active mechanism, but something like the *superfold*, as borne out by the foldings proper to the chains of the genetic code, and the potential of silicon in third-generation machines, as well as by the contours of a sentence in modern literature, when literature "merely turns back on itself in an endless reflexivity."[67]

We have pointed to multiple points of articulation between current developments in bioinformatics and architecture. In our view, they are not merely the result of random coincidences between two disparate fields. Articulated in the recent work of Eisenman, Denari, and Lynn, we find a concern to address what they have called a crisis of the mechanics of vision:

TIMOTHY LENOIR AND CASEY ALT

architecture could not move beyond its own circular process of logic and theory—beyond its own language game—without some force from the outside to move it. They located that external force, we have argued, in the highly automated, massively parallel, stacked multiple-alignment algorithms, in the neural networks, and in the Markov chains that practitioners of bioinformatics draw upon in processing the flow of sequence data into the dynamic folds of protein. When merged with immersive computer-design environments, these new machinic assemblages enable architects to *think architecture* in Deleuze's terms: *thinking architecture* ceases to be a solely human practice.

The overlap produced by the similar technological desires of bio informaticists and architects indexes just one fold in a much larger multiplicity. Building on the work of Foucault, Deleuze conceived of the *outside* as an affective space external to the larger epistemic areas of discourse at any given time: a network of hidden forces that inflects, stratifies, and organizes the systems of discourse it subtends. Foucault's lifework was to map the margins of such networks throughout different periods of history; his metaphor of the panopticon presents one such diagram of the space of the outside. This paper attempts to map a small section of a similar diagram of the outside for our particular historical location. In our diagram, the outside is inscribed in the fluid lines of flight of electronic media that cut across and inflect not only architecture and bioinformatics but also disciplines as diverse as genetics, robotics, psychology, astronomy, physics, philosophy, and engineering. All of these fields either have been or are being remade from the outside by electronic media, and in none of them is *thinking* any longer a solely human practice. Perhaps it never was.

NOTES

1. Gilles Deleuze and Félix Guattari, *A Thousand Plateaus: Capitalism and Schizophrenia* (Minneapolis: University of Minnesota Press, 1987), 144–48.

2. Christian B. Anfinsen, "Principles That Govern the Folding of Protein Chains," *Science* 181, no. 96 (1973): 223–30; C. B. Anfinsen and H. H. Scheraga, "Experimental and Theoretical Aspects of Protein Folding," *Advances in Protein Chemistry* 29 (1975): 205–300; Anfinsen, "The Formation and Stabilization of Protein Structure," *Biochemistry Journal* 128, no. 4 (1972): 737–49.

3. C. J. Epstein, R. F. Goldberger, and C. B. Anfinsen, "The Genetic Control of Tertiary Protein Structure: Studies with Model Systems," *Cold Spring Harbor Symposium on Quantitative Biology* 28 (1963): 439–49.

4. Cyrus Levinthal, "How to Fold Graciously," in *Mossbauer Spectroscopy in Biological Systems: Proceedings of a Meeting Held at Allerton House, Monticello, Illinois*, ed. J. T. P. DeBrunner and E. Munck (Urbana, Ill.: University of Illinois Press, 1969), 22–24.

5. Anthony G. Oettinger, "The Uses of Computers in Science," *Scientific American* 215, no. 3 (1966): 161–72, quote p. 161.

6. See Cyrus Levinthal, "Molecular Model-Building by Computer," *Scientific American* 214, no. 6 (1966): 42–52.

7. Ibid., 48–49. The author (T. L.) therefore decided to develop programs that would make use of a man-computer combination to do a kind of model building that neither a man nor a computer could accomplish alone. This approach implies that one must be able to obtain information from the computer and introduce changes in the way the program is running in a span of time that is appropriate to human operation. This in turn suggests that the output of the computer must be presented not in numbers but in visual form.

8. Lou Katz and Cyrus Levinthal, "Interactive Computer Graphics and the Representation of Complex Biological Structures," *Annual Reviews in Biophysics and Bioengineering* 1 (1972): 465–504.

9. Jean-Claude Latombe, *Robot Motion Planning* (Boston: Kluwer Academic Publishers, 1991). M. S. Apaydin, A. P. Singh, D. L. Brutlag, and J.-C. Latombe, "Capturing Molecular Energy Landscapes with Probabilistic Conformational Roadmaps," in *International Conference on Robotics and Automatons* (2001), 932–39.

10. The Protein Data Bank (PDB) was established in 1971 as a computer-based archival resource for macromolecular structures. But two decades later in April 1990 only 535 atomic coordinate entries were recorded for macromolecules, and in 1999, following a period of rapid improvement in technology for obtaining crystallographic data, the Biological Macromolecule Crystallization Database (BMCD) of the PDB contained entries for a meager 5,400 protein molecules.

11. Indeed, more than 140,000 genes were cloned and sequenced in the twenty years from 1974 to 1994, of which more than 20 percent were human genes. By the early 1990s at the beginning of the Human Genome Initiative, the NIH GenBank database (release #70) contained more than 74,000 sequences, while the Swiss Protein database (Swiss-Prot) included nearly 23,000 sequences. Protein databases were doubling in size every twelve months, and some were predicting that, as a result of the technological impact of the Human Genome Initiative, by the year 2000 ten million base pairs a day would be sequenced, predictions that have been more than borne out.

12. See, for instance, Ram Samudrala, Yu Xia, Enoch Huang, and Michael Levitt, "Ab Initio Protein Structure Prediction Using a Combined Hierarchical Approach," *Proteins: Structure, Function, and Genetics*, suppl. 3 (1999): 194–98. For evidence on this point, see the entries in the Critical Assessment of Protein Prediction competition hosted since 1994 at the Lawrence Livermore National Laboratory.

13. See especially the papers in L. Hunter, ed., *Artificial Intelligence and Molecular Biology* (Menlo Park, Calif: AAAI Press, 1993).

14. Douglas L. Brutlag, "Understanding the Human Genome," in *Scientific American: Introduction to Molecular Medicine*, ed. P. Leder, D. A. Clayton, and E. Rubenstein (New York: Scientific American, Inc., 1994), 153–68. Walter Gilbert characterizes the situation sharply: "The next tenfold increase in the amount of information in the databases will divide the world into haves and have-nots, unless each of us connects to that information and learns how to sift through it for the parts we need."

15. These are the disciplines with which graduate students and postdocs in molecular biology in Brutlag's lab at Stanford are expected to work. See Douglas Brutlag's introductory lecture to Biochemistry 218, Computational Molecular Biology, slide 16, at http://cmgm.stanford.edu/biochem218/01%20Genomics%26Bioinformatics.pdf, Stanford University, January 7, 2003.

16. New disciplinary requirements were imposed on the biologist who wanted to interpret and use the matrix of biological knowledge:

> The development of the matrix and the extraction of biological generalizations from it are going to require a new kind of scientist, a person familiar enough with the subject being studied to read the literature critically, yet expert enough in information science to be innovative in developing methods of classification and search. This implies the development of a new kind of theory geared explicitly to biology with its particular theory structure. It will be tied to the use of computers, which will be required to deal with the vast amount and complexity of the information, but it will be designed to search for general laws and structures that will make general biology much more easily accessible to the biomedical scientist.

Ibid., 67.

17. Ibid., 26–27.

18. Peter Eisenman, "Visions Unfolding: Architecture in the Age of Electronic Media," in *Digital Eisenman: An Office of the Electronic Era*, ed. Luca Galofaro (Basel: Birkhäuser, 1999), 84.

19. Ibid.

20. Ibid, 85.

21. Ibid, 84.

22. Ibid.

23. Neil Denari, *Gyroscopic Horizons* (New York: Princeton Architectural Press, 1999), 11 n. 3.

24. Greg Lynn, 1995, http://www.basilisk.com/aspace/formview.html.

25. Mark Wigley described a deconstructive architect as "not one who dismantles buildings, but one who locates the inherent dilemmas within buildings—the structural flaws." *Deconstructivist Architecture* (Boston: Little, Brown, 1988), 133.

26. Lynn, "The Folded, the Pliant, and the Supple," in *Folds, Bodies and Blobs: Collected Essays* (Brussels: La Lettre Volée, 1998), 115.

27. Frederic Jameson, in his book *Postmodernism, or the Cultural Logic of Late Capitalism*, diagnosed postmodernism as a "depthless" and "schizophrenic" logic doomed to operate only through an ahistorical "pastiche" of past styles. *Postmodernism* (Durham, N.C.: Duke University Press, 1991), 6.

28. Eisenman, "Visions Unfolding," 85.

29. For Eisenman's early embrace of postmodern approaches, see Peter Eisenman, "Cardboard Architecture: House I (1967)," in Peter Eisenman, Michael Graves, Charles Gwathmey, John Hejduk, Richard Meier, Collin Rowe, and Kenneth Frampton, *Five Architects* (New York: Oxford University Press, 1975), 15–23; Eisenman, "Cardboard Architecture: House II (1969)," Ibid., 25–37.

30. Kathryn Henderson, *On Line and on Paper: Visual Representations, Visual Culture, and Computer Graphics in Design Engineering* (Cambridge, Mas s.: MIT Press, 1999), 99.

31. Stephen S. Hall, "Protein Images Update Natural History," *Science* 267, no. 3 (February 1995): 620–24.

32. William J. Mitchell, "Roll Over Euclid: How Frank Gehry Designs and Builds," in *Frank Gehry, Architect*, ed. J. Fiona Ragheb (New York: Solomon R. Guggenheim Foundation, 2001), 352–63, quote p. 354.

33. Ibid., 354.

34. Ibid., 358.

35. Ibid., 363.

36. Ibid., 357.

37. Dennis Dollens, "Fish, Snake, Gehry & Guggenheim," www.sitesarch.org/reviews/GehryBil.html.

38. Gehry describes the impressive degree to which CAD/CAM applications allow mass customization of building materials by listing the project's components (e.g., number of aluminum and stainless steel shingles: over 21,000). There are over 3,000 panels, each composed of an average of seven metal shingles. Each is uniquely shaped; there are no repeating patterns. The panels that sheath EMP were milled in Germany; colored in England; shaped, cut, and assembled in Kansas City; and brought to Seattle to be attached. The gold-colored stainless-steel panels have a special beaded-glass finish that reflects and changes with varying light and weather conditions. *Experience Music Project: The Building* (Seattle: EMP, 2000), 30.

39. Dollens, "Fish, Snake, Gehry & Guggenheim."

40. Selim Koder, "Interview with Peter Eisenman," from "Intelligente Ambiente," *Ars Electronica* (1992), http://xarch.tu-graz.ac.at/home/rurban/course/intelligent_ambiente/interview_eisenman.en.html.

41. Greg Lynn, *Animate Form* (New York: Princeton Architectural Press, 1999), 17.

42. Koder, "Interview with Peter Eisenman."

43. Peter Eisenman, *Unfolding Frankfurt* (Berlin: Ernst & Sohn Verlag, 1991), 10.

44. Lynn, "The Folded, the Pliant, and the Supple," 117.

45. On René Thom, see his *Structural Stability and Morphogenesis: An Outline of a General Theory of Models*, trans. D. H. Fowler, rev. ed. (Cambridge, Mass.: Perseus Books, 1989).

46. Eisenman, *Unfolding Frankfurt*, 10.

47. Ibid.

48. John Rajchman, "Perplications: On the Space and Time of Rebstockpark," in Eisenman, *Unfolding Frankfurt*, 23.

49. Ibid., 25.

50. Ibid.

51. Gilles Deleuze, *The Fold: Leibniz and the Baroque* (Minneapolis: University of Minnesota Press, 1993), 6. Deleuze is referencing Leibniz's statement in *Pacidus philalethi* (c. 614–15): "The division of the continuous must not be taken as of sand dividing into grains, but as that of a sheet of paper or of a tunic in folds, in such a way that an infinite number of folds can be produced, some smaller than others, but without the body ever dissolving into points or minima."

52. Eisenman, "Visions Unfolding," 87 n. 18.

53. Amit P. Singh, Jean-Claude Latombe, Douglas L. Brutlag, "A Motion-Planning Approach to Flexible Ligand Binding," *Proceedings of the Seventh International Conference on Intelligent Systems for Molecular Biology* (Menlo Park, Calif.: AAAI Press, 1999), 253 (emphasis added).

54. Ibid., 254.

55. Greg Lynn, "Multiplicitous and Inorganic Bodies," *Folds, Bodies & Blobs* (Brussels: La Lettre volée, 1998), 53.

56. Denari, *Gyroscopic Horizons*, 83.

57. Eisenman, "Visions Unfolding," 88.

58. Ibid.

TIMOTHY LENOIR AND CASEY ALT

III. TOOLS AND METAPHORS

59. Lynn, "Multiplicitous and Inorganic Bodies," 56.

60. Lynn, *Animate Form*, 11.

61. Lynn, "The Folded, the Pliant, and the Supple," 117.

62. As an example of this view, see Alicia Imperiale's "Time Frozen/Time Liberated?" in *New Flatness: Surface Tension in Digital Architecture* (Basel: Birkhäuser, 2000), 74–78.

63. Lynn, *Animate Form*, 10.

64. Eisenman, "Visions Unfolding," 87.

65. Lynn, *Animate Form*, 103.

66. PCR paper, 6.

67. Gilles Deleuze, *Foucault*, trans. Seán Hand (Minneapolis: University of Minnesota Press, 1988), 131.

BIOGRAPHIES

Casey Alt received his B.A. from Stanford University in 1999, where he majored in human biology and minored in art. He is currently pursuing a Ph.D. in history and philosophy of science at Stanford, focusing on the history of computational biology and electronic media.

Martin Bressani is associate professor of architecture at McGill University and is currently a guest scholar at the Study Center at the Canadian Center for Architecture in Montreal. He has published widely on modern French architecture and is completing a book entitled *Surface into Depth: A Tracing of Viollet-le-Duc's Constructive Imagination*.

Denis Cosgrove is the Alexander Von Humboldt Professor of Geography at the University of California at Los Angeles. His published work has concentrated on landscape meanings, mappings, and histories in the modern world, with special attention to Italy. His books include *Social Formation and Symbolic Landscape* (1984), *The Iconography of Landscape* (1988), *The Palladian Landscape* (1994), *Mappings* (1999), and *Apollo's Eye: A Cartographic Genealogy of the Earth in the Western Imagination* (2001).

Edward Eigen received his M.Arch from Columbia University in 1991 and his Ph.D. in the history and theory of architecture from MIT in 2000. He is currently a lecturer at the Princeton University School of Architecture and is preparing the book *An Anomalous Plan*, which discusses the evolution of laboratory spaces in nineteenth-century France.

Peter Galison is the Mallinckrodt Professor of the History of Science and of Physics at Harvard University. He has published extensively on the history and philosophy of science and serves as advisory editor for numerous scholarly journals. In 1999 he edited a collection of essays with Emily Thompson entitled *The Architecture of Science* (1999).

Catherine Ingraham is the director of graduate programs in architecture and urban design at Pratt Institute, where she also teaches. An architectural theorist, she writes and lectures widely on architecture and is the author of *Architecture and the Burdens of Linearity* (1998).

Timothy Lenoir is professor of the history of science and technology and chair of the program in history and philosophy of science at Stanford University. He has published on the history of the biomedical sciences in the nineteenth and twentieth centuries and, most recently, on the history of interactive simulation and video games.

Reinhold Martin is an assistant professor of architecture at Columbia University, a partner in the firm of Martin/Baxi Architects, and an editor of the journal *Grey Room*. His published work on the history and theory of postwar modern architecture will soon include *The Organizational Complex: Architecture, Media, and Corporate Space* (forthcoming).

Antoine Picon is professor of the history of architecture and technology at the Harvard University Graduate School of Design and has published extensively on French architecture and engineering. He is the author of *French Architects and Engineers in The Age of Enlightenment* (1992) and is currently working on an essay on digital culture and architecture.

Alessandra Ponte is visiting assistant professor at the College of Art, Architecture and Planning, Cornell University. She has also taught at the Princeton University School of Architecture and at the Istituto Universitario di Architettura di Venezia. She has published a book on Richard Payne Knight and the picturesque (2000) and is currently writing another, on the American desert.

Felicity D. Scott is currently a J. Paul Getty postdoctoral fellow in the history of art and the humanities, 2002–03, and an editor of the journal *Grey Room*. She has published on modern architecture and design as well as postwar experimental practices and is currently writing a book on the dissident modernism of Bernard Rudofsky entitled *Underneath Aesthetics and Utility*.

Georges Teyssot is an architect and a scholar. He has taught in the Department of the History of Architecture at the Instituto Universitario di Architettura di Venezia and at the Princeton University School of Architecture. He currently teaches at the Université Laval's School of Architecture in Québec and recently edited a collection of essays entitled *The American Lawn* (1999).

CREDITS

Archives Historique de la Station Biologique de Roscoff, 73

Archives Historique de l'Observatoire Océanologique de Banyuls, Laboratoire Arago, Université Pierre et Marie Curie, 56, 74 (left and right)

Bibliothèque Centrale du Muséum d'Histoire Naturelle, Paris, 55

Carmel, James H., *Exhibition Techniques: Traveling and Temporary* (New York: Reinhold Publishing Corporation, 1962), 267, 269, 278

Corbis, 231

Denari, Neil, *Gyroscopic Horizons* (New York: Princeton Architectural Press, 1999), 343

Eisenman, Peter, *Unfolding Frankfurt* (Berlin: Ernst & Sohn Verlag,1991), 339, 341

©Estate of Robert Smithson/VAGA, New York, NY, 176, 186, 187

Film-maker's Cooperative, 191

Frank Gehry, Architect, ed. J. Fiona Ragheb (New York: The Solomon R. Guggenheim Foundation, 2001), 332

http://robotics.stanford.edu/~latombe/projects/#F, 321

http://www.accelrys.com/support/life/images/2sod.jpg, 320

Lynn, Greg, *Animate Form* (New York: Princeton Architectural Press, 1999), 305, 347

Lynn, Greg, FORM Web site, http://www.basilisk.com/aspace/imajj/glowblobs.jpeg, 345

Museum of Modern Art, New York, 233

Reiser+Umemoto, 308

Royal Library, Windsor, Great Britain, 234

Rudofsky, Mrs. Berta, 258, 260, 265, 279

Stoller, Ezra ©Esto, 189 (top and bottom), 192

This is America (Washington, D.C.: Office of the United States Commissioner General, Brussels World's Fair, 1958), 259, 268

UN Studio, 306

ARCHITECTURE AND THE SCIENCES: EXCHANGING METAPHORS
is the fourth volume in the series
PRINCETON PAPERS ON ARCHITECTURE
Princeton University School of Architecture
Princeton, New Jersey 08544-5264

Published by
Princeton Architectural Press
37 East Seventh Street
New York, New York 10003

For a free catalog of books, call 1.800.722.6657.
Visit our Web site at www.papress.com.

Editing: Nancy Eklund Later
Copyediting: Moira Duggan
Design: Jan Haux
Layout: Nicola Bednarek and Linda Lee

Special thanks to: Nettie Aljian, Ann Alter, Janet Behning, Megan Carey, Penny (Yuen Pik) Chu,
Russell Fernandez, Clare Jacobson, Mark Lamster, Nancy Levinson, Katharine Myers,
Jane Sheinman, Scott Tennent, Jennifer Thompson, Joe Weston, and Deb Wood of Princeton
Architectural Press—Kevin C. Lippert, publisher

Library of Congress Cataloging-in-Publication Data

Architecture and the sciences : exchanging metaphors / Antoine Picon and
Alessandra Ponte, editors.—1st ed.
    p. cm. — (Princeton papers on architecture)
Book emerged from a symposium sponsored by the School of Architecture at
Princeton University during November 2000.
 ISBN 1–56898–365–4 (alk. paper)
 1. Architecture and science. 2. Architectural design. I. Picon,
Antoine. II. Ponte, Alessandra. III. Series.
 NA2543.S35 A727 2003
 720'.1'05—dc21
                                        2003002305